SECOND EDITION

Practical C++ Programming

Steve Oualline

O'REILLY®

Beijing · Cambridge · Farnham · Köln · Paris · Sebastopol · Taipei · Tokyo

Practical C++ Programming, Second Edition
by Steve Oualline

Copyright © 2003, 1995 O'Reilly Media, Inc. All rights reserved.
Printed in the United States of America.

Published by O'Reilly Media, Inc., 1005 Gravenstein Highway North, Sebastopol, CA 95472.

O'Reilly & Associates books may be purchased for educational, business, or sales promotional use. On-line editions are also available for most titles (*safari.oreilly.com*). For more information, contact our corporate/institutional sales department: (800) 998-9938 or *corporate@oreilly.com*.

Editor:	Robert Denn
Cover Designer:	Edie Freedman
Interior Designer:	David Futato

Printing History:

August 1995:	First Edition.
January 2003:	Second Edition.

 This book uses RepKover™, a durable and flexible lay-flat binding.

ISBN: 0-596-00419-2

[M] [3/04]

Table of Contents

Part I. The Basics

Part II. Simple Programming

Part III.   Advanced Types and Classes

Part V.   Other Language Features

Preface

This book is devoted to practical C++ programming. It teaches you not only the mechanics of the language, but also style and debugging. The entire life cycle of a program is discussed, including conception, design, writing, debugging, release, documentation, maintenance, and revision.

Style is emphasized. Creating a good program involves more than just typing code. It is an art in which writing and programming skills blend to form a masterpiece. A well-written program not only functions correctly, but also is simple and easy to understand. Comments allow programmers to include descriptive text in their programs. Clearly written, well-commented programs are highly prized.

A program should be as simple as possible. Avoid the use of clever tricks. Cleverness and complexity can kill programs. This book stresses simple, practical rules. For example, the 15 operator-precedence rules in C++ can be simplified to 2:

1. Multiply and divide before you add and subtract.
2. Put parentheses around everything else.

Consider two programs. One was written by a clever programmer, using all the tricks. The program contains no comments, but it works. The other is nicely commented and well structured, but doesn't work. Which program is more useful? In the long run, the "broken" one is more useful because it can be fixed and maintained easily. Although the clever one works now, sooner or later it will have to be modified. The hardest work you will ever have to do is modifying a cleverly written program.

Scope of This Handbook

This handbook is written for people with no previous programming experience, for programmers who know C and want to upgrade their skills to C++, and for those who already know C++ and want to improve their programming style and reliability. You should have access to a computer and know how to use the basic functions such as the text editor and file system.

Computer languages are best learned by writing and debugging programs. Sweating over a broken program at two o'clock in the morning only to find that you typed = where you should have typed == is a very effective teaching tool. This book contains many examples of common programming errors. (They are labeled as broken programs in the text.) You are encouraged to enter these programs into your computer and then run and debug them. This process introduces you to common errors using short programs so you will know how to spot and correct such errors in your own larger programs. (Instructions for obtaining copies of the programs presented in this book are located at the end of this preface.)

Several dialects of C++ are presented:

- A "generic" Unix compiler that should work on most Unix systems
- The GNU C++ compiler, named g++ (available for most Unix systems*)
- Borland C++ for MS-DOS/Windows
- Microsoft's Visual C++ for MS-DOS/Windows

As far as standard C++ is concerned, there are only minor differences among the various compilers. This book clearly indicates where compiler differences can affect the programmer. Specific instructions are given for producing and running programs using each of these compilers. The book also gives examples of using the programming utility *make* for automated program production.

How This Book Is Organized

You must crawl before you walk. In Part I, , you learn how to crawl. These chapters teach you enough to write very simple programs. You start with the mechanics of programming and programming style. Next, you learn how to use variables and very simple decision and control statements.

At this point you will have learned enough to create very simple programs; therefore, in Chapter 7, *The Programming Process*, you embark on a complete tour of the programming process that shows you how real programs are created.

- Chapter 1, *What Is C++?*, gives you an overview of C++, describes its history and uses, and explains how the language is organized.
- Chapter 2, *The Basics of Program Writing*, explains the basic programming process and gives you enough information to write a very simple program.
- Chapter 3, *Style*, discusses programming style. How to comment a program is covered, as well as how to write clear and simple code.

---

* The GNU g++ compiler can be obtained from *http://www.gnu.org*, or you can contact the Free Software Foundation, Inc., at 675 Massachusetts Avenue, Cambridge, MA 02139, (617) 876-3296.

- Chapter 4, *Basic Declarations and Expressions*, introduces simple C++ statements. Basic variables and the assignment statement are covered in detail along with the arithmetic operators: +, -, *, /, and %.

- Chapter 5, *Arrays, Qualifiers, and Reading Numbers*, covers arrays and more complex variables. The shorthand operators ++, --, *=, =, +=, -=, /=, and %= are described.

- Chapter 6, *Decision and Control Statements*, explains simple decision statements including **if**, **else**, and **for**. The problem of == versus = is discussed.

- Chapter 7, *The Programming Process*, takes you through the steps required for creating a simple program, from specification through release. Fast prototyping and debugging are discussed.

Part II, *Simple Programming*, describes all the other simple statements and operators that are used in programming. You also learn how to organize these statements into simple functions.

- Chapter 8, *More Control Statements*, describes additional control statements. Included are **while**, **break**, and **continue**. The **switch** statement is discussed in detail.

- Chapter 9, *Variable Scope and Functions*, introduces local variables, namespaces, functions, and parameters.

- Chapter 10, *The C++ Preprocessor*, describes the C++ preprocessor, which gives you great flexibility in creating code. It also provides a tremendous number of ways for you to screw up. Simple rules that help keep the preprocessor from becoming a problem are described.

- Chapter 11, *Bit Operations*, discusses the logical C++ operators that work on bits.

In Part III, *Advanced Types and Classes*, you learn how basic declarations and statements can be used in the construction of advanced types such as structures, unions, and classes. You also learn about the concept of pointers.

- Chapter 12, *Advanced Types*, explains structures and other advanced types. The **sizeof** operator and the **enum** type are included.

- Chapter 13, *Simple Classes*, introduces the concept of a **class**. This is one of the more powerful features of C++. Classes allow you to group data and the operations that can be performed on that data into one object.

- Chapter 14, *More on Classes*, describes additional operations that can be performed with classes.

- Chapter 15, *Simple Pointers*, introduces C++ pointer variables and shows some of their uses.

Advanced programming techniques are explored in Part IV, *Advanced Programming Concepts*. In this section, you explore a number of C++ features that let you create complex, yet easy-to-use objects or classes.

- Chapter 16, *File Input/Output*, describes both buffered and unbuffered input/output (I/O). ASCII and binary files are discussed and you are shown how to construct a simple file. Old C-style I/O operations are also included.

- Chapter 17, *Debugging and Optimization*, describes how to debug a program and how to use an interactive debugger. You are shown not only how to debug a program, but also how to write a program so that it is easy to debug. This chapter also describes many optimization techniques to make your programs run faster and more efficiently.

- Chapter 18, *Operator Overloading*, explains that C++ allows you to extend the language by defining additional meanings for the language's operators. In this chapter, you create a complex type and the operators that work on it.

- Chapter 19, *Floating Point*, uses a simple decimal floating-point format to introduce the problems inherent in using floating points, such as roundoff errors, precision loss, overflow, and underflow.

- Chapter 20, *Advanced Pointers*, describes advanced use of pointers to construct dynamic structures such as linked lists and trees.

- Chapter 21, *Advanced Classes*, shows how to build complex, derived classes out of simple, base ones.

Several miscellaneous features are described in Part V, *Other Language Features*.

- Chapter 22, *Exceptions*, explains how to handle unexpected conditions within a program.

- Chapter 23, *Modular Programming*, shows how to split a program into several files and use modular programming techniques. The make utility is explained in more detail.

- Chapter 24, *Templates*, allows you to define a generic function or class that generates a family of functions.

- Chapter 25, *Standard Template Library*, describes the template library that comes with C++. This library consists of a number of "container templates" and related data structures which let you create very complex and robust data structures with very little work.

- Chapter 26, *Program Design,* discusses some of the methodologies used to design programs, such as structured programming and object-oriented design. Not only are the design methods discussed, but also the reasoning that went into the design of the program.

- Chapter 27, *Putting It All Together,* details the steps necessary to take a complex program from conception to completion. Information hiding and modular programming techniques, as well as object-oriented programming, are stressed.

- Chapter 28, *From C to C++*, describes how to turn C code into C++ code and addresses many of the traps lurking in C code that bite the C++ programmer.
- Chapter 29, *C++'s Dustier Corners*, describes the little used **do/while** statement, the comma operator, and the ?: operators.
- Chapter 30, *Programming Adages*, lists programming adages that will help you construct good C++ programs.

Part VI, *Appendixes*, contains additional C++ reference information.

- Appendix A, *ASCII Table*, contains a list of character codes and their values.
- Appendix B, *Ranges*, lists the numeric ranges of some C++ variable types.
- Appendix C, *Operator Precedence Rules*, lists the rules that determine the order in which operators are evaluated.
- Appendix D, *Computing Sine Using a Power Series*, contains a program that shows how the computer can compute the value of the sine function.
- Appendix E, *Resources*, lists information on the programming resources mentioned in the book.

How to Read This Book If You Already Know C

C++ is built on the C language. If you know C, you will find much of the material presented in Chapters 2 through 12 familiar.

C++ does introduce a number of new minor improvements to C++, including:

- An entirely new I/O system. (The basics are described in Chapter 4, *Basic Declarations and Expressions*. The new file system is discussed in detail in Chapter 16, *File Input/Output*.)
- Constants and reference variables (described in Chapter 5, *Arrays, Qualifiers, and Reading Numbers*).
- Function overloading, **inline** functions, reference parameters, and default parameters. (Read Chapter 9, *Variable Scope and Functions*.)

So you can use C++ as a better C. But C++ has added some entirely new features such as objects, templates, and exceptions. So starting with Chapter 13, *Simple Classes*, you will begin to learn entirely new concepts.

Font Conventions

The following conventions are used in this book:

Italic

Used for directories and to emphasize new terms and concepts when they are introduced. Italic is also used to highlight comments in examples.

Bold

Used for C++ keywords.

`Constant width`

Used for programs and the elements of a program and in examples to show the contents of files or the output from commands. A reference in text to a word or item used in an example or code fragment is also shown in constant width font.

`Constant bold`

Used in examples to show commands or other text that should be typed literally by the user. (For example, **`rm foo`** means to type "rm foo" exactly as it appears in the text or the example.)

`Constant italic`

Used in examples to show variables for which a context-specific substitution should be made. (The variable *filename*, for example, would be replaced by some actual filename.)

"Quotes"

Used to identify system messages or code fragments in explanatory text.

%   The Unix C shell prompt.

$ The Unix Bourne shell or Korn shell prompt.

[ ] Surround optional values in a description of program syntax. (The brackets themselves should never be typed.)

... Stands for text (usually computer output) that's been omitted for clarity or to save space.

The notation CTRL-X or ^X indicates use of *control* characters. It means hold down the "control" key while typing the character "x". We denote other keys similarly (e.g., RETURN indicates a carriage return).

All examples of command lines are followed by a RETURN unless otherwise indicated.

How to Contact Us

Please address comments and questions concerning this book to:

O'Reilly & Associates, Inc.
1005 Gravenstein Highway North
Sebastopol, CA 95472
1-800-998-9938 (in the United States or Canada)
1-707-829-0515 (international or local)
1-707-829-0104 (fax)

There is a web page for this book, which lists errata, examples, or any additional information. You can access this page at:

http://www.oreilly.com/catalog/cplus2

To comment or ask technical questions about this book, send email to:

bookquestions@oreilly.com

For more information about books, conferences, Resource Centers, and the O'Reilly Network, see the O'Reilly web site at:

http://www.oreilly.com/

Acknowledgments for the First Edition

Thanks to Peg Kovar for her proofreading and editing help. Special thanks to Dale Dougherty for ripping apart my first book and forcing me to put it together correctly. I greatly appreciate the hard work put in by Phil Straite and Gregory Satir. I especially thank all those people who reviewed and edited my book. My thanks also go to the production group at O'Reilly & Associates—Nicole Gipson, project manager and production editor; John Files, Juliette Muellner, and Jane Ellin, production assistants; and Mike Sierra, book design implementor. Finally, special thanks go to all the hard-working programmers out there whose code has taught me so much.

Acknowledgments for the Second Edition

For the second edition I wish to thank my editor, Robert J. Denn, for his patience and hard work in getting the book done. Thanks to Ray Lischner for his technical insight. Al Stevens deserves special recognition for his extensive knowledge of C++ and his exacting standards. His efforts helped me to tighten the terminology and refine the examples in the book, resulting in a much more precise manuscript. Any errors in this book are my own and are not the fault of the reviewers or of the staff at O'Reilly.

Also I wish to give credit to all the sales and marketing people at O'Reilly who work so hard to sell my book.

## PART I

The Basics

## CHAPTER 1

What Is C++?

Profanity is the one language that all programmers understand.
—Anonymous

The ability to organize and process information is the key to success in the modern age. Computers are designed to handle and process large amounts of information quickly and efficiently. However, they can't do anything until someone tells them what to do. That's where C++ comes in. C++ is a high-level programming language that allows a software engineer to efficiently communicate with a computer.

C++ is a highly flexible and adaptable language. Since its creation in 1980, it has been used for a wide variety of programs including firmware for microcontrollers, operating systems, applications, and graphics programming. C++ is the programming language of choice for a tremendous number of applications. There is a tremendous demand for people who can tell computers what to do, and C++ lets you do so quickly and efficiently.

A Brief History of C++

In 1970 two programmers, Brian Kernighan and Dennis Ritchie, created a new language called C. (The name came about because C was preceded by the old programming language they were using called B.) C was designed with one goal in mind: writing operating systems. The language was extremely simple and flexible and soon was used for many different types of programs. It quickly became one of the most popular programming languages in the world.

C had one major problem, however. It was a procedure-oriented language. This meant that in designing a typical C program, the programmer would start by describing the data and then write procedures to manipulate that data.

Programmers eventually discovered that it made a program clearer and easier to understand if they were able to take a bunch of data and group it together with the operations that worked on that data. Such a grouping is called an *object* or *class*. Designing programs by designing classes is known as *object-oriented design (OOD)*.

In 1980 Bjarne Stroustrup started working on a new language, called "C with Classes." This language improved on C by adding a number of new features, the most important of which was classes. This language was improved, augmented, and finally became C++.

C++ owes its success to the fact that it allows the programmer to organize and process information more effectively than most other languages. Also, it builds on the work already done with the C language. In fact, most C programs can be transformed into C++ programs with little trouble. These programs usually don't use all the new features of C++, but they do work. In this way, C++ allows programmers to build on an existing base of C code.

C++ Organization

C++ is designed as a bridge between the programmer and the raw computer. The idea is to let the programmer organize a program in a way that he can easily understand. The compiler then translates the language into something the machine can use.

Computer programs consist of two main parts: data and instructions. The computer imposes little or no organization on these two parts. After all, computers are designed to be as general as possible. The idea is for the programmer to impose his or her own organization on the computer and not the other way around.

The data in a computer is stored as a series of bytes. C++ organizes those bytes into useful data. Data declarations are used by the programmer to describe the information he or she is working with. For example:

```
int total;    // Total number accounts
```

tells C++ that you want to use a section of the computer's memory to store an integer named total. You can let the compiler decide what particular bytes of memory to use; that's a minor bookkeeping detail you don't need to worry about.

The variable total is a *simple variable*. It can hold only one integer and describe only one total. A series of integers can be organized into an array. Again, C++ will handle the details, imposing that organization on the computer's memory.

```
int balance[100];    // Balance (in cents) for all 100 accounts
```

Finally, there are more complex data types. For example, a rectangle might have a width, a height, a color, and a fill pattern. C++ lets you organize these four attributes into one group called a *structure*.

```
struct rectangle {
    int width;      // Width of rectangle in pixels
    int height;     // Height of rectangle in pixels
```

```
        color_type color; // Color of the rectangle
        fill_type fill;   // Fill pattern
    };
```

However, data is only one part of a program; you also need instructions. As far as the computer is concerned, it knows nothing about the layout of the instructions. It knows only what it's doing for the current instruction and where to get the next instruction.

C++ is a high-level language. It lets you write a high-level statement such as:

```
    area = (base * height) / 2.0;    // Compute area of triangle
```

The compiler translates this statement into a series of cryptic machine instructions. This sort of statement is called an *assignment statement*. It is used to compute and store the value of an arithmetic expression.

You can also use *control statements* to control the order of processing. Statements such as the **if** and **switch** statements enable the computer to make simple decisions. Statements can be repeated by using looping statements such as **while** and **for.**

Groups of statements can be wrapped to form *functions*. Thus you only need to write a general-purpose function to draw a rectangle once, and you can reuse that function whenever you want to draw a new rectangle. C++ provides a rich set of *standard functions* that perform common functions such as searching, sorting, input, and output. A set of related functions can be grouped together to form a *module*, and modules are linked to form *programs*.

One of the major goals of the C++ language is to organize instructions into reusable components. After all, you can write programs much faster if you "borrow" most of your code from somewhere else. Groups of reusable modules can be combined into a *library*. For example, if you need a sort routine, you can use the standard function qsort from the library and link it into your program.

A computer divides the world into data and instructions. For a long time, high-level languages such as C kept that dividing line in place. In C you can define data or write instructions, but you can't combine the two.

One of C++'s major innovations is the idea of combining data and instructions together in a construct called a class or object. Object-oriented programming allows you to group data with the operations that can be performed on that data. This concept is taken a step further in C++ by letting you derive new classes from existing ones.

This last feature is extremely powerful. It allows you to build complex classes on top of smaller, simpler ones. It also allows you to define a basic, abstract class and then derive specific classes from it. For example, an abstract class of shape might be used to define the shapes rectangle, triangle, and circle.

Organization is the key to writing good programs. In this book, you know that the table of contents is in the front and the index is in the back, because that's the way books are organized. Organization makes this book easier to use.

The C++ language lets you organize your programs using a simple yet powerful *syntax*. This book goes beyond the C++ syntax and teaches you style rules that enable you to create highly readable and reliable programs. By combining a powerful syntax with good programming style, you can create powerful programs that perform complex and wonderful operations.

How to Learn C++

The only way to learn how to program is to write programs. You'll learn a lot more by writing and debugging programs than you ever will by reading this book. This book contains many programming exercises, and you should try to do as many of them as possible. When doing the exercises, keep good programming style in mind. Always comment your programs, even if you're doing the exercises only for yourself. Commenting helps you organize your thoughts, and commenting your own programs is good practice for when you go into the "real world."

Don't let yourself be seduced by the idea that, "I'm only writing these programs for myself, so I don't need to comment them." First of all, code that looks obvious to you when you write it can often be confusing and cryptic when you revisit it a week later. Writing comments also helps you organize your ideas. (If you can write out an idea in English, you are halfway to writing it in C++.)

Finally, programs tend to be around far longer than expected. I once wrote a highly system-dependent program that was designed to work only on the computer at Caltech. As I was the only one who would ever use the program, it would print the following message if I got the command line wrong:

```
?LSTUIT User is a twit
```

A few years later I was a student at Syracuse University. The chief secretary at the School of Computer Science needed a program similar to my Caltech listing program, so I adapted my program for her use. Unfortunately, I had forgotten about my funny little error message.

Imagine how horrified I was when I came into the Computer Science office and was accosted by the chief secretary. This lady had so much power she could make the dean cringe. She looked at me and said, "User is a twit, huh?" Luckily she had a sense of humor, or I might not be here today.

Sprinkled throughout are not only examples of working programs (to show you how to do things), but also examples of broken programs where we ask you to go through the program and figure out what's wrong. Often the problem is very subtle, such as a misplaced semicolon or use of = instead of ==. These programs let you learn how to spot mistakes in a small program. That way when you make similar mistakes in a big program—and you *will* make mistakes—you will be trained to spot them.

## CHAPTER 2

The Basics of Program Writing

The first and most important thing of all, at least for writers today, is to strip language clean, to lay it bare down to the bone.

—Ernest Hemingway

Computers are very powerful tools that can store, organize, and process a tremendous amount of information. However, they can't do anything until someone gives them detailed instructions.

Communicating with computers is not easy. They require instructions that are exact and detailed. Wouldn't life be easier if we could write programs in English? Then we could tell the computer, "Add up all my checks and deposits, and tell me the total," and the machine would balance our checkbooks.

But English is a lousy language when you must write exact instructions. The language is full of ambiguity and imprecision. Grace Hopper, the grand old lady of computing, once commented on the instructions she found on a bottle of shampoo:

Wash.
Rinse.
Repeat.

She tried to follow the directions, but she ran out of shampoo. (Wash-rinse-repeat. Wash-rinse-repeat. Wash-rinse-repeat. . . .)

Of course, we can try to write in precise English. We'd have to be careful and make sure to spell everything out and include instructions for every contingency. If we worked really hard, we could write precise English instructions, right?

As it turns out, there is a group of people who spend their time trying to write precise English. They're called the government, and the documents they write are called government regulations. Unfortunately, in their effort to make the regulations precise, the government also has made the documents almost unreadable. If you've ever read the instruction book that comes with your tax forms, you know what precise English can be like.

Still, even with all the extra verbiage the government puts in, problems can occur. A few years ago California passed a law requiring all motorcycle riders to wear a helmet. Shortly after this law went into effect a cop stopped a guy for not wearing a helmet. The man suggested the police officer take a closer look at the law.

The law had two requirements: 1) that motorcycle riders have an approved crash helmet and 2) that it be firmly strapped on. The cop couldn't give the motorcyclist a ticket because the man did have a helmet firmly strapped on—to his knee.

So English, with all its problems, is out as a computer language. Now, how do we communicate with a computer?

The first computers cost millions of dollars, while at the same time a good programmer cost about $6,000 a year. Programmers were forced to program in a language where all the instructions were reduced to a series of numbers, called *machine language*. This language could be directly input into the computer. A typical machine-language program looks like this:

```
1010 1111
0011 0111
0111 0110
.. and so on for several hundred instructions
```

Whereas machines "think" in numbers, people don't. To program these ancient machines, software engineers would write out their programs using a simple language where each word would stand for a single instruction. This was called *assembly language* because the programmers had to manually translate, or assemble, each line into machine code.

A typical program might look like:

```
Program          Translation
MOV A,47         1010 1111
ADD A,B          0011 0111
HALT             0111 0110
.. and so on for several hundred instructions
```

This process is illustrated in Figure 2-1.

Translation was a difficult, tedious, exacting task. One software engineer decided this was a perfect job for a computer, so he wrote a program, called an *assembler*, that would do the job automatically.

He showed his new creation to his boss and was immediately chewed out: "How dare you even think of using such an expensive machine for a mere 'clerical' task?" Given the cost of an hour of computer time versus the cost of an hour of programmer's time, this was not an unreasonable attitude.

Figure 2-1. Assembling a program

Fortunately, as time passed the cost of programmers went up and the cost of computers went down. So it became more cost-effective to let the programmers write programs in assembly language and use a program called an assembler to translate the programs into machine language.

Assembly language organized programs in a way that was easier for the programmers to understand. However, the program was more difficult for the machine to use. The program had to be translated before the machine could execute it. This was the start of a trend. Programming languages became more and more convenient for programmers to use and started requiring more and more computer time to translate them into something useful for computers.

Over the years a series of *high-level languages* has been devised. These languages are attempts to let programmers write in something that is easy for them to understand and also precise and simple enough for computers to understand.

Early high-level languages were designed to handle specific types of applications. FOR-TRAN was designed for number crunching; COBOL, for writing business reports; and PASCAL, for student use. (Many of these languages have far outgrown their initial uses. It is rumored that Nicklaus Wirth has said, "If I had known that PASCAL was going to be so successful, I would have been more careful in its design.")

Later on, Brian Kernighan and Dennis Ritchie developed C and Bjarne Stroustrup turned it into C++.

Programs from Conception to Execution

C++ programs are written in a high-level language using letters, numbers, and the other symbols you find on a computer keyboard. Computers actually execute a very *low-level language* called *machine code* (a series of numbers). So, before a program can be used, it must undergo several transformations.

Programs start out as an idea in a programmer's head. She writes down her thoughts in a file, called a *source file* or *source code*, using a *text editor*. This file is transformed by the *compiler* into an *object file*. Next a program called the *linker* takes the object file, combines it with predefined routines from a *standard library,* and produces an *executable program* (a set of machine-language instructions). In the following sections, you'll see how these various forms of the program work together to produce the final program.

Figure 2-2 shows the steps that must be taken to transform a program written in a high-level language into an executable program.

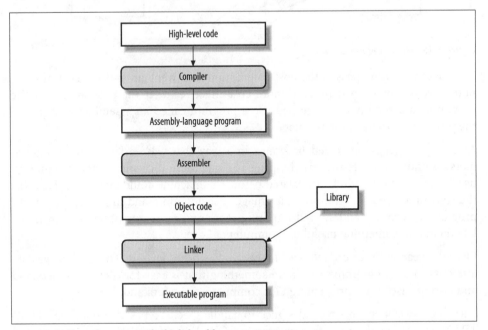

Figure 2-2. Transformation of a high-level language into a program

Fortunately you don't have to run the compiler, assembler, and linker individually. Most C++ compilers use *"wrapper" programs,* which determine which tools need to be run and then run them.

Some programming systems go even further and provide the developer with an integrated development environment (IDE). The IDE contains an editor, compiler, linker, project manager, debugger, and more in one convenient package. Both Borland and Microsoft provide IDEs with their compilers.

Creating a Real Program

Before you can actually start creating your own programs, you need to know how to use the basic programming tools. This section will take you step by step through the process of entering, compiling, and running a simple program.

This section describes how to use two different types of compilers. The first type is the standalone or command-line compiler. This type of compiler is operated from the command line. You type a command, and the compiler turns your source code into an executable program. The other type of compiler is contained in an IDE.

Most Unix systems use command-line compilers. A few IDE-type compilers are available for Unix, but they are rare. On the other hand, almost all the compilers used with Microsoft Windows are part of an IDE. For command-line die-hards, these IDEs contain command-line compilers as well.

Creating a Program Using a Command-Line Compiler

In this section you'll go through the step-by-step process needed to create a program using a command-line compiler. The program you're going to create will display the message "Hello World" on the screen. Instruction is given for using a generic Unix compiler, the Free Software Foundation's g++ compiler, Borland C++, and Microsoft Visual C++.

However, if you are using a Borland or Microsoft compiler, you might want to skip ahead to the section "Creating a Program Using an Integrated Development Environment."

Note that, because compilers are continually being improved, the information in this section may not be accurate by the time you read it. As new compilers come out, we'll update this section and post the update on the O'Reilly web site at *http://www. oreilly.com/catalog/cplus2*.

Step 1: Create a place for your program

It is easier to manage things if you create a separate directory for each program you are working on. In this case you'll create a directory called *hello* to hold your hello program.

In Unix, type:

```
% mkdir hello
% cd hello
```

In MS-DOS, type:

```
C:> MKDIR HELLO
C:> CD HELLO
```

Step 2: Create the program

A program starts out as a text file. Example 2-1 shows the hello program in source form.

Example 2-1. Source for the hello.cpp program

```
#include <iostream>

int main( )
{
    std::cout << "Hello World\n";
    return (0);
}
```

Use your favorite text editor to enter the program. Your file should be named *hello.cpp*.

 Do *not* use a word-processing program such as Microsoft Word or WordPerfect to write your programs. Word-processing programs add formatting codes to files that confuse the compiler. You must use a text editor, such as the notepad program, that is capable of editing ASCII files.

Step 3: Run the compiler

The compiler changes the source file you just created into an executable program. Each compiler has a different command line. The commands for the most popular compilers are listed below.

Unix CC Compiler (Generic Unix). Most Unix-based compilers follow the same generic standard. The C++ compiler is named CC. To compile your hello program, you need the following command:

```
% CC -g -ohello hello.cpp
```

The -g option enables debugging. (The compiler adds extra information to the program to make it easier to debug.) The switch -ohello tells the compiler that the program is to be called hello, and the final hello.cpp is the name of the source file. See your compiler manual for details on all the possible options. There are several different C++ compilers for Unix, so your command line may be slightly different than is shown here.

Free Software Foundation's g++ Compiler. The Free Software Foundation, the GNU people, publishes a number of high-quality programs. (See the glossary entry "Free Software Foundation" for information on how to get their software.) Among their offerings is a C++ compiler called g++.

To compile the *hello* program using the g++ compiler, use the following command line:

```
% g++ -g -Wall -ohello hello.cpp
```

The additional switch -Wall turns on all the warnings. When warnings are turned on, the compiler will warn you when it sees questionable code.

Borland's Turbo C++. Borland International makes a free Microsoft Windows C++ compiler called Borland-C++. This compiler is ideal for learning. The command line for Borland-C++ is:

```
C:> bcc32 -v -N -w -tWC -ehello hello.cpp
```

The -v switch tells Borland-C++ to put debugging information in the program. Warnings are turned on by -w and stack checking by -N. The -tWC option tells Borland-C++ to output a "Console Application." That's a program that uses the standard C++ API (as opposed to the Windows API) and uses a MS-DOS console window for its input and output. Finally, -ehello tells Borland-C++ to create a program named hello, and hello.cpp is the name of the source file. See the Borland-C++ reference manual for a complete list of options.

Microsoft Visual C++ .NET. Microsoft Visual C++ .NET is another C++ compiler for Microsoft Windows. To compile the *HELLO* program, use the following command line:

```
C:> cl /FeHELLO /GZ /RTCsuc /Zi /Wall hello.cpp
```

The /FeHELLO option tells the program to generate a program named *HELLO.exe*. Runtime checking is enabled by /GZ and /RTCsuc, and debugging is turned on with the /Zi option. All warning messages are enabled by /Wall.[*]

Step 4: Execute the program

Now, run the program by typing the following at the command prompt. (This works for both Unix and MS-DOS.)

```
hello
```

The message:

```
Hello World
```

will appear on the screen.

Creating a Program Using an Integrated Development Environment

The IDE provides a one-stop shop when it comes to programming. It take a compiler, editor, and debugger and wraps them into one neat package for the programmer. This package is presented inside a unified graphical interface that allows you to perform most program development operations with a few clicks of the mouse.

---

[*] In the prerelease of Microsoft Visual Studio .NET, compilation with /Wall generated a large number of warnings caused by minor problems in Microsoft's own libraries. I expect these problems to be fixed in the production release of this code.

Since development environments tend to change, the particular version you use may operate slightly differently than is described in this chapter.

Each IDE is a little different, so we've included separate instructions for each one. (Note that compilers change much faster than books, so the information presented in these sections may be outdated. Check this book's page at the O'Reilly web site, *http://www.oreilly.com/catalog/cplus2*, for the latest information on compilation environments.)

Borland C++

1. Create a directory called *HELLO* to hold the files for our `hello` program. You can create a directory using the Windows desktop tools or by typing the following command at the MS-DOS prompt:

   ```
   mkdir \HELLO
   ```

2. From Windows, double-click on the Borland C++ icon to start the IDE, or start the IDE using the "Start" menu. The program begins execution and displays a blank workspace, as shown in Figure 2-3.

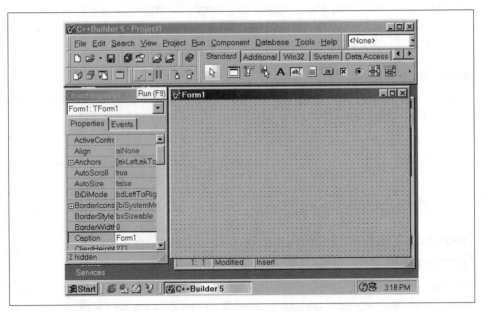

Figure 2-3. Borland C++ initial screen

3. Select the File→New item to create a project for our program. Select Console Wizard as shown in Figure 2-4 and click OK.

4. The Console Wizard dialog appears as shown in Figure 2-5. Select C++ for Source Type and click OK.

5. The initial editing window appears as shown in Figure 2-6.

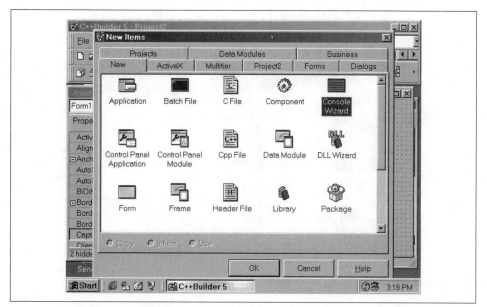

Figure 2-4. New Items selector

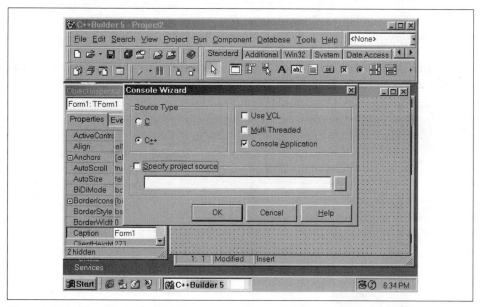

Figure 2-5. Project Options dialog box

6. Add your code to the file *Unit1.cpp*. The resulting code should look like:

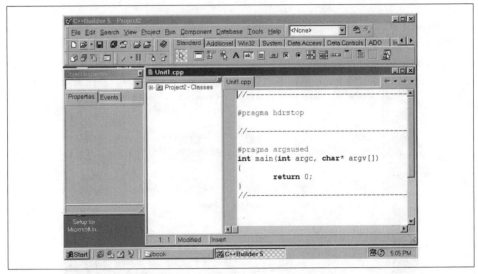

Figure 2-6. Initial editing window

```cpp
#include <iostream>
int main()
{
    std::cout << "Hello World\n";
    return (0);
}
```

You can ignore the #pragma statements and comments that Borland-C++ has added. When you have finished, your screen will look like Figure 2-7.

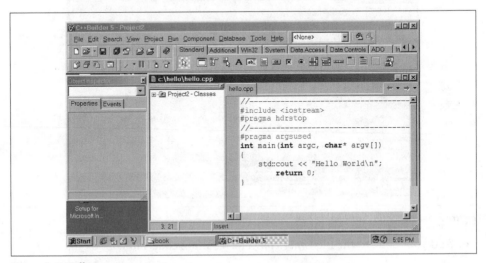

Figure 2-7. Hello program

7. Compile and run the program by selecting the Debug→Run menu item. The program will run and display "Hello World" in a window, as shown in Figure 2-8.

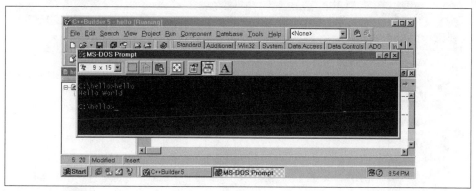

Figure 2-8. Hello program

Microsoft Visual C++

1. From Windows, start Microsoft Visual Studio .NET. A start screen will be displayed, as shown in Figure 2-9.

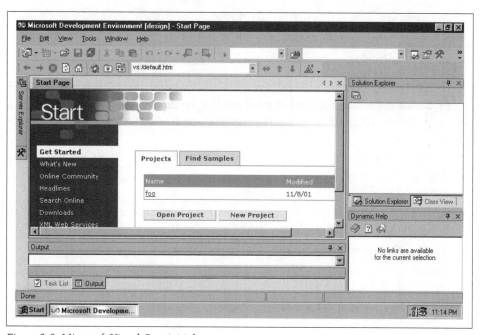

Figure 2-9. Microsoft Visual C++ initial screen

2. Click on File→New→Project to bring up the New Project dialog shown in Figure 2-10.

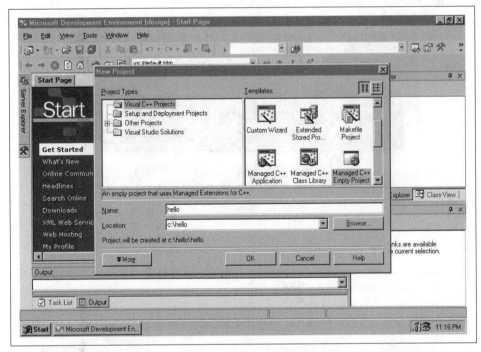

Figure 2-10. New Project dialog

In the Template pane, select "Manage C++ Empty Project." Fill in the Name field with *hello*. Change the Location field to the directory in which you wish to build the project. Click OK. The project screen now appears as shown in Figure 2-11.

3. In the Solution Explorer tab, select Source Files. Now create the program using the File→Add New Item menu. The Add New Item dialog appears as shown in Figure 2-12.

4. Select C++ file as the file type and put *hello.cpp* in the name field. Click Done to bring up the editing window shown in Figure 2-13.

5. Type the following lines into the hello.cpp window.

```
#include <iostream>
int main( )
{
    std::cout << "Hello World\n";
    return (0);
}
```

Your results should look like Figure 2-14.

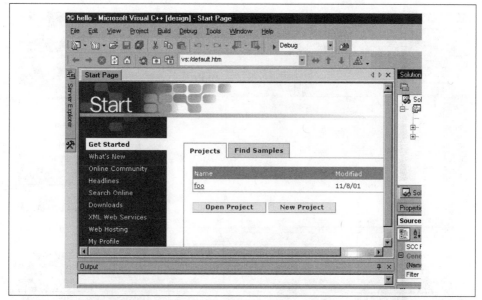

Figure 2-11. Initial project screen

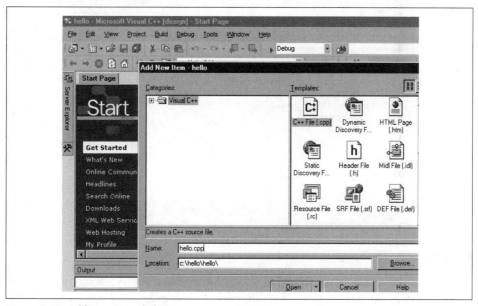

Figure 2-12. Add New Item dialog

6. Compile the program by selecting Build→Build Hello. You may have to resize the windows to view the messages. If everything works, the screen should look something like Figure 2-15.

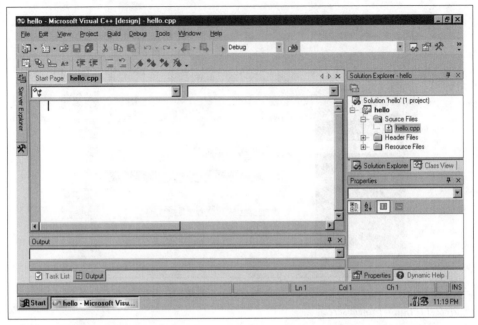

Figure 2-13. Editing window

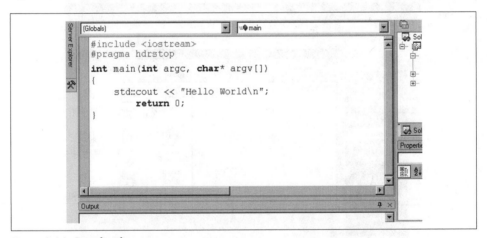

Figure 2-14. Completed program

7. Run the program using the Debug→Start Program without Debugging window menu item. An MS-DOS window appears and the program is run within it. The results are shown in Figure 2-16.

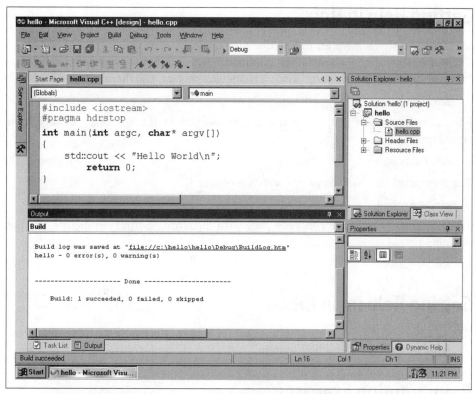

Figure 2-15. Result of the build

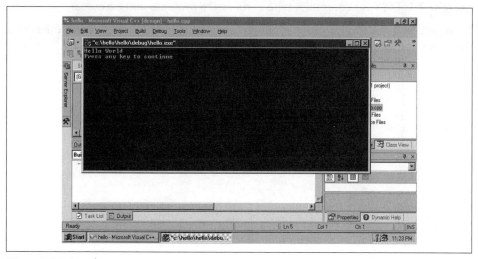

Figure 2-16. Sample run

Getting Help in Unix

Most Unix systems have an online documentation system called the "man pages." These can be accessed using the man command. (Unix uses man as an abbreviation for "manual.") To get information about a particular subject, use the command:

```
man subject
```

For example, to find out about the classes defined in the iostream package, you would type:

```
man iostream
```

The command also has a keyword search mode:

```
man -k keyword
```

To determine the name of every man page with the word "output" in its title, use the command:

```
man -k output
```

Getting Help in an IDE

IDEs such as Borland C++ and Microsoft C++ have a Help menu item. This item activates a hypertext-based help system.

Programming Exercises

Exercise 2-1: On your computer, type in the hello program and execute it.

Exercise 2-2: Take several programming examples from any source, enter them into the computer, and run them.

## CHAPTER 3

Style

*There is no programming language, no matter how
structured, that will prevent programmers from
writing bad programs.*
—L. Flon

*It is the nobility of their style which will make our
writers of 1840 unreadable forty years from now.*
—Stendhal

This chapter discusses how to use good programming style to create a simple, easy-
to-read program. It may seem backward to discuss style before you know how to
program, but style is the most important part of programming. Style is what separates the gems from the junk. It is what separates the programming artist from the
butcher. You must learn good programming style first, before typing in your first line
of code, so everything you write will be of the highest quality.

Contrary to popular belief, programmers do not spend most of their time writing
programs. Far more time is spent maintaining, upgrading, and debugging existing
code than is ever spent on creating new work. The amount of time spent on maintenance is skyrocketing. From 1980 to 1990 the average number of lines in a typical
application went from 23,000 to 1.2 million. The average system age has gone from
4.75 to 9.4 years.

Most software is built on existing software. I recently completed coding for 12 new
programs. Only one of these was created from scratch; the other 11 are adaptations
of existing programs.

Programmers believe that the purpose of a program is only to present the computer
with a compact set of instructions. This is not true. Programs written only for the
machine have two problems:

- They are difficult to correct because sometimes even the author does not understand them.

- Modifications and upgrades are difficult to make because the maintenance programmer must spend a considerable amount of time figuring out what the program does from its code.

Comments

Ideally, a program serves two purposes: First, it presents the computer with a set of instructions, and second, it provides the programmer with a clear, easy-to-read description of what the program does.

Example 2-1 contains a glaring error. It is an error that many programmers still make and one that causes more trouble than any other problem. *The program contains no comments.*

A working but uncommented program is a time bomb waiting to explode. Sooner or later someone will have to modify or upgrade the program, and the lack of comments will make the job ten times more difficult. A well-commented, simple program is a work of art. Learning how to comment is as important as learning how to code properly.

C++ has two flavors of comments. The first type starts with /* and ends with */. This type of comment can span multiple lines as shown:

```
/* This is a single-line comment. */
/*
 * This is a multiline comment.
 */
```

The other form of comment begins with // and goes to the end of the line:

```
// This is another form of comment.
// The // must begin each line that is to be a comment.
```

The advantage of the /* */ comment style is that you can easily span multiple lines, whereas with the // style you have to keep putting the // on each line. The disadvantage of /* */ is that forgetting a */ can really screw up your code. (Remember this because it's the answer to one of the questions later in the book.)

Which flavor should you use? Whichever one makes your program as clear and as easy to read as possible. Mostly, it's a matter of taste. In this book we use the /* */ style comments for big, multiline comments, and the // style is reserved for comments that take up only a single line.

Whatever comment style you decide to use, you *must* comment your programs. Example 3-1 shows how the "hello world" program looks after comments are added.

Example 3-1. hello2/hello2.cpp

```
/********************************************************
 * hello -- program to print out "Hello World".        *
 *       Not an especially earth-shattering program.    *
 *                                                      *
 * Author: Steve Oualline                               *
 *                                                      *
 * Purpose: Demonstration of a simple program           *
 *                                                      *
 * Usage:                                               *
 *       Run the program and the message appears        *
 ********************************************************/
#include <iostream>

int main( )
{
    // Tell the world hello
    std::cout << "Hello World\n";
    return (0);
}
```

In this program, the beginning comments are in a box of asterisks (*) called a *comment box*. This is done to emphasize the more important comments, much like bold characters are used for the headings in this book. Less important comments are not boxed. For example:

```
    // Tell the world hello
    std::cout << "Hello World\n";
```

To write a program, you must have a clear idea of what you are going to do. One of the best ways to organize your thoughts is to write them down in a language that is clear and easy to understand. Once the process has been clearly stated, it can be translated into a computer program.

Understanding what you are doing is the most important part of programming. I once wrote two pages of comments describing a complex graphics algorithm. The comments were revised twice before I even started coding. The actual instructions took only half a page. Because I had organized my thoughts well (and was lucky), the program worked the first time.

Your program should read like an essay. It should be as clear and easy to understand as possible. Good programming style comes from experience and practice. The style described in the following pages is the result of many years of programming experience. It can be used as a starting point for developing your own style. These are not rules, but only suggestions. The only rule is this: Make your program as *clear*, *concise*, and *simple* as possible.

At the beginning of the program is a comment block that contains information about the program. Boxing the comments makes them stand out. The list that follows contains some of the sections that should be included at the beginning of your program. Not all programs will need all sections, so use only those that apply.

Poor Person's Typesetting

In typesetting you can use font style and size, **bold,** and *italic* to make different parts of your text stand out. In programming, you are limited to a single, monospaced font. However, people have come up with ingenious ways to get around the limitations of the typeface.

Here are some of the various commenting tricks:

```
/*****************************************************
 *****************************************************
 ******** WARNING: This is an example of a      *******
 ********    warning message that grabs the     *******
 ********    attention of the programmer.       *******
 *****************************************************
 ****************************************************/


//------------> Another, less important warning <--------


//>>>>>>>>>>>  Major section header  <<<<<<<<<<<<<<<


/*****************************************************
 * We use boxed comments in this book to denote the   *
 * beginning of a section or program                  *
 ****************************************************/


/*---------------------------------------------------*\
 * This is another way of drawing boxes               *
\*---------------------------------------------------*/


/*
 * This is the beginning of a section
 * ^^^^ ^^ ^^^ ^^^^^^^^^ ^^ ^ ^^^^^^^
 *
 * In the paragraph that follows we explain what
 * the section does and how it works.
 */


/*
 * A medium-level comment explaining the next
 * dozen or so lines of code.  Even though we don't have
 * the bold typeface we can **emphasize** words.
 */


// A simple comment explaining the next line
```

Heading

The first comment should contain the name of the program. Also include a short description of what it does. You may have the most amazing program, one that slices, dices, and solves all the world's problems, but it is useless if no one knows what it does.

Author

You've gone to a lot of trouble to create this program. Take credit for it. Also, if someone else must later modify the program, he or she can come to you for information and help.

Purpose

Why did you write this program? What does it do?

Usage

In this section, give a short explanation of how to run the program. In an ideal world, every program comes with a set of documents describing how to use it. The world is not ideal. Oualline's law of documentation states that 90% of the time the documentation is lost. Out of the remaining 10%, 9% of the time the revision of the documentation is different from the revision of the program and therefore completely useless. The 1% of the time you actually have the correct revision of the documentation, the documentation will be written in a foreign language.

To avoid falling prey to Oualline's law of documentation, put the documentation in the program.

References

Creative copying is a legitimate form of programming (if you don't break the copyright laws in the process). In the real world, it doesn't matter how you get a working program, as long as you get it, but give credit where credit is due. In this section you should reference the original author of any work you copied.

File formats

List the files that your program reads or writes and a short description of their format.

Restrictions

List any limits or restrictions that apply to the program, for example, the data file must be correctly formatted or the program does not check for input errors.

Revision history

This section contains a list indicating who modified the program and when and what changes have been made. Many computers have a source control system (RCS, CVS, and SCCS on Unix; MKS-RCS and PCVS on Microsoft Windows) that will keep track of this information for you.

Error handling

If the program detects an error, what does it do with it?

Copyright and license

Some companies require that you include a copyright notice (for example, "Copyright 2002, BB Software Corp.").

On the other hand, many open source programs include a copyright and license. The most popular open source license is the GNU Public License (GPL). (For more information see *http://www.gnu.org.*)

Notes

Include special comments or other information that has not already been covered.

The format of your beginning comments will depend on what is needed for the environment in which you are programming. For example, if you are a student, the instructor may ask you to include in the program heading the assignment number, your name, student identification number, and other information. In industry, a project number or part number might be included.

Comments should explain everything the programmer needs to know about the program, but no more. It is possible to overcomment a program. (This is rare, but it does happen.) When deciding on the format for your heading comments, make sure there is a reason for everything you include.

Inserting Comments—The Easy Way

If you are using the Unix editor vi, put the following in your *.exrc* file to make it easier to construct boxes.

```
:abbr #b /*********************************************
:abbr #e *********************************************/
```

These two lines define vi abbreviations #b and #e, so that typing #b and pressing RETURN at the beginning of a block will cause the string:

```
/*********************************************
```

to appear (for beginning a comment box). Typing #e and hitting RETURN will end a box. The number of stars was carefully selected to align the end of the box on a tab stop.

C++ Code

The actual code for your program consists of two parts: variables and executable instructions. Variables are used to hold the data used by your program. Executable instructions tell the computer what to do with the data. C++ classes are a combination of data and the instructions that work on the data. They provide a convenient way of packaging both instructions and data.

A variable is a place in the computer's memory for storing a value. C++ identifies that place by the variable name. Names can be any length and should be chosen so their meaning is clear. (Actually, a length limit does exist, but it is so large that you probably will never encounter it.) Every variable in C++ must be declared. (Variable declarations are discussed in Chapter 9.) The following declaration tells C++ that you are going to use three integer (**int**) variables named p, q, and r:

```
int p,q,r;
```

But what are these variables for? The reader has no idea. They could represent the number of angels on the head of a pin, or the location and acceleration of a plasma bolt in a game of Space Invaders. Avoid abbreviations. Exs. abb. are diff. to rd. and hd. to ustnd. (Excess abbreviations are difficult to read and hard to understand.)

Now consider another declaration:

```
int account_number;
int balance_owed;
```

Now we know that we are dealing with an accounting program, but we could still use some more information. For example, is the balance_owed in dollars or cents? It would be much better if we added a comment after each declaration explaining what we are doing.

```
int account_number;      // Index for account table
int balance_owed;        // Total owed us (in pennies)
```

By putting a comment after each declaration, we in effect create a mini-dictionary where we define the meaning of each variable name. Since the definition of each variable is in a known place, it's easy to look up the meaning of a name. (Programming tools, such as editors, cross-referencers, and grep, can also help you quickly find a variable's definition.)

Units are very important. I was once asked to modify a program that converted plot data files from one format to another. Many different units of length were used throughout the program and none of the variable declarations was commented. I tried very hard to figure out what was going on, but it was impossible to determine what units were being used in the program. Finally, I gave up and put the following comment in the program:

```
/*******************************************************
 * Note: I have no idea what the input units are, nor  *
 *       do I have any idea what the output units are, *
 *       but I have discovered that if I divide by 3   *
 *       the plots look about the right size.          *
 *******************************************************/
```

One problem many beginning programmers have is that they describe the code, not the variable. For example:

```
int top_limit;   // Top limit is an integer [bad comment]
```

It's obvious from the code that top_limit is an integer. I want to know what top_limit is. Tell me.

```
int top_limit;   // Number of items we can load before losing data
```

You should take every opportunity to make sure your program is clear and easy to understand. Do not be clever. Cleverness makes for unreadable and unmaintainable programs. Programs, by their nature, are extremely complex. Anything you can to do to cut down on this complexity will make your programs better. Consider the following code, written by a very clever programmer.

```
while ('\n' != *p++ = *q++);
```

It is almost impossible for the reader to tell at a glance what this mess does. Properly written this would be:

```
while (true) {
    *destination_ptr = *source_ptr;
    ++destination_ptr;
    ++source_ptr;
    if (*(destination_ptr-1) == '\n')
        break;  // exit the loop if done
}
```

Although the second version is longer, it is much clearer and easier to understand. Even a novice programmer who does not know C++ well can tell that this program has something to do with moving data from a source to a destination.

The computer doesn't care which version is used. A good compiler will generate the same machine code for both versions. It is the programmer who benefits from the verbose code.

Naming Style

Names can contain both uppercase and lowercase letters. In this book we use all lowercase names for variables (e.g., source_ptr, current_index). All uppercase is reserved for constants (e.g., MAX_ITEMS, SCREEN_WIDTH). This convention is the classic convention followed by most C and C++ programs.

Many newer programs use mixed-case names (e.g., RecordsInFile). Sometimes they use the capitalization of the first letter to indicate information about the variable. For example, recordsInFile might be used to denote a local variable while RecordsInFile would denote a global variable. (See Chapter 9 for information about local and global variables.) You should be careful when making up rules for your variables because the more complex the rules, the more likely someone will violate them or get confused.

One additional note on variable names: please use whole words. The problem with abbreviations is that there are too many different ways of abbreviating the same word. This is especially true when programmers think that to abbreviate a word, you write down the word and then cross out random letters. I've seen "Ground Point" named gp, ground_pt, gnd_pt, g_pnt, and many others. On the other hand, there's only one full spelling: ground_point.

Also, I work for a company which has people from 62 different countries working together to produce code. The non-English speakers have real difficulty looking up the more unusual abbreviations. Words in the dictionary make things much easier to understand for people who have to deal with the twin complexities of English and C++.

Which naming convention you use is up to you. It is more a matter of religion than of style. However, using a consistent naming style is extremely important. In this book we have chosen the first style—lowercase variable names and uppercase constants—and we use it throughout the book. (Note that this convention is growing less common as old-style #define constants are being replaced with new-style const ones.)

Coding Religion

Computer scientists have devised many programming styles. These include structured programming, top-down programming, and **goto**-less programming. Each of these styles has its own following or cult. I use the term "religion" because people are taught to follow the rules without knowing the reasons behind them. For example, followers of the **goto**-less cult will never use a **goto** statement, even when it is natural to do so.

The rules presented in this book are the result of years of programming experience. I have discovered that by following these rules, I can create better programs. You do not have to follow them blindly. If you find a better system, by all means use it. (If it really works, drop me a line. I'd like to use it, too.)

Indentation and Code Format

To make programs easier to understand, most programmers indent their programs. The general rule for a C++ program is to indent one level for each new block or conditional. In Example 3-1 there are three levels of logic, each with its own indentation level. The **while** statement is outermost. The statements inside the **while** are at the next level. The statement inside the **if** (**break**) is at the innermost level.

There are two styles of indentation, and a vast religious war is being waged in the programming community as to which is better. The first is the short form:

```
while (! done) {
    std::cout << "Processing\n";
    next_entry( );
}

if (total <= 0) {
    std::cout << "You owe nothing\n";
    total = 0;
} else {
    std::cout << "You owe " << total << " dollars\n";
```

```
        all_totals = all_totals + total;
    }
```

In this case, most of the curly braces are put on the same line as the statements. The other style puts the curly braces on lines by themselves:

```
while (! done)
{
    std::cout << "Processing\n";
    next_entry( );
}

if (total <= 0)
{
    std::cout << "You owe nothing\n";
    total = 0;
}
else
{
    std::cout << "You owe " << total << " dollars\n";
    all_totals = all_totals + total;
}
```

Both formats are commonly used. You should use the format you feel most comfortable with. This book uses the short form. (It saves paper.)

The amount of indentation is left to the programmer. Two, four, and eight spaces are common. Studies have shown that a four-space indent makes the most readable code. You can choose any indent size as long as you are consistent.

Automatic Indenting

The vim editor is a vi-like program with many additional features. This includes the ability to automatically indent C++ programs. To turn on automatic four-space indentation, execute the commands:

```
:set cindent
:set sw=4
```

Clarity

A program should read like a technical paper, organized into sections and paragraphs. Procedures form a natural section boundary. You should organize your code into paragraphs, beginning a paragraph with a topic sentence comment and separating it from other paragraphs with a blank line. For example:

```
// poor programming practice
temp = box_x1;
box_x1 = box_x2;
```

```
box_x2 = temp;
temp = box_y1;
box_y1 = box_y2;
box_y2 = temp;
```

A better version would be:

```
/*
 * Swap the two corners
 */

/* Swap X coordinate */
temp = box_x1;
box_x1 = box_x2;
box_x2 = temp;

/* Swap Y coordinate */
temp = box_y1;
box_y1 = box_y2;
box_y2 = temp;
```

Simplicity

Your program should be simple. Here are some general rules of thumb:

- A single function should not be longer than one or two pages. (See Chapter 9.) If it gets longer, it can probably be split into two simpler functions. This rule comes about because the human mind can hold only so much in short-term memory: three pages is about the maximum for a single sitting.

- Avoid complex logic such as multiple nested **if**s. The more complex your code, the more indentation levels you will need. About the time you start running into the right margin, you should think about splitting your code into multiple procedures and thus decreasing the level of complexity.

- Did you ever read a sentence, like this one, where the author went on and on, stringing together sentence after sentence with the word "and," and didn't seem to understand the fact that several shorter sentences would do the job much better, and didn't it bother you?

  C++ statements should not go on forever. Long statements should be avoided. If an equation or formula looks like it is going to be longer than one or two lines, you probably should split it into two shorter equations.

- Split large single code files into multiple smaller ones. (See Chapter 23 for more information about programming with multiple files.) In general I like to keep my files smaller than 1,500 lines. That way they aren't too difficult to edit and print.

- When using classes (see Chapter 13), put one class per module.

- Finally, the most important rule: make your program as simple and easy to understand as possible, even if it means breaking some of the rules. The goal is clarity, and the rules given in this chapter are designed to help you accomplish that goal. If the rules get in the way, get rid of them. I have seen a program with a single statement that spanned more than 20 pages. However, because of the specialized nature of the program, this statement was simple and easy to understand.

Consistency and Organization

Good style is only one element in creating a high-quality program. Consistency is also a factor. This book is organized with the table of contents at the front and the index at the back. Almost every book printed has a similar organization. This consistency makes it easy to look up a word in the index or find a chapter title in the table of contents.

Unfortunately, the programming community has developed a variety of coding styles. Each has its own advantages and disadvantages. The trick to efficient programming in a group is to pick one style and use it consistently. That way you can avoid the problems and confusion that arise when programs written in different styles are combined.

Good style is nice, but consistency is better.

Further Reading

In this chapter we have touched only the basics of style. Later chapters expand on this base, adding new stylistic elements as you learn new elements of the language.

For a more complete discussion of style, the online book *C Elements of Style* is available from *http://www.oualline.com*.

Summary

A program should be concise and easy to read. It must serve as a set of computer instructions, but also as a reference work describing the algorithms and data used inside it. Everything should be documented with comments. Comments serve two purposes: they describe your program to any maintenance programmer who has to fix it, and they help you remember what you did.

Class discussion 1: Create a style sheet for class assignments. Discuss what comments should go into the programs and why.

Class discussion 2: Analyze the style of an existing program. Is the program written in a manner that is clear and easy to understand? What can be done to improve the style of the program?

## CHAPTER 4

Basic Declarations and Expressions

*A journey of a thousand miles must begin
with a single step.*

—Lao-zi

*If carpenters made buildings the way programmers
make programs, the first woodpecker to come
along would destroy all of civilization.*

—Anonymous

If you are going to construct a building, you need two things: the bricks and a blueprint that tells you how to put them together. In computer programming you also need two things: data (variables) and instructions (code). Variables are the basic building blocks of a program. Instructions tell the computer what to do with the variables.

Comments are used to describe the variables and instructions. They are notes by the author documenting the program so it is clear and easy to read. Comments are ignored by the computer.

In construction, before we can start we must order our materials: "We need 500 large bricks, 80 half-size bricks, and 4 flagstones." Similarly, in C++ you must declare all variables before you can use them. You must name each one of your "bricks" and tell C++ what type of "brick" to use.

After the variables are defined, you can begin to use them. In construction the basic structure is a room. By combining many rooms we form a building. In C++ the basic structure is a function, and functions can be combined to form a program.

An apprentice builder does not start out building the Empire State Building. He starts on a one-room house. In this chapter you will concentrate on constructing simple, one-function programs.

Basic Program Structure

The basic elements of a program are the data declarations, functions, and comments. Let's see how these can be organized into a simple C++ program.

The basic structure of a one-function program is:

```
/*****************************************************
 * Heading comments                                  *
 *****************************************************/
data declarations
int main( )
{
    executable statements
    return(0);
}
```

The heading comments tell the programmer all about the program. The *data declarations* describe the data that the program is going to use.

Our single function is named main. The name main is special, because it is the first function called. Any other functions are called directly or indirectly from main. The function main begins with:

```
int main( )
{
```

and ends with:

```
    return(0);
}
```

The line return(0); is used to tell the operating system that the program exited normally (status=0). A nonzero status indicates an error—the bigger the return value, the more severe the error. Typically 1 is used for most simple errors, such as a missing file or bad command-line syntax.

Now let's take a look at the "Hello World" program (Example 1-1).

At the beginning of the program is a comment box enclosed in /* and */. Next we have the line:

```
#include <iostream>
```

This tells C++ that we want to use the standard input/output system. (The proper name for this is the I/O streams module.) This is a type of data declaration.[*]

The main routine contains the instruction:

```
    std::cout << "Hello World\n";
```

---

[*] Technically, the statement causes a set of data declarations to be taken from an include file. Chapter 10 discusses include files.

This instruction is an executable statement telling C++ to write the message "Hello World" on the screen. The special character sequence \n tells C++ to write out a newline character. C++ uses a semicolon to end a statement in much the same way we use a period to end a sentence. Unlike line-oriented languages such as BASIC, the end of a line does not end a statement. The sentences in this book can span several lines—the end of a line is treated as a space separating words. C++ works the same way. A single statement can span several lines. Similarly, you can put several sentences on the same line, just as you can put several C++ statements on the same line. However, most of the time your program is more readable if each statement starts on a separate line.

We are using the standard object std::cout (console out) to output the message. A standard object is a generally useful C++ object that has already been defined and put in the standard library. A library is a collection of class definitions, functions, and data that have been grouped together for reuse. The standard library contains classes and functions for input, output, sorting, advanced math, and file manipulation. See your C++ reference manual for a complete list of library functions and standard objects.

"Hello World" is one of the simplest C++ programs. It contains no computations, merely sending a single message to the screen. It is a starting point. Once you have mastered this simple program, you have done many things right. The program is not as simple as it looks. But once you get it working, you can move on to create more complex code.

Simple Expressions

Computers can do more than just print strings. They can also perform calculations. Expressions are used to specify simple computations. C++ has the five simple operators listed in Table 4-1.

Table 4-1. Simple operators

Operator	Meaning
*	Multiply
/	Divide
+	Add
–	Subtract
%	Modulus (remainder after division)

Multiply (*), divide (/), and modulus (%) have precedence over addition (+) and subtraction (–). Parentheses may be used to group terms. Thus, the following expression yields 12:

```
(1 + 2) * 4
```

The next expression yields 9:

```
1 + 2 * 4
```

The program in Example 4-1 computes the value of the expression (1 + 2) * 4.

Example 4-1. Simple expression

```
int main( )
{
    (1 + 2) * 4;
    return(0);
}
```

Although we calculate the answer, we don't do anything with it. (This program will generate a "null effect" warning when it's compiled, which indicates that there is a correctly written, but useless, statement in the program.)

If we were constructing a building, think about how confused a worker would be if we said, "Take your wheelbarrow and go back and forth between the truck and the building site."

"Do you want me to carry bricks in the wheelbarrow?"

"No. Just go back and forth."

You need to output the results of your calculations.

The std::cout Output Object

The standard **object** std::cout is used to output data to the console. We'll learn what a object is later in Chapter 13, *Simple Classes*, but for now all we have to know is that the operator <<* tells C++ what to output. So the statement:

```
std::cout << "Hello World\n";
```

tells C++ to take the string "Hello World\n" and write it to the console. Multiple << operators may be used together. For example, both the following lines output the same message:

```
std::cout << "Hello World\n";
std::cout << "Hello " << "World\n";
```

Expressions can also be output this way, such as:

```
std::cout << "Half of " << 64 << " is " << (64 / 2) << "\n";
```

When this is executed, it will write:

```
Half of 64 is 32
```

---

* Technically << is the left shift operator; however, the std::cout object has overloaded this operator and made it the output operator. (See Chapter 16 for a complete discussion of I/O objects and classes and Chapter 18, for a definition of overloading.)

on the console. Note that we had to put a space after the "of" in "Half of". There also is a space on either side of the "is" string. These spaces are needed in the output to separate the numbers from the text. Suppose we didn't put the spaces in, and the code looked like this:

```
// Problem code
std::cout << "Half of" << 64 << "is" << (64 / 2) << "\n";
```

At first glance this code looks perfectly normal. There are spaces around each of the numbers. But these spaces are not inside any string, so they will not be output. The result of this code is:

```
Half of64is32
```

Omitting needed spaces is a common first-time programming mistake. Remember, only the text inside the quotation marks will be output.

Variables and Storage

C++ allows you to store values in *variables*. Each variable is identified by a *variable name*.

Additionally, each variable has a *variable type*. The type tells C++ how the variable is going to be used and what kind of numbers (real, integer) it can hold.

Names start with a letter followed by any number of letters, digits, or underscores (_).* Uppercase is different from lowercase, so the names "sam", "Sam", and "SAM" specify three different variables. To avoid confusion, it is better to use different names for variables and not depend on case differences.

Some C++ programmers use all lowercase variable names. Some names, such as **int**, **while**, **for**, and **float**, have a special meaning to C++ and are considered *reserved words*, also called *keywords*. They cannot be used for variable names.

The following is an example of some variable names:

```
average            // average of all grades
pi                 // pi to 6 decimal places
number_of_students // number of students in this class
```

The following are *not* variable names:

```
3rd_entry   // Begins with a number
all$done    // Contains a "$"
the end     // Contains a space
int         // Reserved word
```

Avoid variable names that are similar. For example, the following illustrates a poor choice of variable names:

---

* System variable names (names defined the by the standard library) can begin with underscore.

```
total      // total number of items in current entry
totals     // total of all entries
```

This is a much better set of names:

```
entry_total // total number of items in current entry
all_total   // total of all entries
```

Variable Declarations

Before you can use a variable in C++, it must be defined in a *declaration statement*. A variable cannot be used unless it is declared.

A variable declaration serves three purposes:

- It defines the name of the variable.
- It defines the type of the variable (integer, real, character, etc.).
- It gives the programmer a description of the variable.

The declaration of a variable answer can be:

```
int answer;    // the result of our expression
```

The keyword **int** tells C++ that this variable contains an integer value. (Integers are defined below.) The variable name is answer. The semicolon is used to indicate the statement end, and the comment is used to define this variable for the programmer.

The general form of a variable declaration is:

```
type  name;  // comment
```

Type is one of the C++ variable types (**int, float**, etc.) *Name* is any valid variable name. The comment explains what the variable is and what it will be used for. Variable declarations come just before the main( ) line at the top of a program. (In Chapter 9 you will see how local variables may be declared elsewhere.)

Integers

One variable type is integer. Integers (also known as whole numbers) have no fractional part or decimal point. Numbers such as 1, 87, and –222 are integers. The number 8.3 is not an integer because it contains a decimal point. The general form of an integer declaration is:

```
int name;  // comment
```

A calculator with an eight-digit display can only handle numbers between 99,999,999 and –99,999,999. If you try to add 1 to 99,999,999, you will get an overflow error. Computers have similar limits. The limits on integers are implementation-dependent, meaning they change from computer to computer.

Calculators use decimal digits (0–9). Computers use binary digits (0–1) called *bits*. Eight bits make a *byte*. The number of bits used to hold an integer varies from machine to machine. Numbers are converted from binary to decimal for printing.

On most machines integers are 32 bits (4 bytes), providing a range of 2,147,483,647 ($2^{31}- 1$) to –2,147,483,648 (-2^{31}). Some systems now use newer processors such as the Intel Itanium, which have 64-bit integers, giving you a range of 9223372036854775807 ($2^{63}-1$) to –9223372036854775807 (-2^{63}) If you are programming using an older MS-DOS compiler, only 16 bits (2 bytes) are used, so the range is 32,767 ($2^{15}-1$) to –32,768 (-2^{15}).

Question 4-1: *The following will work on a Unix machine but will fail on an old MS-DOS system.*

```
int zip;      // zip code for current address

.........

zip = 92126;
```

Why does this fail? What will be the result when this program is run on an MS-DOS system?

Assignment Statements

Variables are given a value through the use of *assignment statements*. Before a variable can be used, it must be declared. For example:

```
int answer;     // Result of a simple computation
```

The variable may then be used in an assignment statement, such as:

```
answer = (1 + 2) * 4;
```

The variable answer on the left side of the equal sign (=) is assigned the value of the expression (1 + 2) * 4 on the right side. The semicolon ends the statement.

When you declare a variable, C++ allocates storage for the variable and puts an unknown value inside it. You can think of the declaration as creating a box to hold the data. When it starts out, it is a mystery box containing an unknown quantity. This is illustrated in Figure 4-1A. The assignment statement computes the value of the expression and drops that value into the box, as shown in Figure 4-1B.

The general form of the assignment statement is:

```
variable = expression;
```

The equal sign (=) is used for assignment, not equality.

In Example 4-2, the variable term is used to store an integer value that is used in two later expressions. Variables, like expressions, can be output using the output operator <<, so we use this operator to check the results.

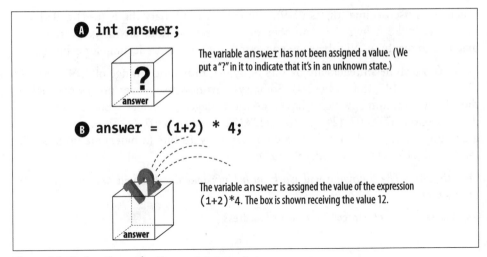

Figure 4-1. Declaration and assignment statements

Example 4-2. tterm/tterm.cpp

```
#include <iostream>

int term;        // term used in two expressions
int main( )
{

    term = 3 * 5;
    std::cout << "Twice " << term << " is " << 2*term << "\n";
    std::cout << "Three times " << term << " is " << 3*term << "\n";
    return (0);
}
```

Floating-Point Numbers

Real numbers are numbers that have a fractional part. Because of the way they are stored internally, real numbers are also known as *floating-point numbers*. The numbers 5.5, 8.3, and −12.6 are all floating-point numbers. C++ uses the decimal point to distinguish between floating-point numbers and integers, so a number such as 5.0 is a floating-point number while 5 is an integer. Floating-point numbers must contain a decimal point. Numbers such as 3.14159, 0.5, 1.0, and 8.88 are floating-point numbers.

Although it is possible to omit digits before the decimal point and specify a number as .5 instead of 0.5, the extra 0 makes it clear that you are using a floating-point number. A similar rule applies to 12. versus 12.0. Floating-point zero should be written as 0.0.

Additionally, a floating-point number may include an exponent specification of the form $e\pm exp$. For example, 1.2e34 is shorthand for 1.2×10^{34}.

The form of a floating-point declaration is:

```
float variable;    // comment
```

Again, there is a limit on the range of floating-point numbers the computer can handle. The range varies widely from computer to computer. Floating-point accuracy is discussed further in Chapter 19.

Floating-point numbers may be output using std::cout. For example:

```
std::cout << "The answer is " << (1.0 / 3.0) << "\n";
```

Floating-Point Divide Versus Integer Divide

The division operator is special. There is a vast difference between an integer divide and a floating-point divide. In an integer divide, the result is truncated (any fractional part is discarded). For example, the integer divide value of 19/10 is 1.

If either the divisor or the dividend is a floating-point number, a floating-point divide is executed. In this case 19.0/10.0 is 1.9. (19/10.0 and 19.0/10 are also floating-point divides; however, 19.0/10.0 is preferred for clarity.) There are several examples in Table 4-2.

Table 4-2. Expression examples

Expression	Result	Result type
19 / 10	1	Integer
19.0 / 10.0	1.9	Floating point
19.0 / 10	1.9	Floating point (for clarity, do not code like this)
19 / 10.0	1.9	Floating point (for clarity, do not code like this)

C++ allows the assignment of an integer expression to a floating-point variable. It will automatically perform the integer-to-floating-point conversion and then make the assignment. A similar conversion is performed when assigning a floating-point number to an integer variable. Floating-point numbers are truncated when assigned to integer variables.

Example 4-3 demonstrates a variety of floating-point and integer operations.

Example 4-3. float1/float1.cpp

```
int    integer;  // an integer
float floating; // a floating-point number

int main( )
{
```

Example 4-3. float1/float1.cpp (continued)

```
    floating = 1.0 / 2.0;        // assign "floating" 0.5

    integer = 1 / 3;             // assign integer 0

    floating = (1 / 2) + (1 / 2); // assign floating 0.0

    floating = 3.0 / 2.0;        // assign floating 1.5

    integer = floating;          // assign integer 1

    return (0);
}
```

Notice that the expression 1/2 is an integer expression resulting in an integer divide and an integer result of 0.

Question 4-2: *Why does Example 4-4 print "The value of 1/3 is 0"? What must be done to this program to fix it?*

Example 4-4. float2/float2.cpp

```
#include <iostream>

float answer;  // the result of the divide

int main( )
{
    answer = 1/3;
    std::cout << "The value of 1/3 is " << answer << "\n";
    return (0);
}
```

Characters

The type **char** represents single characters. The form of a character declaration is:

```
    char variable;   //comment
```

Characters are enclosed in single quotation marks ('). 'A', 'a' and '!' are character constants. The backslash character (\) is called the *escape character*. It is used to signal that a special character follows. For example, the character \t can be used to represent the single character "tab." \n is the newline character. It causes the output device to go to the beginning of the next line, similar to a return key on a typewriter. The character \\ is the backslash itself. Finally, characters can be specified by \\nnn, where *nnn* is the octal code for the character. Table 4-3 summarizes these special characters. For a full list of ASCII character codes, see Appendix A.

Table 4-3. Special characters

Character	Name	Meaning
\b	Backspace	Move the cursor to the left one character.
\f	Form feed	Go to top of a new page.
\n	New line	Go to the next line.
\r	Return	Go to the beginning of the current line.
\t	Tab	Advance to the next tab stop (eight-column boundary).
\'	Apostrophe or single quotation mark	The character ' .
\"	Double quote	The character ".
\\	Backslash	The character \.
\nnn	The character nnn	The character number nnn (octal).
\xNN	The character NN	The character number NN (hexadecimal).

While characters are enclosed in single quotes ('), a different data type, the string literal, is enclosed in double quotes ("). A good way to remember the difference between these two types of quotes is that *single* characters are enclosed in *single* quotes. Strings can have any number of characters (including double quote characters), and they are enclosed in double quotes.

Example 4-5 demonstrates the use of character variables by reversing three characters.

Example 4-5. print3/print3.cpp

```
#include <iostream>

char char1;    // first character
char char2;    // second character
char char3;    // third character

int main( )
{
    char1 = 'A';
    char2 = 'B';
    char3 = 'C';
    std::cout << char1 << char2 << char3 << " reversed is " <<
            char3 << char2 << char1 << "\n";
    return (0);
}
```

When executed, this program prints:

```
ABC reversed is CBA
```

Wide Characters

The problem with the char data type is that it was designed to hold only a basic character set. This is fine for all the American characters, but what about foreign languages? That where the **wchar_t** data type comes in. It is used to specify "wide characters" which include not only the basic American characters, but foreign characters as well. A wide character is declared just like a simple character:

```
char simple;    // A simple character
wchar_t wide;   // A wide character
```

A simple character is declared by putting the character inside single quotes: 'X'. A wide character uses an "L" prefix to indicate that it is a wide character: L'Ω'.

For example:

```
simple = 'X';

wide = L'Ω';
```

Boolean Type

The **bool** type can hold the value **true** or **false**. For example:

```
bool flag; /* Flag can be on or off */
flag = true;
```

This type of variable is extremely useful when dealing with logic statements, as described in Chapter 6.

Legacy Boolean Types

Until recently the C language did not have a **bool**[a] type. Because of this, people used macros and the typedef statements to define their own boolean type. Most of the time they called it **BOOL**, or sometimes **Bool**.

You may see these types in old (and not so old) programs. These names are depreciated and should not be used in current C++ programs.

a. Yes, C does have a **bool** type. See the C standard: ISO/IEC 9899:1999(E) section 7.16.

Programming Exercises

Exercise 4-1: Write a program to print your name, Social Security number, and date of birth.

Exercise 4-2: Write a program to print a block E using asterisks (*), where the E is 7 characters high and 5 characters wide.

Exercise 4-3: Write a program to compute the area and perimeter of a rectangle 3 inches wide by 5 inches long. What changes must be made to the program so it works for a rectangle 6.8 inches wide by 2.3 inches long?

Exercise 4-4: Write a program to print "HELLO" in big block letters where each letter is 7 characters high and 5 characters wide.

Answers to Chapter Questions

Answer 4-1: The largest number that can be stored in an **int** on a Unix machine is 2,147,483,647. When using an old MS-DOS compiler the limit is 32,767. The zip code 92126 is larger than 32,767, so it is mangled and the result is 26,590.

This problem can be fixed by using a **long int** instead of just an **int**. The various types of integers are discussed in Chapter 5.

Answer 4-2: The problem concerns the division: 1/3. The number 1 and the number 3 are both integers, so this is an integer divide. Fractions are truncated in an integer divide. The expression should be written as:

```
answer = 1.0 / 3.0
```

CHAPTER 5

Arrays, Qualifiers, and Reading Numbers

*That mysterious independent variable of political
calculations, Public Opinion.*
—Thomas Henry Huxley

This chapter covers arrays and more complex variables.

Arrays

So far in constructing our building we have named each brick (variable). That is fine
for a small number of bricks, but what happens when we want to construct something larger? We would like to point to a stack of bricks and say, "That's for the left
wall. That's brick 1, brick 2, brick 3. . . ."

Arrays allow us to do something similar with variables. An *array* is a set of consecutive memory locations used to store data. Each item in the array is called an *element*.
The number of elements in an array is called the *dimension* of the array. A typical
array declaration is:

```
// List of data to be sorted and averaged
int    data_list[3];
```

This declares data_list to be an array of the three elements data_list[0], data_
list[1], and data_list[2], which are separate variables. To reference an element of
an array, you use a number called the *subscript* (the number inside the square brackets []). C++ is a funny language and likes to start counting at 0, so these three elements are numbered 0–2.

Common sense tells you that when you declare data_list to be three
elements long, data_list[3] would be valid. Common sense is wrong:
data_list[3] is illegal.

Example 5-1 computes the total and average of five numbers.

Example 5-1. five/five.cpp

```cpp
#include <iostream>

float data[5];    // data to average and total
float total;      // the total of the data items
float average;    // average of the items

int main( )
{
    data[0] = 34.0;
    data[1] = 27.0;
    data[2] = 46.5;
    data[3] = 82.0;
    data[4] = 22.0;

    total = data[0] + data[1] + data[2] + data[3] + data[4];
    average =  total / 5.0;
    std::cout << "Total " << total << " Average " << average << '\n';
    return (0);
}
```

Example 5-1 outputs:

```
Total 211.5 Average 42.3
```

Strings

C++ comes with an excellent string package. Unlike the numbers such as int and float, which are built-in to the core language, the std::string type comes from the C++ library. Before you can use this type, you must bring in the std::string definition with the statement:

```cpp
#include <string>
```

After this you can declare strings like any other variable:

```cpp
std::string my_name;
```

A string constant is any text enclosed in double quotes. So to assign the variable my_name the value "Steve", we use the statement:

```cpp
my_name = "Steve";
```

Strings may be concatenated using the + operator. Example 5-2 illustrates how to combine two strings (and a space) to turn a first and last name into a full name.

Example 5-2. string/string.cpp

```cpp
#include <string>
#include <iostream>
```

Example 5-2. string/string.cpp (continued)

```
std::string first_name; // First name of the author
std::string last_name;  // Last name of the author
std::string full_name;  // Full name of the author

int main()
{
    first_name = "Steve";
    last_name = "Oualline";
    full_name = first_name + " " + last_name;
    std::cout << "Full name is " << full_name << '\n';
    return (0);
}
```

A string can be treated like an array of characters. Each character in the string can be accessed through the [ ] operation. For example:

```
char first_ch;    // First character of the name
    ....
    first_ch = first_name[0];
```

If the subscript is out of range, the result is undefined. That means that sometimes you'll get a random character, sometimes your program will crash, and sometimes something else will happen. You could protect things with an assert statement, which is described later in this chapter, but there's a better way to do it.

That is to access the characters through the at member function. (We'll learn all about what exactly a member function is in Chapter 13.) It works just like [ ] except that if the index is out of range, it throws an exception and shuts your program down in an orderly manner. See Chapter 22 for a description of exceptions.)

So to get the first character of our string safely, we need to use the statement:

```
    first_ch = first_name.at(0);
```

The length of a C++ string can be obtained with the length member function. For example:

```
    std::cout << full_name << " is " << full_name.length() << " long\n";
```

Finally, to extract a portion of a string, there is the substr member function. The general form of this function is:

```
    string.substr(first, last)
```

This function returns a string containing all the characters from *first* to *last*. For example, the following code assigns the variable sub_string the word "is":

```
    //           01234567890123
    main_string = "This is a test";
    sub_string = main_string.substr(5, 6);
```

If first is out of range, an exception is generated and your program is terminated. If last is too big, the substr function returns as much of the string as it can get.

If you omit the last parameter, `substr` returns the rest of the string.

The `std::string` variable type has lots of useful and advanced features. For a full list, see your C++ documentation or help text.

Wide Strings

The **wstring** data type acts just like the **string** data type except that uses wide characters (**wchar_t**) instead of characters (**char**). Wide string constants look just like string constants, but they begin with L" instead of ". For example:

```
wstring name = L"ディアズ・タチアナ";
```

Reading Data

So far you've learned how to compute expressions and output the results. You need to have your programs read numbers as well. The output class object `std::cout` uses the operator `<<` to write numbers. The input object `std::cin` uses the operator `>>` to read them. For example:

```
std::cin >> price >> number_on_hand;
```

This code reads two numbers: `price` and `number_on_hand`. The input to this program should be two numbers, separated by whitespace. For example, if you type:

```
32 5
```

`price` gets the value 32 and `number_on_hand` gets 5.

This does not give you very precise control over your input. C++ does a reasonable job for simple input. If your program expects a number and you type <enter> instead, the program will skip the <enter> (it's whitespace) and wait for you to type a number. Sometimes this may lead you to think your program's stuck.

In Example 5-3, we use `std::cin` to get a number from the user, then we double it.

Example 5-3. double/double.cpp

```
#include <iostream>

int    value;       // a value to double

int main()
{
    std::cout << "Enter a value: ";
    std::cin >> value;
    std::cout << "Twice " << value << " is " << value * 2 << '\n';
```

Example 5-3. double/double.cpp (continued)

```
    return (0);
}
```

Notice that there is no \n at the end of Enter a value:. This is because we do not want the computer to print a newline after the prompt. For example, a sample run of the program might look like this:

```
Enter a value: 12
Twice 12 is 24
```

If we replaced Enter a value: with Enter a value:\n the result would be:

```
Enter a value:
12
Twice 12 is 24
```

Question 5-1: *Example 5-4 is designed to compute the area of a triangle, given its width and height. For some strange reason, the compiler refuses to believe that we declared the variable* width. *The declaration is right there on line two, just after the definition of height. Why isn't the compiler seeing it?*

Example 5-4. comment/comment.cpp

```
#include <iostream>

int  height;    /* the height of the triangle
int  width;     /* the width of the triangle */
int  area;      /* area of the triangle (computed) */

int main()
{
    std::cout << "Enter width height? ";
    std::cin >> width >> height;
    area = (width * height) / 2;
    std::cout << "The area is " << area << '\n';
    return (0);
}
```

The general form of a std::cin statement is:

```
std::cin >> variable;
```

This works for all types of simple variables such as **int**, **float**, **char**, and **wchar_t**.

Reading strings is a little more difficult. To read a string, use the statement:

```
std::getline(std::cin, string);
```

For example:

```
std::string name;    // The name of a person

std::getline(std::cin, name);
```

We discuss the std::getline function in Chapter 16.

When reading a string, the std::cin class considers anything up to the end-of-line part of the string. Example 5-5 reads a line from the keyboard and reports the line's length.

Example 5-5. len/len.cpp

```
#include <string>
#include <iostream>

std::string line;        // A line of data

int main( )
{
    std::cout << "Enter a line:";
    std::getline(std::cin, line);

    std::cout << "The length of the line is: " << line.length( ) << '\n';
    return (0);
}
```

When we run this program we get:

```
Enter a line:test
The length of the line is: 4
```

Initializing Variables

C++ allows variables to be initialized in the declaration statement. For example, the following statement declares the integer counter and initializes it to 0.

```
    int counter(0);    // number cases counted so far
```

The older C-style syntax is also supported:

```
    int counter = 0;    // number cases counted so far
```

Arrays can be initialized in a similar manner. The element list must be enclosed in curly braces ({}). For example:

```
    // Product numbers for the parts we are making
    int product_codes[3] = {10, 972, 45};
```

This is equivalent to:

```
    product_codes[0] = 10;
    product_codes[1] = 972;
    product_codes[2] = 45;
```

The number of elements in the curly braces ({}) does not have to match the array size. If too many numbers are present, a warning will be issued. If there are not enough numbers, the extra elements will be initialized to 0.

If no dimension is given, C++ will determine the dimension from the number of elements in the initialization list. For example, we could have initialized our variable product_codes with the statement:

```
// Product numbers for the parts we are making
int product_codes[] = {10, 972, 45};
```

Bounds Errors

In Example 5-2 the data array has five elements. So what happens if we accidently use an illegal index? For example:

```
int data[5];
// ...
result = data[99];    // Bad
```

The results are undefined. Most of the time you'll get a random number. Other times, your program may abort with an error. Things get worse if you use the bad index on the left side of an assignment:

```
int data[5];
// ...
data[99] = 55;    // Very bad
```

In this case, if you're lucky, the program will abort. If you're not so lucky, the program will change a random memory location. This location could hold another variable, vital system data, or something else important. The result is that your program fails in a strange and hard to debug manner.

Therefore it is extremely important to make sure that any time you use an array index that it's within bounds. Example 5-6 illustrates a program that contains an array bounds error.

Example 5-6. bounds/bound_err.cpp

```
#include <iostream>

const int N_PRIMES = 7; // Number of primes
// The first few prime numbers
int primes[N_PRIMES] = {2, 3, 5, 7, 11, 13, 17};

int main()
{
    int index = 10;

    std::cout << "The tenth prime is " << primes[index] << '\n';
    return (0);
}
```

When this program executes on some machines it outputs:

```
Segmentation violation
Core dumped
```

On others it just gives us funny information:

```
The tenth prime is 0
```

Bounds errors are ugly, nasty things that should be stamped out whenever possible. One solution to this problem is to use the assert statement. The assert statement tells C++, "This can never happen, but if it does, abort the program in a nice way." One thing you find out as you gain programming experience is that things that can "never happen" happen with alarming frequency. So just to make sure that things work as they are supposed to, it's a good idea to put lots of self checks in your program.

The assert statement is one form of self check. When we add it to Example 5-6 we get Example 5-7.

Example 5-7. bounds/bound_c1.cpp

```
#include <iostream>
#include <assert.h>

const int N_PRIMES = 7; // Number of primes
// The first few prime numbers
int primes[N_PRIMES] = {2, 3, 5, 7, 11, 13, 17};

int main()
{
    int index = 10;

    assert(index < N_PRIMES);
    assert(index >= 0);
    std::cout << "The tenth prime is " << primes[index] << '\n';
    return (0);
}
```

The statement:

```
#include <assert.h>
```

tells C++ that we want to use the assert module. Now we know that the index must be in range. After all, our program could never contain an error that might generate a bad index. But just to make sure, we check to see if it's in range using the statement:

```
assert(index < N_PRIMES);
assert(index >= 0);
```

Now when the program hits the assert statement, the assertion fails and an error message is issued:

```
bound_c1: bound_c1.cpp:11: int main(): Assertion `index < 7' failed.
Abort (core dumped)
```

The program then aborts. Aborting is a nasty way of handling an error, but it's better than doing nothing at all. (This is not true in every case; see sidebar.)

There is a problem with our code. The programmer must remember that the array data has a limit of N_PRIMES. This means that he has to count and to keep track of two things: the number of items in data and the value of N_PRIMES. It would be better to do things automatically.

The C++ operation sizeof returns the size of a variable in bytes. So sizeof(data) is 28 (7 elements of 4 bytes each). This assumes that integers are 4 bytes long. (This is system-dependent.)

But we want the number of elements in data, not the number of bytes. The size of the first element is sizeof(data[0]), and since each element is the same size, this is the size of every element. So we have the total number of bytes in the array and the number of bytes in an element. From this we can compute the number of elements in the array:

```
sizeof(data) / sizeof(data[0])
```

Now we can rewrite the code and eliminate the need to count elements. The results are in Example 5-8.

Example 5-8. bounds/bound_c2.cpp

```
#include <iostream>
#include <assert.h>

// The first few prime numbers
int primes[] = {2, 3, 5, 7, 11, 13, 17};

int main()
{
    int index = 10;

    assert(index < (sizeof(primes)/sizeof(primes[0])));
    assert(index >= 0);
```

Example 5-8. bounds/bound_c2.cpp (continued)

```
    std::cout << "The tenth prime is " << primes[index] << '\n';
    return (0);
}
```

Multidimensional Arrays

Arrays can have more than one dimension. The declaration for a two-dimensional array is:

```
type variable[size1][size2]; // comment
```

For example:

```
// a typical matrix
int matrix[2][4];
```

Notice that C++ does *not* follow the notation used in other languages of matrix[10,12].

To access an element of the matrix we use the following notation:

```
matrix[1][2] = 10;
```

C++ allows you to use as many dimensions as needed (limited only by the amount of memory available). Additional dimensions can be tacked on:

```
four_dimensions[10][12][9][5];
```

Initializing multidimensional arrays is similar to initializing single-dimension arrays. A set of curly braces {} encloses each element. The declaration:

```
// a typical matrix
int matrix[2][4];
```

can be thought of as a declaration of an array of dimension 2 whose elements are arrays of dimension 4. This array is initialized as follows:

```
// a typical matrix
int matrix[2][4] =
    {
        {1, 2, 3, 4},
        {10, 20, 30, 40}
    };
```

This is shorthand for:

```
matrix[0][0] = 1;
matrix[0][1] = 2;
matrix[0][2] = 3;
matrix[0][3] = 4;

matrix[1][0] = 10;
matrix[1][1] = 20;
matrix[1][2] = 30;
matrix[1][3] = 40;
```

Question 5-2: *Why does the program in Example 5-9 print incorrect answers?*

Example 5-9. array/array.cpp

```
#include <iostream>

int array[3][5] = {     // Two dimensional array
    { 0,  1,  2,  3,  4 },
    {10, 11, 12, 13, 14 },
    {20, 21, 22, 23, 24 }
};

int main( )
{
    std::cout << "Last element is " << array[2,4] << '\n';
    return (0);
}
```

When run on a Sun 3/50 this program generates:

```
Last element is 0x201e8
```

Your answers may vary.

You should be able to spot the error because one of the statements looks like it has a syntax error in it. It doesn't, however, and the program compiles because we are using a new operator that has not yet been introduced. But even though you don't know about this operator, you should be able to spot something funny in this program.

C-Style Strings

C++ lets you use not only the C++ std::string class, but also older C-style strings, as well. You may wonder why we would want to study a second type of string when the first one does just fine. The answer is that there are a lot of old C programs out there that have been converted to C++, and the use of C-style strings is quite common.

C-style strings are arrays of characters. The special character '\0' (NUL) is used to indicate the end of a string. For example:

```
char    name[4];

int main( )
{
    name[0] = 'S';
    name[1] = 'a';
    name[2] = 'm';
    name[3] = '\0';
    return (0);
}
```

This creates a character array four elements long. Note that we had to allocate one character for the end-of-string marker.

String constants consist of text enclosed in double quotes ("). You may have already noticed that we've used string constants extensively for output with the std::cout standard class. C++ does not allow one array to be assigned to another, so you can't write an assignment of the form:

```
name = "Sam";    // Illegal
```

Instead you must use the standard library function std::strcpy to copy the string constant into the variable. (std::strcpy copies the whole string, including the end-of-string character.) The definition of this function is in the header file *cstring* (note the lack of *.h* on the end).

To initialize the variable name to "Sam" you would write:

```
#include <cstring>

char    name[4];

int main( )
{
    std::strcpy(name, "Sam");    // Legal
    return (0);
}
```

C++ uses variable-length strings. For example, the declaration:

```
#include <cstring>

char a_string[50];

int main( )
{
    std::strcpy(a_string, "Sam");
```

creates an array (a_string) that can contain up to 50 characters. The *size* of the array is 50, but the *length* of the string is 3. Any string up to 49 characters long can be stored in a_string. (One character is reserved for the NUL that indicates the end of the string.)

There are several standard routines that work on string variables. These are listed in Table 5-1.

Table 5-1. String functions

Function	Description
std::strcpy(string1, string2)	Copies string2 into string1
std::strncpy(string1, string2, length)	Copies string2 into string1, but doesn't copy over length characters (including the end of string character)
std::strcat(string1, string2)	Concatenates string2 onto the end of string1

Table 5-1. String functions (continued)

Function	Description
std::strncat(string1, string2, length)	Concatenates string2 onto the end of string1, but only length characters (will not put an end of string character on the result if length characters are copied)
length = std::strlen(string)	Gets the length of a string
std::strcmp(string1, string2)	Returns 0 if string1 equals string2;
	A negative number if string1 < string2
	A positive number if string1 > string2

Example 5-10 illustrates how std::strcpy is used.

Example 5-10. str/sam.cpp

```
#include <iostream>
#include <cstring>

char name[30];  // First name of someone

int main()
{
    std::strcpy(name, "Sam");
    std::cout << "The name is " << name << '\n';
    return (0);
}
```

Example 5-11 takes a first name and a last name and combines the two strings. The program works by initializing the variable first to the first name (Steve). The last name (Oualline) is put in the variable last. To construct the full name, the first name is copied into full_name. Then strcat is used to add a space. We call strcat again to tack on the last name.

The dimensions of the string variables are 100 because we know that no one we are going to encounter has a name more than 98 characters long. (One character is reserved for the space and one for the NUL at the end of the string.) If we get a name more than 99 characters long, our program will overflow the array, corrupting memory.

Example 5-11. name2/name2.cpp

```
#include <cstring>
#include <iostream>

char first[100];         // first name
char last[100];          // last name
char full_name[100];     // full version of first and last name

int main()
{
```

Example 5-11. name2/name2.cpp (continued)

```
    std::strcpy(first, "Steve");      // Initalize first name
    std::strcpy(last, "Oualline");    // Initalize last name

    std::strcpy(full_name, first);    // full = "Steve"
    // Note: strcat not strcpy
    std::strcat(full_name, " ");      // full = "Steve "
    std::strcat(full_name, last);     // full = "Steve Oualline"

    std::cout << "The full name is " << full_name << '\n';
    return (0);
}
```

The output of this program is:

```
The full name is Steve Oualline
```

C++ has a special shorthand for initializing strings, using double quotes (") to simplify the initialization. The previous example could have been written:

```
char name[] = "Sam";
```

The dimension of name is 4, because C++ allocates a place for the '\0' character that ends the string.

C++ uses variable-length strings. For example, the declaration:

```
char long_name[50] = "Sam";
```

creates an array (long_name) that can contain up to 50 characters. The size of the array is 50, and the length of the string is 3. Any string up to 49 characters long can be stored in long_name. (One character is reserved for the NUL that indicates the end of the string.)

Our statement initialized only 4 of the 50 values in long_name. The other 46 elements are not initialized and may contain random data.

Safety and C Strings

The problem with strcpy is that it doesn't check to see if the string being changed is big enough to hold the data being copied into it. For example, the following will overwrite random memory:

```
char name[5];
//...
strcpy(name, "Oualline");  // Corrupts memory
```

There are a number of ways around this problem:

- Use C++ strings. They don't have this problem.
- Check the size before you copy:

```
    assert(sizeof(name) >= sizeof("Oualline"));
    strcpy(name, "Oualline");
```

Although this method prevents us from corrupting memory, it does cause the program to abort.

- Use the `strncpy` function to limit the number of characters copied. For example:

```
std::strncpy(name, "Oualline", 4);
```

In this example, only the first four characters of "Oualline" (Oual) are copied into name. A null character is then copied to end the string for a total of 5 characters—the size of name.

A more reliable way of doing the same thing is to use the `sizeof` operator:

```
std::strncpy(name, "Oualline", sizeof(name)-1);
```

In this case we've had to add an adjustment of −1 to account for the null at the end of the string.

This method does not corrupt memory, but strings that are too long will be truncated.

The `strcat` function has a similar problem. Give it too much data and it will overflow memory. One way to be safe is to put in `assert` statements:

```
char full_name[10];

assert(sizeof(name) >= sizeof("Steve"));
std::strcpy(name, "Steve");

// Because we're doing a strcat we have to take into account
// the number of characters already in name
assert(sizeof(name) >= ((strlen(name) + sizeof("Oualline"))));
std::strcat(name, "Oualline");
```

The other way of doing things safely is to use `strncat`. But `strncat` has a problem: if it reaches the character limit for the number of characters to copy, it does not put the end-of-string null on the end. So we must manually put it on ourselves. Let's take a look at how to do this. First we set up the program:

```
char full_name[10];

std::strncpy(name, "Steve", sizeof(name));
```

Next we add the last name, with a proper character limit:

```
std::strncat(name, "Oualline", sizeof(name)-strlen(name)-1);
```

If we fill the string, the `strncat` does not put on the end-of-string character. So to be safe, we put one in ourselves:

```
name[sizeof(name)-1] = '\0';
```

If the resulting string is shorter than the space available, `strncat` copies the end-of-string character. In this case our string will have two end-of-string characters. However, since we stop at the first one, the extra one later on does no damage.

Our complete code fragment looks like this:

```
char full_name[10];

std::strncpy(name, "Steve", sizeof(name));
std::strncat(name, "Oualline", sizeof(name)-strlen(name)-1);
name[sizeof(name)-1] = '\0';
```

You may notice that there is a slight problem with the code presented here. It takes the first name and adds the last name to it. It does not put a space between the two. So the resulting string is "SteveOualline" instead of "Steve Oualline" or, more accurately, "SteveOual" because of space limitations.

There are a lot of rules concerning the use of C-style strings. Not following the rules can result in programs that crash or have security problems. Unfortunately, too many programmers don't follow the rules.

One nice thing about C++ strings is that the number of rules you have to follow to use them goes way down and the functionality goes way up. But there's still a lot of C code that has been converted to C++. As a result, you'll still see a lot of C-style strings.

Reading C-Style Strings

Reading a C-style string is accomplished the same way as it is with the C++ string class, through the use of the getline function:

```
char name[50];
// ....
std::getline(std::cin, name, sizeof(name));
```

A new parameter has been introduced: sizeof(name). Because C-style strings have a maximum length, you must tell the getline function the size of the string you are reading. That way it won't get too many characters and overflow your array.

Converting Between C-Style and C++ Strings

To convert a C++ string to a C-style string, use the c_str( ) member function. For example:

```
char c_style[100];
std::string a_string("Something");
....
    std::strcpy(c_style, a_string.c_str());
```

Conversion from C-style to C++-style is normally done automatically. For example:

```
a_string = c_style;
```

or

```
a_string = "C-style string constant";
```

However, sometimes you wish to make the conversion more explicit. This is done through a type change operator called a *cast*. The C++ operator static_cast converts one type to another. The general form of this construct is:

```
static_cast<new-type>(expression)
```

For example:

```
a_string = static_cast<std::string>(c_style);
```

 There are actually four flavors of C++-style casts: static_cast, const_cast, dynamic_cast, and reinterpret_cast. The other three are discussed later in the book.

The Differences Between C++ and C-Style Strings

C++ style strings are easier to use and are designed to prevent problems. For example, the size of C-style strings is limited by the size of the array you declare. There is no size limit when you use a C++ std::string (other than the amount of storage in your computer). That's because the C++ string automatically manages the storage for itself.

Size is a big problem in C-style strings. The std::strcpy and std::strcat functions do not check the size of the strings they are working with. This means that it is possible to copy a long string into a short variable and corrupt memory. It's next to impossible to corrupt memory using C++ strings because size checking and memory allocation is built into the class.

But there is overhead associated with the C++ std::string class. Using it is not as fast as using C-style strings. But for almost all the programs you will probably write, the speed difference will be negligible. And since the risk associated with using C-style strings is significant, it's better to use the C++ std::string class.

Types of Integers

C++ is considered a medium-level language because it allows you to get very close to the actual hardware of the machine. Some languages, such as Perl, go to great lengths to completely isolate the user from the details of how the processor works. This consistency comes at a great loss of efficiency. C++ lets you give detailed information about how the hardware is to be used.

For example, most machines let you use different-length numbers. Perl allows you to use only one simple data type (the string*). This simplifies programming, but Perl

---

* Perl does have numbers such as 5, 8.3, and 20.8, but they are identical to the strings "5", "8.3", and "20.8".

programs are inefficient. C++ allows you to specify many different kinds of integers so you can make best use of the hardware.

The type specifier **int** tells C++ to use the most efficient size (for the machine you are using) for the integer. This can be 2 to 4 bytes depending on the machine. Sometimes you need extra digits to store numbers larger than what is allowed in a normal **int**. The declaration:

```
long int answer;        // the answer of our calculations
```

is used to allocate a long integer. The **long** qualifier informs C++ that you wish to allocate extra storage for the integer. If you are going to use small numbers and wish to reduce storage, use the qualifier **short**.

```
short int year;         // Year including the century
```

C++ guarantees that the storage for **short** <= **int** <= **long**. In actual practice, **short** almost always allocates 2 bytes; **long,** 4 bytes; and **int,** 2 or 4 bytes. (See Appendix B for numeric ranges.)

Long integer constants end with the character "L". For example:

```
long int var = 1234L;    // Set up a long variable
```

Actually you can use either an uppercase or a lowercase "L". Uppercase is preferred since lowercase easily gets confused with the digit "1".

```
long int funny = 12l;    // Is this 12<long> or one hundred twenty-one?
```

The type **short int** usually uses 2 bytes, or 16 bits. Normally, 15 bits are used for the number and 1 bit for the sign. This results in a range of $-32{,}768$ (-2^{15}) to 32,767 ($2^{15} - 1$). An **unsigned short int** uses all 16 bits for the number, giving it a range of 0 to 65,535 ($2^{16} - 1$). All **int** declarations default to **signed**, so the declaration:

```
signed long int answer;     // final result
```

is the same as:

```
long int answer;            // final result
```

Finally there is the very short integer, the type **char**. Character variables are usually 1 byte long. They can also be used for numbers in the range of -128 to 127 or 0 to 255. Unlike integers, they do not default to **signed**; the default is compiler-dependent.[*]

Question: Is the following character variable signed or unsigned?

```
char foo;
```

Answers:

a.   It's signed.

b.   It's unsigned.

---

[*] Borland-C++ even has a command-line switch to make the default for type **char** either **signed** or **unsigned**.

c. It's compiler-dependent.

d. If you always specify **signed** or **unsigned,** you don't have to worry about problems like this.

Reading and writing very short integers is a little tricky. If you try to use a **char** variable in an output statement, it will be written—*as a character.* You need to trick C++ into believing that the char variable is an integer. This can be accomplished with the static_cast operator. Example 5-12 shows how to write a very short integer as a number.

Example 5-12. two2/twoc.cpp

```
#include <iostream>

signed char ch; // Very short integer
             // Range is -128 to 127

int main()
{
    std::cout << "The number is " << static_cast<int>(ch) << '\n';
    return (0);
}
```

We start by declaring a character variable ch. This variable is assigned the value 37. This is actually an integer, not a character, but C++ doesn't care. On the next line, we write out the value of the variable. If we tried to write ch directly, C++ would treat it as a character. The code static_cast<int>(ch) tells C++, "Treat this character as an integer."

Reading a very short integer is not possible. You must first read in the number as a **short int** and then assign it to a very short integer variable.

Summary of Integer Types

long int declarations allow the programmer to explicitly specify extra precision where it is needed (at the expense of memory). **short int** numbers save space but have a more limited range. The most compact integers have type **char**. They also have the most limited range.

unsigned numbers provide a way of doubling the range at the expense of eliminating negative numbers. The kind of number you use will depend on your program and storage requirements. The ranges of the various types of integers are listed in Appendix B.

Types of Floats

The **float** type also comes in various flavors. **float** denotes normal precision (usually 4 bytes). **double** indicates double precision (usually 8 bytes), giving the programmer twice the range and precision of single-precision (**float**) variables.

The quantifier **long double** denotes extended precision. On some systems this is the same as **double**; on others, it offers additional precision. All types of floating-point numbers are always signed.

On most machines, single-precision floating-point instructions execute faster (but less accurately) than double precision. Double precision gains accuracy at the expense of time and storage. In most cases **float** is adequate; however, if accuracy is a problem, switch to **double** (see Chapter 19).

Constant and Reference Declarations

Sometimes you want to use a value that does not change, such as π. The keyword **const** indicates a variable that never changes. To declare a value for pi, we use the statement:

```
const float PI = 3.1415926;    // The classic circle constant
```

 By convention variable names use lowercase only while constants use uppercase only. However, there is nothing in the language that requires this, and some programming projects use a different convention.

In fact, there are major programming environments such as the X Windows System that use their own naming conventions with mixed-case constants and variables (VisibilityChangeMask, XtConvertAndStore, etc.). The Microsoft Windows API also uses its own unique naming convention.

Constants must be initialized at declaration time and can never be changed. For example, if we tried to reset the value of PI to 3.0 we would generate an error message:

```
PI = 3.0;    // Illegal
```

Integer constants can be used as a size parameter when declaring an array:

```
const int TOTAL_MAX = 50;    // Max. number of elements in total list
float total_list[TOTAL_MAX]; // Total values for each category
```

Another special variable type is the reference type. The following is a typical reference declaration:

```
int count;                   // Number of items so far
int& actual_count = count;   // Another name for count
```

The special character & is used to tell C++ that actual_count is a reference. The declaration causes the names count and actual_count to refer to the same variable. For example, the following two statements are equivalent:

```
count = 5;          // "Actual_count" changes too
actual_count = 5;   // "Count" changes too
```

In other words, a simple variable declaration declares a box to put data in. A reference variable slaps another name on the box, as illustrated in Figure 5-1.

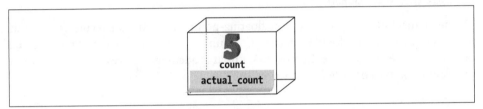

Figure 5-1. Reference variables

This form of the reference variable is not very useful. In fact, it is almost never used in actual programming. In Chapter 9, you'll see how another form of the reference variable can be very useful.

Qualifiers

As you've seen, C++ allows you to specify a number of qualifiers for variable declarations. Qualifiers may be thought of as adjectives that describe the type that follows. Table 5-2 summarizes the various qualifiers; they are explained in detail in the following sections.

Table 5-2. Qualifiers and simple types

Special	Constant	Storage class	Size	Sign	Type
volatile	const	register	long	signed	int
<blank>	<blank>	static	short	unsigned	float
		extern	double	<blank>	char
		auto	<blank>		wchar_t
		<blank>			<blank>

Special

The **volatile** keyword is used for specialized programming such as I/O drivers and shared memory applications. It is an advanced modifier whose use is far beyond the scope of this book.

volatile
　　Indicates a special variable whose value may change at any time

<blank>
   Normal variable

Constant

The **const** keyword indicates a value that cannot be changed.

const
   Indicates that this is a declaration of constant data

<blank>
   Normal variable

Storage Class

The class of a variable is discussed in detail in Chapter 9. A brief description of the various classes follows:

register
   This indicates a frequently used variable that should be kept in a machine register. See Chapter 17.

static
   The meaning of this word depends on the context. This keyword is described in Chapter 9 and Chapter 23.

extern
   The variable is defined in another file. See Chapter 23 for more information.

auto
   A variable allocated from the stack. This keyword is hardly ever used.

<blank>
   Indicates that the default storage class is selected. For variables declared outside a function, this makes the variable global. Variables inside a function are declared **auto**.

Size

The **size** qualifier allows you to select the most efficient size for the variable.

long
   Indicates a larger than normal number.

short
   Indicates a smaller than normal integer.

double
   Indicates a double-size floating-point number.

<blank>
> Indicates a normal-size number.

Sign

Numbers can be **signed** or **unsigned**. This qualifier applies only to **char** and **int** types. Floating-point numbers are always signed. The default is **signed** for **int** and undefined for characters.

Type

This specifies the type of the variable. Simple types include:

int
> Integer.

float
> Floating-point number.

char
> Single character, but can also be used for a very short integer.

wchar_t
> Single wide character. Can also be used for a short integer, but most people don't because the other integer types are more appropriate to use.

Hexadecimal and Octal Constants

Integer numbers are specified as a string of digits, such as 1234, 88, –123, and so on. These are decimal (base 10) numbers: 174 or 174_{10}. Computers deal with binary (base 2) numbers: 10101110_2. The octal (base 8) system easily converts to and from binary. Each group of three digits ($2^3 = 8$) can be transformed into a single octal digit. Thus 10101110_2 can be written as 10 101 110 and changed to the octal 256_8. Hexadecimal (base 16) numbers have a similar conversion, but 4 bits at a time are used. For example, 10010100_2 is 1001 0100, or 94_{16}.

The C++ language has conventions for representing octal and hexadecimal values. Leading zeros are used to signal an octal constant. For example, 0123 is 123 (octal) or 83 (decimal). Starting a number with "0x" indicates a hexadecimal (base 16) constant. So 0x15 is 21 (decimal). Table 5-3 shows several numbers in all three bases.

Table 5-3. Integer examples

Base 10	Base 8	Base 16
6	06	0x6
9	011	0x9
15	017	0xF

Table 5-3. Integer examples (continued)

Base 10	Base 8	Base 16
23	027	0x17

Question 5-3: *Why does the following program fail to print the correct Zip code? What does it print instead?*

```
#include <iostream>
long int zip;          // Zip code

int main( )
{
    zip = 02137L;       // Use the Zip code for Cambridge MA

    std::cout << "New York's Zip code is: " << zip << '\n';
    return(0);
}
```

Operators for Performing Shortcuts

C++ not only provides you with a rich set of declarations, but also gives you a large number of special-purpose operators. Frequently a programmer wants to increment (add 1 to) a variable. Using a normal assignment statement, this would look like:

```
total_entries = total_entries + 1;
```

C++ provides you a shorthand for performing this common task. The ++ operator is used for incrementing:

```
++total_entries;
```

A similar operator, --, can be used for decrementing (subtracting 1 from) a variable.

```
--number_left;
// Is the same as
number_left = number_left - 1;
```

But suppose you want to add 2 instead of 1. Then you can use the following notation:

```
total_entries += 2;
```

This is equivalent to:

```
total_entries = total_entries + 2;
```

Each of the simple operators shown in Table 5-4 can be used in this manner.

Table 5-4. Shorthand operators

Operator	Shorthand	Equivalent statement
+=	x += 2;	x = x + 2;

Table 5-4. Shorthand operators (continued)

Operator	Shorthand	Equivalent statement
-=	x -= 2;	x = x - 2;
*=	x *= 2;	x = x * 2;
/=	x /= 2;	x = x / 2;
%=	x %= 2;	x = x % 2;
++	++x;	x = x + 1;
--	--x;	x = x - 1;

Side Effects

Unfortunately, C++ allows you to use *side effects*. A side effect is an operation that is performed in addition to the main operation executed by the statement. For example, the following is legal C++ code:

```
size = 5;
result = ++size;
```

The first statement assigns size the value of 5. The second statement:

1. Increments size (side effect)
2. Assigns result the value of size (main operation)

But in what order? There are three possible answers:

1. result is assigned the value of size (5), then size is incremented.

   result is 5 and size is 6.

2. size is incremented, then result is assigned the value of size (6).

   result is 6 and size is 6.

3. If you don't write code like this, you don't have to worry about these sorts of questions.

The correct answer is 2: The increment occurs before the assignment. However, 3 is a much better answer. The main effects of C++ are confusing enough without having to worry about side effects.

 Some programmers highly value compact code. This is a holdover from the early days of computing when storage cost a significant amount of money. It is my view that the art of programming has evolved to the point where clarity is much more valuable than compactness. (Great novels, which a lot of people enjoy reading, are not written in shorthand.)

C++ actually provides two forms of the ++ operator. One is *variable++* and the other is *++variable*. The first:

```
number = 5;
result = number++;
```

evaluates the expression and then increments the number, so result is 5. The second:

```
number = 5;
result = ++number;
```

increments first and then evaluates the expression. In this case result is 6. However, using ++ or -- in this way can lead to some surprising code:

```
o = --o - o--;
```

The problem with this is that it looks like someone is writing Morse code. The programmer doesn't read this statement; she decodes it. If you never use ++ or -- as part of any other statement, but always put them on a line by themselves, the difference between the two forms of these operators is not noticeable.

The prefix form ++*variable* is preferred over the suffix form *variable*++ because it allows the compiler to generate slightly simpler code.

(Actually, the code for simple integers is not more complex, but when we get into operator overloading, we'll see that it takes more code to write the suffix version of the increment operator (*variable*++) than it does to write the prefix version (++*variable*). (See Chapter 18.) To be constant, we always use the prefix form.)

More complex side effects can confuse even the C++ compiler. Consider the following code fragment:

```
value = 1;
result = (value++ * 5) + (value++ * 3);
```

This expression tells C++ to perform the following steps:

1. Multiply value by 5 and add 1 to value.
2. Multiply value by 3 and add 1 to value.
3. Add the results of the two multiples together.

Steps 1 and 2 are of equal priority, unlike the previous example, so *the compiler can execute them in any order it wants to*. It may decide to execute step 1 first, as shown in Figure 5-2, but it may execute step 2 first, as shown in Figure 5-3.

Using the first method, we get a result of 11; using the second method, the result is 13. The result of this expression is ambiguous. By using the operator ++ in the middle of a larger expression, we created a problem. (This is not the only problem that ++ and -- can cause. We will get into more trouble in Chapter 1.)

To avoid trouble and keep programs simple, always put ++ and -- on a line by themselves.

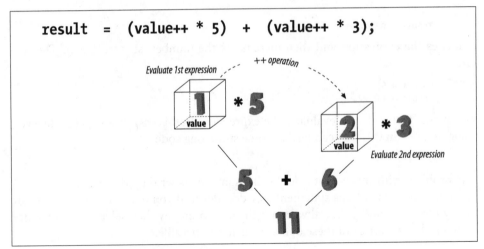

Figure 5-2. Expression evaluation, method 1

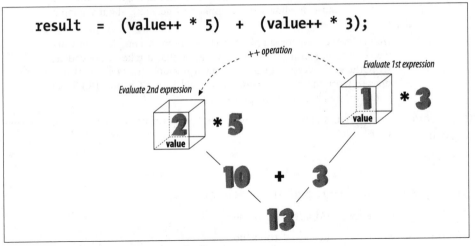

Figure 5-3. Expression evaluation, method 2

Programming Exercises

Exercise 5-1: Write a program that converts Celsius to Fahrenheit. The formula is $F = \frac{9}{5}C + 32$.

Exercise 5-2: Write a program to calculate the volume of a sphere, $\frac{4}{3}\pi r^3$.

Exercise 5-3: Write a program to print out the perimeter of a rectangle given its height and width.

$$perimeter = 2 \cdot (width + height)$$

Exercise 5-4: Write a program that converts kilometers per hour to miles per hour.

$$miles = (kilometers \cdot 0.6213712)$$

Exercise 5-5: Write a program that takes hours and minutes as input and outputs the total number of minutes (e.g., 1 hour 30 minutes = 90 minutes).

Exercise 5-6: Write a program that takes an integer as the number of minutes and outputs the total hours and minutes (e.g., 90 minutes = 1 hour 30 minutes).

Answers to Chapter Questions

Answer 5-1: The programmer accidentally omitted the end-comment symbol (*/) after the comment for height. The comment continues onto the next line and engulfs the width variable declaration. Example 5-13 shows the program with the comments underlined.

Example 5-13. Triangle area program

```
#include <iostream>

int height;    /* The height of the triangle
int width;     /* The width of the triangle*/
int area;      /* Area of the triangle (computed) */

int main()
{
    std::cout << "Enter width and height? ";
    std::cin >> width >> height;
    area = (width * height) / 2;
    std::cout << "The area is " << area << '\n';
    return (0);
}
```

Some people may think that it's unfair to put a missing comment problem in the middle of a chapter on basic declarations. But no one said C++ was fair. You will hit surprises like this when you program in C++ and you'll hit a few more in this book.

Answer 5-2: The problem is with the way we specified the element of the array: array[2,4]. This should have been written: array[2] [4].

The reason that the specification array[2,4] does not generate a syntax error is that it is legal (but strange) C++. There is a comma operator in C++ (see Chapter 29), so the expression 2,4 evaluates to 4. So array[2,4] is the same as array[4]. C++ treats this as a pointer (see Chapter 15), and what's printed is a memory address, which on most systems looks like a random hexadecimal number.

Answer 5-3: The problem is that the Zip code 02137 begins with a zero. That tells C++ that 02137 is an octal constant. When we print it, we print in decimal. Because 02137_8 is 1119_{10} the program prints:

```
New York's Zip code is: 1119
```

## CHAPTER 6

Decision and Control Statements

Once a decision was made, I did not worry about it
afterward.
—Harry Truman

Calculations and expressions are only a small part of computer programming. Decision and control statements also are needed, to specify the order in which statements are to be executed.

So far you have constructed *linear programs*, which are programs that execute in a straight line, one statement after another. In this chapter you will see how to change the *control flow* of a program with *branching statements* and *looping statements*. Branching statements cause one section of code to be executed or not, depending on a *conditional clause*. Looping statements are used to repeat a section of code a number of times or until some condition occurs.

if Statement

The **if** statement allows you to put some decision-making into your programs. The general form of the **if** statement is:

```
if (condition)
    statement;
```

If the expression is true (nonzero), the statement is executed. If the expression is false (zero), the statement is not executed. For example, suppose you are writing a billing program. At the end, if the customer owes nothing or if he has credit (owes a negative amount), you want to print a message. In C++ this is written:

```
if (total_owed <= 0)
    std::cout << "You owe nothing.\n";
```

The operator <= is a *relational operator* that represents less than or equal to. This statement reads, "If the total_owed is less than or equal to zero, print the message." The complete list of relational operators is found in Table 6-1.

Table 6-1. Relational operators

Operator	Meaning
<=	Less than or equal to
<	Less than
>	Greater than
>=	Greater than or equal to
==	Equal
!=	Not equal

Multiple relational expressions may be grouped together with *logical operators*. For example, the statement:

```
if ((oper_char == 'Q') || (oper_char == 'q'))
    std::cout << "Quit\n";
```

uses the *logical OR operator* (||) to cause the **if** statement to print "Quit" if oper_char is either a lowercase "q" *or* an uppercase "Q". Table 6-2 lists the logical operators.

Table 6-2. Logical operators

Operator	Usage	Meaning
Logical OR (||)	(*expr1*) || (*expr2*)	True if *expr1* or *expr2* is true
Logical AND (&&)	(*expr1*) && (*expr2*)	True if *expr1* and *expr2* are true
Logical NOT (!)	!(*expr*)	Returns false if *expr* is true; returns true if *expr* is false

Multiple statements after the **if** may be grouped by putting them inside curly braces ({}). For example:

```
if (total_owed <= 0) {
    ++zero_count;
    std::cout << "You owe nothing.\n";
}
```

For readability, the statements enclosed in curly braces are usually indented. This allows the programmer to quickly tell which statements are to be conditionally executed. As you will see later, mistakes in indentation can result in programs that are misleading and hard to read.

else Statement

An alternative form of the **if** statement is:

```
if (condition)
    statement;
else
    statement;
```

If the condition is true, the first statement is executed. If it is false, the second statement is executed. In our accounting example, we wrote out a message only if nothing was owed. In real life, we probably want to tell the customer how much he owes if there is a balance due.

```
if (total_owed <= 0)
    std::cout << "You owe nothing.\n";
else
    std::cout << "You owe " << total_owed << " dollars\n";
```

 Note to Pascal programmers: Unlike Pascal, C++ requires you to put a semicolon at the end of the statement before the **else**.

Now consider this program fragment:

```
if (count < 10)      // If #1
    if ((count % 4) == 2)   // If #2
        std::cout << "Condition:White\n";
  else   // (Indentation is wrong)
        std::cout << "Condition:Tan\n";
```

There are two **if** statements and one **else**. To which **if** does the **else** belong? Pick one:

1. It belongs to **if #1**.
2. It belongs to **if #2**.
3. You don't have to worry about this situation if you never write code like this.

The correct answer is 3. According to the C++ syntax rules, the **else** goes with the nearest **if**, so 2 is syntactically correct. But writing code like this violates the KISS principle (Keep It Simple, Stupid). It is best to write your code as clearly and simply as possible. This code fragment should be written as follows:

```
if (count < 10) {      // If #1
    if ((count % 4) == 2)   // If #2
        std::cout << "Condition:White\n";
    else
        std::cout << "Condition:Tan\n";
}
```

From our original example, it was not clear which **if** statement had the **else** clause; however, adding an extra set of braces improves readability, understanding, and clarity.

How Not to Use std::strcmp

The function std::strcmp compares two C-style strings and returns zero if they are equal and nonzero if they are different. To check whether two C-style strings are equal, we use code like the following:

```
    // Check for equal
    if (std::strcmp(string1, string2) == 0)
        std::cout << "Strings equal\n";
    else
        std::cout << "Strings not equal\n";
```

Some programmers omit the comment and the `== 0` clause, leading to the following, confusing code:

```
    if (std::strcmp(string1, string2))
        std::cout << "......";
```

At first glance, this program obviously compares two strings and executes the `std::cout` statement if they are equal. Unfortunately, the obvious is wrong. If the strings are equal, `std::strcmp` returns zero, and the `std::cout` is not executed. Because of this backwards behavior, you should be very careful in your use of `strcmp` and always comment its use.

(The problem with `std::strcmp` is another reason that C++ style strings are easier to use than the old C-style strings.)

Looping Statements

To get a computer to repeat its work, you need a *loop statement*. Looping statements have many uses, such as counting the number of words in a document or the number of accounts that have past due balances.

while Statement

The **while** statement is used when the program needs to perform repetitive tasks. The general form of a **while** statement is:

```
    while (condition)
        statement;
```

The program repeatedly executes the statement inside the **while** until the condition becomes false (0). (If the condition is initially false, the statement will not be executed.)

For example, Example 6-2 computes all the Fibonacci numbers that are less than 100. The Fibonacci sequence is:

1 1 2 3 5 8 . . .

The terms are computed from the equations:

$$1$$
$$1$$
$$2 = 1 + 1$$
$$3 = 2 + 1$$
$$5 = 3 + 2$$

etc.

In general, the Fibonacci sequence is defined as:

$$f_n = f_{n-1} + f_{n-2}$$

This is a mathematical equation using math-style variable names (fn). Mathematicians use this very terse style of naming variables, but in programming, terse is dangerous, so we translate these names into something verbose for C++:

Mathematician	Programmer
fn	next_number
fn-1	current_number
fn-2	old_number

So in C++ code, the equation is expressed as:

```
next_number = current_number + old_number;
```

We want to loop until our current term is 100 or larger. The following **while** loop will repeat our computation until we reach this limit.:

```
while (current_number < 100)
```

In our **while** loop we compute the value of current_number. Next we need to advance one term.

This completes the body of the loop. The first two terms of the Fibonacci sequence are 1 and 1. We initialize our first two terms to these values.

Figure 6-1 shows what happens to the variables during the execution of the program.

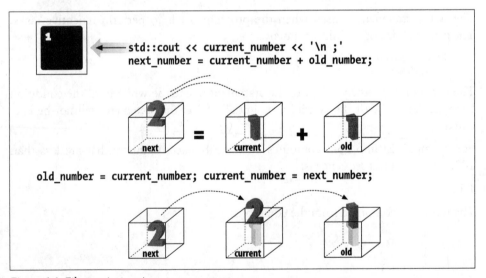

Figure 6-1. Fibonacci execution

At the beginning, current_number and old_number are 1. We print the value of the current term. Then the variable next_number is computed (value 2). Next we advance one term by putting `current_number` into `old_number` and putting `next_number` into `current_number`. This is repeated until we compute the last term and the **while** loop exits. Example 6-1 shows our algorithm written as C++ code.

Example 6-1. fib/fib.cpp

```
#include <iostream>

int   old_number;      // previous Fibonacci number
int   current_number;  // current Fibonacci number
int   next_number;     // next number in the series

int main()
{
    // start things out
    old_number = 1;
    current_number = 1;

    std::cout << "1\n"; // Print first number

    while (current_number < 100) {

        std::cout << current_number << '\n';
        next_number = current_number + old_number;

        old_number = current_number;
        current_number = next_number;
    }
    return (0);
}
```

break Statement

We have used a **while** statement to compute Fibonacci numbers less than 100. The loop exits when the condition at the beginning becomes false. Loops also can be exited at any point through the use of a **break** statement.

Suppose you want to add a series of numbers and you don't know how many numbers are to be added together. You want to read numbers and need some way of letting the program know it has reached the end of the list. Example 6-2 allows you to use the number zero (0) to signal the end of the list.

Note that the **while** statement begins with:

```
while (true) {
```

The program will loop forever because the **while** would exit only when the expression true is false. The only way to exit this loop is through a **break** statement.

We detect the end-of-list indicator (zero) with the statement following if statement, then use break to exit the loop.

```
    if (item == 0)
        break;
```

Example 6-2. total/total.cpp

```cpp
#include <iostream>

int   total;  // Running total of all numbers so far
int   item;   // next item to add to the list

int main()
{
    total = 0;
    while (true) {
        std::cout << "Enter # to add \n";
        std::cout << "  or 0 to stop:";
        std::cin >> item;

        if (item == 0)
            break;

        total += item;
        std::cout << "Total: " << total << '\n';
    }
    std::cout << "Final total " << total << '\n';
    return (0);
}
```

Note that this program makes use of an old programming trick called an indicator to end the input. In this example, our end-of-input indicator is the number 0.

continue Statement

The **continue** statement is similar to the **break** statement, except that instead of terminating the loop, it starts re-executing the body of the loop from the top. For example, let's modify the previous program to total only numbers larger than 0. This means that when you see a negative number, you want to skip the rest of the loop. To do this you need an if to check for negative numbers and a continue to restart the loop. The result is Example 6-3.

Example 6-3. total2/total2.cpp

```cpp
#include <iostream>

int   total;       // Running total of all numbers so far
int   item;        // next item to add to the list
int   minus_items; // number of negative items

int main()
{
    total = 0;
```

Example 6-3. total2/total2.cpp (continued)

```cpp
    minus_items = 0;
    while (true) {
        std::cout << "Enter # to add\n";
        std::cout << "  or 0 to stop:";
        std::cin >> item;

        if (item == 0)
            break;

        if (item < 0) {
            ++minus_items;
            continue;
        }
        total += item;
        std::cout << "Total: " << total << '\n';
    }

    std::cout << "Final total " << total << '\n';
    std::cout << "with " << minus_items << " negative items omitted\n";
    return (0);
}
```

The Assignment Anywhere Side Effect

C++ allows the use of assignment statements almost anyplace. For example, you can put an assignment statement inside another assignment statement:

```cpp
// don't program like this
average = total_value / (number_of_entries = last - first);
```

This is the equivalent of saying:

```cpp
// program like this
number_of_entries = last - first;
average = total_value / number_of_entries;
```

The first version buries the assignment of `number_of_entries` inside the expression. Programs should be clear and simple and should not hide anything. The most important rule of programming is *KEEP IT SIMPLE*.

C++ also allows you to put assignment statements in the **while** conditional. For example:

```cpp
// do not program like this
while ((current_number = last_number + old_number) < 100)
    std::cout << "Term " << current_number << '\n';
```

Avoid this type of programming. Notice how much clearer the logic is in the following version:

```
    // program like this
    while (true) {
        current_number = last_number + old_number;

        if (current_number >= 100)
            break;

        std::cout << "Term " << current_number << '\n';
    }
```

Question 6-1: *For some strange reason, the program in Example 6-4 thinks that every-one owes a balance of 0 dollars. Why?*

Example 6-4. balance/balance.cpp

```
#include <iostream>

int   balance_owed;      // amount owed

int main()
{
    std::cout << "Enter number of dollars owed:";
    std::cin >> balance_owed;

    if (balance_owed = 0)
        std::cout << "You owe nothing.\n";
    else
        std::cout << "You owe " << balance_owed << " dollars.\n";

    return (0);
}
```

Sample output:

```
Enter number of dollars owed: 12
You owe 0 dollars.
```

Programming Exercises

Exercise 6-1: A professor generates letter grades using Table 6-3.

Table 6-3. Grade values

% Correct	Grade
0–60	F
61–70	D
71–80	C
81–90	B
91–100	A

Write a program that accepts a numeric grade and displays the corresponding letter grade.

Exercise 6-2: Modify the previous program to print out a + or − after the letter grade based on the last digit of the score. The modifiers are listed in Table 6-4.

Table 6-4. Grade-modification values

Last digit	Modifier
1–3	−
4–7	<blank>
8–0	+

For example, 81=B−, 94=A, and 68=D+. Note that an F is only an F; there is no F+ or F−.

 Programmers frequently have to modify code that someone else wrote. A good exercise is to take someone else's Exercise 6-2 and modify it.

Exercise 6-3: Given an amount less than $1.00, compute the number of quarters, dimes, nickels, and pennies needed.

Exercise 6-4: A leap year is any year divisible by 4 unless it is divisible by 100, but not 400. Write a program to tell whether a year is a leap year.

Exercise 6-5: Write a program that, given the number of hours an employee worked and her hourly wage, computes her weekly pay. Count any hours over 40 as overtime at time-and-a-half.

Answers to Chapter Questions

Answer 6-1: This program illustrates one of the most common and most frustrating errors a beginning C++ programmer makes. The problem is that C++ allows assignment statements inside **if** conditionals. The statement:

```
if (balance_owed = 0)
```

uses a single equal sign instead of the double equal. C++ will assign `balance_owed` the value 0 and then test the result (which is zero). If the result were nonzero (true), the **if** clause would be executed. Since the result is zero (false), the **else** clause is executed and the program prints the wrong answer.

The statement

```
if (balance_owed = 0)
```

is equivalent to

```
balance_owed = 0;
if (balanced_owed != 0)
```

The statement should be written:

```
if (balance_owed == 0)
```

I once taught a course in C programming. One day about a month after the course had ended, I saw one of my former students on the street. He greeted me and said, "Steve, I have to tell you the truth. During the class I thought you were going a bit overboard on this single equal versus double equal bug, until now. You see, I just wrote the first C program for my job, and guess what mistake I made."

One trick many programmers use is to put the constant first in any == statement. For example:

```
if (0 == balanced_owed)
```

This way, if the programmer makes a mistake and puts in = instead of ==, the result is:

```
if (0 = balanced_owed)
```

which causes a compiler error. (You can't assign balance_owed to 0.)

## CHAPTER 7

The Programming Process

It's just a simple matter of programming.
—Any boss who has never written a program

Programming is more than just writing code. Software has a life cycle. It is born, grows up, becomes mature, and finally dies, only to be replaced by a newer, younger product. Understanding this cycle is important because as a programmer you will spend only a small amount of time actually writing new code. Most programming time is spent modifying and debugging existing code. Software does not exist in a vacuum; it must be documented, maintained, enhanced, and sold. In this chapter we take a look at a small programming project using one programmer. Larger projects that involve many people are discussed in Chapter 23. Although the final code is fewer than a hundred lines, the principles used in its construction can be applied to programs with thousands of lines of code. Figure 7-1 illustrates the software life cycle.

The major steps in making a program are:

Assignment
> It all starts when someone gets a bright idea. Then they usually assign someone else to implement it.

Requirements
> Programs start when someone gets an idea and assigns you to implement it. This is written down in a requirements document, which describes, in very general terms, what is wanted.

Specification
> This is a description of what the program does. In the beginning, a Preliminary Specification is used to describe what the program is going to do. Later, as the program becomes more refined, so does the specification. Finally, when the program is finished, the specification serves as a complete description of what the program does.

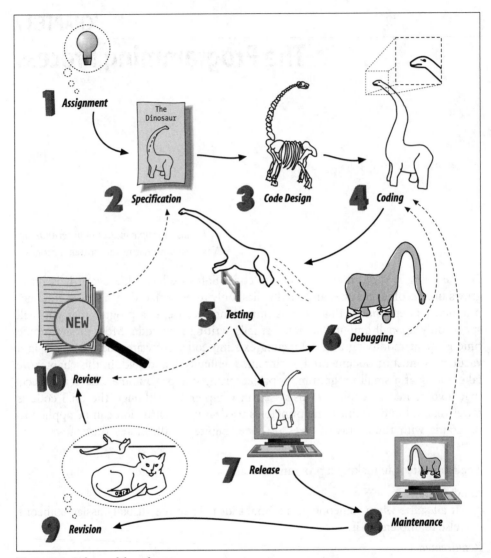

Figure 7-1. Software life cycle

Code design

The programmer does an overall design of the program. The design should include major algorithms, class definitions, module specifications, file formats, and data structures.

One thing cannot be over-stressed: *Think before you act.* Studies have shown that a good design can result in a program that is one tenth the size of a poorly designed one. This is especially true when using C++, where designing good objects is critical to writing a good program. (You will find out what objects are in Chapter 13.)

Note: "Think before you act" is good advice not only for coding, but also for life in general.

See Chapter 26, *Program Design*, for information on code design techniques.

Coding
The next step is writing the program. This involves first writing a prototype and then filling it in to create the full program.

Testing
The programmer should design a test plan and use it to test the program. This is the first level of testing.

The next level involves having someone else test the program. Testing can result in bug reports, which means that you need to do some debugging. It can also uncover flaws in the original specification, in which case you need to review the results and see if a revised specification is needed.

Finally, testing can show the absence of bugs. (Experienced programmers never say a program works; they say only that it has no observed bugs.) When testing shows that the number of bugs is acceptably low, the software is released.

Debugging
Unfortunately, very few programs work the first time. They must be corrected and tested again.

Release
The program is packaged, documented, and sent out into the world to be used.

Maintenance
Programs are never perfect. Bugs will be found and will need correction.

Revising and updating
After a program has been working for a while, the users will want changes, such as more features or more intelligent algorithms. At this point, a new specification is created and the process starts again.

Setting Up Your Work Area

The operating system allows you to group files in directories. Just as file folders serve to keep papers together in a filing cabinet, directories serve to keep files together. In this chapter you will be creating a simple calculator program. All the files for this program will be stored in a directory named *calc*. To create a directory in Unix, execute the following commands:

```
% cd ~
% mkdir calc
```

In MS-DOS, type:

```
C:\> cd \
C:\> mkdir calc
```

To tell the operating system which directory you want to use, in Unix type the command:

```
% cd ~/calc
```

In MS-DOS, type:

```
C:\> cd \calc
C:\CALC>
```

More information on how to organize directories can be found in your operating system documentation.

 Some IDEs will create the directory for you as part of the project creation process.

The Specification

For this chapter we are going to assume that you have been given the assignment to "write a program that acts like a four-function calculator." Typically, the specification you are given is vague and incomplete. It is up to you to refine it into something that exactly defines the program you are going to produce.

The first step is to write a document called *The Preliminary Users' Specification,* which describes what your program is going to do and how to use it. This document does not describe the internal structure of the program or the algorithm you plan to use. Following is a sample specification for the four-function calculator:

Calc

A four-function calculator

Preliminary Users' Specification

Dec. 10, 2002 Steve Oualline

Warning: This is a preliminary specification. Any resemblance to any software living or dead is purely coincidental.

Calc is a program that allows the user to turn his $10,000 computer into a $1.98 four-function calculator. The program adds, subtracts, multiplies, and divides simple integers.

When the program is run, it zeros the result register and displays its contents. The user can then type in an operator and number. The result is updated and displayed. The following operators are valid:

Operator	Meaning
+	Addition
-	Subtraction
*	Multiplication
/	Division

Example (user input is in boldface):

```
calc
Result: 0
Enter operator and number: + 123
Result: 123
Enter operator and number: - 23
Result: 100
Enter operator and number: / 25
Result: 4
Enter operator and number: * 4
Result: 16
```

The preliminary specification serves two purposes. First, you should give it to your boss (or customer) to ensure agreement between what he thought he said and what you thought he said. Second, you can circulate it among your colleagues to see whether they have any suggestions or corrections.

This preliminary specification was circulated and received two comments: "How are you going to get out of the program?" and "What happens when you try to divide by 0?"

So a new operator is added to the Preliminary Users' Specification:

```
q – quit
```

We also add another paragraph:

Dividing by 0 results in an error message and the result register is left unchanged.

IV + III = VII

A college instructor once gave his students an assignment to "write a four-function calculator." One of his students noticed that this was a pretty loose specification and decided to have a little fun. The professor didn't say what sort of numbers had to be used, so the student created a program that worked only with Roman numerals (IV + III = VII). The program came with a complete user manual—written in Latin.

Code Design

After the preliminary specification has been approved, you can start designing code. In the code-design phase, you plan your work. In large programming projects involving many people, the code would be broken up into modules for each programmer. At this stage, file formats are planned, data structures are designed, and major algorithms are decided upon.

This simple calculator uses no files and requires no fancy data structures. What's left for this phase is to design the major algorithm, which we can outline in *pseudocode*, a shorthand halfway between English and code. In pseudocode, our code design looks like this:

```
Loop
    Read an operator and number
    Do the calculation
    Display the result
End-Loop
```

The Prototype

Once the code design is completed, you can begin writing the program. But rather than try to write the entire program at once and then debug it, you will use a method called *fast prototyping*. This consists of writing the smallest portion of the specification you can implement that will still do something. In our case, you will cut the four functions down to a one-function calculator. Once you get this small part working, you can build the rest of the functions onto this stable foundation. Also, the prototype gives the boss something to look at and play around with so he has a good idea of the direction the project is taking. Good communication is the key to good programming, and the more you can show someone, the better. The code for the first version of the four-function calculator is found in Example 7-1.

Example 7-1. calc1/calc.cpp

```cpp
#include <iostream>

int    result;    // the result of the calculations
char   oper_char; // operator the user specified
int    value;     // value specified after the operator

int main( )
{
    result = 0; // initialize the result

    // Loop forever (or till we hit the break statement)
    while (true) {
        std::cout << "Result: " << result << '\n';

        std::cout << "Enter operator and number: ";
        std::cin >> oper_char >> value;

        if (oper_char = '+') {
            result += value;
        } else {
            std::cout << "Unknown operator " << oper_char << '\n';
        }
    }
    return (0);
}
```

The program begins by initializing the variable result to zero. The main body of the program is a loop starting with:

```
while (true) {
```

This will loop until a **break** statement is reached. The code:

```
std::cout << "Enter operator and number: ";
std::cin >> oper_char >> value;
```

asks the user for an operator and number. These are parsed and stored in the variables oper_char and value. (The full set of I/O operations such as << and >> are described in Chapter 16.) Finally, you start checking the operators. If the operator is a plus (+), you perform an addition using the line:

```
if (oper_char = '+') {
    result += value;
```

So far you recognize only the plus operator. As soon as this works, you will add more operators by adding more **if** statements.

Finally, if an illegal operator is entered, the line:

```
} else {
    std::cout << "Unknown operator " << oper_char << '\n';
}
```

writes an error message telling the user he made a mistake.

The Makefile

Once the source has been entered, it needs to be compiled and linked. Up to now we have been running the compiler manually. This is somewhat tedious and prone to error. Also, larger programs consist of many modules and are extremely difficult to compile by hand. Fortunately, both Unix and Borland-C++ have a utility called make that handles the details of compilation. Microsoft Visual C++ comes with the same thing, but the program is named nmake.

Basically, make looks at the file called *Makefile* for a description of how to compile your program and then runs the compiler for you. The make program is discussed in detail in Chapter 23. For now, just use one of the examples below as a template and substitute the name of your program in place of calc.

The following examples contain *Makefiles* for various C++ compilation environments. These include:

- The Unix operating system using a generic CC compiler (Example 7-2)
- The Unix or Linux operating system using the Free Software's g++ compiler (Example 7-3)
- The Microsoft Windows operating system using the Borland C++ compiler (Example 7-4)

- The Microsoft Windows operating system using the Microsoft Visual Studio .NET C++ compiler (Example 7-5)

Example 7-2. Makefile for CC under Unix

```
#
# Makefile for many Unix compilers using the
# "standard" command name CC
#
CC=CC
CFLAGS=-g
all: calc

calc: calc.cpp
$(CC) $(CFLAGS) -o calc calc.cpp

clean:
rm calc
```

Example 7-3. Makefile for GNU g++ under Linux or Unix

```
#
# Makefile for the Free Software Foundation's g++ compiler
#
CC=g++
CFLAGS=-g -Wall
all: calc

calc: calc.cpp
        $(CC) $(CFLAGS) -o calc calc.cpp

clean:
        rm calc
```

Example 7-4. Makefile for Borland C++ on Windows

```
#
# Makefile for Borland's Borland-C++ compiler
#
CC=bcc32
#
# Flags
#       -N  -- Check for stack overflow
#       -v  -- Enable debugging
#       -w  -- Turn on all warnings
#       -tWC -- Console application
#
CFLAGS=-N -v -w -tWC
all: calc.exe

calc.exe: calc.cpp
        $(CC) $(CFLAGS) -ecalc calc.cpp
```

Example 7-4. Makefile for Borland C++ on Windows (continued)
```
clean:
        erase calc.exe
```

Example 7-5. Makefile for Microsoft Visual Studio .NET C++ on Windows
```
#
# Makefile for Microsoft Visual C++
#
CC=cl
#
# Flags
#       GZ -- Enable stack checking
#       RTCsuc -- Enable all runtime checks
#       Zi -- Enable debugging
#       Wall -- Turn on warnings (Omitted)
#       EHsc -- Turn exceptions on

#
CFLAGS=/GZ /RTCsuc /Zi /EHsc
all: calc.exe

calc.exe: calc.cpp
        $(CC) $(CFLAGS)  calc.cpp

clean:
        erase calc.exe
```

To compile the program, just execute the command make. (Under Microsoft Visual C++ use the command nmake.) The make program determines what compilation commands are needed and executes them.

For example, on Linux and Unix we compile our program with the command:
```
$ make
g++ -g -Wall -o calc calc.c
calc.cpp: In function 'int main( )':
calc.cpp:19: warning: suggest parenthesis around assignment used as truth value
$
```

Using Microsoft Visual C++ the command is:
```
C:> nmake
Microsoft (R) Program Maintenance Utility Version 7.00.9392
Copyright (C) Microsoft Corporation. All rights reserved.

cl /FeCALC /RTCsuc /Zi /Wall calc.cpp
Microsoft (R) 32-bit C/C++ Compiler Ver. 13.00.9392 for 80x86
Copyright (C) Microsoft Corporation 1984-2001. All rights reserved.
/out:CALC.exe
/debug
calc.obj
LINK : LNK6004: CALC.exe not found or not built by the last incremental link;
performing full link
```

The make program uses the modification dates of the files to determine whether a compilation is necessary. Compilation creates an object file. The modification date of the object file is later than the modification date of its source. If the source is edited, its modification date is updated, making the object file out of date. make checks these dates, and if the source was modified after the object, make recompiles the object.

Testing

Once the program is compiled without errors, you can move on to the testing phase. Now is the time to start writing a test plan. This document is simply a list of the steps you perform to make sure the program works. It is written for two reasons:

- If a bug is found, you want to be able to reproduce it.
- If you ever change the program, you will want to retest it to make sure new code did not break any of the sections of the program that were previously working.

The test plan starts out as something like this:

```
Try the following operations

+ 123     Result should be 123
+ 52      Result should be 175
x 37      Error message should be output
```

Running the program you get the following results:

```
Result: 0
Enter operator and number: + 123
Result: 123
Enter operator and number: + 52
Result: 175
Enter operator and number: x 37
Result: 212
```

Something is clearly wrong. The entry x 37 should have generated an error message but didn't. There is a bug in the program, so you begin the debugging phase. One advantage to making a small working prototype is that you can isolate errors early.

Debugging

First you inspect the program to see if you can detect the error. In such a small program it is not difficult to spot the mistake. However, let's assume that instead of a 21-line program, you have a much larger one containing 5,000,000 lines. Such a program would make inspection more difficult, so you need to proceed to the next step.

Most systems have C++ debugging programs, but each debugger is different. Some systems have no debugger. In that case you must resort to a diagnostic print statement. (More advanced debugging techniques are discussed in Chapter 17.) The technique is simple: put a std::cout where you're sure the data is good (just to make sure it really *is* good). Then put a std::cout where the data is bad. Run the program and keep putting in std::cout statements until you isolate the area in the program that contains the mistake. The program, with diagnostic std::cout lines added, looks like:

```
std::cout << "Enter oper_char and number: ";
std::cin >> value;
std::cin >> oper_char;

std::cout << "## after cin " << oper_char << '\n';

if (oper_char = '+') {
    std::cout << "## after if " << oper_char << '\n';
    result += value;
```

 The ## at the beginning of each std::cout line is my trick to flag the line as a debug line. This makes it easy to tell the temporary debug output from the real program output. Also, when you finally find the bug, the ## makes it easy to find and remove the debug lines with your editor.

Running the program again results in:

```
Result: 0
Enter operator and number: + 123
## after cin +
## after if +
Result: 123
Enter operator and number: + 52
## after cin +
## after if +
Result: 175
Enter operator and number: x 37
## after cin x
## after if +
Result: 212
```

From this you see that something is going wrong with the **if** statement. Somehow the variable operator is an x going in and a + coming out. Closer inspection reveals that you have the old mistake of using = instead of ==. After you fix this bug, the program runs correctly. Building on this working foundation, you add in the code for the other operators, -, *, and /, to create Example 7-6.

Example 7-6. calc3/calc3.cpp

```
#include <iostream>

int    result;    // the result of the calculations
char   oper_char; // operator the user specified
int    value;     // value specified after the operator

int main()
{
```

Example 7-6. calc3/calc3.cpp (continued)

```
    result = 0; // initialize the result

    // loop forever (or until break reached)
    while (true) {
        std::cout << "Result: " << result << '\n';
        std::cout << "Enter operator and number: ";

        std::cin >> oper_char >> value;

        if ((oper_char == 'q') || (oper_char == 'Q'))
            break;

        if (oper_char == '+') {
            result += value;
        } else if (oper_char == '-') {
            result -= value;
        } else if (oper_char == '*') {
            result *= value;
        } else if (oper_char == '/') {
            if (value == 0) {
                std::cout << "Error:Divide by zero\n";
                std::cout << "  operation ignored\n";
            } else
                result /= value;
        } else {
            std::cout << "Unknown operator " << oper_char << '\n';
        }
    }
    return (0);
}
```

You expand the test plan to include the new operators and try it again:

```
+ 123    Result should be 123
+ 52     Result should be 175
x 37     Error message should be output
- 175    Result should be zero
+ 10     Result should be 10
/ 5      Result should be 2
/ 0      Divide by zero error
* 8      Result should be 16
q        Program should exit
```

Testing the program, you find much to your surprise that it works. The word "Preliminary" is removed from the specification and the program, test plan, and specification are released.

Maintenance

Good programmers put their programs through a long and rigorous testing process before releasing them to the outside world. Then the first user tries the program and almost immediately finds a bug. This starts the maintenance phase. Bugs are fixed, the program is tested (to make sure the fixes didn't break anything), and the program is released again.

Revisions

Although the program is officially finished, you are not finished with it. After it is in use for a few months, someone will come to you and ask, "Can you add a modulus operator?" So you revise the specifications, add the change to the program, update the test plan, test the program, and release it again.

As time passes, more people will come to you with additional requests for changes. Soon the program has trig functions, linear regressions, statistics, binary arithmetic, and financial calculations. The design is based on the idea of one-character operators. Soon you find yourself running out of characters to use. At this point the program is doing work far beyond what it was initially designed to do. Sooner or later you reach the point where the program needs to be scrapped and a new one written from scratch. At this point you write a new Preliminary Specification and start the process over again.

Electronic Archaeology

Unfortunately, most programmers don't start a project at the design step. Instead they are immediately thrust into the maintenance or revision stage. This means most programmers are faced with the worst possible job: understanding and modifying someone else's code.

Contrary to popular belief, most C++ programs are not written by disorganized orangutans using Zen programming techniques and poorly commented in Esperanto. They just look that way. Electronic archeology is the art of digging through old code to discover amazing things (like how and why the code works).

Your computer can aid greatly in your search to discover the true meaning of someone else's code. Many tools are available for examining and formatting code. Some of these tools include:

Cross-referencers
> These programs have names like xref, cxref, and cross. System V Unix has the utility cscope. They print out a list of variables and where the variables are used.

Program indenters
> Programs such as cb and indent indent a program "correctly" (correct indentation is something defined by the tool maker).

Pretty printers
> A pretty printer such as vgrind or cprint typesets source code for printing on a laser printer.

Call graphs
> On System V Unix, the program `cflow` analyzes the structure of a program. On other systems there is a public domain utility, `calls`, that produces call graphs, showing who calls whom and who is called by whom.

Class browsers
> A class browser allows you to display the class hierarchy so you can tell what components went into building the class, as well as its structure. You'll learn what a class is in Chapter 13.

IDEs
> Both Borland-C++ Builder and Microsoft Visual C++ .NET contain an integrated development environment (IDE). This means that the tool has both an editor and source browsing tools built in. Commercial and free IDEs are available for Unix as well. One of the better free ones is Source Navigator, which can be obtained from *http://sources.redhat.com/sourcenav* (Appendix E gives the location of this and many other freely available tools).

Which tools should you use? Whichever ones work for you. Different programmers work in different ways. Some techniques for examining code are listed in the following sections. Choose the ones that work for you and use them.

Mark Up the Program

Take a printout of the program you are trying to figure out and make notes all over it. Use red or blue ink so you can tell the difference between the printout and the notes. Use a highlighter to emphasize important sections. These notes are useful; put them in the program as comments, and then make a new printout and start the process over again.

Use the Debugger

The debugger is a great tool for understanding how something works. Most debuggers allow you to step through a program one line at a time, examining variables and discovering how things really work. Once you find out what the code does, make notes and put them in as comments.

Use the Text Editor as a Browser

One of the best tools for going through someone else's code is your text editor. Suppose you want to find out what the variable `sc` is used for. Use the search command to find the first place `sc` is used. Search again and find the second. Continue searching until you know what the variable does.

Suppose you find out that `sc` is used as a sequence counter. Since you're already in the editor, you can easily do a global search-and-replace to change the variable `sc` to sequence_counter. (Disaster warning: make sure sequence_counter is not already defined as a variable *before* you make the change. Also make sure you do a *word* replacement or you'll find you replaced sc in places you didn't intend.) Comment the declaration, and you're on your way to creating an understandable program.

Add Comments

Don't be afraid to put any information you have, no matter how little, into the comments. Some of the comments I've used include:

```
int state;  // Controls some sort of state machine
int rmxy;   // Something to do with color correction?
```

Finally, there is a catch-all comment:

```
int idn;    // ???
```

which means, "I have no idea what this variable does." Even though its purpose is unknown, the variable is now marked as something that needs more work.

As you go through someone else's code, adding comments and improving style, the structure will become clearer to you. By inserting notes (comments), you make the code better and easier to understand for future programmers.

Suppose you are confronted with the following program written by someone from the "The Terser the Better" school of programming. Your assignment is to figure out what this program does. First you pencil in some comments, as shown in Figure 7-2.

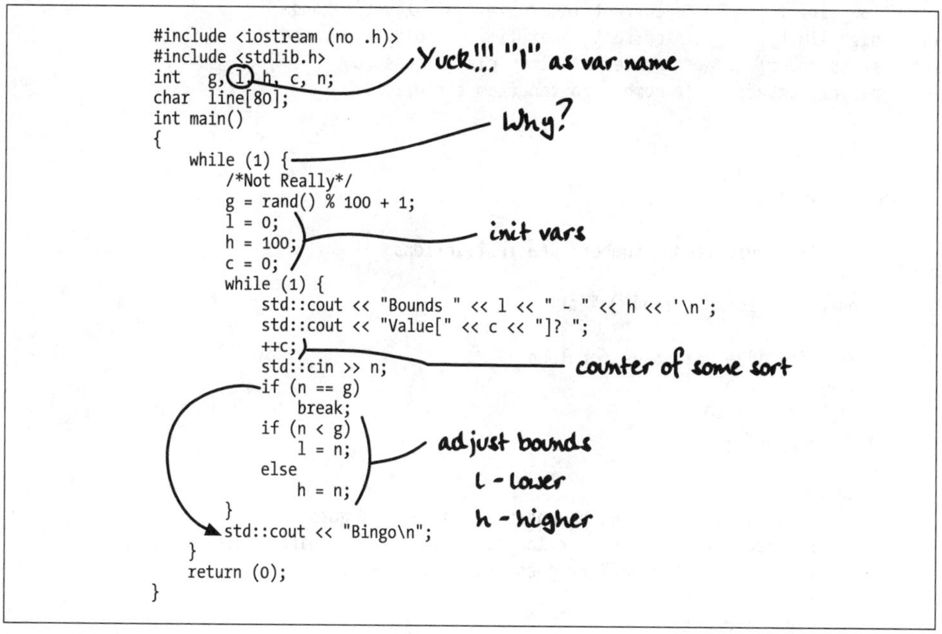

```
#include <iostream (no .h)>
#include <stdlib.h>
int    g, l, h, c, n;          Yuck!!! "l" as var name
char   line[80];
int main()
{                              Why?
    while (1) {
        /*Not Really*/
        g = rand() % 100 + 1;
        l = 0;                 init vars
        h = 100;
        c = 0;
        while (1) {
            std::cout << "Bounds " << l << " - " << h << '\n';
            std::cout << "Value[" << c << "]? ";
            ++c;
            std::cin >> n;      counter of some sort
            if (n == g)
                break;
            if (n < g)
                l = n;          adjust bounds
            else
                h = n;          l - lower
        }
        std::cout << "Bingo\n";  h - higher
    }
    return (0);
}
```

Figure 7-2. A terse program

This mystery program requires some work. After going through it and applying the principles described in this section, you get the well-commented, easy-to-understand version shown in Example 7-7.

Example 7-7. guess/good.cpp

```
/*********************************************************
 * guess -- a simple guessing game                      *
 *                                                       *
 * Usage:                                                *
 *     guess                                             *
 *                                                       *
 *     A random number is chosen between 1 and 100.      *
 *     The player is given a set of bounds and           *
 *     must choose a number between them.                *
 *     If the player chooses the correct number, he wins.*
 *     Otherwise the bounds are adjusted to reflect      *
 *     the players guess and the game continues          *
 *                                                       *
 * Restrictions:                                         *
 *     The random number is generated by the statment    *
 *     rand( ) % 100.  Because rand( ) returns a number  *
 *     0 <= rand( ) <= maxint  this slightly favors      *
 *     the lower numbers.                                *
 *********************************************************/
#include <iostream>
#include <cstdlib>

int    number_to_guess;  // random number to be guessed
int    low_limit;        // current lower limit of player's range
int    high_limit;       // current upper limit of player's range
int    guess_count;      // number of times player guessed
int    player_number;    // number gotten from the player

int main( )
{
    while (true) {
        /*
         * Not a pure random number, see restrictions
         */
        number_to_guess = rand( ) % 100 + 1;

        // Initialize variables for loop
        low_limit = 0;
        high_limit = 100;
        guess_count = 0;

        while (true) {
            // tell user what the bounds are and get his guess
            std::cout << "Bounds " << low_limit << " - " << high_limit << '\n';
            std::cout << "Value[" << guess_count << "]? ";

            ++guess_count;
```

Example 7-7. guess/good.cpp (continued)

```
        std::cin >> player_number;

        // did he guess right?
        if (player_number == number_to_guess)
            break;

        // adjust bounds for next guess
        if (player_number < number_to_guess)
            low_limit = player_number;
        else
            high_limit = player_number;

    }
    std::cout << "Bingo\n";
    }
    return (0);
}
```

Programming Exercises

For each assignment, follow the software life cycle from specification through release.

Exercise 7-1: Write a program to convert English units to metric (e.g., miles to kilometers, gallons to liters, etc.). Include a specification and a code design.

Exercise 7-2: Write a program to perform date arithmetic, such as how many days there are between 6/1/90 and 8/3/92. Include a specification and a code design.

Exercise 7-3: A serial transmission line can transmit 960 characters per second. Write a program that will calculate how long it will take to send a file, given the file's size. Try it on a 400MB (419,430,400 byte) file. Use appropriate units. (A 400MB file takes days.)

Exercise 7-4: Write a program to add an 8% sales tax to a given amount and round the result to the nearest penny.

Exercise 7-5: Write a program to tell whether a number is prime.

Write a program that takes a series of numbers and counts the number of positive and negative values.

## PART II

Simple Programming

## CHAPTER 8

More Control Statements

*Grammar, which knows how to control
even kings . . .*
—Molière

At this point we know enough to create very simple programs. In this chapter we move on to more complex statements. For controlled looping we have the **for** statement. We also study the **switch** statement. This statement can be quite powerful and complex, but as we shall see in the following sections, if used right it can be very efficient and effective.

But we start our discussion with a new looping statement, the **for**.

for Statement

The **for** statement allows you to execute a block of code a specified number of times. The general form of the **for** statement is:

```
for (initial-statement; condition; iteration-statement)
    body-statement;
```

This is equivalent to:

```
initial-statement;
while (condition) {
    body-statement;
    iteration-statement;
}
```

For example, Example 8-1 uses a **while** loop to add five numbers.

Example 8-1. total6/total6w.cpp

```
#include <iostream>

int total;     // total of all the numbers
int current;   // current value from the user
```

Example 8-1. total6/total6w.cpp (continued)

```
int counter;    // while loop counter

int main( ) {
    total = 0;

    counter = 0;
    while (counter < 5) {
        std::cout << "Number? ";

        std::cin >> current;
        total += current;

        ++counter;
    }
    std::cout << "The grand total is " << total << '\n';
    return (0);
}
```

The same program can be rewritten using a **for** statement, as seen in Example 8-2.

Example 8-2. total6/total6.cpp

```
#include <iostream>

int total;      // total of all the numbers
int current;    // current value from the user
int counter;    // for loop counter

int main( ) {
    total = 0;
    for (counter = 0; counter < 5; ++counter) {
        std::cout << "Number? ";

        std::cin >> current;
        total += current;
    }
    std::cout << "The grand total is " << total << '\n';
    return (0);
}
```

Note that counter goes from 0 to 4. Normally you count five items as 1, 2, 3, 4, 5. You will get along much better in C++ if you change your thinking to zero-based counting and count five items as 0, 1, 2, 3, 4. (One-based counting is one of the main causes of array overflow errors. See Chapter 5.)

Careful examination of the two flavors of this program reveals the similarities between the two versions, as shown in Figure 8-1.

Many older programming languages do not allow you to change the control variable (in this case counter) inside the loop. C++ is not so picky. You can change the control variable anytime you wish—you can jump into and out of the loop and generally do things that would make a PASCAL or FORTRAN programmer cringe. (Even

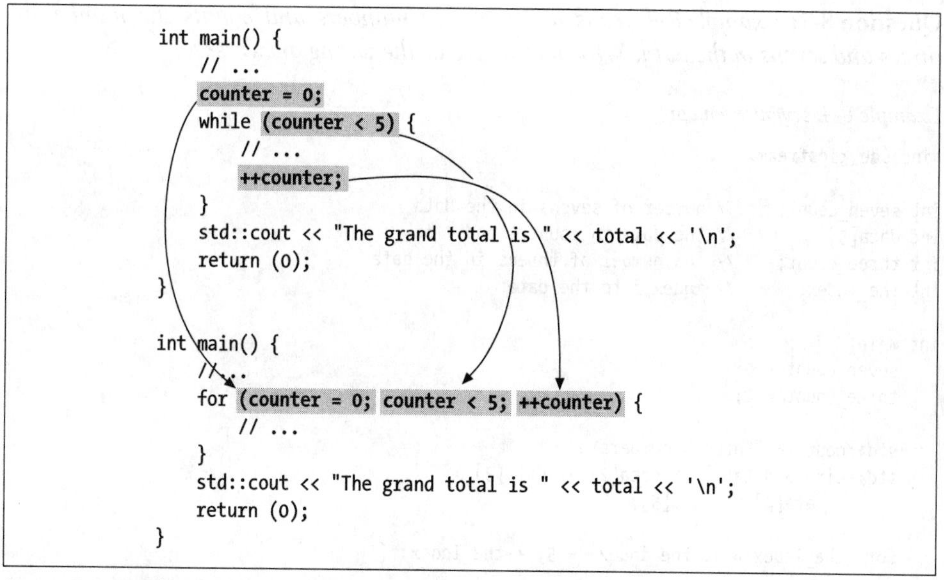

```
int main() {
    // ...
    counter = 0;
    while (counter < 5) {
        // ...
        ++counter;
    }
    std::cout << "The grand total is " << total << '\n';
    return (0);
}

int main() {
    // ...
    for (counter = 0; counter < 5; ++counter) {
        // ...
    }
    std::cout << "The grand total is " << total << '\n';
    return (0);
}
```

Figure 8-1. Similarities between while and for

though C++ gives you the freedom to do such insane things, that doesn't mean you should do them.)

Question 8-1: *What is the error in Example 8-3?*

Example 8-3. cent/cent.cpp

```
#include <iostream>
/*
 * This program produces a Celsius to Fahrenheit conversion
 *    chart for the numbers 0 to 100.
 *
 * Restrictions:
 *     This program deals with integers only, so the
 *     calculations may not be exact.
 */

// the current Celsius temperature we are working with
int celsius;

int main() {
    for (celsius = 0; celsius <= 100; ++celsius);
        std::cout << "celsius: " << celsius <<
                " Fahrenheit: " << ((celsius * 9) / 5 + 32) << '\n';
    return (0);
}
```

When run, this program prints out:

```
Celsius: 101 Fahrenheit: 213
```

and nothing more. Why?

Question 8-2: *Example 8-4 reads a list of five numbers and counts the number of threes and sevens in the data. Why does it give us the wrong answers?*

Example 8-4. seven/seven.cpp

```
#include <iostream>

int seven_count;    // number of sevens in the data
int data[5];        // the data to count 3 and 7 in
int three_count;    // the number of threes in the data
int the_index;      // index into the data

int main( ) {
    seven_count = 0;
    three_count = 0;

    std::cout << "Enter 5 numbers\n";
    std::cin >> data[1] >> data[2] >> data[3] >>
            data[4] >> data[5];

    for (the_index = 1; the_index <= 5; ++the_index) {

        if (data[the_index] == 3)
            ++three_count;

        if (data[the_index] == 7)
            ++seven_count;
    }
    std::cout << "Threes " << three_count <<
        " Sevens " << seven_count << '\n';
    return (0);
}
```

When we run this program with the data 3 7 3 0 2, the results are:

```
Threes 4 Sevens 1
```

(Your results may vary.)

switch Statement

The **switch** statement is similar to a chain of **if-else** statements. The general form of a **switch** statement is:

```
switch (expression) {
    case constant1:
        statement
        . . . .
        break;

    case constant2:
        statement
        . . . .
```

```
        // Fall through
    default:
        statement
        . . . .
        break;

    case constant3:
        statement
        . . . .
        break;
}
```

The **switch** statement evaluates the value of an expression and branches to one of the case statements. Duplicate statements are not allowed, so only one **case** will be selected. The expression must evaluate to an integer, character, or enumeration.

The **case** statements can be in any order and must be constants. The **default** statement can be put anywhere in the **switch**.

When C++ sees a **switch** statement, it evaluates the expression and then looks for a matching **case** statement. If none is found, the **default** statement is used. If no **default** is found, the statement does nothing.

A **break** statement inside a **switch** tells the computer to continue the execution after the **switch**. If the **break** is not there, execution continues with the next statement.

 The **switch** statement is very similar to the PASCAL case statement. The main differences are that while PASCAL allows only one statement after the label, C++ allows many. C++ keeps executing until it hits a **break** statement or the end of the **switch**. In PASCAL you can't "fall through" from one case to another. In C++ you can.

The calculator program in Chapter 7 contains a series of **if-else** statements.

```
    if (operator == '+') {
        result += value;
    } else if (operator == '-') {
        result -= value;
    } else if (operator == '*') {
        result *= value;
    } else if (operator == '/') {
        if (value == 0) {
            std::cout << "Error: Divide by zero\n";
            std::cout << "   operation ignored\n";
        } else
            result /= value;
    } else {
        std::cout << "Unknown operator " << operator << '\n';
    }
```

This section of code can easily be rewritten as a **switch** statement. In this **switch**, we use a different **case** for each operation. The **default** clause takes care of all the illegal operators.

Rewriting the program using a **switch** statement makes it not only simpler, but also easier to read, as seen in Example 8-5.

Example 8-5. calc-sw/calc3.cpp

```
#include <iostream>

int    result;      // the result of the calculations
char   oper_char;   // operator the user specified
int    value;       // value specified after the operator

int main()
{
    result = 0;                   // initialize the result

    // loop forever (or until break reached)
    while (true) {
        std::cout << "Result: " << result << '\n';
        std::cout << "Enter operator and number: ";

        std::cin >> oper_char >> value;

        if ((oper_char == 'q') || (oper_char == 'Q'))
            break;

        switch (oper_char) {
            case '+':
                result += value;
                break;
            case '-':
                result -= value;
                break;
            case '*':
                result *= value;
                break;
            case '/':
                if (value == 0) {
                    std::cout << "Error:Divide by zero\n";
                    std::cout << "   operation ignored\n";
                } else
                    result /= value;
                break;
            default:
                std::cout << "Unknown operator " << oper_char << '\n';
                break;
        }
    }
    return (0);
}
```

A **break** statement is not required at the end of a **case**. If the **break** is not there, execution will continue with the next statement.

For example:

```
control = 0;

// A not so good example of programming
switch (control) {
    case 0:
        std::cout << "Reset\n";
    case 1:
        std::cout << "Initializing\n";
        break;
    case 2:
        std::cout "Working\n";
}
```

In this case, when control == 0, the program prints:

```
Reset
Initializing
```

Case 0 does not end with a **break** statement. After printing "Reset" the program falls through to the next statement (case 1) and prints "Initializing".

But there is a problem with this syntax. You can't be sure that the program is supposed to fall through from case 0 to case 1, or if the programmer forgot to put in a **break** statement. To clear up this confusion, a **case** section should always end with a **break** statement or the comment // fall through.

```
// A better example of programming
switch (control) {
    case 0:
        std::cout << "Reset\n";
        // Fall through
    case 1:
        std::cout << "Initializing\n";
        break;
    case 2:
        std::cout << "Working\n";
}
```

Because case 2 is last, it doesn't absolutely need a **break** statement. A **break** would cause the program to skip to the end of the **switch**, but we're already there.

But suppose we modify the program slightly and add another **case** to the **switch**:

```
// We have a little problem
switch (control) {
    case 0:
        std::cout << "Reset\n";
        // Fall through
    case 1:
        std::cout << "Initializing\n";
        break;
```

```
        case 2:
                std::cout << "Working\n";
        case 3:
                std::cout << "Closing down\n";
}
```

Now when control == 2 the program prints:

```
Working
Closing down
```

This is an unpleasant surprise. The problem is caused by the fact that case 2 is no longer the last **case**. We fall through. (Unintentionally, or otherwise we would have included a // Fall through comment.) A **break** is now necessary. If you always put in a **break** statement, you don't have to worry about whether or not it is really needed.

```
// Almost there
switch (control) {
        case 0:
                std::cout << "Reset\n";
                // Fall through
        case 1:
                std::cout << "Initializing\n";
                break;
        case 2:
                std::cout << "Working\n";
                break;
}
```

Finally, we ask the question: What happens when control == 5? In this case, since there is no matching **case** or a **default** clause, the entire **switch** statement is skipped.

In this example, the programmer did not include a **default** statement because control will never be anything but 0, 1, or 2. However, variables can get assigned strange values, so we need a little more defensive programming.

```
// The final version
switch (control) {
    case 0:
        std::cout << "Reset\n";
        // Fall through
    case 1:
        std::cout << "Initializing\n";
        break;
    case 2:
        std::cout << "Working\n";
        break;
    default:
        assert("Internal error: Impossible control value" != 0);
        break;
}
```

In this case we've put in a default that triggers an **assert** failure. The test in this case is a C-style string ("Internal error....") and a comparison (!= 0). Because of the way C++ stores strings, this test will always fail, which in turn will cause the **assert** to abort the program.

Although a **default** is not required, it should be put in every **switch**. Even though the **default** may be just:

```
default:
        // Do nothing
        break;
```

it should be included. This indicates that you want to ignore out-of-range data.

switch, break, and continue

The **break** statement has two uses. Used inside a **switch**, it causes the program to exit the **switch** statement. Inside a **for** or **while** loop, it causes a loop exit. The **continue** statement is valid only inside a loop and causes the program to go to the top of the loop.

To illustrate how these statements work, we've produced a new version of the calculator program. The new program prints the result only after valid data is input, and it has a help command.

The help command is special. We don't want to print the result after the help command, so instead of ending the help **case** with a **break**, we end it with a **continue**. The **continue** forces execution to go to the top of the loop.

When an unknown operator is entered, we print an error message. As with the help **case**, we use a **continue** statement to skip printing the result.

Finally, there is one special command: quit. This command is handled outside the **switch**. It is handled by the **break** at the top of the loop. Since the **break** is outside the **switch**, it belongs to the **while** loop and causes the program to exit the **while**.

The control flow for this program can be seen in Figure 8-2.

Programming Exercises

Exercise 8-1: Print a checkerboard (8-by-8 grid). Each square should be 5-by-3 characters wide. A 2-by-2 example follows:

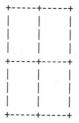

```
#include <iostream>
int    result;      // the result of the calculations
char   oper_char;   // operator the user specified
int    value;       // value specified after the operator
int main()
{
    result = 0;                      // initialize the result

    // loop forever (or until break reached)
    while (true) {◄ - - - - - - - - - - - - - - - - - - - - - - - - - - - - ╮
        std::cout << "Enter operator and number: ";               │

        std::cin >> oper_char >> value;                           │

        if ((oper_char == 'q') || (oper_char == 'Q'))             │
            break;───────────────────────────────────────────────┤

        switch (oper_char) {                                      │
            case '+':                                             │
                result += value;                                  │
                break;                                            │
            case '-':                                             │
                result -= value;                                  │
                break;                                            │
            case '*':                                             │
                result *= value;                                  │
                break;                                            │
            case '/':                                             │
                if (value == 0) {                                 │
                    std::cout << "Error: Divide by zero\n";       │
                    std::cout << "   operation ignored\n";        │
                } else                                            │
                    result /= value;                              │
                break;                                            │
            case 'h':                                             │
            case 'H':                                             │
                std::cout << "Operator    Meaning\n";             │
                std::cout << "  +         Add\n";                 │
                std::cout << "  -         Subtract\n";            │
                std::cout << "  *         Multiply\n";            │
                std::cout << "  /         Divide\n";              │
                continue; - - - - - - - - - - - - - - - - - - - - ┤
            default:                                              │
                std::cout << "Unknown operator " << oper_char << '\n';
                continue; - - - - - - - - - - - - - - - - - - - - ┘
        }
        std::cout << "Result: " << result << '\n';
    }
    return (0); ◄
}
```

"break" (inside switch) *"continue" (inside switch)* *"break" (outside switch)*

Figure 8-2. switch/continue

Exercise 8-2: The total resistance of *n* resistors in parallel is:

$$\frac{1}{R} = \frac{1}{R_1} + \frac{1}{R_2} + \frac{1}{R_3} + \dots + \frac{1}{R_n}$$

Suppose we have a network of two resistors with the values 400Ω and 200Ω. Our equation would be:

$$\frac{1}{R} = \frac{1}{R_1} + \frac{1}{R_2}$$

Substituting in the value of the resistors we get:

$$\frac{1}{R} = \frac{1}{400} + \frac{1}{200}$$

$$\frac{1}{R} = \frac{3}{400}$$

$$R = \frac{400}{3}$$

So the total resistance of our two-resistor network is 133.3Ω.

Write a program to compute the total resistance for any number of parallel resistors.

Exercise 8-3: Write a program to average *n* numbers.

Exercise 8-4: Write a program to print out the multiplication table.

Exercise 8-5: Write a program that reads a character and prints out whether it is a vowel or a consonant.

Exercise 8-6: Write a program that converts numbers to words. Example: 895 results in "eight nine five."

Exercise 8-7: The number 85 is said "eighty-five," not "eight five." Modify the previous program to handle the numbers 0–100 so all numbers come out as we really say them. For example, 13 is "thirteen," and 100 is "one hundred."

Answers to Chapter Questions

Answer 8-1: The problem lies with the semicolon (;) at the end of the **for** statement. The body of the **for** statement is between the closing parentheses and the semicolon. In this case it is nothing. Even though the std::cout statement is indented, it is not part of the **for** statement. The indentation is misleading. The C++ compiler does not look at indentation. The program does nothing until the expression celsius <= 100 becomes false (celsius == 101). Then the std::cout is executed.

Answer 8-2: The problem is that we read the number into data[1] through data[5]. In C++ the range of legal array indices is 0 to <array size>–1, or in this case 0 to 4. data[5] is illegal. When we use it strange things happen; in this case the variable three_count is changed. The solution is to use only data[0] through data[4].

## CHAPTER 9

Variable Scope and Functions

But in the gross and scope of my opinion,
This bodes some strange eruption to our state.
—Shakespeare
  Hamlet, Act I, Scene I

So far you have been using only global variables. These are variables that can be set or used almost anywhere in the program. In this chapter you learn about other kinds of variables and how to use them. This chapter also tells you how to divide your code into functions. Many aspects of functions are detailed, including function overloading, using functions to build structured programs, and the use of recursive function calls.

Scope and Storage Class

All variables have two attributes, *scope* and *storage class*. The scope of a variable is the area of the program where the variable is valid. A *global variable* is valid from the point it is declared to the end of the program. A *local variable's* scope is limited to the block where it is declared and cannot be accessed (set or read) outside that block. A *block* is a section of code enclosed in curly braces ({ }). Figure 9-1 illustrates the difference between local and global variables.

It is possible to declare a local variable with the same name as a global variable. Normally, the scope of the variable count (first declaration in Figure 9-2) would be the whole program. The declaration of a second, local count takes precedence over the global declaration inside the small block where the local count is declared. In this block, the global count is said to be *hidden*. You can also nest local declarations and hide local variables. These "very local" variables have an even smaller and more local scope than the "normal local" variables. (The clarity of the previous sentence gives you some idea why using nesting to hide local variables does not make your program easy to understand.) Figure 9-2 illustrates a hidden variable.

```
                        int global;              // a global variable
                        int main()
                        {
                            int  local;          // a local variable

                            global = 1;          // global can be used here
                            local = 2;           // so can local

                            {                    // beginning a new block
                                int  very_local  // this is local to the block

                                very_local = global+local;
                            }

                            // We just closed the block
                            // very_local can not be used
                        }
```

Scope of global — Scope of local — Scope of very_local

Figure 9-1. Local and global variables

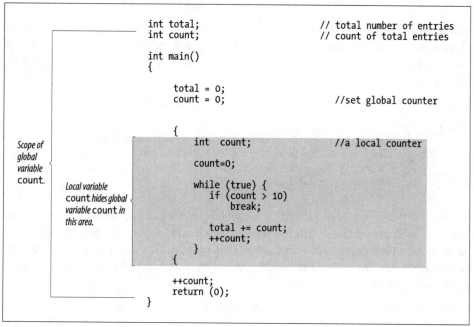

```
                        int total;               // total number of entries
                        int count;               // count of total entries

                        int main()
                        {
                            total = 0;
                            count = 0;            //set global counter


                            {
                                int  count;       //a local counter

                                count=0;

                                while (true) {
                                    if (count > 10)
                                        break;

                                    total += count;
                                    ++count;
                                }
                            {
                            ++count;
                            return (0);
                        }
```

Scope of global variable count.

Local variable count *hides global* variable count *in this area.*

Figure 9-2. Hidden variables

The variable count is declared both as a local variable and as a global variable. Normally the scope of count (global) would be the entire program, but when a variable is declared inside a block, that instance of the variable becomes the active one for the length of the block. The global count has been hidden by the local count for the scope of this block. The shaded area in the figure shows where the scope of count (global) is hidden.

It is not good programming practice to hide variables. The problem is that when you have the statement:

```
count = 1;
```

it is difficult to tell which count you are referring to. Is it the global count—the one declared at the top of main—or the one in the middle of the **while** loop? It is better to give these variables different names, such as total_count, current_count, and item_count.

The **storage class** of a variable may be either *permanent* or *temporary*. Global variables are always permanent. They are created and initialized before the program starts and remain until it terminates. Temporary variables are allocated from a section of memory called the *stack* at the beginning of the block. If you try to allocate too many temporary variables, you will get a stack overflow error. The space used by the temporary variables is returned to the stack at the end of the block. Each time the block is entered, the temporary variables are initialized.

The size of the stack depends on the system and compiler you are using. On many Unix systems, the program is automatically allocated the largest possible stack. On other systems, a default stack size is allocated that can be changed by a compiler switch.

Local variables are temporary unless they are declared **static**.

 static has an entirely different meaning when used with global variables. (It indicates that a variable is local to the current file.) See Chapter 23. For a complete discussion of the many meanings of the word **static**, see Table 14-1.

Example 9-1 illustrates the difference between permanent and temporary variables. We have chosen obvious variable names; temporary is a temporary variable and permanent is permanent. C++ initializes temporary each time it is created (at the beginning of the **for** statement block); permanent gets initialized only once, at program start-up time.

In the loop both variables are incremented. However, at the top of the loop—temporary is initialized to 1.

Example 9-1. perm/perm.cpp

```
#include <iostream>

int main() {
    int counter;     // loop counter

    for (counter = 0; counter < 3; ++counter) {
        int temporary = 1;
        static int permanent = 1;
```

Example 9-1. perm/perm.cpp (continued)

```
        std::cout << "Temporary " << temporary <<
                " Permanent " << permanent << '\n';
        ++temporary;
        ++permanent;
    }
    return (0);
}
```

The output of this program looks like:

```
Temporary 1 Permanent 1
Temporary 1 Permanent 2
Temporary 1 Permanent 3
```

 Temporary variables are sometimes referred to as *automatic variables* because the space for them is allocated automatically. The qualifier **auto** can be used to denote a temporary variable; however, in practice **auto** is almost never used.

Table 9-1 describes the different ways a variable can be declared.

Table 9-1. Declaration modifiers

Declared	Scope	Storage class	Initialized
Outside all blocks	Global	Permanent	Once
static outside all blocks	File	Permanent	Once
Inside a block	Local	Temporary	Each time block is entered
static inside a block	Local	Permanent	Once

 The keyword **static** is the most overloaded C++ keyword. It means a lot of different things depending on how it is used. For a complete list see Table 14-1.

The for Scope

The **for** statement is similar to a set of curly braces in that you can declare variables inside the statement whose scope goes from the start of the **for** to the end of the statement. (This includes the statement or block controlled by the **for**.) In the following statement:

```
for (int count = 0; count < MAX; ++count)
    sum += count;
// count is out of scope from here on.
```

the variable count is declared inside the **for**. Its scope is to the end of the statement; the scope ends with the first semicolon after the **for**.

Namespaces

The size of programs has grown steadily, and as the number of lines of code in a program grows larger and larger, so does the number of global variables. As a result, the global namespace has become very crowded.

One solution is to use stylized variable names. For example, in one program, all variables in the data processing module would begin with dp_ and all variables in the storage module would begin with st_.

This works after a fashion, but things get a little hairy as more and more modules are added. When you're dealing with the core software system, the user interface module, the game group, and the backgammon module, and you have to prefix all your variables with core_ui_games_back_, things have gotten out of hand.

The C++ solution to this problem is to divide the program into namespaces. You deal with namespaces every day in real life. For example, chances are that you refer to the members of your family by their first names, such as Steve, Bill, Sandra, and Fred. Someone outside the family would use more formal names, like Steve Smith, Bill Smith, and so on.

C++ lets you define something called a **namespace**. All the variables declared inside a **namespace** are considered to be members of the same family, or namespace. For example, the following code declares three integers that are members of the namespace display:

```
namespace display {
    int width;      // The width of the display
    int height;     // Height of the display in lines
    bool visible;   // Is the display visible?
};
```

A family member's full name might be Stephen Douglas Smith. The C++ equivalent of a full name is something called a fully qualified name. In this case, the fully qualified name of the variable width is display::width. Functions that belong to the family (i.e., functions that are part of the namespace display) can use the less formal name width.

Namespace std

We started out using the object std::cout for output. What this actually means is that we are using the variable cout in the namespace std. This namespace is used by C++ to define its standard library objects and functions.

You may remember that we began most of our programs with the statement:

```
#include <iostream>
```

The first statement causes the compiler to read in a file called *iostream*, which contains the definitions of the C++ standard variables. For example, a simplified *iostream* might look like this:

```
namespace std {
    istream cin;    // Define the input stream cin
    ostream cout;   // Define the output stream cout
    ostream cerr;   // Define the standard error stream
    // Lots of other stuff
}
```

Once the compiler has seen these definitions, `std::cin`, `std::cout`, and `std::cerr` are available for our use.

Global Namespace

If you do not enclose your code or variables in any namespace, a blank namespace is assigned to them. For example, the expression:

```
::global = 45;
```

assigns 45 to the variable `global`, which was declared outside any namespace declaration.

File-Specific Namespace

Let's suppose you want to define a module and you want most of the functions and variables in the file to exist in their own unique namespace.

You could put the following statement at the top of your file:

```
namespace my_file_vars {
```

But what happens if, by some strange quirk of fate, someone else defines a namespace with the same name? The result is a namespace collision.

To avoid this, C++ has invented the unnamed namespace. The declaration:

```
namespace {
```

with no name specified, puts all the enclosed declarations in a namespace unique to the file.

Nested Namespaces

Namespaces may be nested. For example, we could declare some variables as follows:

```
namespace core {
    namespace games {
        namespace dice {
            int roll;    // The value of the last roll
```

Nesting this deep is a little verbose (`core::games::dice::roll`), but if you have a lot of code to organize, nested namespaces may be useful.

The using Statement

Let's assume we have a program with a command module (with the namespace `command`) and a command parsing module (with the namespace `command_parser`). These two modules are very closely related, and the command module makes frequent references to variables inside the parsing module. (We'll also ignore the fact that tight coupling like this is a bad design.)

When writing the command module, if you want to refer to a variable in the parsing module, you have to prefix it with the namespace identifier:

```
if (command_parser::first_argument == "ShowAll")
```

Because these modules are tightly coupled, you have to write out `command_parser::first_argument` a lot of times. This can get tiring after a while.

But you can tell C++, "I know that `first_argument` is in the `command_parser` module, but pretend that it's in mine too." This is accomplished through the **using** statement:

```
using command_parser::first_argument;
```

C++ will now let you use the name `first_argument` instead of `command_parser::first_argument`.

```
using command_parser::first_argument;

if (first_argument == "ShowAll")
```

> The scope of a **using** declaration is the same as any other variable declaration. It ends at the end of the block in which it is declared.

Now let's suppose there are a lot of variables that we wish to import from the module `command_parser`. We could put a **using** statement in our code for each one, but this would require a lot of statements. Or we can do things wholesale and tell C++ that all the names in the namespace `command_parser` are to be imported into our module. This is done with the statement:

```
using namespace command_parser;
```

The problem with the using statement

The use of the **using** statement should be avoided in most cases. The example we presented here had many interconnects between the two namespaces which necessitated the use of the **using** statement. But it's considered bad program design to have so many interconnects.

The **using** statement also causes namespace confusion. Normally if you see a variable without a scope declaration (e.g., signal_curve) you can assume it belongs to the current namespace. If there are **using** statements in the program, this assumption is no longer valid and your life just got more complex. Programs are complex enough already, and this complication is not welcome.

Functions

Functions allow you to group commonly used code into a compact unit that can be used repeatedly. You have already encountered one function, main. It is a special function called at the beginning of the program after all static and global variables have been initialized.

Suppose you want to write a program to compute the area of three triangles. You could write out the formula three times, or you could create a function to do the work and then use that function three times. Each function should begin with a comment block containing the following:

Name
    Name of the function
Description
    Description of what the function does
Parameters
    Description of each parameter to the function
Returns
    Description of the return value of the function

Additional sections may be added, such as file formats, references, or notes. Refer to Chapter 1 for other suggestions.

The function to compute the area of a triangle could begin with the following comment block:

```
/****************************************
 * Triangle -- compute area of a triangle  *
 *                                          *
 * Parameters                               *
 *   width -- width of the triangle         *
 *   height -- height of the triangle       *
 *                                          *
 * Returns                                  *
 *   area of the triangle                   *
 ****************************************/
```

The function proper begins with the line:

```
float triangle(float width, float height)
```

float is the function type. This defines the type of data returned by the function. width and height are the parameters to the function. Parameters are variables local to the function that are used to pass information into the function.

We first check the parameters from the caller. Everybody knows that a triangle can't have a negative width or height. But programming is a world of its own, and you can trust nothing. So let's verify the input with a couple of **assert** statements:

```
assert(width >= 0.0);
assert(height >= 0.0);
```

This sort of paranoia is extremely useful when debugging large programs. **assert** statements like these can be a tremendous help when tracking down bad code. They serve to stop the program at the earliest possible time, thus saving you lots of time tracing bad data back to its source. Remember: just because you're paranoid, it doesn't mean they aren't out to get you.

The function computes the area with the statement:

```
area = width * height / 2.0;
```

What's left is to give the result to the caller. This is done with the **return** statement:

```
return (area)
```

The full triangle function can be seen in Example 9-2.

Example 9-2. tri/tri-sub.cpp

```
/********************************************
 * triangle -- compute area of a triangle  *
 *                                          *
 * Parameters                               *
 *  width -- width of the triangle          *
 *  height -- height of the triangle        *
 *                                          *
 * Returns                                  *
 *  area of the triangle                    *
 ********************************************/
float triangle(float width, float height)
{
    float area; // area of the triangle

    assert(width >= 0.0);
    assert(height >= 0.0);
    area = width * height / 2.0;
    return (area);
}
```

The line:

```
size = triangle(1.3, 8.3);
```

is a call to the function triangle. When C++ sees this function call, it performs the following operations:

triangle's variable width = 1.3
triangle's variable height = 8.3

Begin execution of the first line of the function triangle.

The technical name for this type of parameter passing is "call by value." The assignment occurs only when the function is called, so data flows through the parameters only one way: in.

The **return** statement is how you get data out of the function. In the triangle example, the function assigns the local variable area the value 5.4 and then executes the statement return (area), so the return value of this function is 5.4. This value is assigned to size.

```
    return(area);          5.4 (The value of area)
    // ......
    size = triangle(1.3, 8.3)
```

Example 9-3 computes the area of three triangles.

Example 9-3. tri/tri.cpp

```cpp
#include <iostream>
#include <assert.h>

int main( )
{
    // function to compute area of triangle
    float triangle(float width, float height);

    std::cout << "Triangle #1 " << triangle(1.3, 8.3) << '\n';
    std::cout << "Triangle #2 " << triangle(4.8, 9.8) << '\n';
    std::cout << "Triangle #3 " << triangle(1.2, 2.0) << '\n';
    return (0);
}
/******************************************
 * triangle -- compute area of a triangle  *
 *                                         *
 * Parameters                              *
 *  width -- width of the triangle         *
 *  height -- height of the triangle       *
 *                                         *
 * Returns                                 *
 *  area of the triangle                   *
 ******************************************/
float triangle(float width, float height)
{
    float area; // area of the triangle

    assert(width >= 0.0);
    assert(height >= 0.0);
    area = width * height / 2.0;
```

Example 9-3. tri/tri.cpp (continued)
```
    return (area);
}
```

Functions must be declared just like variables. The declaration tells the C++ compiler about the function's return value and parameters. There are two ways of declaring a function. The first is to write the entire function before it's used. The other is to define what's called a *function prototype,* which gives the compiler just enough information to call the function. A function prototype looks like the first line of the function, but the prototype has no body. For example, the prototype for the triangle function is:

```
    float triangle(float width, float height);
```

Note the semicolon at the end of the line. This is used to tell C++ that this is a prototype and not a real function.

C++ allows you to leave out the parameter names when declaring a prototype. This function prototype could just as easily have been written:

```
    float triangle(float, float);
```

However, this technique is not commonly used, because including the parameter names gives the reader more information about what the function is doing and makes the program easier to understand. Also, it's very easy to create a prototype by simply using the editor to copy the first line of a function and putting that line where you want the prototype. (Many times this will be in a header file, as described in Chapter 23.)

Functions that have no parameters are declared with a parameter list of ( ). For example:

```
    int get_value( );
```

You can also use the parameter list (void). This is a holdover from the old C days when an empty parameter list "()" signaled an old K&R-style C function prototype. Actually, C++ will accept both an empty list and a **void** declaration.

Almost all C++ programmers prefer the empty list. The advantages of the (void) form are:

- It provides an obvious indicator that there is no parameter list. (In other words, if the programmer puts in the void she tells the world, "This function really takes no arguments, and I didn't forget the parameter list."
- It is compatible with the older C language.

The advantages of the empty list are:

- The syntax ( ) is more sane and consistent with the way we declare parameters than that of (void).

- The void list is a historical hack put into C to solve a syntax problem that existed because the empty list was used for something else. It was ported from C to C++ for compatibility.
- We are programming C++, not C, so why should we use relics from the past in our code?

For these reasons most people use the empty list. This author is one exception. I prefer the (void) construct, but when three reviewers and an editor tell you you're wrong, it's time to rethink your choices. The empty list is used throughout this book.

Returning void

The keyword **void** is also used to indicate a function that does not return a value (similar to the FORTRAN SUBROUTINE or PASCAL Procedure). For example, this function just prints a result; it does not return a value:

```
void print_answer(int answer)
{
    if (answer < 0) {
        std::cout << "Answer corrupt\n";
        return;
    }
    std::cout << "The answer is " << answer '\n';
}
```

Namespaces and Functions

Namespaces affect not only variables but functions as well. A function belongs to the namespace in which it is declared. For example:

```
namespace math {

int square(const int i) {
    return (i * i);
}

} // End namespace

namespace body {

int print_value()
{
    std::cout << "5 squared is " << math::square(5) << '\n';
}

}
```

All the functions in a namespace can access the variables in that namespace directly and don't need a **using** clause or a **namespace** qualification. For example:

```
namespace math {

const double PI = 3.14159;

double area(const double radius)
{
    return (2.0 * PI * radius);
}

}
```

const Parameters and Return Values

A parameter declared **const** cannot be changed inside the function. Ordinary parameters can be changed inside functions, but the changes will not be passed back to the calling program.

For example, in the triangle function, we never change width or height. These could easily be declared **const**. Since the return value is also something that cannot be changed, it can be declared **const** as well. The **const** declarations serve to notify the programmer that the parameters do not change inside the function. If you do attempt to change a **const** parameter, the compiler generates an error. The improved triangle function with the **const** declarations can be seen in Example 9-4.

Example 9-4. tri/tri-sub2.cpp
```
const float triangle(const float width, const float height)
{
    float area; // area of the triangle

    assert(width >= 0.0);
    assert(height >= 0.0);
    area = width * height / 2.0;
    return (area);
}
```

As it stands now, the **const** declaration for the return value is merely a decoration. In the next section you'll see to how to return references and make the **const** return declaration useful.

Reference Parameters and Return Values

Remember that in Chapter 5 we discussed reference variables. A reference variable is a way of declaring an additional name for a variable. For global and local variables, reference variables are not very useful. However, they take on an entirely new meaning when used as parameters.

Suppose you want to write a subroutine to increment a counter. If you write it like Example 9-5, it won't work.

Example 9-5. value/value.cpp

```
#include <iostream>

// This function won't work
void inc_counter(int counter)
{
    ++counter;
}

int main()
{
    int a_count = 0;      // Random counter

    inc_counter(a_count);
    std::cout << a_count << '\n';
    return (0);
}
```

Why doesn't it work? Because C++ defaults to call by value. This means that values go in, but they don't come out.

What happens if you convert the parameter counter to a reference? References are just another way of giving the same variable two names. When inc_counter is called, counter becomes a reference to a_count. Thus, anything done to counter results in changes to a_count. Example 9-6, using a reference parameter, works properly.

Example 9-6. value/ref.cpp

```
#include <iostream>

// Works
void inc_counter(int& counter)
{
    ++counter;
}

int main()
{
    int a_count = 0;      // Random counter

    inc_counter(a_count);
    std::cout << a_count << '\n';
    return (0);
}
```

Reference declarations can also be used for return values. Example 9-7 finds the biggest element in an array.

Example 9-7. value/big.cpp

```
int& biggest(int array[], int n_elements)
{
```

Example 9-7. value/big.cpp (continued)

```
    int index;  // Current index
    int biggest; // Index of the biggest element

    // Assume the first is the biggest
    biggest = 0;
    for (index = 1; index < n_elements; ++index) {
        if (array[biggest] < array[index])
            biggest = index;
    }

    return (array[biggest]);
}
```

If you wanted to print the biggest element of an array, all you would have to do is this:

```
    int item_array[5] = {1, 2, 5000, 3, 4}; // An array

    std::cout << "The biggest element is " <<
            biggest(item_array, 5) << '\n';
```

Let's examine this in more detail. First of all, consider what happens when you create a reference variable:

```
    int& big_reference = item_array[2]; // A reference to element #2
```

The reference variable big_reference is another name for item_array[2]. You can now use this reference to print a value:

```
    std::cout << big_reference << '\n';   // Print out element #2
```

But since this is a reference, you can use it on the left side of an assignment statement as well. (Expressions that can be used on the left side of the = in an assignment are called *lvalues*.)

```
    big_reference = 0;      // Zero the largest value of the array
```

The function biggest returns a reference to item_array[2]. Remember that in the following code, biggest( ) is item_array[2]. The following three code sections all perform equivalent operations. The actual variable, item_array[2], is used in all three:

```
    // Using the actual data
    std::cout << item_array[2] << '\n';
    item_array[2] = 0;

    // Using a simple reference
    int big_reference = &item_array[2];
    std::cout << big_reference << '\n';
    big_reference = 0;

    // Using a function that returns a reference
    std::cout << biggest() << '\n';
    biggest() = 0;
```

Because biggest returns a reference, it can be used on the left side of an assignment operation (=). But suppose you don't want that to happen. You can accomplish this by returning a **const** reference:

```
const int& biggest(int array[], int n_elements);
```

This tells C++ that even though you return a reference, the result cannot be changed. Thus, code like the following is illegal:

```
biggest() = 0;                // Now it generates an error
```

Dangling References

Be careful when using return by reference, or you could wind up with a reference to a variable that no longer exists. Example 9-8 illustrates this problem.

Example 9-8. ref/ref.cpp

```
 1: const int& min(const int& i1, const int& i2)
 2: {
 3:     if (i1 < i2)
 4:         return (i1);
 5:     return (i2);
 6: }
 7:
 8: int main()
 9: {
10:     const int& i = min(1+2, 3+4);
11:
12:     return (0);
13: }
```

Line 1 starts the definition of the function min. It returns a reference to the smaller of two integers.

In line 10 we call this function. Before the function min is called, C++ creates a temporary integer variable to hold the value of the expression 1 + 2. A reference to this temporary variable is passed to the min function as the parameter i1. C++ creates another temporary variable for the i2 parameter.

The function min is then called and returns a reference to i1. But what does i1 refer to? It refers to a temporary variable that C++ created in main. At the end of the statement, C++ can destroy all the temporaries.

Let's look at the call to min (line 10) in more detail. Here's a pseudo-code version of line 10, including the details that C++ normally hides from the programmer:

```
create integer tmp1, assign it the value 1 + 2
create integer tmp2, assign it the value 3 + 4
bind parameter i1 so it refers to tmp1
bind parameter i2 so it refers to tmp2
call the function "min"
```

```
bind main's variable i so it refers to
        the return value (i1-a reference to tmp1)
// At this point i is a reference to tmp1
destroy tmp1
destroy tmp2

//   At this point i still refers to tmp1
//   It doesn't exist, but i refers to it
```

At the end of line 10 we have a bad situation: i refers to a temporary variable that has been destroyed. In other words, i points to something that does not exist. This is called a *dangling reference* and should be avoided.

Array Parameters

So far you've dealt only with simple parameters. C++ treats arrays a little differently. First of all, you don't have to put a size in the prototype declaration. For example:

```
int sum(int array[]);
```

C++ uses a parameter-passing scheme called "call by address" to pass arrays. Another way of thinking of this is that C++ automatically turns all array parameters into reference parameters. This allows any size array to be passed. The function sum we just declared may accept integer arrays of length 3, 43, 5,000, or any length.

However, you can put in a size if you want to. C++ allows this, although it ignores whatever number you put there. But by putting in the size, you alert the people reading your program that this function takes only fixed-size arrays.

```
int sum(int array[3]);
```

For multidimensional arrays you are *required* to put in the size for each dimension except the last one. That's because C++ uses these dimensions to compute the location of each element in the array.

```
int sum_matrix(int matrix1[10][10]);   // Legal
int sum_matrix(int matrix1[10][]);     // Legal
int sum_matrix(int matrix1[][]);       // Illegal
```

Question 9-1: *The function in Example 9-9 should compute the length of a C-style string.* *Instead it insists that all strings are of length zero. Why?*

Example 9-9. length/length.cpp

```
/********************************************************
 * length -- compute the length of a string            *
 *                                                      *
 * Parameters                                           *
 *     string -- the string whose length we want        *
 *                                                      *
```

---

* This function (when working properly) performs the same function as the library function strlen.

Example 9-9. length/length.cpp (continued)

```
* Returns                                              *
*        the length of the string                      *
*******************************************************/
int  length(char string[])
{
    int index;        // index into the string

    /*
     * Loop until we reach the end of string character
     */
    for (index = 0; string[index] != '\0'; ++index)
        /* do nothing */
    return (index);
}
```

Function Overloading

Let's define a simple function to return the square of an integer:

```
int square(int value) {
    return (value * value);
}
```

We also want to square floating-point numbers:

```
float square(float value) {
    return (value * value);
}
```

Now we have two functions with the same name. Isn't that illegal? In older languages, such as C and PASCAL, it would be. In C++ it's not. C++ allows *function overloading*, which means you can define multiple functions with the same names. Thus you can define a square function for all types of things: **int**, **float**, **short int**, **double**, and even **char**, if we could figure out what it means to square a character.

To keep your code consistent, all functions that use the same name should perform the same basic function. For example, you could define the following two square functions:

```
// Square an integer
int square(int value);

// Draw a square on the screen
void square(int top, int bottom, int left, int right);
```

This is perfectly legal C++ code, but it is confusing to anyone who has to read the code.

There is one limitation to function overloading: C++ must be able to tell the functions apart. For example, the following is illegal:

```
int get_number();
float get_number();  // Illegal
```

The problem is that C++ uses the parameter list to tell the functions apart. But the parameter list of the two get_number routines is the same: ( ). The result is that C++ can't tell these two routines apart and flags the second declaration as an error.

Default Arguments

Suppose you want to define a function to draw a rectangle on the screen. This function also needs to be able to scale the rectangle as needed. The function definition is:

```
void draw(const int width, const int height, double scale)
```

After using this function for a while, you discover that 90% of the time you don't use the draw's scale ability. In other words, 90% of the time the scale factor is 1.0.

C++ allows you to specify a default value for scale. The statement:

```
void draw(const int width, const int height, double scale = 1.0)
```

tells C++, "If scale is not specified, make it 1.0." Thus the following are equivalent:

```
draw(3, 5, 1.0);    // Explicit specify scale
draw(3, 5);         // Let it default to 1.0
```

There are some style problems with default arguments. Study the following code:

```
draw(3, 5);
```

Can you tell whether the programmer intended for the scale to be 1.0 or just forgot to put it in? Although sometimes useful, the default argument trick should be used sparingly.

Unused Parameters

If you define a parameter and fail to use it, most good compilers will generate a warning. For example, consider the following code:

```
void exit_button(Widget& button) {
    std::cout << "Shutting down\n";
    exit (0);
}
```

This example generates the message:

```
Warning: line 1.  Unused parameter "button"
```

But what about the times you really don't want to use a parameter? Is there a way to get C++ to shut up and not bother you? There is. The trick is to leave out the name of the parameter:

```
// No warning, but style needs work
void exit_button(Widget&) {
    std::cout << "Shutting down\n";
    exit (0);
}
```

This is nice for C++, but not so nice for the programmer who has to read your code. We can see that exit_button takes a Widget& parameter, but what is the name of the parameter? A solution to this problem is to reissue the parameter name as a comment:

```
// Better
void exit_button(Widget& /*button*/) {
    std::cout << "Shutting down\n";
    exit (0);
}
```

Some people consider this style ugly and confusing. They're right that it's not that easy to read. There ought to be a better way; I just wish I could think of one.

One question you might be asking by now is, "Why would I ever write code like this? Why not just leave the parameter out?"

It turns out that many programming systems make use of *callback functions*. For example, you can tell the X Window System, "When the EXIT button is pushed, call the function exit_button." Your callback function may handle many buttons, so it's important to know which button is pushed. So X supplies button as an argument to the function.

What happens if you know that button can only cause X to call exit_button? Well, X is still going to give it to you, you're just going to ignore it. That's why some functions have unused arguments.

Inline Functions

Looking back at the square function for integers, we see that it is a very short function, just one line. Whenever C++ calls a function, there is some overhead generated. This includes putting the parameters on the stack, entering and leaving the function, and stack fix-up after the function returns.

For example, consider the following code:

```
int square(int value) {
    return (value * value);
}
int main( ) {
    // .....
    x = square(x);
```

The code generates the following assembly code on a 68000 machine (paraphrased):

```
label "int square(int value)"
        link a6,#0              // Set up local variables

        // The next two lines do the work
        movel a6@(8),d1        // d1 = value
        mulsl a6@(8),d1        // d1 = value * d1
```

```
        movel d1,d0          // Put return value in d0
        unlk a6              // Restore stack
        rts                  // Return(d0)

label "main"
//....
//      x = square(x)
//
        movel a6@(-4),sp@-   // Put the number x on the stack
        jbsr "void square(int value)"
                             // Call the function

        addqw #4,sp          // Restore the stack
        movel d0,a6@(-4)     // Store return value in X
// ...
```

As you can see from this code, there are eight lines of overhead for two lines of work. C++ allows you to cut out that overhead through the use of an inline function. The **inline** keyword tells C++ that the function is very small. This means that it's simpler and easier for the C++ compiler to put the entire body of the function in the code stream instead of generating a call to the function. For example:

```
inline int square(int value) {
    return (value * value);
}
```

Changing the square function to an inline function generates the following, much smaller, assembly code:

```
label "main"
// ...
//      x = square(x)
//
        movel d1,a6@(-4)     // d1 = x
        movel a6@(-4),d0     // d0 = x
        mulsl d0,d0          // d0 = (x * x)

        movel d0,a6@(-4)     // Store result
```

Expanding the function inline has eliminated the eight lines of overhead and results in much faster execution.

The **inline** specifier provides C++ a valuable hint it can use when generating code, telling the compiler that the code is extremely small and simple. Like **register**, the **inline** specifier is a hint. If the C++ compiler can't generate a function inline, it will create it as an ordinary function.

Summary of Parameter Types

Table 9-2 lists the various parameter types.

Table 9-2. Parameter types

Type	Declaration
Call by value	`function(int var)`
	Value is passed into the function and can be changed inside the function, but the changes are not passed to the caller.
Constant call by value	`function(const int var)`
	Value is passed into the function and cannot be changed.
Reference	`function(int& var)`
	Reference is passed to the function. Any changes made to the parameter are reflected in the caller.
Constant reference	`function(const int& var)`
	Value cannot be changed in the function. This form of parameter is more efficient than "constant call by value" for complex data types. (See Chapter 12.)
Array	`function(int array[])`
	Value is passed in and may be modified. C++ automatically turns arrays into reference parameters.
Call by address	`function(int *var)`
	Passes a pointer to an item. Pointers are covered in Chapter 15.

Recursion

Recursion occurs when a function calls itself directly or indirectly. Some programming functions lend themselves naturally to recursive algorithms, such as the factorial.

A recursive function must follow two basic rules:

- It must have an ending point.
- It must reduce the amount of work to be done each time it's called.

A definition of factorial is:

```
fact(0) = 1
fact(n) = n * fact(n-1)
```

In C++, this definition translates to:

```
int fact(int number)
{
    if (number == 0)
        return (1);
    /* else */
    return (number * fact(number-1));
}
```

This satisfies the two rules. First, it has a definite ending point (when `number == 0`). Second, it reduces the amount of work to be done because computing `fact(number-1)` is simpler than `fact(number)`.

Factorial is legal only for number >= 0. But what happens if we try to compute fact(–3)? The program aborts with a stack overflow or similar message. fact(–3) calls fact(–4) calls fact(–5) and so on. There is no ending point. This is called an *infinite recursion error*. In this case it was caused by a bad parameter. We should check for that:

```
int fact(int number)
{
    assert(number >= 0);
    if (number == 0)
        return (1);
    /* else */
    return (number * fact(number-1));
}
```

Many things we do iteratively can be done recursively, like summing the elements of an array. You can define a function to add elements *m* through *n* of an array as follows:

If you have only one element, the sum is simple.
Otherwise, it is the sum of the first element and the sum of the rest.

In C++ this is:

```
int sum(const int first, const int last, const int array[],
        const int array_size)
{
    assert((first > 0) && (first < array_size));
    assert((last > 0) && (last < array_size));

    if (first == last)
        return (array[first]);
    /* else */
        return (array[first] + sum(first + 1, last, array));
}
```

For example:

$$Sum(1\ 8\ 3\ 2) =$$
$$1 + Sum(8\ 3\ 2) =$$
$$8 + Sum(3\ 2) =$$
$$3 + Sum(2) =$$
$$2$$
$$3 + 2 = 5$$
$$8 + 5 = 13$$
$$1 + 13 = 14$$
$$Answer = 14$$

This is not to say that this is the clearest or fastest way to sum a loop. In this case, a loop would be much faster. But it does illustrate how recursion can be used to create a nontraditional solution to a problem.

Structured Programming Basics

Computer scientists spend a great deal of time and effort studying how to program. The result is that they come up with the absolutely, positively, best programming methodology—a new one each month. Some of these systems include flow charts, top-down programming, bottom-up programming, structured programming, and object-oriented programming.

Now that you have learned about functions, we can talk about using *structured programming techniques* to design programs. This is a way of dividing up or structuring a program into small, well-defined functions. It makes the program easy to write and easy to understand. I don't claim that this system is the absolute best way to program, but it happens to be the system that works best for me. If another system works better for you, use it.

Structured programming focuses on a program's code. Later you'll see how to merge code and data to form classes and begin to perform object-oriented programming.

The first step in programming is to decide what you are going to do. This has already been described in Chapter 1. Next, decide how you are going to structure your data.

Finally, the coding phase begins. When writing a paper, you start with an outline, with each section in the paper described by a single sentence. The details are filled in later. Writing a program is similar. You start with an outline, but this outline is your main function. The details can be hidden within other functions. For example, the program in Example 9-10 solves all of the world's problems.

Example 9-10. A global solution

```
int main( )
{

    init( );
    solve_problems( );
    finish_up( );
    return (0);
}
```

Of course, some of the details remain to be filled in.

Start by writing the main function. It should be less than two pages long. If it grows longer, consider splitting it up into two smaller, simpler functions. The size of the function should be limited to three pages, because that is about the maximum amount of information a human being can store in short-term memory at one time. After the main function is complete, you can start on the other functions. This type of structured programming is called *top-down programming*. You start at the top (main) and work your way down.

Another type of coding is called *bottom-up programming*. This involves writing the lowest-level function first, testing it, and then building on that working set. I tend to use some bottom-up techniques when I'm working with a new standard function that I haven't used before. I write a small function to make sure I really know how the function works and continue from there. This is the approach used in Chapter 1 to construct the calculator program.

Later on, in Chapter 13, we'll learn about object-oriented programming. That's where you design your data and the things that can be done with it together in something called a class.

Real-World Programming

Over the years I've used a lot of different programming techniques. The one I use depends on the problem I'm trying to solve. I've discovered a few things about what it take to create a successful program.

The first step is to think about what you are doing before you do it. Resist the urge to start coding, and sit down and do some design. Make things as simple as possible. The simpler your code, the less that can go wrong with it.

Also try to make your design as flexible as possible. After all, you may know things tomorrow that you don't know today.

Next, organize the information you need for your program in a way that makes it as clear as possible. Depending on what you are doing, this may involve documentation, charts, diagrams, or something else. It all depends on the problem you're trying to solve and how you think. Do whatever works for you.

When you code, make sure that you are able to test your code at every step of the way. A bunch of small, correct steps will get you there much faster than one great leap in the wrong direction.

Finally, realize that there's not one "right" coding technique. Different systems work for different problems. Use whatever works best for you.

Programming Exercises

Exercise 9-1: Write a procedure that counts the number of words in a string. (Your documentation should describe exactly how you define a word.) Write a program to test your new procedure.

Exercise 9-2: Write a function begins(string1, string2) that returns true if string1 begins string2. Write a program to test the function.

Exercise 9-3: Write a function count(number, array, length) that will count the number of times number appears in array. The array has length elements. The function should be recursive. Write a test program to go with the function.

Nontraditional Coding Techniques

Traditional coding techniques describe how coding should ideally be done. But when you enter the real world, you quickly learn the difference between the way things should be done and the way they really are done. In real life, a number of nontraditional coding techniques are frequently employed:

Programming by creative copying

> This is where the programmer finds a program that does most of what he wants and copies and adapts it to his purposes. There's a lot of free code out there and "borrowing" is allowed in most cases.

Programming by successive experimentation

> Frequently you will find systems that are poorly or incorrectly documented. This programming technique involves creating a set of experiments to see how the system really works. As you learn more about the system, your refine your research efforts. When you finally figure out how the system functions, your remove the debug code and put the system into production.

Continual editing

> You start with a small, simple program and then edit it over and over again, several hundred times—maybe several thousand times. Each time, you make small edits, adding features and improving the program. There are programs out there that have had several hundred thousand edits made to them. And they work!

Exercise 9-4: Write a function that will take a character string and return a primitive hash code by adding up the value of each character in the string.

Exercise 9-5: Write a function that returns the maximum value of an array of numbers.

Exercise 9-6: Write a function that scans a string for the character "-" and replaces it with "_".

Answers to Chapter Questions

Answer 9-1: The programmer went to a lot of trouble to explain that the **for** loop did nothing (except increment the index). However, there is no semicolon at the end of the **for**. C++ keeps reading until it sees a statement (in this case `return(index)`) and puts it in the **for** loop. Example 9-11 contains a correctly written version of the program.

Example 9-11. length/rlen.cpp

```
int  length(char string[])
{
    int index;      // index into the string
```

Example 9-11. length/rlen.cpp (continued)

```
    /*
     * Loop until we reach the end of string character
     */
    for (index = 0; string[index] != '\0'; ++index)
        /* do nothing */ ;
    return (index);
}
```

## CHAPTER 10

The C++ Preprocessor

*The speech of man is like embroidered tapestries, since
like them this has to be extended in order to display its
patterns, but when it is rolled up it conceals and
distorts them.*
—Themistocles

The first C compilers had no constants or inline functions. When C was still being developed, it soon became apparent that it needed a facility for handling named constants, macros, and include files. The solution was to create a preprocessor that is run on the programs before they are passed to the C compiler. The preprocessor is nothing more than a specialized text editor. Its syntax is completely different from C's, and it has no understanding of C constructs. It is merely a dumb text editor.

The preprocessor was soon merged into the main C compiler. The C++ compiler kept this preprocessor. On some systems, such as Unix, it is still a separate program, automatically executed by the compiler wrapper `cc`. Some of the newer compilers, such as Borland-C++ Builder, have the preprocessor built in.

#define Statement

The **#define** statement can be used to define a constant. For example, the following two lines perform similar functions:

```
#define SIZE 20      // The array size is 20
const int SIZE = 20; // The array size is 20
```

Actually the line #define SIZE 20 acts as a command to the preprocessor to globally change SIZE to 20. This takes the drudgery and guesswork out of making changes.

All preprocessor commands begin with a hash mark (#) as the first character of the line. (You can put whitespace before the #, but this is rarely done.) C++ is free-format. Language elements can be placed anywhere on a line, and the end-of-line is treated just like a space. The preprocessor is not free-format. It depends on the hash mark (#) being the first character on the line. As you will see, the preprocessor knows nothing about C++ and can be (and is) used to edit things other than C++ programs.

> The preprocessor is not part of the core C++ compiler. It uses an entirely different syntax and requires an entirely different mindset to use it well. Most problems you will see occur when the preprocessor is treated like C++.

Preprocessor directives terminate at the end of the line. In C++ a semicolon (;) ends a statement. The preprocessor directives do not end in a semicolon, and putting one in can lead to unexpected results. A preprocessor directive can be continued by putting a backslash (\) at the end of the line. The simplest use of the preprocessor is to define a replacement macro. For example, the command:

```
#define FOO bar
```

causes the preprocessor to replace the word "FOO" with the word "bar" everywhere "FOO" occurs. It is common programming practice to use all uppercase letters for macro names. This makes it very easy to tell the difference between a variable (all lowercase) and a macro (all uppercase).

The general form of a simple **#define** statement is:

```
#define Name Substitute-Text
```

Name can be any valid C++ identifier. *Substitute-Text* can be anything as long as it fits on a single line. The *Substitute-Text* can include spaces, operators, and other characters.

Consider the following definition:

```
#define FOR_ALL for (i = 0; i < ARRAY_SIZE; ++i)
```

It is possible to use it like this:

```
/*
 * Clear the array
 */
FOR_ALL {
    data[i] = 0;
}
```

It is considered bad programming practice to define macros in this manner. Doing so tends to obscure the basic control flow of the program. In this example, if the programmer wants to know what the loop does, he must search the beginning of the program for the definition of FOR_ALL.

It is even worse to define macros that do large-scale replacement of basic C++ programming constructs. For example, you can define the following:

```
#define BEGIN {
#define END }

. . .

    if (index == 0)
    BEGIN
        std::cout << "Starting\n";
    END
```

The problem is that you are no longer programming in C++, but in a half C++, half-PASCAL mongrel.

The preprocessor can cause unexpected problems because it does not check for correct C++ syntax. For example, Example 10-1 generates an error on line 11.

Example 10-1. big/big.cpp

```
1:#define BIG_NUMBER 10 ** 10
2:
3:int main()
4:{
5:    // index for our calculations
6:    int    index;
7:
8:    index = 0;
9:
10:    // syntax error on next line
11:    while (index < BIG_NUMBER) {
12:        index = index * 8;
13:    }
14:    return (0);
15:
```

The problem is in the **#define** statement on line 1, but the error message points to line 11. The definition in line 1 causes the preprocessor to expand line 11 to look like:

```
    while (index < 10 ** 10)
```

Because ** is an illegal operator, this generates a syntax error.

Question 10-1: *The following program generates the answer 47 instead of the expected answer 144. Why? (Hint below.)*

Example 10-2. first/first.cpp

```
#include <iostream>

#define FIRST_PART     7
#define LAST_PART      5
#define ALL_PARTS      FIRST_PART + LAST_PART
```

Example 10-2. first/first.cpp (continued)

```cpp
int main( ) {
    std::cout << "The square of all the parts is " <<
        ALL_PARTS * ALL_PARTS << '\n';
    return (0);
}
```

Hint:

```
CC -E prog.cc
```

sends the output of the preprocessor to the standard output.

In MS-DOS/Windows, the command:

```
cpp prog.cpp
```

creates a file called prog.i containing the output of the preprocessor.

Running the program for Example 10-2 through the preprocessor gives you the code shown in Example 10-3.

Example 10-3. first/first-ed.out

```
# 1 "first.cpp"
# 1 "/usr/local/lib/g++-include/iostream" 1 3

// About 900 lines of #include stuff omitted

inline ios& oct(ios& i)
{ i.setf(ios::oct, ios::dec|ios::hex|ios::oct); return i; }

# 1 "first.cpp" 2

int main( ) {
    std::cout << "The square of all the parts is " <<
                7 + 5 * 7 + 5 << '\n';
    return (0);
}
```

 The output of the C++ preprocessor contains a lot of information, most of which can easily be ignored. In this case, you need to scan the output until you reach the std::cout line. Examining this line will give you an idea of what caused the error.

Question 10-2: *Example 10-4 generates a warning that counter is used before it is set. This is a surprise because the **for** loop should set it. You also get a very strange warning, "null effect," for line 11. What's going on?*

Example 10-4. max/max.cpp

```cpp
// warning, spacing is VERY important
```

Example 10-4. max/max.cpp (continued)

```
#include <iostream>

#define MAX =10

int main()
{
    int  counter;

    for (counter =MAX; counter > 0; --counter)
        std::cout << "Hi there\n";

    return (0);
}
```

Hint: *Take a look at the preprocessor output.*

Some preprocessors, such as the one that comes with the g++ compiler, add spaces around the tokens, which makes this program fail with a syntax error instead of compiling and generating strange code.

Question 10-3: *Example 10-5 computes the wrong value for* size. *Why?*

Example 10-5. size/size.cpp

```
#include <iostream>

#define SIZE     10;
#define FUDGE    SIZE -2;

int main()
{
    int size;// size to really use

    size = FUDGE;
    std::cout << "Size is " << size << '\n';
    return (0);
}
```

Question 10-4: *Example 10-6 is supposed to print the message* Fatal Error: Abort *and exit when it receives bad data. But when it gets good data, it exits. Why?*

Example 10-6. die/die.cpp

```
#include <iostream>
#include <cstdlib>

#define DIE \
    std::cerr << "Fatal Error:Abort\n";exit(8);

int main() {
    // a random value for testing
```

Example 10-6. die/die.cpp (continued)

```
    int value;

    value = 1;
    if (value < 0)
        DIE;

    std::cerr << "We did not die\n";
    return (0);
}
```

#define Versus const

The **const** keyword is relatively new. Before **const**, **#define** was the only way to define constants, so most older code uses **#define** directives. However, the use of **const** is preferred over **#define** for several reasons. First, C++ checks the syntax of **const** statements immediately. The **#define** directive is not checked until the macro is used. Also, **const** uses C++ syntax, while **#define** has a syntax all its own. Finally, **const** follows normal C++ scope rules, whereas constants defined by a **#define** directive continue on forever.

In most cases a **const** statement is preferred over **#define**. Here are two ways of defining the same constant:

```
#define MAX 10 // Define a value using the pre-processor
               // (This can easily cause problems)

const int MAX = 10; // Define a C++ constant integer
                    // (Safer)
```

The **#define** directive is limited to defining simple constants. The **const** statement can define almost any type of C++ constant, including things such as structure classes. For example:

```
struct box {
    int width, height;    // Dimensions of the box in pixels
};

// Size of a pink box to be used for input
const box pink_box(1, 4);
```

The **#define** directive is, however, essential for things such as conditional compilation and other specialized uses.

Conditional Compilation

One problem programmers have is writing code that can work on many different machines. In theory, C++ code is portable; in practice, many machines have little quirks that must be accounted for. For example, this book covers Unix, MS-DOS, and Windows compilers. Although they are almost the same, there are some differences.

Through the use of *conditional compilation*, the preprocessor allows you great flexibility in changing the way code is generated. Suppose you want to put debugging code in the program while you are working on it and then remove the debugging code in the production version. You could do this by including the code in an **#ifdef**-**#endif** section, like this:

```
#ifdef DEBUG
    std::cout << "In compute_hash, value " << value << " hash " << hash << "\n";
#endif /* DEBUG */
```

You do not have to put the /* DEBUG */ after the **#endif**, but it is very useful as a comment.

If the beginning of the program contains the following directive, the std::cout is included:

```
#define DEBUG       /* Turn debugging on */
```

If the program contains the following directive, the std::cout is omitted:

```
#undef DEBUG        /* Turn debugging off */
```

Strictly speaking, the #undef DEBUG is unnecessary. If there is no #define DEBUG statement, DEBUG is undefined. The #undef DEBUG statement is used to indicate explicitly to anyone reading the code that DEBUG is used for conditional compilation and is now turned off.

The directive **#ifndef** causes the code to be compiled if the symbol is *not* defined:

```
#ifndef STACK_SIZE /* Is stack size defined? */
#define STACK_SIZE 100 /* It's not defined, so define it here */
#endif /* STACK_SIZE */
```

#else reverses the sense of the conditional. For example:

```
#ifdef DEBUG
    std::cout << "Test version. Debugging is on\n";
#else /* DEBUG */
    std::cout << "Production version\n";
#endif /* DEBUG  */
```

A programmer may wish to temporarily remove a section of code. A common method of doing this is to comment out the code by enclosing it in /* */. This can cause problems, as shown by the following example:

```
/***** Comment out this section
    section_report();
    /* Handle the end-of-section stuff */
    dump_table();
**** End of commented out section */
```

This generates a syntax error for the fifth line. Why? Because the */ on the third line ends the comment that started on the first line, and the fifth line :

```
**** End of commented out section */
```

is not a legal C++ statement.

A better method is to use the **#ifdef** construct to remove the code.

```
#ifdef UNDEF
    section_report( );
    /* Handle the end-of-section stuff */
    dump_table( );
#endif /* UNDEF */
```

(Of course the code will be included if anyone defines the symbol UNDEF; however, anyone who does so should be shot.)

The compiler switch –D*symbol* allows symbols to be defined on the command line. For example, the command:

```
CC -DDEBUG -g -o prog prog.cc
```

compiles the program *prog.c* and includes all the code in #ifdef DEBUG/#endif /* DEBUG */ pairs, even though there is no #define DEBUG in the program. The Borland-C++ equivalent is:

```
bcc32 -DDEBUG -g -N -eprog.exe prog.c
```

The general form of the option is –D*symbol* or –D*symbol=value*. For example, the following sets MAX to 10:

```
CC -DMAX=10 -o prog prog.c
```

Most C++ compilers automatically define some system-dependent symbols. For example, Borland-C++ defines the symbol __BORLANDC__, and Windows-based compilers define __WIN32. The ANSI standard compiler C defines the symbol __STDC__. C++ compilers define the symbol __cplusplus. Most Unix compilers define a name for the system (e.g., Sun, VAX, Linux, etc.); however, they are rarely documented. The symbol unix is always defined for all Unix machines

 Command-line options specify the initial value of a symbol only. Any #define and #undef directives in the program can change the symbol's value. For example, the directive #undef DEBUG results in DEBUG being undefined whether or not you use -DDEBUG .

#include Files

The **#include** directive allows the program to use source code from another file.

For example, you have been using the following directive in your programs:

```
#include <iostream>
```

This tells the preprocessor to take the file *iostream* and insert it in the current program. Files that are included in other programs are called *header files.* (Most **#include** directives come at the head of a program.) The angle brackets indicate that the file is a standard header file. In Unix, these files are usually located in */usr/include.* In MS-DOS/Windows, they are located in an installation-dependent directory.

Standard include files are used for defining data structures and macros used by library routines. For example, std::cout is a standard object that (as you know by now) prints data on the standard output. The std::ostream class definition used by std::cout and its related routines is defined in *iostream.*[*]

Sometimes you may want to write your own set of include files. Local include files are particularly useful for storing constants and data structures when a program spans several files, which can be helpful for information sharing when a team of programmers is working on a single project. (See Chapter 23.)

Local include files may be specified by using double quotation marks (") around the filename.

```
#include "defs.h"
```

The filename ("defs.h") can be any valid filename. By convention, local C++ headers end in *.h.* The file specified by the #include can be a simple file, "defs.h"; a relative path, "../../data.h"; or an absolute path, "/root/include/const.h". (In MS-DOS/Windows, you should use backslash (\) instead of slash (/) as a directory separator. For some reason though, you can still use slash (/) and things work.)

Include files may be nested, but this can cause problems. Suppose you define several useful constants in the file *const.h.* If the files *data.h* and *io.h* both include *const.h,* and you put the following in your program:

```
#include "data.h"
#include "io.h"
```

you generate errors because the preprocessor sets the definitions in *const.h* twice. Defining a constant twice is not a fatal error; however, defining a data structure or union twice is an error and must be avoided.

One way around this problem is to have *const.h* check to see whether it has already been included and not define any symbols that have already been defined.

Look at the following code:

```
#ifndef _CONST_H_INCLUDED_

/* Define constants */
```

[*] Actually, the ostream class is defined in the header *ostream.* However, this file is included by the *iostream* header. The result is that by including this single header, you get the definitions of standard objects such as std::cin and standard classes such as std::ostream.

```
#define _CONST_H_INCLUDED_
#endif   /* _CONST_H_INCLUDED_ */
```

When *const.h* is included, it defines the symbol _CONST_H_INCLUDED_. If that symbol is already defined (because the file was included earlier), the **#ifdef** conditional hides all the other defines so they don't cause trouble.

It is possible to put code in a header file, but this is considered poor programming practice. By convention, code goes in *.cpp* files and definitions, declarations, macros, and inline functions go in the *.h* files. You could include a *.cpp* file in another *.cpp* file, but this is considered bad practice.

Parameterized Macros

So far we have discussed only simple **#define**s or macros. Macros can take parameters. The following macro computes the square of a number:

```
#define SQR(x)  ((x) * (x))     /* Square a number */
```

There can be no space between the macro name (SQR in this example) and the open parenthesis.

When used, the macro replaces x with the text of its argument. SQR(5) *expands to* ((5) * (5)). It is a good rule always to put parentheses around the parameters of a macro. Example 10-7 illustrates the problems that can occur if this rule is not followed:

Example 10-7. sqr/sqr.cpp

```
#include <iostream>

#define SQR(x) (x * x)

int main( )
{
    int counter;    // counter for loop

    for (counter = 0; counter < 5; ++counter) {
        std::cout << "x " << (counter+1) <<
                " x squared " << SQR(counter+1) << '\n';
    }
    return (0);
}
```

Question 10-5: *What does the above program output? (Try running it on your machine.) Why did it output what it did? (Try checking the output of the preprocessor.)*

The keep-it-simple system of programming prevents us from using the increment (++) and decrement (--) operators except on a line by themselves. When used in an expression, they cause side effects, and this can lead to unexpected results, as illustrated in Example 10-8.

Example 10-8. sqr-i/sqr-i.cpp

```
#include <iostream>

#define SQR(x) ((x) * (x))

int main()
{
    int counter;    /* counter for loop */

    counter = 0;
    while (counter < 5)
        std::cout << "x " << (counter+1) <<
                " x squared " << SQR(++counter) << '\n';
    return (0);
}
```

Why does this not produce the expected output? How much does the counter go up each time?

In the program shown in Example 10-8, the SQR(++counter) *is expanded to* ((++counter) * (++counter)) *in this case. The result is that* counter *goes up by 2 each time through the loop. The actual result of this expression is system-dependent.*

Question 10-6: *Example 10-9 tells us we have an undefined variable, but our only variable name is* counter. *Why?*

Example 10-9. rec/rec.cpp

```
#include <iostream>

#define RECIPROCAL (number) (1.0 / (number))

int main()
{
    float   counter;

    for (counter = 0.0; counter < 10.0;
         counter += 1.0) {

        std::cout << "1/" << counter << " = " <<
                RECIPROCAL(counter) << "\n";
    }
    return (0);
}
```

The # Operator

The # operator is used inside a parameterized macro to turn an argument into a string. For example:

```
#define STR(data) #data
STR(hello)
```

This code generates:

```
"hello"
```

For a more extensive example of how to use this operator, see Chapter 27.

Parameterized Macros Versus Inline Functions

In most cases, to avoid most of the traps caused by parameterized macros, it is better to use inline functions. But there are cases where a parameterized macro may be better than an inline function. For example, the SQR macro works for both **float** and **int** data types. We'd have to write two inline functions to perform the same functions, or we could use a template function. (See Chapter 24.)

```
#define SQR(x) ((x) * (x))   // A parameterized macro
// Works, but is dangerous

// Inline function to do the same thing
inline int sqr(const int x) {
    return (x * x);
}
```

Advanced Features

This book does not cover the complete list of C++ preprocessor directives. Among the more advanced features are an advanced form of the **#if** directive for conditional compilations and the **#pragma** directive for inserting compiler-dependent commands into a file. See your C++ reference manual for more information on these features.

Summary

The C++ preprocessor is a very useful part of the C++ language. It has a completely different look and feel from C++. However, it must be treated apart from the main C++ compiler.

Problems in macro definitions often do not show up where the macro is defined, but result in errors much further down in the program. By following a few simple rules, you can decrease the chances of having problems:

- Put parentheses around everything. In particular they should enclose **#define** constants and macro parameters.

- When defining a macro with more than one statement, enclose the code in {}.

- The preprocessor is not C++. Don't use = or ;.

```
#define X = 5 // Illegal
#define X 5;  // Illegal
#define X = 5; // Very illegal
#define X 5    // Correct
```

Finally, if you got this far, be glad that the worst is over.

Programming Exercises

Note that the solutions to all the exercises below can be obtained using standard C++ syntax such as inline and enum. In general, using C++ construction is preferred over using macro definitions. However since this is the chapter on the preprocessor, macros should be used for these exercises.

Exercise 10-1: Create a set of macros to define a type called RETURN_STATUS and the following values: RETURN_SUCCESS, RETURN_WARNING, and RETURN_ERROR. Define a macro, CHECK_RETURN_FATAL,,, that takes a RETURN_STATUS as its argument and returns true if you have a fatal error.

Exercise 10-2: Write a macro that returns true if its parameter is divisible by 10 and false otherwise.

Exercise 10-3: Write a macro is_digit that returns true if its argument is a decimal digit. Write a second macro is_hex that returns true if its argument is a hex digit (0–9, A–F, a–f). The second macro should reference the first.

Exercise 10-4: Write a preprocessor macro that swaps two integers. (If you're a real hacker, write one that does not use a temporary variable declared outside the macro.)

Answers to Chapter Questions

Answer 10-1: After the program has been run through the preprocessor, the std::cout statement is expanded to look like:

```
std::cout << "The square of all the parts is " << 7 + 5 * 7 + 5 << '\n';
```

The equation 7 + 5 * 7 + 5 evaluates to 47. It is a good rule to put parentheses () around all expressions in macros. If you change the definition of ALL_PARTS to:

```
#define ALL_PARTS (FIRST_PART + LAST_PART)
```

the program executes correctly.

Answer 10-2: The preprocessor is a very simple-minded program. When it defines a macro, everything past the identifier is part of the macro. In this case, the definition of MAX is literally =10. When the **for** statement is expanded, the result is:

```
for (counter==10; counter > 0; --counter)
```

C++ allows you to compute a result and throw it away. For this statement, the program checks to see whether counter is 10 and discards the answer. Removing the = from the macro definition will correct the problem.

Answer 10-3: As with the previous problem, the preprocessor does not respect C++ syntax conventions. In this case, the programmer used a semicolon to end the statement, but the preprocessor included it as part of the definition for size. The assignment statement for size, expanded, is:

```
size = 10; -2;;
```

The two semicolons at the end do not hurt anything, but the one in the middle is a killer. This line tells C++ to do two things: assign 10 to size and compute the value −2 and throw it away (this results in the null effect warning). Removing the semicolons will fix the problem.

Answer 10-4: The output of the preprocessor looks like:

```
int main( ) {
    int value;

    value = 1;
    if (value < 0)
        std::cout << "Fatal Error: Abort\n"; exit(8);

    std::cout << "We did not die\n";
    return (0);
}
```

The problem is that two statements follow the **if** line. Normally they would be put on two lines. If we properly indent this program we get:

Example 10-10. die3/die.cpp

```
#include <iostream>
#include <cstdlib>

int main( ) {
    int value;   // a random value for testing

    value = 1;
    if (value < 0)
        std::cout << "Fatal Error:Abort\n";

    exit(8);

    std::cout << "We did not die\n";
```

Example 10-10. die3/die.cpp (continued)

```
    return (0);
}
```

From this it is obvious why we always exit. The fact that there were two statements after the **if** was hidden by using a single preprocessor macro. The cure for this problem is to put curly braces around all multistatement macros.

```
#define DIE \
    {std::cout << "Fatal Error: Abort\n"; exit(8);}
```

Answer 10-5: The problem is that the preprocessor does not understand C++ syntax. The macro call:

```
SQR(counter+1)
```

expands to:

```
(counter+1 * counter+1)
```

The result is not the same as ((counter+1) * (counter+1)). To avoid this problem, use inline functions instead of parameterized macros:

```
inline int SQR(int x) { return (x*x);}
```

If you must use parameterized macros, enclose each instance of the parameter in parentheses:

```
#define SQR(x) ((x) * (x))
```

Answer 10-6: The only difference between a parameterized macro and one without parameters is the parentheses immediately following the macro name. In this case, a space follows the definition of RECIPROCAL, so it is not a parameterized macro. Instead it is a simple text replacement macro that replaces RECIPROCAL with:

```
(number) (1.0 / number)
```

Removing the space between RECIPROCAL and (number) corrects the problem.

CHAPTER 11

Bit Operations

To be or not to be, that is the question.
—Shakespeare on Boolean algebra

This chapter discusses bit-oriented operations. A bit is the smallest unit of information; normally represented by the values 1 and 0. (Other representations include on/off, true/false, and yes/no.) Bit manipulations are used to control the machine at the lowest level. They allow the programmer to get "under the hood" of the machine. Many higher-level programs will never need bit operations. Low-level coding such as writing device drivers or pixel-level graphic programming requires bit operations.

Eight bits together form a byte, represented by the C++ data type **char**. A byte might contain the following bits: 01100100.

The binary number 01100100 can also be written as the hexadecimal number 0x64. (C++ uses the prefix "0x" to indicate a hexadecimal—base 16—number.) Hexadecimal is convenient for representing binary data because each hexadecimal digit represents 4 binary bits. Table 11-1 gives the hexadecimal (hex) to binary conversion.

Thus, the hexadecimal number 0xAF represents the binary number 10101111.

Table 11-1. Hex and binary

Hex	Binary	Hex	Binary
0	0000	8	1000
1	0001	9	1001
2	0010	A	1010
3	0011	B	1011
4	0100	C	1100
5	0101	D	1101
6	0110	E	1110
7	0111	F	1111

Bit Operators

Bit, or *bitwise, operators* allow the programmer to work on individual bits. For example, a short integer holds 16 bits (on most machines). The bit operators treat each of these as an independent bit. By contrast, an add operator treats the 16 bits as a single 16-bit number.

Bit operators allow you to set, clear, test, and perform other operations on bits. The bit operators are listed in Table 11-2.

Table 11-2. Bit operators

Operator	Meaning
&	Bitwise AND
|	Bitwise OR
^	Bitwise exclusive OR
~	Complement
<<	Shift left
>>	Shift right

These operators work on any integer or character-data type.

The AND Operator (&)

The AND *operator* compares two bits. If they both are 1, the result is 1. The results of the AND operator are defined in Table 11-3.

Table 11-3. AND operator

Bit1	Bit2	Bit1 & Bit2
0	0	0
0	1	0
1	0	0
1	1	1

When two 8-bit variables (char variables) are "ANDed" together, the AND operator works on each bit independently. The following program segment illustrates this operation. (In the output statement below, hex tells the system to output numbers in hexadecimal format, and dec tells it to return to decimal. For more information, see Chapter 16.)

```
int    c1, c2;

c1 = 0x45;
c2 = 0x71;
```

```
    std::cout << "Result of " << hex << c1 << " & " << c2 << " = " <<
                          (c1 & c2) << dec << '\n';
```

The output of this program is:

```
Result of 45 & 71 = 41
```

This is because:

	c1 = 0x45	binary 01000101
&	c2 = 0x71	binary 01110001
=	0x41	binary 01000001

The bitwise AND (&) is similar to the logical AND (&&). In the logical AND if both operands are true (nonzero), the result is true (1). In bitwise AND (&), if the corresponding bits of both operands are true (1), the corresponding bits of the results are true (1). So the bitwise AND (&) works on each bit independently, while the logical AND (&&) works on the operands as a whole.

However, & and && are different operators, as Example 11-1 illustrates.

Example 11-1. and/and.cpp

```cpp
#include <iostream>

int main()
{
    int i1, i2; // two random integers

    i1 = 4;
    i2 = 2;     // set values

    // Nice way of writing the conditional
    if ((i1 != 0) && (i2 != 0))
        std::cout << "Both are not zero #1\n";

    // Shorthand way of doing the same thing
    // Correct C++ code, but rotten style
    if (i1 && i2)
        std::cout << "Both are not zero #2\n";

    // Incorrect use of bitwise and resulting in an error
    if (i1 & i2)
        std::cout << "Both are not zero #3\n";
    return (0);
}
```

Question: Why does test #3 fail to print Both are not zero #3?

Answer: The operator & is a bitwise AND. The result of the bitwise AND is zero:

$$
\begin{array}{r r l}
 & \text{i1=4} & \text{00000100} \\
\text{\&} & \text{i2=2} & \text{00000010} \\
\hline
 & 0 & \text{00000000}
\end{array}
$$

The result of the bitwise AND is 0, and the conditional is false. If the programmer had used the first form:

```
if ((i1 != 0) && (i2 != 0))
```

and made the mistake of using & instead of &&:

```
if ((i1 != 0) & (i2 != 0))
```

the program would still have executed correctly.

| (i1 != 0) | is true (result = 1) |
| (i2 != 0) | is true (result = 1) |

1 bitwise AND 1 is 1, so the expression is true.

 Soon after discovering the bug illustrated by this program, I told my officemate, "I now understand the difference between AND and AND AND), and he understood me. How we understand language has always fascinated me, and the fact that I could utter such a sentence and have someone understand it without trouble amazed me.

You can use the bitwise AND operator to test whether a number is even or odd. In base 2, the last digit of all even numbers is zero and the last digit of all odd numbers is one. The following function uses the bitwise AND to pick off this last digit. If it is zero (an even number), the result of the function is true.

```
inline int even(const int value)
{
    return ((value & 1) == 0);
}
```

Bitwise OR (|)

The inclusive OR operator (also known as just the OR operator) compares its two operands. If one or the other bit is a 1, the result is 1. Table 11-4 lists the truth table for the OR operator.

Table 11-4. Bitwise OR operator

Bit1	Bit2	Bit1	Bit2
0	0	0
0	1	1

Table 11-4. Bitwise OR operator (continued)

Bit1	Bit2	Bit1 | Bit2
1	0	1
1	1	1

Here's an example of bitwise OR performed on a byte:

```
      i1=0x47    01000111
  |   i2=0x53    01010011
      0x57       01010111
```

The Bitwise Exclusive OR (^)

The exclusive OR (also known as XOR) operator results in a 1 when either of its two operands is a 1, but not both. The truth table for the exclusive OR operator is listed in Table 11-5.

Table 11-5. Bitwise exclusive OR operator

Bit1	Bit2	Bit1 ∧ Bit2
0	0	0
0	1	1
1	0	1
1	1	0

Here's an example of bitwise exclusive OR performed on a byte:

```
      i1=0x47    01000111
  ∧   i2=0x53    01010011
      0x14       00010100
```

The Ones Complement Operator (NOT) (~)

The NOT operator (also called the invert operator or bit flip) is a unary operator that returns the inverse of its operand, as shown in Table 11-6.

Table 11-6. NOT operator

Bit	~Bit
0	1
1	0

Here's an example of NOT performed on a byte:

c=	0x45	01000101
~c=	0xBA	10111010

The Left and Right Shift Operators (<<, >>)

The left shift operator moves the data left a specified number of bits. Any bits that are shifted out the left side disappear. New bits coming in from the right are zeros. The right shift does the same thing in the other direction. For example:

	c=0x1C	00011100
c << 1	c=0x38	00111000
c >> 2	c=0x07	00000111

Shifting left by one (x << 1) is the same as multiplying by 2 (x * 2). Shifting left by two (x << 2) is the same as multiplying by 4 (x * 4, or x * 2^2). You can see a pattern forming here. Shifting left by n places is the same as multiplying by 2^n. Why shift instead of multiply? Shifting is faster than multiplication, so:

```
i = j << 3;     // Multiply j by 8 (2**3)
```

is faster than:

```
i = j * 8;
```

Or it would be faster if compilers weren't smart enough to turn "multiply by power of two" into "shift."

Many clever programmers use this trick to speed up their programs at the cost of clarity. Don't do it. The compiler is smart enough to perform the speedup automatically. This means that putting in a shift gains you nothing at the expense of clarity.

The left shift operator multiplies; the right shift divides. So:

```
q = i >> 2;
```

is the same as:

```
q = i / 4;
```

Again, this clever trick should not be used in modern code.

Right Shift Details

Right shifts are particularly tricky. When a variable is shifted to the right, C++ needs to fill the space on the left side with something. For signed variables, C++ uses the value of the sign bit. For unsigned variables, C++ uses zero. Table 11-7 illustrates some typical right shifts.

Table 11-7. Right shift examples

	Signed character	Signed character	Unsigned character
Expression	9 >> 2	−8 >> 2	248 >> 2
Binary value >> 2	0000 1010₂ >> 2	1111 1000₂ >> 2	1111 1000₂ >> 2
Result	??00 0010₂	??11 1110₂ >> 2	??11 1110₂ >> 2
Fill	Sign bit (0)	Sign bit (1)	Zero
Final result (binary)	0000 0010₂	1111 1110₂	0011 1110₂
Final result (short int)	2	−2	62

Setting, Clearing, and Testing Bits

A character contains eight bits.* Each of these can be treated as a separate flag. Bit operations can be used to pack eight single-bit values in a single byte. For example, suppose you are writing a low-level communications program. You are going to store the characters in an 8K buffer for later use. With each character, you will also store a set of status flags. The flags are listed in Table 11-8.

Table 11-8. Communications status values

Name	Description
ERROR	True if any error is set
FRAMING_ERROR	A framing error occurred for this character
PARITY_ERROR	Character had the wrong parity
CARRIER_LOST	The carrier signal went down
CHANNEL_DOWN	Power was lost on the communication device

You could store each flag in its own character variable. That would mean that for each character buffered, you would need five bytes of status storage. For a large buffer, that adds up. By instead assigning each status flag its own bit within an eight-bit status character, you cut storage requirements down to 1/5 of the original need.

You can assign the flags the bit numbers listed in Table 11-9.

Table 11-9. Bit assignments

Bit	Name
0	ERROR
1	FRAMING_ERROR
2	PARITY_ERROR

---

* This is true on every machine I know in use today, but there's nothing in the C++ standard that mandates how many bits must be in a character.

Table 11-9. Bit assignments (continued)

Bit	Name
3	CARRIER_LOST
4	CHANNEL_DOWN

Bits are numbered 76543210 by convention. The constants for each bit are defined in Table 11-10.

Table 11-10. Bit values

Bit	Binary value	Hex constant
7	10000000	0x80
6	01000000	0x40
5	00100000	0x20
4	00010000	0x10
3	00001000	0x08
2	00000100	0x04
1	00000010	0x02
0	00000001	0x01

Here's one way we can define constants for the bits that make up the communication status values:

```
// True if any error is set
const int ERROR = 0x01;

// A framing error occurred for this character
const int FRAMING_ERROR = 0x02;

// Character had the wrong parity
const int PARITY_ERROR = 0x04;

// The carrier signal went down
const int CARRIER_LOST = 0x08;

// Power was lost on the communication device
const int CHANNEL_DOWN = 0x10;
```

This method of defining bits is somewhat confusing. Can you tell (without looking at the table) which bit number is represented by the constant 0x10? Table 11-11 shows how you can use the left shift operator (<<) to define bits.

Table 11-11. The left shift operator and bit definition

C++ representation	Base 2 equivalent	Result (base 2)	Bit number
1 << 0	00000001₂ << 0	00000001₂	Bit 0
1 << 1	00000001₂ << 1	00000010₂	Bit 1

Table 11-11. The left shift operator and bit definition (continued)

C++ representation	Base 2 equivalent	Result (base 2)	Bit number
1 << 2	$00000001_2 << 2$	00000100_2	Bit 2
1 << 3	$00000001_2 << 3$	00001000_2	Bit 3
1 << 4	$00000001_2 << 4$	00010000_2	Bit 4
1 << 5	$00000001_2 << 5$	00100000_2	Bit 5
1 << 6	$00000001_2 << 6$	01000000_2	Bit 6
1 << 7	$00000001_2 << 7$	10000000_2	Bit 7

Although it is hard to tell what bit is represented by 0x10, it's easy to tell what bit is meant by 1 << 4.

Here's another way of defining the constants for testing the communication status bits:

```
// True if any error is set
const int ERROR =        (1 << 0);

// A framing error occurred for this character
const int FRAMING_ERROR =  (1 << 1);

// Character had the wrong parity
const int PARITY_ERROR =   (1 << 2);

// The carrier signal went down
const int CARRIER_LOST =   (1 << 3);

// Power was lost on the communication device
const int CHANNEL_DOWN =   (1 << 4);
```

Now that you have defined the bits, you can manipulate them. To set a bit, use the | operator. For example:

```
char    flags = 0;  // Start all flags at 0

    flags |= CHANNEL_DOWN; // Channel just died
```

To test a bit, use the & operator to "mask out" the bits:

```
if ((flags & ERROR) != 0)
    std::cerr << "Error flag is set\n";
else
    std::cerr << "No error detected\n";
```

Clearing a bit is a little harder. Suppose you want to clear the bit PARITY_ERROR. In binary this bit is 00000100. You want to create a mask that has all bits set *except* for the bit you want to clear (11111011). This is done with the NOT operator (~). The mask is then ANDed with the number to clear the bit.

```
PARITY_ERROR                 00000100
~PARITY_ERROR                11111011
```

flags	00000101
flags & ~PARITY_ERROR	00000001

In C++ this is:

```
flags &= ~PARITY_ERROR; // Who cares about parity
```

Question 11-1: *In the following program, the* HIGH_SPEED *flag works, but the* DIRECT_CONNECT *flag does not. Why?*

```
#include <iostream>

const int HIGH_SPEED = (1<<7);      /* modem is running fast */
                                    // we are using a hardwired connection
const int DIRECT_CONNECT = (1<<8);

char flags = 0;                     // start with nothing

int main( )
{
    flags |= HIGH_SPEED;            // we are running fast
    flags |= DIRECT_CONNECT;        // because we are wired together

    if ((flags & HIGH_SPEED) != 0)
        std::cout <<"High speed set\n";

    if ((flags & DIRECT_CONNECT) != 0)
        std::cout <<"Direct connect set\n";
    return (0);
}
```

Bitmapped Graphics

In black and white bitmapped graphics, each pixel in the image is represented by a single bit in memory. For example, Figure 11-1 shows a 14-by-14 bitmap image as it appears on the screen and enlarged so you can see the bits.

Suppose we have a small graphic device—a 16-by-16 pixel monochrome display. We want to set the bit at (4, 7). The bitmap for this device is shown as an array of bits in Figure 11-2.

But we have a problem. There is no data type for an array of bits in C++. The closest we can come is an array of bytes. Our 16-by-16 array of bits now becomes a 2-by-16 array of bytes, as shown in Figure 11-3.

To set the pixel at bit number (4, 7), we need to set the fourth bit of byte (0, 7). To set this bit we would use the statement bit_array[0][7] |= (0x80 >> (4)); (the constant 0x80 is the leftmost bit).

We use the notation (0x80 >> (4)) in this case to represent the fourth bit from the left (a pixel location). Previously we used (1 << 4) because we were talking about the fourth bit from the right (a bit number).

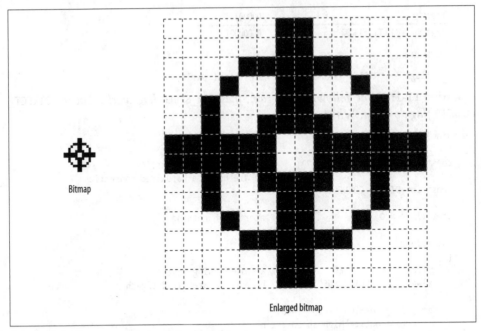

Figure 11-1. Bitmap, actual size and enlarged

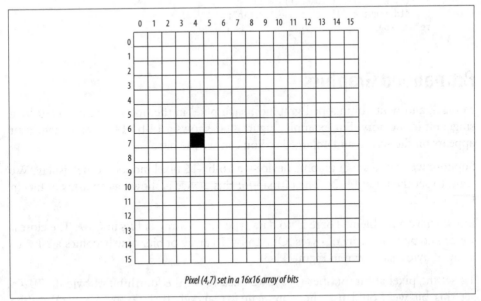

Pixel (4,7) set in a 16x16 array of bits

Figure 11-2. Array of bits

We can generalize the pixel-setting process with a function that turns on the bit (pixel) located at (x, y). We need to compute two values: the coordinate of the byte and the number of the bit within the byte.

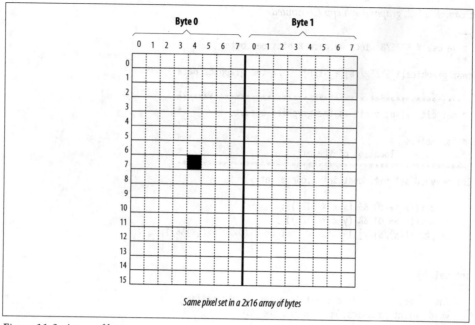

Figure 11-3. Array of bytes

Our bit address is (*x, y*). Bytes are groups of eight bits, so our byte address is (*x/8, y*).

Answer 11-1: The bit within the byte is not so simple. We want to generate a mask consisting of the single bit we want to set. For the leftmost bit this should be 1000 0000₂, or 0x80. This occurs when (x%8) == 0. The next bit is 0100 0000₂, or (0x80 >> 1), and occurs when (x%8) == 1. Therefore, to generate our bit mask we use the expression (0x80 >> (x%8)).

Now that we have the byte location and the bit mask, all we have to do is set the bit. The following function sets a given bit in a bitmapped graphics array named *graphics*:

```
void inline set_bit(const int x ,const int y)
{
    assert((x >= 0) && (x < X_SIZE));
    assert((y < Y_SIZE));
    graphics[x/8][y] | = (0x80) >> (x%8);
}
```

Example 11-2 draws a diagonal line across the graphics array and then prints the array on the console.

Example 11-2. graph/graph.cpp

```
#include <iostream>
#include <assert.h>

const int X_SIZE = 40; // size of array in the X direction
const int Y_SIZE = 60; // size of the array in Y direction
```

Example 11-2. graph/graph.cpp (continued)

```cpp
/*
 * We use X_SIZE/8 since we pack 8 bits per byte
 */
char graphics[X_SIZE / 8][Y_SIZE];   // the graphics data

/**********************************************************
 * set_bit -- set a bit in the graphics array.           *
 *                                                        *
 * Parameters                                             *
 *      x,y -- location of the bit.                       *
 **********************************************************/
inline void set_bit(const int x,const int y)
{
    assert((x >= 0) && (x < X_SIZE));
    assert((y >= 0) && (y < Y_SIZE));
    graphics[(x)/8][y] |= static_cast<char>(0x80 >>((x)%8));
}

int main()
{
    int    loc;        // current location we are setting
    void   print_graphics(); // print the data

    for (loc = 0; loc < X_SIZE; ++loc)
        set_bit(loc, loc);

    print_graphics();
    return (0);
}
/**********************************************************
 * print_graphics -- print the graphics bit array        *
 *                 as a set of X and .'s.                 *
 **********************************************************/
void print_graphics()
{
    int x;     // current x BYTE
    int y;     // current y location
    int bit;   // bit we are testing in the current byte

    for (y = 0; y < Y_SIZE; ++y) {

        // Loop for each byte in the array
        for (x = 0; x < X_SIZE / 8; ++x) {

            // Handle each bit
            for (bit = 0x80; bit > 0; bit = (bit >> 1)) {
                assert((x >= 0) && (x < (X_SIZE/8)));
                assert((y >= 0) && (y < Y_SIZE));

                if ((graphics[x][y] & bit) != 0)
                    std::cout << 'X';
                else
```

Example 11-2. graph/graph.cpp (continued)

```
                std::cout << '.';
        }
    }
    std::cout << '\n';
    }
}
```

The program defines a bitmapped graphics array:

```
char graphics[X_SIZE / 8][Y_SIZE];   // The graphics data
```

The constant X_SIZE/8 is used since we have X_SIZE bits across, which translates to X_SIZE/8 bytes.

The main **for** loop:

```
for (loc = 0; loc < X_SIZE; ++loc)
        set_bit(loc, loc);
```

draws a diagonal line across the graphics array.

Since we do not have a bitmapped graphics device we will simulate it with the subroutine print_graphics.

The following loop prints each row:

```
for (y = 0; y < Y_SIZE; ++y) {
    ....
```

This loop goes through every byte in the row:

```
    for (x = 0; x < X_SIZE / 8; ++x) {
        ...
```

There are eight bits in each byte handled by the following loop:

```
        for (bit = 0x80; bit > 0; bit = (bit >> 1))
```

which uses an unusual loop counter. This loop causes the variable bit to start with bit 7 (the leftmost bit). For each iteration of the loop, bit = (bit >> 1) moves the bit to the right one bit. When we run out of bits, the loop exits.

The loop counter cycles through the values listed in the following table:

Binary	Hex
0000 0000 1000 0000	0x80
0000 0000 0100 0000	0x40
0000 0000 0010 0000	0x20
0000 0000 0001 0000	0x10
0000 0000 0000 1000	0x08
0000 0000 0000 0100	0x04
0000 0000 0000 0010	0x02
0000 0000 0000 0001	0x01

Finally, at the heart of the loops is the code:

```
if ((graphics[x][y] & bit) != 0)
    std::cout <<"X";
else
    std::cout << ".";
```

This tests an individual bit and writes "X" if the bit is set or "." if the bit is not set.

Question 11-2: *In Example 11-3 the first loop works, but the second fails. Why?*

Example 11-3. loop/loop.cpp

```cpp
#include <iostream>

int main()
{
    short int i;

    // Works
    for (i = 0x80; i != 0; i = (i >> 1)) {
        std::cout << "i is " << std::hex << i << std::dec << '\n';
    }

    signed char ch;

    // Fails
    for (ch = 0x80; ch != 0; ch = (ch >> 1)) {
        std::cout << "ch is " << std::hex <<
            static_cast<int>(ch) << std::dec << '\n';
    }
    return (0);
}
```

Programming Exercises

Exercise 11-1: Write a set of inline functions, clear_bit and test_bit, to go with the set_bit operation defined in Example 11-2. Write a main program to test these functions.

Exercise 11-2: Write a program to draw a 10-by-10 bitmapped square.

Exercise 11-3: Change Example 11-1 so it draws a white line across a black background.

Exercise 11-4: Write a program that counts the number of bits set in an integer. For example, the number 5 (decimal), which is 0000000000000101 (binary), has two bits set.

Exercise 11-5: Write a program that takes a 32-bit integer (**long int**) and splits it into eight 4-bit values. (Be careful of the sign bit.)

Exercise 11-6: Write a program that will take all the bits in a number and shift them to the left end. For example, 01010110 (binary) would become 11110000 (binary).

Answers to Chapter Questions

Answer 11-2: DIRECT_CONNECT is defined to be bit number 8 by the expression (1 << 8); however, the eight bits in a character variable are numbered 76543210. There is no bit number 8. A solution to this problem is to make flags a short integer with 16 bits.

Answer 11-3: The problem is that ch is a character (8 bits). The value 0x80 represented in 8 bits is 1000 0000₂. The first bit, the sign bit, is set. When a right shift is done on this variable, the sign bit is used for fill, so 1000 0000₂ >> 1 is 1100 0000₂.

The variable i works even though it is signed because it is 16 bits long. So 0x80 in 16 bits is 0000 0000 1000 0000₂. Notice that the bit we've got set is nowhere near the sign bit.

The solution to the problem is to declare ch as an **unsigned** variable.

## PART III

Advanced Types and Classes

## CHAPTER 12

Advanced Types

> *Total grandeur of a total edifice,*
> *Chosen by an inquisitor of structures.*
> —Wallace Stevens

C++ provides a rich set of data types. Through the use of structures, unions, enumerations, and class types, the programmer can extend the language with new types.

Structures

Suppose you are writing an inventory program for a warehouse. The warehouse is filled with bins, each containing a bunch of parts. All the parts in a bin are identical, so you don't have to worry about mixed bins or partials.

For each bin you need to know:

- The name of the part it holds (30-character string).
- The quantity on hand (integer).
- The price (integer cents).

In previous chapters you have used arrays for storing a group of similar data types, but in this example you have a mixed bag: two integers and a string.

Instead of an array, you will use a new data type called a *structure*. In an array, all the elements are of the same type and are numbered. In a structure, each element, or *member*, is named and has its own data type.

The general form of a structure definition is:

```
struct structure-name {
    member-type member-name;  // Comment
    member-type member-name;  // Comment
    . . . .
} variable-name;
```

For example, say you want to define a bin to hold printer cables. The structure definition is:

```
struct bin {
    char    name[30];     // Name of the part
    int     quantity;     // How many are in the bin
    int     cost;         // The cost of a single part (in cents)
} printer_cable_box;      // Where we put the print cables
```

This definition actually tells C++ two things. The first is what a struct bin looks like. This statement defines a new data type that can be used in declaring other variables. This statement also declares the variable printer_cable_box. Since the structure of a bin has been defined, you can use it to declare additional variables:

```
struct bin terminal_cable_box;  // Place to put terminal cables
```

The *structure-name* part of the definition may be omitted:

```
struct {
    char    name[30];     // Name of the part
    int     quantity;     // How many are in the bin
    int     cost;         // The cost of a single part (in cents)
} printer_cable_box;      // Where we put the print cables
```

The variable printer_cable_box is still to be defined, but no data type is created. The data type for this variable is an *anonymous structure*.

The *variable-name* part also may be omitted. This would define a structure type but no variables:

```
struct bin {
    char    name[30];     // Name of the part
    int     quantity;     // How many are in the bin
    int     cost;         // The cost of a single part (in cents)
};
```

In an extreme case, both the *variable-name* and the *structure-name* parts may be omitted. This creates a section of correct but totally useless code.

Once the structure type has been defined you can use it to define variables:

```
struct bin printer_cable_box; // Define the box holding printer cables
```

C++ allows the struct to be omitted, so you can use the following declaration:

```
bin printer_cable_box; // Define the box holding printer cables
```

You have defined the variable printer_cable_box containing three named members: name, quantity, and cost. To access them you use the syntax:

```
variable.member
```

For example, if you just found out that the price of the cables went up to $12.95, you would do the following:

```
printer_cable_box.cost = 1295;    // $12.95 is the new price
```

To compute the value of everything in the bin, you can simply multiply the cost by the number of items using the following:

```
total_cost = printer_cable_box.cost * printer_cable_box.quantity;
```

Structures may be initialized at declaration time by putting the list of elements in curly braces ({ }):

```
/*
 * Printer cables
 */
struct bin {
    char    name[30];    // Name of the part
    int     quantity;    // How many are in the bin
    int     cost;        // The cost of a single part (in cents)
};
struct bin printer_cable_box = {
    "Printer Cables",    // Name of the item in the bin
    0,                   // Start with empty box
    1295                 // Cost -- $12.95
};
```

The definition of the structure bin and the variable printer_cable_box can be combined in one step:

```
struct bin {
    char    name[30];    // Name of the part
    int     quantity;    // How many are in the bin
    int     cost;        // The cost of a single part (in cents)
} printer_cable_box = {
    "Printer Cables",    // Name of the item in the bin
    0,                   // Start with empty box
    1295                 // Cost -- $12.95
};
```

Unions

A structure is used to define a data type with several members. Each member takes up a separate storage location. For example, the structure:

```
struct rectangle {
    int width;
    int height;
};
```

appears in memory as shown in Figure 12-1.

A *union* is similar to a structure; however, it defines a single location that can be given many different member names:

```
union value {
    long int i_value;    // Long integer version of value
    float f_value;       // Floating version of value
}
```

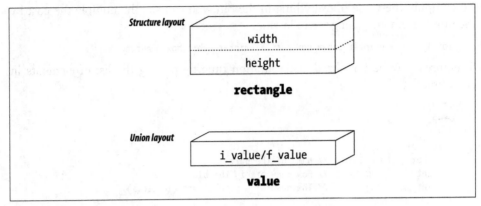

Figure 12-1. Structure and union layout

The members i_value and f_value share the same space. You might think of a structure as a large box divided up into several different compartments, each with its own name. A union is a box, not divided at all, with several different labels placed on the single compartment inside.

In a structure, the members do not interact. Changing one member does not change any others. In a union, all members occupy the same space, so only one may be active at a time. In other words, if you put something in i_value, assigning something to f_value wipes out the old value of i_value.

The following shows how a union may be used:

```
/*
 * Define a variable to hold an integer or
 * a real number (but not both)
 */
union value {
    long int i_value;   // The real number
    float f_value;      // The floating point number
} data;

int i;                  // Random integer
float f;                // Random floating point number

int main( )
{
    data.f_value = 5.0;
    data.i_value = 3;   // Data.f_value overwritten

    i = data.i_value;   // Legal

    f = data.f_value;   // Not legal; will generate unexpected results

    data.f_value = 5.5; // Put something in f_value/clobber i_value
    i = data.i_value;   // Not legal; will generate unexpected results
    return (0);
}
```

Suppose you want to store the information about a shape. The shape can be any standard shape such as a circle, rectangle, or triangle. The information needed to draw a circle is different from the data needed to draw a rectangle, so you need to define different structures for each shape:

```
struct circle {
    int radius;          // Radius of the circle in pixels
};
struct rectangle {
    int height, width;   // Size of the rectangle in pixels
};
struct triangle {
    int base;            // Length of the triangle's base in pixels
    int height;          // Height of the triangle in pixels
};
```

Now you define a structure to hold the generic shape. The first member is a code that tells you what type of shape you have. The second is a union that holds the shape information:

```
const int SHAPE_CIRCLE    = 0;    // Shape is a circle
const int SHAPE_RECTANGLE = 1;    // Shape is a rectangle
const int SHAPE_TRIANGLE  = 2;    // Shape is a triangle

struct shape {
    int kind;                     // What kind of shape is stored
    union shape_union {           // Union to hold shape information
        struct circle    circle_data;     // Data for a circle
        struct rectangle rectangle_data;  // Data for a rectangle
        struct triangle  triangle_data;   // Data for a triangle
    } data;
};
```

Graphically you can represent shape as a large box. Inside the box is the single integer kind and our union shape_union. The union is a box with three labels on it. The question is which one is the "real" label. You can't tell from looking at the union, but that's why you defined kind. It tells us which label to read. The layout of the shape structure is illustrated by Figure 12-2.

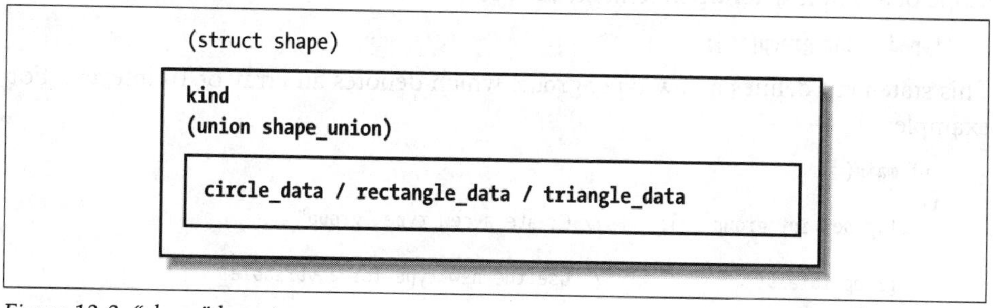

Figure 12-2. "shape" layout

Now you can store a circle in the generic shape:

```
struct shape a_shape;
//...
a_shape.kind = SHAPE_CIRCLE;
a_shape.data.circle_data.radius = 50;   // Define the radius of the circle
```

In this example we are define one basic data type (a shape) and adding in specific information for a bunch of different types of shapes. Although we are using a union to organize our data, this sort of data can be better organized using base and derived classes. (See Chapter 21.)

typedef

C++ allows you to define your own variable types through the typedef statement. This provides a way for you to extend C++'s basic types. The general form of the typedef statement is:

```
typedef type-declaration;
```

The *type-declaration* is the same as a variable declaration except a type name is used instead of a variable name. For example:

```
typedef int width; // Define a type that is the width of an object
```

defines a new type, width, that is the same as an integer. So the declaration:

```
width box_width;
```

is the same as:

```
int box_width;
```

At first glance, this is not much different from:

```
#define width int

width box_width;
```

However, typedefs can be used to define more complex objects that are beyond the scope of a simple **#define** statement, such as:

```
typedef int group[10];
```

This statement defines a new type, group, which denotes an array of 10 integers. For example:

```
int main( )
{
    typedef int group[10];      // Create a new type "group"

    group totals;               // Use the new type for a variable

    // Initialize each element of total
    for (i = 0; i < 10; ++i)
        totals[i] = 0;
```

enum Type

The *enumerated* (enum) data type is designed for variables that can contain only a limited set of values. These values are referenced by name (*tag**). The compiler assigns each tag an integer value internally, such as the days of the week. You could use the directive **const** to create values for the days of the week (day_of_the_week) as follows:

```
typedef int day_of_the_week;    // Define the type for days of the week

const int SUNDAY    = 0;
const int MONDAY    = 1;
const int TUESDAY   = 2;
const int WEDNESDAY = 3;
const int THURSDAY  = 4;
const int FRIDAY    = 5;
const int SATURDAY  = 6;

/* Now to use it */
day_of_the_week today = TUESDAY;
```

This method is cumbersome. A better method is to use the enum type:

```
enum day_of_the_week {SUNDAY, MONDAY, TUESDAY, WEDNESDAY, THURSDAY,
    FRIDAY, SATURDAY};

/* Now use it */
enum day_of_the_week today = TUESDAY;
```

The general form of an enum statement is:

```
enum enum-name {tag-1, tag-2, . . .} variable-name;
```

As with structures, the *enum-name* or the *variable-name* may be omitted. The tags may be any valid C++ identifier; however, tags are usually all uppercase.

An additional advantage of using an enum type is that C++ will restrict the values that can be used to the ones listed in the enum declaration. Thus, the following will result in a compiler error:

```
today = 5;  // 5 is not a day_of_the_week
```

If we want to force the issue, we have to use a static_cast to transform 5 into a day:

```
today = static_cast<enum day_of_the_week>(5);
```

So far we've let C++ do the mapping from enum tags to integers. For example, our enum declaration:

```
enum day_of_the_week {SUNDAY, MONDAY, TUESDAY, WEDNESDAY, THURSDAY,
    FRIDAY, SATURDAY};
```

results in SUNDAY being assigned 0, MONDAY gets 1, and so on. This works great if we don't care about the mapping. But suppose we are interfacing to a device that returns

---

* Tags are also called "named constants" or "enumerators."

a set of error codes. We would like to define an enum to hold them. The problem is that the device returns error numbers and we need to map them precisely to our enum tags. C++ lets you specify the mapping values in your enum declaration:

```
enum ERROR_RETURNS {
    MOTOR_FAILURE = 55,
    POSITION_ERROR = 58,
    OIL_FAILURE = 33
};
```

Bit Members or Packed Structures

So far all the structures you've been using have been *unpacked. Packed structures* allow you to declare structures in a way that takes up a minimum of storage. For example, the following structure takes up 6 bytes (using a 16-bit compiler):

```
struct item {
    unsigned int list;      // True if item is in the list
    unsigned int seen;      // True if this item has been seen
    unsigned int number;    // Item number
};
```

The storage layout for this structure can be seen in Figure 12-3. Each structure uses 6 bytes of storage (2 bytes for each integer).

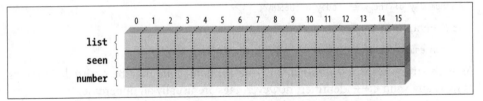

Figure 12-3. Unpacked structure

However, the members list and seen can have only two values, 0 and 1, so only 1 bit is needed to represent them. You never plan on having more than 16383 items (0x3fff or 14 bits). You can redefine this structure using bit members, so that it takes only 2 bytes, by following each member with a colon and the number of bits to be used for that member:

```
struct item {
    unsigned int list:1;      // True if item is in the list
    unsigned int seen:1;      // True if this item has been seen
    unsigned int number:14;   // Item number
};
```

In this example, you tell the compiler to use 1 bit for list, 1 bit for seen and 14 bits for number. Using this method you can pack data into only 2 bytes, as seen in Figure 12-4.

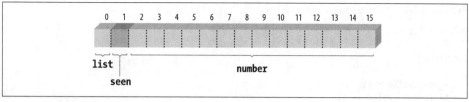

Figure 12-4. Packed structure

You can add a bit field only to an `int` or `enum` variable. It doesn't work on floating-point members, strings, or other complex types.

Packed structures should be used with care. The machine code to extract data from bit members is relatively large and slow. Unless storage is a problem, packed structures should not be used.

Also, the C++ standard does not define how packing must be implemented. The compiler is free to pack things together in any order it wants to. There is no guarantee that our structure will be stored in two 8-bit bytes. (Some cheap compilers treat packed structures the same an normal structures and leave everything unpacked. This is legal under the C++ standard.)

In Chapter 1, you needed to store character data and five status flags for 8,000 characters. In this case, using a different byte for each flag would eat up a lot of storage (five bytes for each incoming character). You used bitwise operations to pack the five flags into a single byte. Alternatively, a packed structure could have accomplished the same thing:

```
struct char_and_status {
    char character;       // Character from device
    unsigned int error:1;         // True if any error is set
    unsigned int framing_error:1;// A framing error occurred
    unsigned int parity_error:1; // Character had the wrong parity
    unsigned int carrier_lost:1; // The carrier signal went down
    unsigned int channel_down:1; // Power was lost on the channel
};
```

Using packed structures for flags is clearer and less error-prone than using bitwise operators. However, bitwise operators allow additional flexibility. You should use the approach that is clearest and easiest for you to use.

Question 12-1: *Why does Example 12-1 fail?*

Example 12-1. info/info.cpp

```
#include <iostream>

struct info {
    int valid:1;       // If 1, we are valid
    int data:31;       // The data
};
```

Example 12-1. info/info.cpp (continued)

```
info a_info;

int main( )
{
    a_info.valid = 1;
    if (a_info.valid == 1)
        std::cout << "a_info is valid\n";
    return (0);
}
```

The GNU compiler does try to give a hint as to what's going on. Now if we could only understand what it is trying to say:

```
info.cpp: In function `int main( )':
info.cpp:13: warning: comparison is always 0 due to width of bitfield
```

Arrays of Structures

Structures and arrays can be combined. Suppose you want to record the time a runner completes each lap of a four-lap race. You define a structure to store the time:

```
struct time {
    int hour;   // Hour (24-hour clock)
    int minute; // 0-59
    int second; // 0-59
};

const int MAX_LAPS = 4; /* We will have only 4 laps*/

/* The time of day for each lap*/
struct time lap[MAX_LAPS];
```

The statement:

```
struct time lap[MAX_LAPS];
```

defines lap as an array of four elements. Each element consists of a single time structure.

You can use this as follows:

```
/*
 * Runner just past the timing point
 */

assert((count >= 0) && (count <= sizeof(lap)/sizeof(lap[0])));
lap[count].hour = hour;
lap[count].minute = minute;
lap[count].second = second;
++count;
```

This array can also be initialized when the variable is declared. Initialization of an array of structures is similar to the initialization of multidimensional arrays:

```
struct time start_stop[2] = {
    {10, 0, 0},
    {12, 0, 0}
};
```

Suppose you want to write a program to handle a mailing list. Mailing labels are 5 lines high and 60 characters wide. You need a structure to store names and addresses. The mailing list will be sorted by name for most printouts, and in Zip-code order for actual mailings. The mailing list structure looks like this:

```
struct mailing {
    char name[60];      // Last name, first name
    char address1[60];// Two lines of street address
    char address2[60];
    char city[40];      // Name of the city
    char state[2];      // Two-character abbreviation*
    long int zip;       // Numeric zip code
};
```

You can now declare an array to hold the mailing list:

```
/* Our mailing list */
struct mailing list[MAX_ENTRIES];
```

Programming Exercises

Exercise 12-1: Design a data structure to handle the data for a mailing list.

Exercise 12-2: Design a structure to store time and date. Write a function to find the difference between two times in minutes.

Exercise 12-3: Design an airline reservation data structure that contains the following data:

    Flight number
    Originating airport code (3 characters)
    Destination airport code (3 characters)
    Departure time
    Arrival time

Write a program that lists all planes leaving from two airports specified by the user.

Answers to Chapter Questions

Answer 12-1: The problem is that we have a single signed-integer-bit field. A three-bit-wide signed-integer field can take on the following values:

---

* To store the state abbreviation as a C-style string, three characters are needed; two for the data and one for the end-of-string character. This is not a C-style string. Instead it is just two characters. So the dimension 2 is correct.

```
struct foo {
    int three_bits:3;
};
```

Bit pattern	Decimal value
100	-4
110	-3
101	-2
111	-1
000	0
001	1
010	2
011	3

A two-bit-wide signed-integer field can take on the following values:

```
struct foo {
    int two_bits:3;
};
```

Bit pattern	Decimal value
10	-2
11	-1
000	0
001	1

A one-bit-wide signed-integer field can take on the following values:

```
struct foo {
    int one_bit:1;
};
```

Bit pattern	Decimal value
1	−1
0	0

So the two values of this bit field are 0 and −1. That means that 1 can never be stored in this field.

A *unsigned* bit field of width 1 can hold the values 0 and 1. Using the declaration unsigned int valid:1 makes the program work correctly.

## CHAPTER 13

Simple Classes

She thinks that even up in heaven
Her class lies late and snores.
—Cyril Connolly

So far you've used simple variables and structures to hold data and functions to process the data. C++ *classes* allow you to combine data and the functions that use it.

In this chapter you'll see how a class can improve your code; you'll implement a simple stack two ways: first using a structure and functions, then using a class.

Stacks

A *stack* is an algorithm for storing data. Data can be put in the stack using a *push operation*. The *pop operation* removes the data. Data is stored in last-in-first-out (LIFO) order.

You can think of a stack as a stack of papers. When you perform a push operation, you put a new paper on top of the stack. You can push as many times as you want; each time the new data goes on top of the stack. You get data out of a stack using the pop operation, which takes the top paper off the stack and gives it to the caller.

Suppose you start with an empty stack and put three elements on it, 4, 5, and 8, using three push operations. The first pop would return the top element, 8. The elements 4 and 5 remain in the stack. Popping again gives you 5. You then push another value, 9, on the stack. Popping twice gives you the numbers 9 and 4, in that order. This is illustrated by Table 13-1.

Table 13-1. Stack operation

Operation	Stack after operation
Push (4)	4
Push (5)	5 4

Table 13-1. Stack operation (continued)

Operation	Stack after operation
Push (8)	8 5 4
Pop (returns 8)	5 4
Pop (returns 5)	4
Push (9)	9 4
Pop (returns 9)	4
Pop (returns 4)	<empty>

Designing a Stack

The easiest way to design a stack is to let someone else do it. C++ comes with a very nice stack class as part of the Standard Template Library (See Chapter 25.) But to learn about simple classes, in this chapter we are going to create our own.

We start a stack design by designing the data structure. This structure will need a place to put the data (called data) and a count of the number of items currently pushed on the stack (called count):

```
const int STACK_SIZE = 100;    // Maximum size of a stack

// The stack itself
struct stack {
    int count;                 // Number of items in the stack
    int data[STACK_SIZE];      // The items themselves
};
```

Next you need to create the routines to handle the push and pop operations. The push function stores the item on the stack and then increases the data count:

```
inline void stack_push(struct stack& the_stack, const int item)
{
    assert((the_stack.count >= 0) &&
           (the_stack.count <=
                sizeof(the_stack.data)/sizeof(the_stack.data[0])));

    the_stack.data[the_stack.count] = item;
    ++the_stack.count;
}
```

 This version of the program does not do a good job of checking for stack overflow or other error conditions. Later, in Chapter 14, you'll see how you can use this simple stack to make a safer, more complex one.

Popping simply removes the top item and decreases the number of items in the stack:

```
inline int stack_pop(struct stack&the_stack)
{
    // Stack goes down by one
```

```
        --the_stack.count;

    assert((the_stack.count >= 0) &&
        (the_stack.count <=
            sizeof(the_stack.data)/sizeof(the_stack.data[0])));
    // Then we return the top value
    return (the_stack.data[the_stack.count]);
}
```

There is one item you've overlooked: initializing the stack. You must set up the stack before you can use it. Keeping with the spirit of putting everything in a stack_*xxxx* routine, create the stack_init function:

```
inline void stack_init(struct stack& the_stack)
{
    the_stack.count = 0;        // Zero the stack
}
```

Notice that you don't need to zero the data field in the stack, since the elements of data are overwritten by the push operation.

You are now finished. To actually use the stack, you declare it and initialize it, then you can push and pop to your heart's content (or at least within the limits of the stack):

```
stack a_stack;      // Declare the stack

stack_init(a_stack);      // Initialize the stack
// Stack is ready for use
```

Example 13-1 contains a complete implementation of the structure version of the stack and a short test routine.

Example 13-1. stack_s/stack_s.cpp

```
/**********************************************************
 * Stack                                                  *
 *      A set of routines to implement a simple integer   *
 *      stack.                                             *
 *                                                        *
 * Procedures                                              *
 *      stack_init -- initalize the stack.                *
 *      stack_push -- put an item on the stack.           *
 *      stack_pop -- remove an item from the stack.       *
 **********************************************************/
#include <assert.h>
#include <cstdlib>
#include <iostream>

const int STACK_SIZE = 100;     // Maximum size of a stack

// The stack itself
struct stack {
    int count;                  // Number of items in the stack
```

Example 13-1. stack_s/stack_s.cpp (continued)

```cpp
    int data[STACK_SIZE];        // The items themselves
};

/*********************************************************
 * stack_init -- initialize the stack.                   *
 *                                                       *
 * Parameters                                            *
 *      the_stack -- stack to initalize                  *
 *********************************************************/
inline void stack_init(struct stack& the_stack)
{
    the_stack.count = 0;         // Zero the stack
}
/*********************************************************
 * stack_push -- push an item on the stack.              *
 *                                                       *
 * Warning: We do not check for overflow.                *
 *                                                       *
 * Parameters                                            *
 *      the_stack -- stack to use for storing the item   *
 *      item -- item to put in the stack                 *
 *********************************************************/
inline void stack_push(struct stack& the_stack,
                        const int item)
{
    assert((the_stack.count >= 0) &&
           (the_stack.count <
             sizeof(the_stack.data)/sizeof(the_stack.data[0])));

    the_stack.data[the_stack.count] = item;
    ++the_stack.count;
}
/*********************************************************
 * stack_pop -- get an item off the stack.               *
 *                                                       *
 * Warning: We do not check for stack underflow.         *
 *                                                       *
 * Parameters                                            *
 *      the_stack -- stack to get the item from          *
 *                                                       *
 * Returns                                               *
 *      The top item from the stack.                     *
 *********************************************************/
inline int stack_pop(struct stack& the_stack)
{
    // Stack goes down by one
    --the_stack.count;

    assert((the_stack.count >= 0) &&
           (the_stack.count <
             sizeof(the_stack.data)/sizeof(the_stack.data[0])));
```

Example 13-1. stack_s/stack_s.cpp (continued)

```
    // Then we return the top value
    return (the_stack.data[the_stack.count]);
}

// A short routine to test the stack
int main( )
{
    struct stack a_stack;        // Stack we want to use

    stack_init(a_stack);

    // Push three value on the stack
    stack_push(a_stack, 1);
    stack_push(a_stack, 2);
    stack_push(a_stack, 3);

    // Pop the item from the stack
    std::cout << "Expect a 3 ->" << stack_pop(a_stack) << '\n';
    std::cout << "Expect a 2 ->" << stack_pop(a_stack) << '\n';
    std::cout << "Expect a 1 ->" << stack_pop(a_stack) << '\n';

    return (0);
}
```

Improved Stack

The structure version of the stack works but has a few drawbacks. The first is that the data and the functions are defined separately, forcing you to pass a struct stack variable into each procedure.

There is also the problem of data protection. The fields data and count are accessible to anyone. The design states that only the stack functions should have access to these fields, but there is nothing to prevent rogue code from modifying them.

A C++ struct is a mixed collection of data. The C++ class not only holds data like a structure, but also adds a set of functions for manipulating the data and access protection.

Turning the struct stack into a class you get:

```
class stack {
    private:
        int count;           // Number of items in the stack
        int data[STACK_SIZE];  // The items themselves
    public:
        // Initialize the stack
        void init( );

        // Push an item on the stack
        void push(const int item);

        // Pop an item from the stack
        int pop( );
};
```

Let's go into this `class` declaration in more detail. The beginning looks much like a structure definition, except that you're using the word `class` instead of `struct`:

```
class stack {
    private:
        int count;            // Number of items in the stack
        int data[STACK_SIZE]; // The items themselves
```

This declares two fields: `count` and `data`. In a class these items are not called fields; they are called *member variables*. The keyword **private** indicates the access privileges associated with these two member variables.

There are three levels of access privileges: **public, private**, and **protected**. Class members, both data and functions, marked **private** cannot be used outside the class. They can be accessed only by functions within the class. The opposite of **private** is **public**, which indicates members that anyone can access.

Finally, **protected** is similar to **private** except that it allows access by derived classes. (We discuss derived classes in Chapter 21.)

You've finished defining the data for this class. Now you need to define the functions that manipulate the data:

```
    public:
        // Initialize the stack
        void init( );

        // Push an item on the stack
        void push(const int item);

        // Pop an item from the stack
        int pop( );
};
```

This section starts with the keyword **public**. This tells C++ that you want all these member functions to be available to the outside. In this case, you just define the function prototypes. The code for the functions will be defined later.

Next comes the body of the `init` function. Since this function belongs to the stack class, you prefix the name of the procedure with `stack::`. (We discuss the scope operator `::` in more detail in Chapter 14.)

The definition of the `init` function looks like this:

```
inline void stack::init( )
{
    count = 0;  // Zero the stack
}
```

This procedure zeroes the stack's count. In the structure version of the `stack_init` function, you must pass the stack in as a parameter. Since this function is part of the stack class, that's unnecessary. This also means that you can access the member variables directly. In other words, instead of having to say the_stack.count, you just say count.

The functions push and pop are implemented in a similar manner:

```
inline void stack::push(const int item)
{
    data[count] = item;
    ++count;
}

inline int stack::pop()
{
    // Stack goes down by one
    --count;

    // Then we return the top value
    return (data[count]);
}
```

The stack class is now complete. All you have to do is use it.

Using a Class

Using a class is much like using a structure. Declaring a class variable is the same, except you use the word class instead of struct:

```
class stack a_stack;        // Stack we want to use
```

The word class is not needed and is frequently omitted:

```
stack a_stack;        // Stack we want to use
```

You access the members of a structure using a dot; for example:

```
structure.field = 5;
```

Accessing the members of a class is similar, except that the members of a class can be both data and functions. Also, you can access only the members that are public.

To call the init member function of the stack class, all you need to do is this:

```
a_stack.init();
```

The push and pop member functions can be accessed in a similar manner:

```
a_stack.push(1);
result = a_stack.pop();
```

Example 13-2 contains a class version of the stack.

Example 13-2. stack_c/stack_c.cpp

```
/*****************************************************
 * Stack                                             *
 *      A file implementing a simple stack class     *
 *****************************************************/
```

Example 13-2. stack_c/stack_c.cpp (continued)

```cpp
#include <cstdlib>
#include <iostream>
#include <assert.h>

const int STACK_SIZE = 100;      // Maximum size of a stack

/*****************************************************
 * Stack class                                       *
 *                                                   *
 * Member functions                                  *
 *      init -- initialize the stack.                *
 *      push -- put an item on the stack.            *
 *      pop -- remove an item from the stack.        *
 *****************************************************/
// The stack itself
class stack {
    private:
        int count;               // Number of items in the stack
        int data[STACK_SIZE];    // The items themselves
    public:
        // Initialize the stack
        void init();

        // Push an item on the stack
        void push(const int item);

        // Pop an item from the stack
        int pop();
};

/*****************************************************
 * stack::init -- initialize the stack.              *
 *****************************************************/
inline void stack::init()
{
    count = 0;  // Zero the stack
}
/*****************************************************
 * stack::push -- push an item on the stack.         *
 *                                                   *
 * Warning: We do not check for overflow.            *
 *                                                   *
 * Parameters                                        *
 *      item -- item to put in the stack             *
 *****************************************************/
inline void stack::push(const int item)
{
    assert((count >= 0) &&
            (count < sizeof(data)/sizeof(data[0])));
    data[count] = item;
    ++count;
}
```

Example 13-2. stack_c/stack_c.cpp (continued)

```
/*****************************************************
 * stack::pop -- get an item off the stack.          *
 *                                                    *
 * Warning: We do not check for stack underflow.      *
 *                                                    *
 * Returns                                            *
 *      The top item from the stack.                  *
 *****************************************************/
inline int stack::pop( )
{
    // Stack goes down by one
    --count;

    assert((count >= 0) &&
            (count < sizeof(data)/sizeof(data[0])));

    // Then we return the top value
    return (data[count]);
}

// A short routine to test the stack
int main( )
{
    stack a_stack;        // Stack we want to use

    a_stack.init( );

    // Push three value on the stack
    a_stack.push(1);
    a_stack.push(2);
    a_stack.push(3);

    // Pop the item from the stack
    std::cout << "Expect a 3 ->" << a_stack.pop( ) << '\n';
    std::cout << "Expect a 2 ->" << a_stack.pop( ) << '\n';
    std::cout << "Expect a 1 ->" << a_stack.pop( ) << '\n';

    return (0);
}
```

Introduction to Constructors and Destructors

This stack class has one minor inconvenience. The programmer must call the init member function before using the stack. However, programmers are terribly forgetful, and sooner or later someone is going to forget to initialize the stack. Wouldn't it be nice if C++ had an automatic way of initializing the stack?

It does. Actually C++ will automatically call a number of member functions. The first you are concerned about is called when stack is created. In C++ language this is referred to as "creating an instance of the class *stack*."

The function C++ calls to create a instance of the class is called the *constructor* and has the same name as the class. For example, the constructor for the stack class is named stack (also known as stack::stack outside the class body).

A variable, or instance of a class, is created when it is defined. (It can also be created by the new operator, as described in Chapter 20.)

You want to have this stack initialized automatically, so you remove the init function and replace it with the constructor, stack::stack:

```
class stack {
    // ...
  public:
    // Initialize the stack
    stack( );
    // ...
};

inline stack::stack( )
{
    count = 0;  // Zero the stack
}
```

You may have noticed that the return type **void** has been omitted in the constructor declaration. Constructors can never return a value, so the **void** is not needed. In fact, the compiler will complain if it's present.

Since the constructor is called automatically, the program is now simpler. Instead of writing:

```
int main( )
{
    stack a_stack;       // Stack we want to use

    a_stack.init( );
```

you can just write:

```
int main( )
{
    stack a_stack;       // Stack we want to use

    // Use the stack
```

Also, since you no longer have to count on the programmer putting in the init call, the program is more reliable.

Destructors

The constructor is automatically called when a variable is created. The *destructor* is automatically called when a variable is destroyed. This occurs when a variable goes out of scope or when a pointer variable is deleted. (The delete operator is defined in Chapter 20.)

The special name for a destructor is the class name with a tilde (~) in front of it. So, for the stack class, the destructor would be named ~stack.

Suppose you make the rule that the stack should be empty when the programmer is finished with it. In other words, for every push you do, a pop must be done. If this doesn't happen, it's an error and you should warn the user.

All you have to do is create a destructor for the stack that checks for an empty stack and issues a warning if the stack is not empty. The destructor looks like this:

```
inline stack::~stack( ) {
    if (count != 0)
        std::cerr << "Error: Destroying a nonempty stack\n";
}
```

Parameterized Constructors

The constructor for a class can take parameters. Suppose you want to define a class that holds a person's name and phone number. The data members for this class would look like this:

```
class person {
    public:
        std::string name;      // Name of the person
        std::string phone;     // Person's phone number
```

You want the constructor for this class to automatically initialize both the name and the phone number:

```
    public:
        person(const std::string i_name, const std::string i_phone);
    // ... rest of class
};

person::person(const std::string i_name, const std::string i_phone)
{
    name = i_name;
    phone = i_phone;
}
```

Now you are ready to use the class. When you declare variables of this class, you must put two parameters in the declaration. For example:

```
int main( )
{
    person sam("Sam Jones", "555-1234");
```

Like other functions, constructors can be overloaded. Using the person example, you can take care of the case where you have a person with no phone by creating a constructor that takes a name as its only parameter:

```
class person {
    // ... rest of the class
    public:
```

```
        person(const std::string i_name);
};

person::person(const std::string i_name)
{
    name = i_name;
    phone = "No Phone";
}
```

In this case, you have two constructors, one that takes one parameter and one that takes two parameters. You haven't defined a constructor that takes zero parameters, so you can't declare a variable of type person without specifying at least one parameter. In other words:

```
    person unnamed_source;      // Illegal
```

will generate an error message.

Parameterized Destructors

There is no such thing as a parameterized destructor. Destructors take no parameters and supply no return value. All they do is destroy the variable. So there is one and only one destructor for a class.

Copy Constructor

The copy constructor is a special constructor that is used to make an exact copy of a class. For example, a copy constructor for the stack class would look like this:

```
    stack::stack(const stack& old_stack)
    {
        int i;      // Index used to copy the data

        for (i = 0; i < old_stack.count; ++i) {
            data[i] = old_stack.data[i];
        }
        count = old_stack.count;
    }
```

Let's examine this function in more detail. The declaration:

```
    stack::stack(const stack& old_stack)
```

identifies this as a copy constructor. The single parameter (const stack& old_stack) identifies this particular constructor as the copy constructor. This function is expected to turn the current instance of the class into an exact copy of the parameter.

The code:

```
    for (i = 0; i < old_stack.count; ++i) {
        data[i] = old_stack.data[i];
    }
    count = old_stack.count;
```

takes all the data from the old stack and puts it into the new stack.

The copy constructor can be invoked explicitly, as illustrated in the following example:

```
stack a_stack;        // A simple stack

a_stack.push(1);      // Put a couple of elements on the stack
a_stack.push(2);

stack b_stack(a_stack);  // Create a copy of the stack
```

On the face of it, the copy constructor doesn't seem that important. But if you remember, back in Chapter 1, I discussed the various ways C++ can pass parameters to a function. One of these was call by value. That's where a copy of the parameter is made and passed to the function.

When a stack or any other class is passed as a call-by-value parameter, a copy is made of that class using the copy constructor.

In the following code, we've added some commentary to show you the functions that C++ will automatically call behind your back:

```
void use_stack(stack local_stack)
{
    local_stack.push(9);
    local_stack.push(10);
    .. Do something with local_stack          local_stack::~stack( ) called
}


int main( )
{
    stack a_stack;        // Generate a default stack
                                          a_stack.stack()
    a_stack.push(1);
    a_stack.push(2);

    use_stack(a_stack);          local_stack.stack(a_stack) called
                                 (This is part of the parameter-passing mechanism)
    // Prints "2"
    std::cout << a_stack.pop( ) << '\n';
```

As you can see, C++ does a lot of work behind the scenes. It starts when a_stack is declared. C++ calls the default constructor to create a_stack.

The variable a_stack is used, and then passed to the function use_stack. Since a_stack is passed by value, a copy must be made of the stack using the copy constructor local_stack.stack(a_stack).

The function then adds a few items to local_stack. Note that this is a copy of a_stack, so anything you do to local_stack does not affect a_stack. At the end of the function, local_stack contains four items—1, 2, 9, 10—and a_stack contains two items: 1 and 2.

Finally after the function call, the program prints out the top element of a_stack, which is 2.

Automatically Generated Member Functions

Every class has a constructor and a destructor. If the programmer does not write these member functions, C++ will automatically generate them. Also, there are several member functions, such as the copy constructor, that can be called automatically.

Automatically Generated and Used Functions

The following are the automatically generated and called functions:

class::class( )
> Default constructor.
>
> Automatically generated if no other constructors are defined. The generated code fills the data members of the class with random values.
>
> Automatically called when a variable of a class is declared with no parameters, such as:
>
> ```
> class_type var;
> ```

class::class(const class& old_class)
> Copy constructor.
>
> Automatically generated unless the programmer explicitly defines a copy constructor. The function C++ copies all of the data members from the old class to the new one.
>
> Automatically called when passing a call-by-value parameter to a function. This member function will also be called when creating a duplicate of a variable:
>
> ```
> class_type first_var;
> // Call copy constructor to
> // make duplicate of first_var
> class_type second_var(first_var);
> ```

class::~class( )
> Destructor.
>
> Automatically generated unless the programmer defines one.
>
> Automatically called when a variable is destroyed. For automatic variables, this occurs at the end of the block in which the variable is defined. Global and static variables are destroyed when the program exits. (The destructor is also called by the delete operator, discussed in Chapter 20.)

class class::operator = (const class& old_class)
> Assignment operator. (Operator overloading is discussed in Chapter 18.)
>
> Automatically generated to handle assignment of one object to another. The function C++ copies all the data members from the old object to the new one:
>
> ```
> class_type var1;
> class_type var2;
> var1 = var2;   // "operator =" called
> ```

Explicit Constructors

Suppose you have the following class:

```
class int_array {
    public:
        int_array(unsigned int size);
```

We can create an instance of this class using the statement:

```
int_array example(10);
```

But we can also initialize the array using the statement:

```
int_array example = 10;
```

Both do the same thing because C++ is smart enough to automatically convert the assignment to a constructor call.

But what if you don't want this conversion to be done? You can tell C++, "Don't play games with the constructor; do exactly what I say!" This is done by declaring the constructor as an explicit construction:

```
class int_array {
    public:
        explicit int_array(unsigned int size);
```

Now the we can initialize our variable using the constructor:

```
int_array example(10);    // Works with explicit
```

But the statement:

```
int_array example = 10; // Illegal because of "explicit"
```

is now illegal.

It is a good idea to limit the number of side effects and other things that can happen behind your back. For that reason, you should declare your constructors explicit whenever possible.

Shortcuts

So far you have used only function prototypes in the classes you've created. It is possible to define the body of the function inside the class itself. Consider the following code:

```
class stack {
    public:
        // .... rest of class

        // Push an item on the stack
        void push(const int item);
};
inline void stack::push(const int item)
{
```

```
        data[count] = item;
        ++count;
    }
```

This code can instead be written as:

```
class stack {
    public:
        // .... rest of class

        // Push an item on the stack
        void push(const int item) {
            data[count] = item;
            ++count;
        }
};
```

The **inline** directive is not required in the second case since all functions declared inside a class are automatically declared inline.

Style

Programming style for classes looks pretty much like the style for structures and functions. Every member variable should be followed by a comment explaining it, and every member function should be commented like a function.

However, you comment the prototypes for member functions differently from normal function prototypes. For normal functions you put a full function comment block in front for the prototype. If you did this for the member functions of a class, the comments would obscure the structure of the class. This is one of the few cases when too many comments can cause trouble. So you put a one-line comment in front of each member function prototype and full comments in front of the function itself.

But what about inline-member functions, where the entire body of the function is declared inside the class? How do you comment that? If you put in full comments, you obscure the structure of the class. If you put in one-liners, you omit a lot of useful information. Proper commenting is a balancing act. You need to put in what's useful and leave out what's not.

The solution is to keep the size of the inline-member function small. There are two reasons for this: first, all inline functions should be small, and second, large functions declared inside a class make the class excessively complex. A good rule of thumb is that if the function requires more than about five lines of code, put a prototype in the class and put the body of the function elsewhere.

The structure of very small member functions should be obvious and thus not require a full-blown comment block. If the function is not obvious and requires extensive comments, you can always put in a prototype and comment the body of the function later in the program.

C++ does not require an access specifier (**public**, **private**, or **protected**) before the first *member variable*. The following is perfectly legal:

```
class example {
    int data;
    // ...
};
```

But what is the access protection of data? Is it **public**, **private**, or **protected**? If you put in an explicit specification, you don't have to worry about questions like this. (For those of you who are curious, the access specification defaults to **private**.)

Finally, C++ will automatically generate some member functions, such as the default constructor, the copy constructor, and the assignment operator. Suppose you have a class that does not specify a copy constructor, such as this:

```
// Comments describing the class
// Note: The style of this class leaves something to be desired
class queue {
    private:
        int data[100];     // Data stored in the queue
        int first;         // First element in the queue
        int last;          // Last element in the queue
    public:
        queue();           // Initialize the queue
        void put(int item);// Put an item in the queue
        int get();         // Get an item from the queue
};
```

Did the programmer who created this class forget the copy constructor? Will the copy constructor automatically generated by C++ work, or did the programmer design this class knowing that the copy constructor would never be called? These important questions are not answered by the class as written.

All classes have a default constructor, copy constructor, assignment operator, and destructor. If you do not create one of these special member functions, C++ will generate one automatically for you. If you expect to use any of these automatic functions, you should put a comment in the class to indicate the default is being used:

```
// Comments describing the class
class queue {
    private:
        int data[100];     // Data stored in the queue
        int first;         // First element in the queue
        int last;          // Last element in the queue
    public:
        queue();           // Initialize the queue
        // queue(const queue& old_queue)
        //     Use automatically generated copy constructor

        // queue operator = (const queue& old_queue)
        //     Use automatically generated assignment operator

        // ~queue()
```

```
    //   Use automatically generated destructor

    void put(int item);// Put an item in the queue
    int get();     // Get an item from the queue
};
```

Now it is obvious what member functions the programmer wanted to let C++ generate automatically, and being obvious is very important in any programming project.

The copy constructor automatically generated by C++ is rather simple and limited. It doesn't work in all cases, as you'll see later when you start to construct more complex classes. But what happens when the automatic copy constructor won't work as you desire, and you don't want to go to the trouble to create your own? After all, you may decide that a class will never be copied (or that if it is, it's an error).

One solution is to create a dummy copy constructor that prints an error message and aborts the program:

```
class no_copy {
        // Body of the class
    public:
        // Copy constructor
        no_copy(const no_copy& old_class) {
            std::cerr <<
              "Error: Copy constructor for 'no_copy' called. Exiting\n";
            exit(8);
        }
};
```

This works, sort of. The problem is that errors are detected at runtime instead of compile time. You want to catch errors as soon as possible, so this solution is at best a hack.

However, you can prevent the compiler from automatically calling the copy constructor. The trick is to declare it private. That's your way of saying to the world, "Yes, there is a copy constructor, but no one can ever use it":

```
class no_copy {
        // Body of the class
    private:
        // There is no copy constructor
        no_copy(const no_copy& old_class);
};
```

Now when the compiler attempts to use the copy constructor, you will get an error message like "Error: Attempt to access private member function."

Note that in this example, you have defined the prototype for a copy constructor, but no body. Since this function is never called, a body is not needed.

Structures Versus Classes

In C++ a structure is just like a class, except that all the data fields and member functions are public. For example, the following two are the same:

```
struct data {                          public data {
    int status;                            public:
    int data;                                  int status;
                                               int data;
    void start() {
        status = 1;                        void start() {
    }                                          status = 1;
};                                         }
                                       };
```

As you can see, a structure is merely a class with all the protections removed. This means that in most cases a class is superior to a structure.

In actual practice, most programmers use structures for data only. You'll hardly ever see a structure with member functions.

Programming Exercises

Exercise 13-1: Write a parity class. The class supplies a member function named put, which counts the number of elements supplied. The other member function test returns true if an even number of put calls have been made and false otherwise.

Member functions:

```
void parity::put();    // Count another element
bool parity::test();   // Return true if an even number of
                       // puts have been done. Return false
                       // for an odd number.
```

Exercise 13-2: Write a "checkbook" class. You put a list of numbers into this class and get a total out.

Member functions:

```
void check::add_item(int amount);   // Add a new entry to the checkbook
int check::total();                 // Return the total of all items
```

Exercise 13-3: Write a class to implement a simple queue. A queue is similar to a stack except that the data is removed in first-in-first-out (FIFO) order.

Member functions:

```
void queue::put(int item);   // Insert an item in the queue
int queue::get();            // Get the next item from the queue
```

Sample usage:

```
queue a_queue;

a_queue.put(1);    // Queue contains: 1
a_queue.put(2);    // Queue contains: 1 2
a_queue.put(3);    // Queue contains: 1 2 3

std::cout << a_queue.get() << '\n';   // Prints 1, queue contains 2 3
std::cout << a_queue.get() << '\n';   // Prints 2, queue contains 3
```

Exercise 13-4: Define a class that will hold the set of integers from 0 to 31. An element can be set with the set member function and cleared with the clear member function. It is not an error to set an element that's already set or clear an element that's already clear. The function test is used to tell whether an element is set.

Member functions:

```
void small_set::set(int item);     // Set an element in the set
void small_set::clear(int item);   // Clear an element in the set
int small_set::test(int item);     // See whether an element is set
```

Sample usage:

```
small_set a_set;

a_set.set(3);       // Set contains [3]
a_set.set(5);       // Set contains [3,5]
a_set.set(5);       // Legal (set contains [3,5])

std::cout << a_set.test(3) << '\n';    // Prints "1"
std::cout << a_set.test(0) << '\n';    // Prints "0"

a_set.clear(5);    // Set contains [3]
```

Exercise 13-5: I have a simple method of learning foreign vocabulary words. I write the words down on flash cards. I then go through the stack of cards one at a time. If I get a word right, that card is discarded. If I get it wrong, the card goes to the back of the stack.

Write a class to implement this system.

Member functions:

```
struct single_card {
    std::string question;     // English version of the word
    std::string answer;       // Other language version of the word
};

// Constructor -- takes a list of cards to
//                initialize the flash card stack
void flash_card::flash_card(single_card list[]);

// Get the next card
const single_card& flash_card::get_card();

//The student got the current card right
void flash_card::right();

// The student got the current card wrong
void flash_card::wrong();

//Returns true -- done / false -- more to do
bool done();
```

## CHAPTER 14

More on Classes

*This method is, to define as the number of a class the
class of all classes similar to the given class.*
—Bertrand Russell
Principles of Mathematics, Part II,
Chapter 11, Section iii, 1903

C++ has many bells and whistles that give you a lot of flexibility in designing your classes. For example, the **friend** keyword lets a class specify ordinary functions that are allowed to access its private data. This section also covers constant members as well as how to constrain specific data using the keyword **static**.

Friends

In Chapter 13, you defined a basic stack class. Suppose you want to write a function to see whether two stacks are equal. At first glance this is simple. The function looks like Example 14-1.

Example 14-1. stack_c/s_equal.cpp

```
/********************************************************
 * stack_equal -- Test to see if two stacks are equal   *
 *                                                      *
 * Parameters                                           *
 *      s1, s2 -- the two stacks                        *
 *                                                      *
 * Returns                                              *
 *      0 -- stacks are not equal                       *
 *      1 -- stacks are equal                           *
 ********************************************************/
int stack_equal(const stack& s1, const stack& s2)
{
    int index;  // Index into the items in the array
```

Example 14-1. stack_c/s_equal.cpp (continued)

```
    // Check number of items first
    if (s1.count != s2.count)
        return (0);

    for (index = 0; index < s1.count; ++index) {

        assert((index >= 0) &&
               (index < sizeof(s1.data)/sizeof(s1.data[0])));

        assert((index >= 0) &&
               (index < sizeof(s2.data)/sizeof(s2.data[0])));

        if (s1.data[index] != s2.data[index])
            return (0);
    }
    return (1);
}
```

Like many programs, this solution is simple, clear, and *wrong*. The problem is that the member variables count and data are private. That means you can't access them.

So what do you do? One solution is to make these variables public. That gives the function stack_equal access to count and data. The problem is that it also gives everyone else access, and you don't want that.

Friend Functions

Fortunately C++ gives you a way to say, "Let stack_equal and only stack_equal have access to the private data of the class stack." This is accomplished through the **friend** directive. Classes must declare their friends. No function from the outside may access the private data from the class, unless the class allows it.

Example 14-2. stack_c/f_stack.cpp

```
// The stack itself
class stack {
    private:
        int count;                  // Number of items in the stack
        int data[STACK_SIZE];       // The items themselves
    public:
        // Initialize the stack
        void init();

        // Push an item on the stack
        void push(const int item);

        // Pop an item from the stack
        int pop();
```

Example 14-2. stack_c/f_stack.cpp (continued)

```
        friend int stack_equal(const stack& s1, const stack& s2);
};
```

stack_equal is *not* a member function of the class stack. It is a normal, simple function. The only difference is that because the function is a friend, it has access to private data for any class that calls it a friend.

Friend Classes

Friends are not restricted to just functions. One class can be a friend of another. For example:

```
class item {
    private:
        int data;

    friend class set_of_items;
};
class set_of_items {
    // ...
};
```

In this case, since the class set_of_items is a friend of item, it has access to all the members of item.

Constant Functions

C++ lets you define two types of numbers: constant and nonconstant. For example:

```
int index;                  // Current index into the data array
const int DATA_MAX(100);   // Maximum number of items in the array
```

These two items are treated differently. For example, you can change the value of index, but you can't change DATA_MAX.

Now let's consider a class to implement a set of numbers from 0 to 31. The definition of this class is:

```
// Warning: The member functions in this class are incomplete
//          See below for a better definition of this class
class int_set {
    private:
        // ... whatever
    public:
        int_set();                          // Default constructor
        int_set(const int_set& old_set);   // Copy constructor
        void set(int value);                // Set a value
        void clear(int value);              // Clear an element
        int test(int value);                // See whether an element is set
};
```

As with numbers, C++ will let you define two types of int_set objects: constant and nonconstant:

```
int_set var_set;      // A variable set (we can change this)

var_set.set(1);       // Set an element in the set

// Define a constant version of the set (we cannot change this)
const int_set const_set(var_set);
```

In the int_set class, there are member functions such as set and clear that change the value of the set. There is also a function test that changes nothing.

Obviously you don't want to allow set and clear to be used on a constant. However, it is okay to use the test member function.

But how does C++ know what can be used on a constant and what can't? The trick is to put the keyword const at the end of the function header. This tells C++ that this member function can be used for a constant variable. So if you put const *after* the member function test, C++ will allow it to be used in a constant. The member functions set and clear do not have this keyword, so they can't be used in a constant.

```
class int_set {
    private:
        // ... whatever
    public:
        int_set();              // Default constructor
        int_set(const int_set& old_set); // Copy constructor
        void set(int value);    // Set a value
        void clear(int value);  // Clear an element
        int test(int value) const;   // See whether an element is set
};
```

Thus, in your code you can do the following:

```
int_set var_set;      // A variable set (we can change this)

var_set.set(1);       // Set an element in the set (legal)

// Define a constant version of the set (we cannot change this)
const int_set const_set(var_set);

// In the next statement we use the member function "test" legally
std::cout << "Testing element 1. Value=" << const_set.test() << '\n';
```

However, you cannot do the following:

```
const_set.set(5);    // Illegal (set is not allowed on a const)
```

The member function set was not declared const, so it cannot be invoked on a const int_set object.

Constant Members

Classes may contain constant members. The problem is that constants behave a little differently inside classes than outside. Outside, a constant variable declaration must be initialized. For example:

```
const int data_size = 1024; // Number of data items in the input stream
```

Inside a class, constants are not initialized when they are declared. For example:

```
class data_list {
    public:
        const int data_size;    // Number of items in the list
    // ... rest of the class
};
```

Constant member variables are initialized by the constructor. However, it's not as simple as this:

```
class data_list {
    public:
        const int data_size;    // Number of items in the list

        data_list() {
            data_size = 1024;    // This code won't work
        };
    // ... rest of the class
};
```

Instead, because data_size is a constant, it must be initialized with a special syntax:

```
        data_list() : data_size(1024) {
        };
```

But what happens if you want just a simple constant inside your class? Unfortunately C++ doesn't allow you to do the following:

```
class foo {
    public:
        const int foo_size = 100;  // Illegal
```

You are left with two choices:

- Put the constant outside the code:

```
const int foo_size = 100;    // Number of data items in the list

class foo {
```

This makes foo_size available to all the world.

- Use a syntax trick to fool C++ into defining a constant:

```
class foo {
    public:
        enum {foo_size = 100};  // Number of data items in the list
```

This defines foo_size as a constant whose value is 100. It does this by actually declaring foo_size as a element of an enum type and giving it the explicit value 100. Because C++ treats enums as integers, this works for defining integer constants.

The drawbacks to this method are that it's tricky, it works only for integers, and it exploits some holes in the C++ syntax that may go away as the language is better defined. Such code can easily cause difficulties for other programmers trying to maintain your code who aren't familiar with the trick.

Static Member Variables

Suppose you want to keep a running count of the number of stacks in use at any given time. One way to do this is to create a global variable stack_count that is incremented in the stack constructor and decremented in the destructor:

```
int stack_count = 0; // Number of stacks currently in use

class stack {
    private:
        int count;          // Number of items in the stack
        // ... member variables
    public:
        int data_count;  // Number of items in the stack
        // ... member variables
        stack( ) {
            // We just created a stack
            ++stack_count;
            count = 0;
        }
        ~stack( ) {
            // We now have one less stack
            --stack_count;
        }
        // ... other member functions
};
```

Note that stack_count is a single global variable. No matter how many different stacks you create, there is one and only one stack_count.

Although this system works, it has some drawbacks. The definition of the class stack contains everything about the stack, except the variable stack_count. It would be nice to put stack_count in the class, but if you define it as a member variable, you'll get a new copy of stack_count each time you declare a stack class variable.

C++ has a special modifier for member variables: static. This tells C++ that one and only one variable is to be defined for the class:

```
class stack {
    private:
        static int stack_count; // Number of stacks currently in use
```

```
        int count;         // Number of items in the stack
        // ... member variables
    public:
        stack( ) {
            // We just created a stack
            ++stack_count;
            count = 0;
        }
        ~stack( ) {
            // We now have one less stack
            --stack_count;
        }
        // ... other member functions
};
```

This new version looks almost the same as the global variable version. There is, however, one thing missing: the initialization of stack_count. This is done with the statement:

```
int stack::stack_count = 0; // No stacks have been defined
```

The difference between static and nonstatic member variables is that member variables belong to the object, while static member variables belong to the class. Thus if you create three stacks, you get three copies of the ordinary member variable data_count. However, since there is only one definition of the class, only one stack_count is created.

So if you have:

```
stack a_stack;
stack b_stack;
```

a_stack.stack_count is the same as b_stack.stack_count. There is only one stack_count for the class stack. C++ allows you to access static member variables using the syntax:

```
<class>::<variable>
```

Thus you can get to stack_count with the statement:

```
std::cout << "The number of active stacks is " <<
        stack::stack_count << '\n';
```

(Or at least you could if stack_count was not private.)

You can use the dot notation (a_stack.stack_count), but this is considered poor programming style. That's because it implies that stack_count belongs to the object a_stack. But because it's static, the variable belongs to the class stack.

Static Member Functions

The member variable stack_count is defined as private. This means that nothing outside the class can access it. You want to know how many stacks are defined, so you need a function to get the value of stack_count. A first cut might be:

```
class stack {
        static int stack_count; // Number of stacks currently in use
        // ... member variables
    public:
        // Not quite right
        int get_count() {
            return (stack_count);
        }
        // ... other member functions
};
```

This works, but you need a stack type variable to access this function.

```
{
    stack temp_stack;     // Stack for getting the count
    std::cout << "Current count " << temp_stack.get_count() << '\n';
}
```

Because get_count doesn't use any nonstatic data from stack, it can be made a *static member function*:

```
class stack {
        static int stack_count; // Number of stacks currently in use
        // ... member variables
    public:
        // Right
        static int get_count() {
            return (stack_count);
        }
        // ... other member functions
};
```

You can now access the static member function get_count much like you access the static member variable stack_count:

```
std::cout << "The number of active stacks is " <<
            stack::get_count() << '\n';
```

Static member functions are very limited. They can't access nonstatic member variables or functions in the class. They can access static member data, static member functions, and functions and data outside the class.

The Meaning of static

The keyword **static** has many different meanings in C++. Table 14-1 is a complete list of the various ways **static** can be used.

Table 14-1. *The meanings of static*

Usage	Meaning
Variable outside the body of any function	The scope of the variable is limited to the file in which it is declared.
Variable declaration inside a function	The variable is permanent. It is initialized once, and only one copy is created even if the function is called recursively.
Function declaration	The scope of the function is limited to the file in which it is declared.
Member variable	One copy of the variable is created per class (not one per object).
Member function	Function can only access static members of the class.

Programming Exercises

Exercise 14-1: Two classes share a file. Other areas of the program need to know when this file is busy. Create a function that returns 1 when the file is being used by either of these two classes.

Exercise 14-2: You are asked to write a booking program for the veterinarian; Dr. Able Smith, PHD (Pigs, Horses, Dogs). Define a class type for each animal. Each class should keep track in a private static variable of the number of animals that have been defined using that class. Define a function that returns the total number of animals (all three types combined).

Exercise 14-3: Write a class in which each instance of the class can access a stack—not one stack per instance, but one stack, period. Any instance of the class can lock the stack for its own exclusive use and unlock it later. Define member functions to perform the lock and unlock functions.

As an added attraction, make the unlock function check to see that the current instance of the class was the same instance that locked the stack in the first place.

Exercise 14-4: You need to supply some I/O routines for handling lines in a file. The basic definition of the line-number class is:

```
class line_number {
    public:
        void goto_line(int line);
        int get_current_line( );
        long int get_char_pos( );
}
```

The member functions are defined as:

```
void goto_line(int line);
```
Positions the input file at specified line.

```
int get_current_line( );
```
Returns the current line number (as set by `goto_line`).

```
long int get_char_pos( );
```
Returns the character position of the current line. (This is the tricky one.)

Several `line_number` classes may be in use at any time. The class maintains its own internal list so that it knows which `line_number` classes are in use. When `goto_line` is called, the function will scan the list of `line_number` classes to find the one nearest the given line number and use it to start scanning for the given line number.

For example, suppose there are four active `line_number` variables:

Variable	Position
beginning	Line 0
chapter_start	Line 87
current_heading	Line 112
current_location	Line 52

You wish to move `current_location` to line 90. The `goto_line` function would search the list for the line nearest the new location (in this case `chapter_start`) and use it to jump to line 87. It then would read the file, character by character, until it saw three end-of-line characters to position itself at line 90.

## CHAPTER 15

Simple Pointers

> The choice of a point of view is the initial act of
> culture.
>
> —Ortega y Gasset

There are things, and there are pointers to things (Figure 15-1).

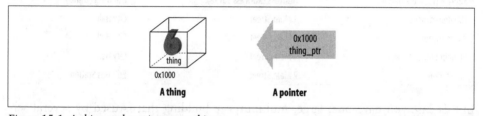

Figure 15-1. A thing and a pointer to a thing

Things can come in any size; some may be big, some may be small. Pointers come in only one size (relatively small).

Throughout this book I use a box to represent a thing. The box may be large or small, but things are always a box. Pointers are represented by arrows.

Most novice programmers get pointers and their contents confused. To limit this problem, all pointer variables in this book end with the extension _ptr. You probably want to follow this convention in your own programs. Although not as common as it should be, this notation is extremely useful.

Figure 15-1 shows one thing: a variable named thing. The name of the variable is written on the box that represents it. This variable contains the value 6. The actual address of this variable is 0x1000. C++ automatically assigns an address to each variable at compile time. The actual addresses differ from machine to machine. Most of the time you don't have to worry about variable addresses, as the compiler takes care of that detail. (After all, you've gotten through 14 chapters of programming without knowing anything about addresses.)

The pointer (thing_ptr) points to the variable thing. Pointers are also called *address variables* since they contain the addresses of other variables. In this case, the pointer contains the address 0x1000. Since this is the address of thing, you say that thing_ptr points to thing. (You could put another address in thing_ptr and force it to point to something else.)

You use "things" and "addresses" in everyday life. For example, you might live in a house (a thing). The street address might be "123 W. Main Street." An address is a small thing that can be written down on a piece of paper. Putting a house on a piece of paper is something else, requiring a lot of work and a very large crane.

Street addresses are approximately the same size: one line. Houses come in various sizes. So while "1600 Pennsylvania Ave." might refer to a big house and "8347 Skid Row" might refer to a one-room shack, both addresses are the same size.[*]

Many different address variables can point to the same thing. This is true for street addresses as well. Table 15-1 lists the location of important services in a small town.

Table 15-1. Small-town directory

Service (variable name)	Address (address value)	Building (thing)
Fire department	1 Main Street	City Hall
Police station	1 Main Street	City Hall
Planning office	1 Main Street	City Hall
Gas station	2 Main Street	Ed's Gas Station

In this case you have one, large, multipurpose building that is used by several services. Although there are three address variables (Services), there is only one address (1 Main Street) pointing to one building (City Hall).

As you will see in this chapter, pointers can be used as a quick and simple way to access arrays. In later chapters you will discover how pointers can be used to create new variables and complex data structures, such as linked lists and trees. As you go through the rest of the book, you will be able to understand these data structures as well as create your own.

A pointer is declared by putting an asterisk (*) in front of the variable name in the declaration statement:

```
int thing;      // Define "thing" (see Figure 15-2A)
int *thing_ptr; // Define "pointer to a thing" (see Figure 15-2B)
```

Table 15-2 lists the operators used in conjunction with pointers.

---

[*] For readers not familiar with American culture, 1600 Pennsylvania Ave. is the address of the President's mansion, while 8347 Skid Row is the typical address of a very poor family.

Table 15-2. Pointer operators

Operator	Meaning
*	Dereference (given a pointer, get the thing referenced)
&	Address of (given a thing, point to it)

The ampersand operator (&) changes a thing into a pointer. The * changes a pointer into a thing. These operators can easily cause confusion. Let's look at some simple uses of these operators in detail:

thing

A thing. The declaration int thing does *not* contain an asterisk, so thing is not a pointer. For example:

```
thing = 4;
```

&thing

A pointer to thing. thing is an object. The & (address of) operator gets the address of an object (a pointer), so &thing is a pointer. For example:

```
thing_ptr = &thing;// Point to the thing
                            // (See Figure 15-2A)
*thing_ptr = 5; // Set "thing" to 5
                            // (See Figure 15-2B)
```

thing_ptr

Thing pointer. The asterisk (*) in the declaration indicates this is a pointer. Also, you have put the extension _ptr onto the name.

*thing_ptr

A thing. The variable thing_ptr is a pointer. The * (dereference operator) tells C++ to look at the data pointed to, not at the pointer itself. Note that this points to an integer, any integer. It may or may not point to the specific variable thing.

```
*thing_ptr = 5;   // Assign 5 to an integer
                  // We may or may not be pointing
                  to the specific integer "thing"
```

The following examples show misuse of pointer operators.

*thing

Illegal. Asks C++ to get the object pointed to by the variable thing. Since thing is not a pointer, this is an invalid operation.

&thing_ptr

Legal, but strange. thing_ptr is a pointer. The & (address of) operator gets a pointer to the object (in this case thing_ptr). The result is a pointer to a pointer. (Pointers to pointers do occur in more complex programs.)

Example 15-1 illustrates a very simple use of pointers. It declares one object, thing_var, and a pointer, thing_ptr. thing_var is set explicitly by the line:

```
thing_var = 2;
```

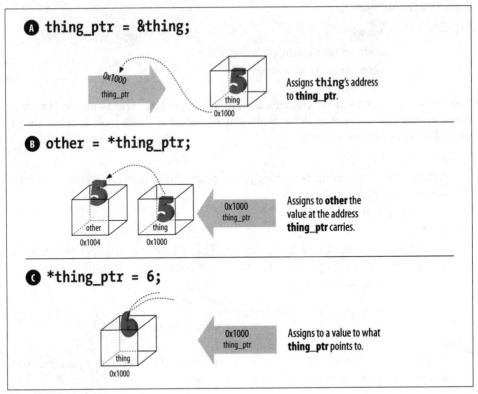

A `thing_ptr = &thing;`

Assigns **thing**'s address to **thing_ptr**.

B `other = *thing_ptr;`

Assigns to **other** the value at the address **thing_ptr** carries.

C `*thing_ptr = 6;`

Assigns to a value to what **thing_ptr** points to.

Figure 15-2. Pointer operators

The line:

```
thing_ptr = &thing_var;
```

causes C++ to set thing_ptr to the address of thing_var. From this point on, thing_var and *thing_ptr are the same.

Example 15-1. thing/thing.cpp

```
#include <iostream>

int main( )
{
    int   thing_var; // define a variable
    int *thing_ptr; // define a pointer

    thing_var = 2;      // assigning a value to thing
    std::cout <<"Thing " << thing_var << '\n';

    thing_ptr = &thing_var; // make the pointer point to thing
    *thing_ptr = 3;         // thing_ptr points to thing_var so
                            // thing_var changes to 3
    std::cout << "Thing " << thing_var << '\n';
```

Example 15-1. thing/thing.cpp (continued)

```
    // another way of printing the data
    std::cout << "Thing " << *thing_ptr << '\n';
    return (0);
}
```

Several pointers can point to the same thing:

```
1:      int     something;
2:
3:      int     *first_ptr;     // One pointer
4:      int     *second_ptr;    // Another pointer
5:
6:      something = 1;          // Give the thing a value
7:
8:      first_ptr = &something;
9:      second_ptr = first_ptr;
```

In line 8 you use the & operator to change a simple variable (something) into a pointer that can be assigned to first_ptr. Because first_ptr and second_ptr are both pointers, you can do a direct assignment in line 9.

After executing this program fragment, you have the situation illustrated by Figure 15-3.

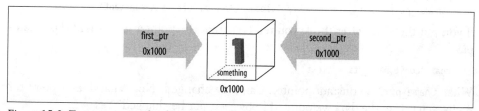

Figure 15-3. Two pointers and a thing

It is most important to note that while you have three variables, there is only one integer (thing). The following are all equivalent:

```
something = 1;
*first_ptr = 1;
*second_ptr = 1;
```

Finally, there is a special pointer called NULL that points to nothing. (The actual numeric value is 0.) The standard include file, *stddef.h*, defines the constant NULL. (Most standard include files that have anything to do with pointers automatically include NULL as well.) The NULL pointer is represented graphically in Figure 15-4.

Figure 15-4. NULL

const Pointers

Declaring constant pointers is a little tricky. For example, although the declaration:

```
const int result = 5;
```

tells C++ that result is a constant, so:

```
result = 10;      // Illegal
```

is illegal. The declaration:

```
const char *answer_ptr = "Forty-Two";
```

does *not* tell C++ that the variable answer_ptr is a constant. Instead it tells C++ that the data pointed to by answer_ptr is a constant. The data cannot be changed, but the pointer can. Again we need to make sure we know the difference between "things" and "pointers to things."

What's answer_ptr? A pointer. Can it be changed? Yes, it's just a pointer. What does it point to? A const char array. Can the data pointed to by answer_ptr be changed? No, it's constant.

Translating these rules into C++ syntax we get the following:

```
answer_ptr = "Fifty-One";     // Legal (answer_ptr is a variable)
*answer_ptr = 'X';            // Illegal (*answer_ptr is a constant)
```

If you put the const after the *, you tell C++ that the pointer is constant. For example:

```
char *const name_ptr = "Test";
```

What's name_ptr? A constant pointer. Can it be changed? No. What does it point to? A character. Can the data we pointed to by name_ptr be changed? Yes.

```
name_ptr = "New";             // Illegal (name_ptr is constant)
*name_ptr = 'B';              // Legal (*name_ptr is a char)
```

Finally, we put const in both places, creating a pointer that cannot be changed to a data item that cannot be changed:

```
const char *const title_ptr = "Title";
```

One way of remembering whether the const modifies the pointer or the value is to remember that *const reads "constant pointer" in English.

Pointers and Printing

In C++ you can display the value of a pointer just like you can display the value of a simple variable such as an integer or floating point number. For example:

```
int an_integer = 5;         // A simple integer
int *int_ptr = &an_integer; // Pointer to an integer
```

```
    std::cout << "Integer pointer " << int_ptr << '\n';
```
outputs
```
    Integer pointer 0x58239A
```
In this case, the value 0x58239A represents a memory address. This address may vary from program to program.

C++ treats character pointers a little differently from other pointers. A character pointer is treated as a pointer to a C-style string. For example:
```
    char some_characters[10] = "Hello";   // A simple set of characters
    char *char_ptr = &some_characters[0];  // Pointer to a character

    std::cout << "String pointer " << char_ptr << '\n';
```
outputs
```
    String pointer Hello
```
So with string pointers, the string itself is printed.

Pointers and Arrays

C++ allows pointer arithmetic. Addition and subtraction are allowed with pointers. Suppose you have the following:
```
    char array[10];
    char *array_ptr = &array[0];
```
This is represented graphically in Figure 15-5.

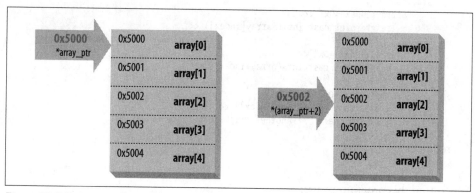

Figure 15-5. Pointers and an array

In this example, *array_ptr is the same as array[0], *(array_ptr+1) is the same as array[1], and so on. Note the use of parentheses. (*array_ptr)+1 is *not* the same as array[1]. The +1 is outside the parentheses, so it is added after the dereference. Thus (*array_ptr)+1 is the same as array[0]+1.

At first glance this may seem like a complex way of representing simple array indices. You are starting with simple pointer arithmetic. In later chapters you will use more complex pointers to handle more difficult functions efficiently.

Pointers are merely variables that contain memory addresses. In an array each element is assigned to consecutive addresses. For example, array[0] may be placed at address 0xff000024. Then array[1] would be placed at address 0xff000025 and so on. Example 15-3 prints out the elements and addresses of a simple character array. (Note: The I/O manipulators hex and dec are described in Chapter 16. The reinterpret_cast is discussed later in this chapter.)

Example 15-2. array-p/array-p.cpp

```
#include <assert.h>
#include <iostream>
#include <iomanip>

const int ARRAY_SIZE  = 10; // Number of characters in array
// Array to print
char array[ARRAY_SIZE] = "012345678";

int main( )
{
    int index;  /* Index into the array */

    for (index = 0; index < ARRAY_SIZE; ++index) {
        std::cout << std::hex;  // Trick to print hex numbers
        assert(index >= 0);
        assert(index < sizeof(array)/sizeof(array[0]));
        std::cout <<
            "&array[index]=0x" <<
                reinterpret_cast<int>(&array[index]) <<

            " (array+index)=0x" <<
                reinterpret_cast<int>(array+index) <<

            " array[index]=0x" <<
                static_cast<int>(array[index]) << '\n',
        std::cout << std::dec;  // Another trick to go back to decimal
    }
    return (0);
}
```

When run, this program prints:

```
&array[index]=0x20090 (array+index)=0x20090 array[index]=0x30
&array[index]=0x20091 (array+index)=0x20091 array[index]=0x31
&array[index]=0x20092 (array+index)=0x20092 array[index]=0x32
&array[index]=0x20093 (array+index)=0x20093 array[index]=0x33
&array[index]=0x20094 (array+index)=0x20094 array[index]=0x34
&array[index]=0x20095 (array+index)=0x20095 array[index]=0x35
&array[index]=0x20096 (array+index)=0x20096 array[index]=0x36
&array[index]=0x20097 (array+index)=0x20097 array[index]=0x37
```

```
&array[index]=0x20098 (array+index)=0x20098 array[index]=0x38
&array[index]=0x20099 (array+index)=0x20099 array[index]=0x0
```

Characters usually take up one byte, so the elements in a character array will be assigned consecutive addresses. A short int takes up two bytes, so in an array of short ints, the addresses increase by two. Does this mean short_array+1 will not work for anything other than characters? No. C++ automatically scales pointer arithmetic so it works correctly. In this case short_array+1 will point to element number 1.

C++ provides a shorthand for dealing with arrays. Rather than write:

```
array_ptr = &array[0];
```

you can write:

```
array_ptr = array;
```

C++ blurs the distinction between pointers and arrays by treating them the same in many cases. Here you used the variable array as a pointer, and C++ automatically did the necessary conversion.

Example 15-3 counts the number of elements that are nonzero and stops when a zero is found. No limit check is provided, so there must be at least one zero in the array.

Example 15-3. ptr2/ptr2a.cpp

```cpp
#include <assert.h>
#include <iostream>

int array[10] = {4, 5, 8, 9, 8, 1, 0, 1, 9, 3};
int the_index;

int main()
{
    the_index = 0;
    while (true) {
        assert(the_index >= 0);
        assert(the_index < sizeof(array)/sizeof(array[0]));

        if (array[the_index] == 0)
            break;

        ++the_index;
    }

    std::cout << "Number of elements before zero " << the_index << '\n';
    return (0);
}
```

Rewriting this program to use pointers gives us Example 15-4.

Example 15-4. ptr2/ptr2.cpp

```cpp
#include <iostream>

int array[10] = {4, 5, 8, 9, 8, 1, 0, 1, 9, 3};
int *array_ptr;

int main()
{
    array_ptr = array;

    while ((*array_ptr) != 0)
        ++array_ptr;

    std::cout << "Number of elements before zero " <<
        (array_ptr - array) << '\n';
    return (0);
}
```

 In the second example, we lost the safety provided by the **assert** statement.

The first program uses the expression (array[index] != 0). This requires the compiler to generate an index operation, which takes longer than a simple pointer dereference: ((*array_ptr) != 0). The expression at the end of this program, array_ptr - array, computes how far array_ptr is into the array.

When passing an array to a procedure, C++ will automatically change the array into a pointer. In fact, if you put an & before the array, C++ will issue a warning. Example 15-5 illustrates array passing.

Example 15-5. init-a/init-a.cpp

```cpp
#include <assert.h>

const int MAX = 10;

/****************************************************
 * init_array_1 -- Zero out an array               *
 *                                                  *
 * Parameters                                       *
 *      data -- the array to zero                   *
 ****************************************************/
void init_array_1(int data[])
{
    int  index;

    for (index = 0; index < MAX; ++index) {
        assert(index >= 0);
        assert(index < MAX);
        data[index] = 0;
```

Example 15-5. init-a/init-a.cpp (continued)

```
}

/*********************************************************
 * init_array_2 -- Zero out an array                     *
 *                                                       *
 * Parameters                                            *
 *      data_ptr -- pointer to array to zero             *
 *********************************************************/
void init_array_2(int *data_ptr)
{
    int index;

    for (index = 0; index < MAX; ++index)
        *(data_ptr + index) = 0;
}
int main()
{
    int  array[MAX];

    // one way of initializing the array
    init_array_1(array);

    // another way of initializing the array
    init_array_1(&array[0]);

    // Similar to the first method but
    //    function is different
    init_array_2(array);

    return (0);
}
```

Splitting a C-Style String

Suppose you are given a C-style string (character array) of the form "Last/First". You want to split this into two strings, one containing the first name and one containing the last name.

Example 15-6 reads in a single line, stripping the newline character from it. The function strchr is called to find the location of the slash (/). (The function strchr is actually a standard function. I have duplicated it for this example so you can see how it works.)

At this point last_ptr points to the beginning character of the last name (with the first tacked on) and first_ptr points to a slash. You then split the string by replacing the slash (/) with an end-of-string (NUL or "\0"). Now last_ptr points to just the last name and first_ptr points to a null string. Moving first_ptr to the next character makes first_ptr point to the beginning of the first name.

Graphically what you are doing is illustrated in Figure 15-6. Example 15-6 contains the full program.

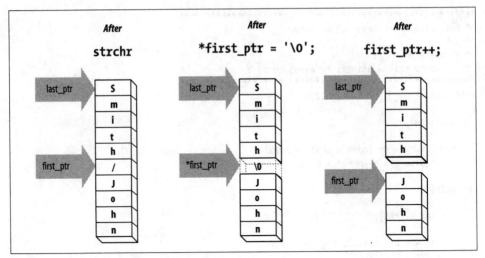

Figure 15-6. Splitting a string

Example 15-6. split/split.cpp

```
/********************************************************
 * split -- split a entry of the form Last/First       *
 *      into two parts.                                 *
 ********************************************************/
#include <iostream>
#include <cstring>
#include <cstdlib>

int main()
{
    char line[80];      // The input line
    char *first_ptr;    // pointer we set to point to the first name
    char *last_ptr;     // pointer we set to point to the last name

    std::cin.getline(line, sizeof(line));

    last_ptr = line;    // last name is at beginning of line

    first_ptr = strchr(line, '/');      // Find slash

    // Check for an error
    if (first_ptr == NULL) {
        std::cerr << "Error: Unable to find slash in " << line << '\n';
        exit (8);
    }

    *first_ptr = '\0';  // Zero out the slash
```

Example 15-6. split/split.cpp (continued)

```
    ++first_ptr;            // Move to first character of name

    std::cout << "First:" << first_ptr << " Last:" << last_ptr << '\n';
    return (0);
}
/************************************************************
 * strchr -- find a character in a string                 *
 *      Duplicate of a standard library function,         *
 *      put here for illustrative purposes.               *
 *                                                        *
 * Parameters                                             *
 *      string_ptr -- string to look through              *
 *      find -- character to find                         *
 *                                                        *
 * Returns                                                *
 *      pointer to 1st occurrence of character in string* *
 *      or NULL for error                                 *
 ************************************************************/
char *strchr(char * string_ptr, char find)
{
    while (*string_ptr != find) {

        // Check for end

        if (*string_ptr == '\0')
            return (NULL);        // not found

        ++string_ptr;
    }
    return (string_ptr);          // Found
}
```

This program illustrates how pointers and character arrays may be used for simple string processing.

Question 15-1: *Example 15-7 is supposed to print out:*

```
Name: tmp1
```

but instead you get:

```
Name: !_@$#ds80
```

(Your results may vary.) Why does this happen? Would this happen if we used the C++ string class instead of the old C-style strings?

Example 15-7. tmp-name/tmp-name.cpp

```
#include <iostream>
#include <cstring>

/************************************************************
 * tmp_name -- return a temporary file name               *
 *                                                        *
```

Example 15-7. tmp-name/tmp-name.cpp (continued)

```
 * Each time this function is called, a new name will    *
 * be returned.                                          *
 *                                                       *
 * Returns                                               *
 *      Pointer to the new file name.                    *
 ********************************************************/
char *tmp_name()
{
    char name[30];            // The name we are generating
    static int sequence = 0;  // Sequence number for last digit

    ++sequence; // Move to the next file name

    strcpy(name, "tmp");

    // Put in the sequence digit
    name[3] = static_cast<char>(sequence + '0');

    // End the string
    name[4] = '\0';

    return(name);
}

int main()
{
    std::cout << "Name: " << tmp_name() << '\n';
    return(0);
}
```

The reinterpret_cast

The reinterpret_cast is used to tell C++ to interpret a value as a different type. It is used to convert pointers to integers, integers to pointers, and pointers from one type to another. The syntax is:

```
reintepret_cast<type>(expression)
```

where type is of the result of the conversion.

Pointers and Structures

In Chapter 1, you defined a structure for a mailing list:

```
struct mailing {
    std::string   name;     // Last name, first name
    std::string   address1;// Two lines of street address
    std::string   address2;
    std::string   city;
```

```
    char    state[2];    // Two-character abbreviation*
    long int zip;        // Numeric zip code
} list[MAX_ENTRIES];
```

Mailing lists must frequently be sorted in name order and Zip-code order. You could sort the entries themselves, but each entry is 226 bytes long. That's a lot of data to move around. A way around this problem is to declare an array of pointers and then sort the pointers:

```
// Pointer to the data
struct mailing *list_ptrs[MAX_ENTRIES];

int current;    // Current mailing list entry

// ....

for (current = 0; current = number_of_entries; ++current) {
    list_ptrs = &list[current];
    ++list_ptrs;
}

// Sort list_ptrs by zip code
```

Now instead of having to move a large structure around, you are moving 4-byte pointers. This sorting is much faster. Imagine that you had a warehouse full of big heavy boxes and you needed to locate any box quickly. One way of doing this would be to put the boxes in alphabetical order. But that would require a lot of moving, so you assign each location a number, write down the name and number on index cards, and sort the cards by name.

Command-Line Arguments

The procedure main actually takes two arguments. They are called argc and argv. (They don't have to be called argc and argv; however, 99.99% of C++ programs use these names.)

```
int main(int argc, char *argv[])
{
```

It's easy to remember which comes first when you realize that they are in alphabetical order.

The parameter argc is the number of arguments on the command line (including the program name). The array argv contains the actual arguments. For example, if the program args were run with the command line:

---

* Every once in a while, someone will send in a bug report stating that the size of the character array should be 3: two for the state abbreviation and one for the end of string character. In this example, the state is a character array, not a C-style string. We know that it contains two and only two characters, so we can represent it as two-character array.

```
args this is a test
```

then:

```
argc         = 5
argv[0]      = "args"
argv[1]      = "this"
argv[2]      = "is"
argv[3]      = "a"
argv[4]      = "test"
```

 The Unix shell expands wildcard characters like *, ?, and [] before sending the command line to the program. See your sh or csh manual for details.

Borland-C++ will expand wildcard characters if the file *WILDARG.OBJ* is linked with your program. See the Borland-C++ manual for details.

Almost all Unix commands use a standard command-line format. This "standard" has carried over into other environments. A standard UNIX command has the form:

```
command options file1 file1 file3 ...
```

Options are preceded by a hyphen (-) and are usually a single letter. For example, the option -v might turn on verbose mode. If the option takes a parameter, the parameter follows the letter. For example, the switch –m1024 sets the maximum number of symbols to 1024, and –ooutfile sets the output file name to *outfile*.

You have been given the assignment to write a program that will format and print files. Part of the documentation for the program looks like:

```
print_file [-v] [-l<length>] [-o<name>] [file1] [file2] ...
```

In this line, -v sets verbose options, which turns on a lot of progress information messages. The option -l<length> sets page size to <length> lines (default = 66), and -o<name> sets the output file to <name> (default = *print.out*). A list of files to print follows these options ([file1], [file2], etc.). If no files are specified, print the file *print.in*.

The while loop cycles through the options. The actual loop is:

```
while ((argc > 1) && (argv[1][0] == '-')) {
```

There is always one argument, the program name. The expression (argc > 1) checks for additional arguments. The first one will be numbered 1. The first character of the first argument is argv[1][0]. If this character is a dash, you have an option.

At the end of the loop is the code:

```
        --argc;
        ++argv;
    }
```

This consumes an argument. The number of arguments is decremented to indicate one fewer option, and the pointer to the first option is incremented, shifting the list to the left one place. (Note that after the first increment, argv[0] no longer points to the program name.)

The switch statement is used to decode the options. Character 0 of the argument is the hyphen (-). Character 1 is the option character, so you use the following expression to decode the option:

```
switch (argv[1][1]) {
```

The option -v has no arguments; it just causes a flag to be set.

The -1 option takes an integer argument. The library function atoi is used to convert the string into an integer. From the previous example, you know that argv[1][2] starts the string containing the number. This string is passed to atoi.

The option -o takes a filename. Rather than copy the whole string, you set the character pointer out_file to point to the name part of the string. By this time you know that:

```
argv[1][0] = '-'
argv[1][1] = 'o'
argv[1][2] = first character of the file name
```

You set out_file to point to the string with the statement:

```
out_file = &argv[1][2];
```

Finally all the options are parsed, and you fall through to the processing loop. This merely executes the function do_file for each file argument.

Example 15-8 contains the complete option-decoding program.

Example 15-8. print/print.cpp

```
/*******************************************************
 * print -- format files for printing                 *
 *******************************************************/
#include <iostream>
#include <cstdlib>

int verbose = 0;              // verbose mode (default = false)
char *out_file = "print.out"; // output file name
char *program_name;           // name of the program (for errors)
int line_max = 66;            // number of lines per page

/*******************************************************
 * do_file -- dummy routine to handle a file          *
 *                                                    *
 * Parameter                                          *
 *      name -- name of the file to print             *
 *******************************************************/
void do_file(const char *const name)
{
    std::cout << "Verbose " << verbose << " Lines " << line_max <<
```

Example 15-8. print/print.cpp (continued)

```
            " Input " << name << " Output " << out_file << '\n';
}
/*********************************************************
 * usage -- tell the user how to use this program and   *
 *          exit                                        *
 *********************************************************/
void usage()
{
    std::cerr << "Usage is " << program_name <<
        " [options] [file-list]\n";
    std::cerr << "Options\n";
    std::cerr << "   -v          verbose\n";
    std::cerr << "   -l<number>  Number of lines\n";
    std::cerr << "   -o<name>    Set output file name\n";
    exit (8);
}

int main(int argc, char *argv[])
{
    // save the program name for future use
    program_name = argv[0];

    /*
     * loop for each option.
     *    Stop if we run out of arguments
     *    or we get an argument without a dash.
     */
    while ((argc > 1) && (argv[1][0] == '-')) {
        /*
         * argv[1][1] is the actual option character.
         */
        switch (argv[1][1]) {
            /*
             * -v verbose
             */
            case 'v':
                verbose = 1;
                break;
            /*
             * -o<name>  output file
             *    [0] is the dash
             *    [1] is the "o"
             *    [2] starts the name
             */
            case 'o':
                out_file = &argv[1][2];
                break;
            /*
             * -l<number> set max number of lines
             */
            case 'l':
                line_max = atoi(&argv[1][2]);
```

Example 15-8. print/print.cpp (continued)

```
                break;
            default:
                std::cerr << "Bad option " << argv[1] <<'\n';
                usage();
        }
        /*
         * move the argument list up one
         * move the count down one
         */
        ++argv;
        --argc;
    }

    /*
     * At this point all the options have been processed.
     * Check to see if we have no files in the list
     * and if so, we need to list just standard in.
     */
    if (argc == 1) {
        do_file("print.in");
    } else {
        while (argc > 1) {
            do_file(argv[1]);
            ++argv;
            --argc;
        }
    }
    return (0);
}
```

This is one way of parsing the argument list. The use of the while loop and switch statement is simple and easy to understand. This method does have a limitation. The argument must immediately follow the options. For example, -odata.out will work, but -o data.out will not. An improved parser would make the program more friendly, but this works for simple programs. (See your system documentation for information on the getopt function.)

Programming Exercises

Exercise 15-1: Write a program that uses pointers to set each element of an array to zero.

Exercise 15-2: Write a function that takes a single C-style string as its argument and returns a pointer to the first nonwhitespace character in the string.

Answers to Chapter Questions

Answer 15-1: The problem is that the variable name is a temporary variable. The compiler allocates space for the name when the function is entered and reclaims the space when the function exits. The function assigns name the correct value and returns a pointer to it. However, the function is over, so name disappears and you have a pointer with an illegal value.

The solution is to declare name static. Consequently, it is a permanent variable and will not disappear at the end of the function.

If we had used the C++ string class we would not have had this problem. That's because the string class's copy constructor and memory allocation logic prevents the destruction of memory before we finish using it.

Question 15-2: *After fixing the function, you try using it for two filenames. Example 15-9 should print out:*

```
Name: tmp1
Name: tmp2
```

but it doesn't. What does it print and why?

Example 15-9. tmp2/tmp2.cpp

```cpp
#include <iostream>
#include <cstring>

/********************************************************
 * tmp_name -- return a temporary file name            *
 *                                                      *
 * Each time this function is called, a new name will   *
 * be returned.                                         *
 *                                                      *
 * Warning: There should be a warning here, but if we   *
 *      put it in we would answer the question.         *
 *                                                      *
 * Returns                                              *
 *      Pointer to the new file name.                   *
 ********************************************************/
char *tmp_name()
{
    static char name[30];       // The name we are generating
    static int sequence = 0;    // Sequence number for last digit

    ++sequence; // Move to the next file name

    strcpy(name, "tmp");

    // But in the squence digit
    name[3] = static_cast<char>(sequence + '0');

    // End the string
```

Example 15-9. tmp2/tmp2.cpp (continued)

```
    name[4] = '\0';

    return(name);
}

int main()
{
    char *name1;                    // name of a temporary file
    char *name2;                    // name of a temporary file

    name1 = tmp_name();
    name2 = tmp_name();

    std::cout <<"Name1: " << name1 << '\n';
    std::cout <<"Name2: " << name2 << '\n';
    return(0);
}
```

The first call to `tmp_name` *returns a pointer to* name. *There is only one* name. *The second call to* `tmp_name` *changes* name *and returns a pointer to it. So you have two pointers, and they point to the same thing,* name.

Several library functions return pointers to static strings. A second call to one of these routines will overwrite the first value. A solution to this problem is to copy the values:

```
    char name1[100];
    char name2[100];

    strncpy(name1, tmp_name(), sizeof(name1));
    strncpy(name2, tmp_name(), sizeof(name1));
```

OK, we decided to finally give up on C-style strings and enter the 21st century. So we've rewritten our function to use the C++ string class. Yet it still doesn't work. Why?

Example 15-10. tmp3/tmp3.cpp

```
#include <iostream>
#include <string>

/*******************************************************
 * tmp_name -- return a temporary file name            *
 *                                                     *
 * Each time this function is called, a new name will  *
 * be returned.                                        *
 *                                                     *
 * Returns                                             *
 *      String containing the name.                    *
 *******************************************************/
std::string& tmp_name()
{
    std::string name;    // The name we are generating
```

Example 15-10. tmp3/tmp3.cpp (continued)

```
    static int sequence = 0;     // Sequence number for last digit

    ++sequence; // Move to the next file name

    name = "tmp";

    // Put in the squence digit
    name += static_cast<char>(sequence + '0');

    return(name);
}

int main( )
{
    std::string name1 = tmp_name( );

    std::cout <<"Name1: " << name1 << '\n';
    return(0);
}
```

The function returns a reference to name, which is a local variable. The problem is that C++ destroys the variable name at the end of the function. It then returns a reference to the variable (which just got destroyed), and that's what's assigned to name1.

You should never return references to local variables or parameters unless they are declared **static**.

Advanced Programming Concepts

## CHAPTER 16

File Input/Output

> *I am the heir of all the ages, in the foremost*
> *files of time.*
> —Tennyson

A file is a collection of related data. C++ treats a file as a series of bytes. Many files reside on disk; however, devices such as printers, magnetic tapes, and communication lines are also considered files.

This chapter discusses three different I/O packages. The first is the C++ I/O stream classes. This is the most commonly used I/O system and the one we've been using up to now. Next, we examine the raw I/O routines that give us direct access to the low-level I/O. Finally we look at the C I/O system. Although it is somewhat outdated, C I/O calls still appear in old code. Also, in some cases, the C-style I/O routines are superior to the ones provided with C++.

C++ File I/O

C++ file I/O is based on three classes: the istream class for input, the ostream class for output, and the iostream class for input/output. C++ refers to files as *streams* since it considers them a stream of bytes. Four class variables are automatically created when you start a program. These are listed in Table 16-1.

Table 16-1. Predefined I/O class variables

Variable	Use
cin	Console input (standard input)
cout	Console output (standard output)
cerr	Console error (standard error)
clog	Console log

These variables are defined in the standard include file <iostream>. Normally, std::cin is assigned to the keyboard and std::cout, std::cerr, and std::clog are assigned to the screen. Most operating systems allow you to change these assignments through I/O redirection (see your operating system manual for details).

For example, the command:

```
my_prog <file.in
```

runs the program my_prog and assigns std::cin to the file *file.in*.

When doing I/O to disk files (except through redirection), you must use the file version of the stream classes. These are std::ifstream, std::ofstream, and std::fstream and are defined in the include file <fstream>.

Suppose you want to read a series of 100 numbers from the file *numbers.dat*. You start by declaring the input file variable:

```
std::ifstream data_file;    // File we are reading the data from
```

Next you need to tell C++ what disk file to use. This is done through the open member function:

```
data_file.open("numbers.dat");
```

Now you can read the file using the same statements you've been using to read std::cin:

```
for (i = 0; i < 100; ++i) {
    assert(i >= 0);
    assert(i < sizeof(data_array)/sizeof(data_array[0]));
    data_file >> data_array[i];
}
```

Finally you need to tell the I/O system that you are done with the file:

```
data_file.close();
```

Closing the file frees resources that can then be used again by the program.

C++ allows the open call to be combined with the constructor. For example, instead of writing:

```
std::ifstream data_file;    // File we are reading the data from
data_file.open("numbers.dat");
```

you can write:

```
std::ifstream data_file("numbers.dat"); // File we are reading the data from
```

Additionally, the destructor automatically calls close.

But what if the file *numbers.dat* is missing? How can you tell if there is a problem? The member function fail returns true if there is a problem, and false otherwise. So to test for problems, all you need is:

```
if (data_file.fail()) {
    std::cerr << "Unable to open numbers.dat\n";
    exit (8);
}
```

A better version of the program for reading numbers is listed in Example 16-1.

Example 16-1. read/read.cpp

```cpp
/**********************************************************
 * read -- read in 100 numbers and sum them              *
 *                                                        *
 * Usage:                                                 *
 *     read                                               *
 *                                                        *
 * Numbers are in the file "numbers.dat"                  *
 *                                                        *
 * Warning: No check is made for a file with less than    *
 * 100 numbers in it.                                     *
 **********************************************************/
#include <iostream>
#include <fstream>
#include <cstdlib>

int main()
{
    const int DATA_SIZE = 100;  // Number of items in the data
    int data_array[DATA_SIZE];  // The data
    std::ifstream data_file("numbers.dat"); // The input file
    int i;                      // Loop counter

    if (data_file.bad()) {
        std::cerr << "Error: Could not open numbers.dat\n";
        exit (8);
    }

    for (i = 0; i < DATA_SIZE; ++i) {
        assert(i >= 0);
        assert(i < sizeof(data_array)/sizeof(data_array[0]));

        data_file >> data_array[i];
    }

    int total;  // Total of the numbers

    total = 0;
    for (i = 0; i < DATA_SIZE; ++i) {
        assert(i >= 0);
        assert(i < sizeof(data_array)/sizeof(data_array[0]));

        total += data_array[i];
    }

    std::cout << "Total of all the numbers is " << total << '\n';
    return (0);
}
```

If you want to read a line of data, you need to use the getline function. It is defined as:[*]

```
std::istream& getline(std::istream& input_file,
                      std::string& the_string);
std::istream& getline(std::istream& input_file,
                      std::string& the_string, char delim)
```

This function reads a line and stores it in a string. The function returns a reference to the input stream. The second form of the function allows you to specify your own end-of-line delimiter. If this is not specified, it defaults to newline ('\n').

Reading C-Style Strings

To read C-style strings, you can use the getline function. (This is an overload version of the getline function discussed in the previous section.) This getline member function is defined as:

```
std::istream& getline(char *buffer, int len, char delim = '\n')
```

The parameters to this function are:

buffer
> A C-style string in which to store the data that has been read.

len
> Length of the buffer in bytes. The function reads up to len-1 bytes of data into the buffer. (One byte is reserved for the terminating null character \0.) This parameter is usually sizeof(buffer).

delim
> The character used to signal end-of-line.

This function returns a reference to the input file. The function reads up to and including the end-of-line character ('\n'). The end-of-line character is not stored in the buffer. (An end-of-string ('\0') is store in to terminate the string.)

For example:

```
char buffer[30];

std::cin.getline(buffer, sizeof(buffer));
```

Output Files

The functions for output files are similar to input files. For example, the declaration:

```
std::ofstream out_file("out.dat");
```

---

[*] If you take a look at the C++ standard, you'll notice that the formal definition of these functions is somewhat more complex. I've simplified the definition for this book, but this definition is compatible with the formal one.

creates a file named *out.dat* and lets you write to the file using the file variable out_file.

Actually, the constructor can take two additional arguments. The full definition of the output file constructor is:

```
std::ofstream::ofstream(const char *name, int mode=std::ios::out,
                        int prot = filebuf::openprot);
```

The parameters for this function are:

name
> The name of the file.

mode
> A set of flags ORed together that determine the open mode. The flag std:: ios::out is required for output files. Other flags are listed in Table 16-2. (The std::ios:: prefix is used to indicate the scope of the constant. This operator is discussed in more detail in Chapter 21.)

prot
> File protection. This is an operating system–dependent value that determines the protection mode for the file. In Unix the protection defaults to 0644 (read/write owner, group read, others read). For MS-DOS/Windows this defaults to 0 (normal file).

Table 16-2. Open flags

Flag	Meaning
std::ios::app	Append data to the end of the output file.
std::ios::ate	Go to the end of the file when opened.
std::ios::in	Open for input (must be supplied to the open member function of std::ifstream variables).
std::ios::out	Open file for output (must be supplied to the open member function of std:: ofstream variables).
std::ios::binary	Binary file (if not present, the file is opened as an ASCII file). See the later section "Binary I/O" for a definition of a binary file.
std::ios::trunc	Discard contents of existing file when opening for write.
std::ios::nocreate	Fail if the file does not exist. (Output files only. Opening an input file always fails if there is no file.)

For example, the statement:

```
std::ofstream out_file("data.new", std::ios::out|std::ios::binary|std::ios::nocreate|
                       std::ios::app);
```

appends (std::ios::app) binary data (std::ios::binary) to an existing file (std::ios::nocreate) named *data.new*.

Example 16-2 contains a short function that writes a message to a log file. The first thing the function does is to open the file for output (std::ios::out), appending (std::ios::app), with the writing to start at the end of the file (std::ios::ate). It then writes the message and closes the file (the destructor for out_file performs the close).

This function was designed to be simple, which it is. But also we didn't care about efficiency, and as a result this function is terribly inefficient. The problem is that we open and close the file every time we call log_message. Opening a file is an expensive operation, and things would go much faster if we opened the file only once and remembered that we had it open in subsequent calls.

Example 16-2. log/log.cpp

```
#include <iostream>
#include <fstream>

void log_message(const string& msg)
{
    std::ofstream out_file("data.log",
                           std::ios::out|std::ios::app|std::ios::ate);
    if (out_file.bad())
        return; /* Where do we log an error if there is no log */
    out_file << msg << endl;
}
```

Conversion Routines

So far we have just considered writing characters and strings. In this section, we consider some of the more sophisticated I/O operations: conversions.

To write a number to a printer or terminal, you must convert the number to characters. The printer understands only characters, not numbers. For example, the number 567 must be converted to the three characters "5", "6", and "7" to be printed.

The << operator is used to convert data to characters and put them in a file. This function is extremely flexible. It can convert a simple integer into a fixed- or variable-size string as a hex, octal, or decimal number with left or right justification. So far you've been using the default conversion for your output. It serves pretty well, but if you want to control your output exactly, you need to learn about conversion flags.

The member functions setf and unsetf are used to set and clear the flags that control the conversion process. The general form of the functions is:

```
file_var.setf(flags);   // Set flags
file_var.unsetf(flags); // Clear flags
```

Table 16-3 lists the various flags and their meanings.

Table 16-3. I/O conversion flags

Flag	Meaning
std::ios::skipws	Skip leading whitespace characters on input.
std::ios::left	Output is left justified.
std::ios::right	Output is right justified.
std::ios::internal	Numeric output is padded by inserting a fill character between the sign or base character and the number itself.
std::ios::boolalpha	Use the character version of true and false ("true", "false") for input and output.
std::ios::dec	Output numbers in base 10, decimal format.
std::ios::oct	Output numbers in base 8, octal format.
std::ios::hex	Output numbers in base 16, hexadecimal format.
std::ios::showbase	Print out a base indicator at the beginning of each number. For example, hexadecimal numbers are preceded with "0x".
std::ios::showpoint	Show a decimal point for all floating-point numbers whether or not it's needed.
std::ios::uppercase	When converting hexadecimal numbers, show the digits A–F as uppercase.
std::ios::showpos	Put a plus sign before all positive numbers.
std::ios::scientific	Convert all floating-point numbers to scientific notation on output.
std::ios::fixed	Convert all floating-point numbers to fixed point on output.
std::ios::unitbuf	Buffer output. (More on this later.)

If you want to output a number in hexadecimal format, all you have to do is this:

```
number = 0x3FF;
std::cout << "Dec: " << number << '\n';

std::cout.setf(std::ios::hex);
std::cout << "Hex: " << number << '\n';

std::cout.setf(std::ios::dec);
```

When run, this program produces the output:

```
Dec: 1023
Hex: 3ff
```

People normally expect the output mode to be decimal, so it is a good idea to reset the mode after each output to avoid later confusion.

When converting numbers to characters, the member function:

```
int file_var.width(int size);
```

determines the minimum characters to use. For example, the number 3 would normally convert to the character string "3" (note the lack of spaces). If the width is set to four, the result would be "␣␣␣3" where ␣ represents a single space.

The member function:

```
int file_var.precision(int digits);
```

controls how many digits are printed after the decimal point.

Finally, the function:

```
char file_var.fill(char pad);
```

determines the fill character. This character is used for padding when a number is smaller than the specified width.

 Some of these flags and parameters are reset after each output call and some are not. Which flags are permanent and which are temporary seems to change from compiler to compiler. In general, don't assume anything is going to remain set and you'll be okay. (Just because you're paranoid doesn't mean the compiler isn't out to get you.)

These functions can be called directly, or you can use an *I/O manipulator*. An I/O manipulator is a special function that can be used in an I/O statement to change the formatting. You can think of a manipulator as a magic bullet that, when sent through an input or output file, changes the state of the file. A manipulator doesn't cause any output; it just changes the state. For example, the manipulator hex changes the output conversion to hexadecimal.

```
#include <iostream>

number = 0x3FF;
std::cout << "Number is " << std::hex << number << std::dec << '\n';
```

The header file <iostream> defines a basic set of manipulators. Table 16-4 contains a list of these manipulators.

Table 16-4. I/O manipulators

Manipulator	Description
std::dec	Output numbers in decimal format.
std::hex	Output numbers in hexadecimal format.
std::oct	Output numbers in octal format.
std::ws	Skip whitespace on input.
std::endl	Output end-of-line
std::ends	Output end-of-string ('\0').
std::flush	Force any buffered output out. (See Chapter 17, for an explanation of how to use this function).

The more advanced set of manipulators (see Table 16-5) is defined in the header file <iomanip>.

Table 16-5. I/O manipulators

Manipulator	Description
std::setiosflags(long flags)	Set selected conversion flags.
std::resetiosflags(long flags)	Reset selected flags.
std::setbase(int base)	Set conversion base to 8, 10, or 16. Sort of a generalized std::dec, std::hex, std::oct.
std::setw(int width)	Set the width of the output.
std::setprecision(int precision)	Set the precision of floating-point output.
std::setfill(char ch)	Set the fill character.

Example 16-3 shows how some of the I/O manipulators may be used.

Example 16-3. io/io.cpp

```
#include <iostream>
#include <iomanip>

int main( )
{
    int number = 12;    // A number to output
    float real = 12.34; // A real number

    std::cout << "12345678901234567890123456789 0\n"; // output ruler
    std::cout << number << "<-\n";
    std::cout << std::setw(5) << number << "<-\n";
    std::cout << std::setw(5) << std::setfill('*') <<
        number << "<-\n";
    std::cout << std::setiosflags(std::ios::showpos|std::ios::left) <<
        std::setw(5) << number << "<-\n";

    std::cout << real << "<-\n";
    std::cout << std::setprecision(1) <<
        std::setiosflags(std::ios::fixed) << real << "<-\n";

    std::cout << std::setiosflags(std::ios::scientific) << real << "<-\n";
    return (0);
}
```

The output of this program is:

```
12345678901234567890123456789 0
12<-
   12<-
***12<-
+12**<-
12.34<-
12.3<-
1e+01<-
```

Binary and ASCII Files

So far we have limited ourselves to ASCII files. "ASCII" stands for American Standard Code for Information Interchange. It is a set of 95 printable characters and 33 control codes. (A complete list of ASCII codes can be found in Appendix A.) ASCII files are human-readable. When you write a program, the *prog.cc* file is ASCII.

Terminals, keyboards, and printers deal with character data. When you want to write a number like 1234 to the screen, it must be converted to four characters ("1", "2", "3", and "4") and written.

Similarly, when you read a number from the keyboard, the data must be converted from characters to integers. This is done by the >> operator.

The ASCII character "0" has the value 48, "1" the value 49, and so on. When you want to convert a single digit from ASCII to integer, you must subtract 48:

```
int integer;
char ch;

ch = '5';
integer = ch - 48;
std::cout << "Integer " << integer << '\n';
```

Rather than remember that the character "0" is 48, you can just subtract '0':

```
integer = ch - '0';
```

Computers work on binary data. When reading numbers from an ASCII file, the program must process the character data through a conversion routine like the integer conversion routine just defined. This is expensive. Binary files require no conversion. They also generally take up less space than ASCII files. The drawback is that they cannot be directly printed on a terminal or printer. (If you've ever seen a long printout coming out of the printer displaying pages with a few characters at the top that look like "!E#(@$%@^Aa^AA^^JHC%^X", you know what happens when you try to print a binary file.)

ASCII files are portable (for the most part). They can be moved from machine to machine with very little trouble. Binary files are almost certainly nonportable. Unless you are an expert programmer, it is almost impossible to make a portable binary file.

Which file type should you use? In most cases, ASCII is best. If you have small to medium amounts of data, the conversion time does not seriously affect the performance of your program. (Who cares if it takes 0.5 seconds to start up instead of 0.3?) ASCII files also make it easy to verify the data.

Only when you are using large amounts of data will the space and performance problems force you to use the binary format.

The End-of-Line Puzzle

Back in the dark ages BC (Before Computers), there existed a magical device called a Teletype Model 33. This amazing machine contained a shift register made out of a motor and a rotor as well as a keyboard ROM consisting solely of levers and springs.

The Teletype contained a keyboard, printer, and paper tape reader/punch. It could transmit messages over telephones using a modem at the blazing rate of 10 characters per second.

But Teletype had a problem. It took 0.2 seconds to move the printhead from the right side to the left. 0.2 seconds is two character times. If a second character came while the printhead was in the middle of a return, that character was lost.

The Teletype people solved this problem by making end-of-line two characters: <carriage return> to position the printhead at the left margin, and <line feed> to move the paper up one line. That way the <line feed> "printed" while the printhead was racing back to the left margin.

When the early computers came out, some designers realized that using two characters for end-of-line wasted storage (at this time storage was very expensive). Some picked <line feed> for their end-of-line, and some chose <carriage return>. Some of the die-hards stayed with the two-character sequence.

Unix uses <line feed> for end-of-line. The newline character \n is code 0xA (LF or <line feed>).

MS-DOS/Windows uses the two characters <carriage return><line feed>. Compiler designers had problems dealing with the old C programs that thought newline was just <line feed>. The solution was to add code to the I/O library that stripped out the <carriage return> characters from ASCII input files and changed <line feed> to <carriage return><line feed> on output.

In MS-DOS/Windows, whether or not a file is opened as ASCII or binary is important to note. The flag `std::ios::binary` is used to indicate a binary file:

```
// Open ASCII file for reading
ascii_file.open("name", std::ios::in);

// Open binary file for reading
binary_file.open("name", std::ios::in|std::ios::binary);
```

Unix programmers don't have to worry about the C++ library automatically fixing their ASCII files. In Unix, a file is a file, and ASCII is no different from binary. In fact, you can write a half-ASCII/half-binary file if you want to.

Question 16-1: *The member function* put *can be used to write out a single byte of a binary file. The following program (shown in Example 16-4) writes numbers 0 to 127 to a file called test.out. It works just fine in Unix, creating a 128-byte long file; however, in MS-DOS/Windows, the file contains 129 bytes. Why?*

Example 16-4. wbin/wbin.cpp

```
#include <iostream>
#include <fstream>
#include <cstdlib>

int main( )
{
    int cur_char;    // current character to write
    std::ofstream out_file; // output file

    out_file.open("test.out", std::ios::out);
    if (out_file.bad( )) {
        (std::cerr << "Can not open output file\n");
        exit (8);
    }

    for (cur_char = 0; cur_char < 128; ++cur_char) {
        out_file.put(cur_char);
    }
    return (0);
}
```

Hint: Here is a hex dump of the MS-DOS/Windows file:

```
000:0001 0203 0405 0607 0809 0d0a 0b0c 0d0e
010:0f10 1112 1314 1516 1718 191a 1b1c 1d1e
020:1f20 2122 2324 2526 2728 292a 2b2c 2d2e
030:2f30 3132 3334 3536 3738 393a 3b3c 3d3e
040:3f40 4142 4344 4546 4748 494a 4b4c 4d4e
050:4f50 5152 5354 5556 5758 595a 5b5c 5d5e
060:5f60 6162 6364 6566 6768 696a 6b6c 6d6e
070:6f70 7172 7374 7576 7778 797a 7b7c 7d7e
080:7f
```

Binary I/O

Binary I/O is accomplished through two member functions: read and write. The syntax for read is:

> *in_file*.read(*data_ptr*, *size*);

data_ptr
    Pointer to a place to put the data.

size
    Number of bytes to be read.

The member function gcount returns the number of bytes gotten by the last read. This may be less than the number of bytes requested. For example, the read might encounter an end-of-file or error:

```
struct {
    int     width;
```

```
    int     height;
} rectangle;

in_file.read(static_cast<char *>(&rectangle), sizeof(rectangle));
if (in_file.bad( )) {
    cerr << "Unable to read rectangle\n";
    exit (8);
}
if (in_file.gcount( ) != sizeof(rectangle)) {
    cerr << "Error: Unable to read full rectangle\n";
    cerr << "I/O error of EOF encountered\n";
}
```

In this example you are reading in the structure rectangle. The & operator makes rectangle into a pointer. The cast static_cast<char *> is needed since read wants a character array. The sizeof operator is used to determine how many bytes to read as well as to check that read was successful.

The member function write has a calling sequence similar to read:

```
out_file.write(data_ptr, size);
```

Buffering Problems

Buffered I/O does not write immediately to the file. Instead, the data is kept in a buffer until there is enough for a big write, or until the buffer is flushed. The following program is designed to print a progress message as each section is finished.

```
std::cout << "Starting";
do_step_1( );
std::cout << "Step 1 complete";
do_step_2( );
std::cout << "Step 2 complete";
do_step_3( );
std::cout << "Step 3 complete\n";
```

Instead of writing the messages as each step completes, std::cout puts them in a buffer. Only after the program is finished does the buffer get flushed, and all the messages come spilling out at once.

The I/O manipulator std::flush forces the flushing of the buffers. Properly written, the above example should be:

```
std::cout << "Starting" << std::flush;
do_step_1( );
std::cout << "Step 1 complete" << std::flush;
do_step_2( );
std::cout << "Step 2 complete" << std::flush;
do_step_3( );
std::cout << "Step 3 complete\n" << std::flush;
```

Because each output statement ends with a std::flush, the output is displayed immediately. This means that our progress messages come out on time.

The C++ I/O classes buffer all output. Output to std::cout and std::cerr is line buffered. In other words, each newline forces a buffer flush. Also, C++ is smart enough to know that std::cout and std::cerr are related to std::cin and will automatically flush these two output streams just before reading std::cin. This makes it possible to write prompts without having to worry about buffering:

```
std::cout << "Enter a value: ";    // Note: No flush
std::cin >> value;
```

Unbuffered I/O

In buffered I/O, data is buffered and then sent to the file. In unbuffered I/O, the data is immediately sent to the file.

If you drop a number of paperclips on the floor, you can pick them up in buffered or unbuffered mode. In buffered mode, you use your right hand to pick up a paper clip and transfer it to your left hand. The process is repeated until your left hand is full, then you dump a handful of paperclips into the box on your desk.

In unbuffered mode, you pick up a paperclip and dump it into the box. There is no left-hand buffer.

In most cases, buffered I/O should be used instead of unbuffered. In unbuffered I/O, each read or write requires a system call. Any call to the operating system is expensive. Buffered I/O minimizes these calls.

Unbuffered I/O should be used only when reading or writing large amounts of binary data or when direct control of a device or file is required.

Back to the paperclip example—if you were picking up small items like paperclips, you would probably use a left-hand buffer. But if you were picking up cannon balls (which are much larger), no buffer would be used.

The open system call is used for opening an unbuffered file. The macro definitions used by this call differ from system to system. Since the examples have to work for both Unix and MS-DOS/Windows, conditional compilation (#ifdef/#endif) is used to bring in the correct files:

```
#include <sys/types.h>
#include <sys/stat.h>
#include <fcntl.h>

#ifdef __MSDOS__        // If we are MS-DOS
#include <io.h>         // Get the MS-DOS include file for raw I/O
#else /* __MSDOS__ */
#include <unistd.h>     // Get the Unix include file for raw I/O
#endif /* __MSDOS__ */
```

The syntax for an open call is:

```
file_descriptor = open(name, flags);    // Existing file
int file_descriptor = open(name, flags, mode);//New file
```

file_descriptor

An integer that is used to identify the file for the read, write, and close calls. If file_descriptor is less than 0, an error occurred.

name

Name of the file.

flags

Defined in the *fcntl.h* header file. Open flags are described in Table 16-6.

mode

Protection mode for the file. Normally this is 0666.

Table 16-6. Open flags

Flag	Meaning
O_RDONLY	Open for reading only.
O_WRONLY	Open for writing only.
O_RDWR	Open for reading and writing.
O_APPEND	Append new data at the end of the file.
O_CREAT	Create file (the file *mode* parameter required when this flag is present).
O_TRUNC	If the file exists, truncate it to 0 length.
O_EXCL	Fail if file exists.
O_BINARY	Open in binary mode (older Unix systems may not have this flag).

For example, to open the existing file *data.txt* in text mode for reading, you use the following:

```
data_fd = open("data.txt", O_RDONLY);
```

The next example shows how to create a file called *output.dat* for writing only:

```
out_fd = open("output.dat", O_CREAT|O_WRONLY, 0666);
```

Notice that you combined flags using the OR (|) operator. This is a quick and easy way of merging multiple flags.

When any program is initially run, three files are already opened. These are described in Table 16-7.

Table 16-7. Standard unbuffered files

File number	Description
0	Standard in
1	Standard out
2	Standard error

The format of the read call is:

```
read_size = read(file_descriptor, buffer, size);
```

read_size
>   The actual number of bytes read. A 0 indicates end-of-file, and a negative number indicates an error.

file_descriptor
>   File descriptor of an open file.

buffer
>   Pointer to a place to put the data that is read from the file.

size
>   Size of the data to be read. This is the size of the request. The actual number of bytes read may be less than this. (For example, you may run out of data.)

The format of a write call is:

```
write_size = write(file_descriptor, buffer, size);
```

write_size
>   Actual number of bytes written. A negative number indicates an error.

file_descriptor
>   File descriptor of an open file.

buffer
>   Pointer to the data to be written.

size
>   Size of the data to be written. The system will try to write this many bytes, but if the device is full or there is some other problem, a smaller number of bytes may be written.

Finally, the close call closes the file:

```
flag = close(file_descriptor)
```

flag
>   0 for success, negative for error.

file_descriptor
>   File descriptor of an open file.

Example 16-5 copies a file. Unbuffered I/O is used because of the large buffer size. It makes no sense to use buffered I/O to read 1K of data into a buffer (using an std::ifstream) and then transfer it into a 16K buffer.

Example 16-5. copy2/copy2.cpp

```
/***************************************
 * copy -- copy one file to another.    *
 *                                      *
 * Usage                                *
 *      copy <from> <to>                *
```

Example 16-5. copy2/copy2.cpp (continued)

```
 *                                         *
 * <from> -- the file to copy from         *
 * <to>   -- the file to copy into         *
 ***************************************/
#include <iostream>
#include <cstdlib>

#include <sys/types.h>
#include <sys/stat.h>
#include <fcntl.h>

#ifdef __WIN32__         // if we are Windows32
#include <io.h>          // Get the Windows32 include file for raw i/o
#else /* __WIN32__ */
#include <unistd.h>      // Get the Unix include file for raw i/o
#endif /* __WIN32__ */

const int BUFFER_SIZE = (16 * 1024); // use 16k buffers

int main(int argc, char *argv[])
{
    char  buffer[BUFFER_SIZE]; // buffer for data
    int   in_file;             // input file descriptor
    int   out_file;            // output file descriptor
    int   read_size;           // number of bytes on last read

    if (argc != 3) {
        std::cerr << "Error:Wrong number of arguments\n";
        std::cerr << "Usage is: copy <from> <to>\n";
        exit(8);
    }
    in_file = open(argv[1], O_RDONLY);
    if (in_file < 0) {
        std::cerr << "Error:Unable to open " << argv[1] << '\n';
        exit(8);
    }
    out_file = open(argv[2], O_WRONLY | O_TRUNC | O_CREAT, 0666);
    if (out_file < 0) {
        std::cerr << "Error:Unable to open " << argv[2] << '\n';
        exit(8);
    }
    while (true) {
        read_size = read(in_file, buffer, sizeof(buffer));

        if (read_size == 0)
            break;                  // end of file

        if (read_size < 0) {
            std::cerr << "Error:Read error\n";
            exit(8);
        }
        write(out_file, buffer, (unsigned int) read_size);
```

Example 16-5. copy2/copy2.cpp (continued)

```
    }
    close(in_file);
    close(out_file);
    return (0);
}
```

Several things should be noted about this program. First of all, the buffer size is defined as a constant, so it is easily modified. Rather than have to remember that 16K is 16,384, the programmer used the expression (16 * 1024). This form of the constant is obviously 16K.

If the user improperly uses the program, an error message results. To help the user get it right, the message tells how to use the program.

You may not read a full buffer for the last read. That is why read_size is used to determine the number of bytes to write.

Designing File Formats

Suppose you are designing a program to produce a graph. The height, width, limits, and scales are to be defined in a graph configuration file. You are also assigned to write a user-friendly program that asks the operator questions and writes a configuration file so he or she does not have to learn the text editor. How should you design a configuration file?

One way would be as follows:

    height (in inches)
    width (in inches)
    x lower limit
    x upper limit
    y lower limit
    y upper limit
    x-scale
    y-scale

A typical plotter configuration file might look like:

```
10.0
7.0
0
100
30
300
0.5
2.0
```

This file does contain all the data, but in looking at it, you have trouble identifying what, for example, is the value of the Y lower limit. A solution is to comment the file so the configuration program writes out not only the data, but also a string describing the data.

```
10.0        height (in inches)
7.0         width (in inches)
0           x lower limit
100         x upper limit
30          y lower limit
300         y upper limit
0.5         x-scale
2.0         y-scale
```

Now the file is human-readable. But suppose a user runs the plot program and types in the wrong filename, and the program gets the lunch menu for today instead of a plot configuration file. The program is probably going to get very upset when it tries to construct a plot whose dimensions are "BLT on white" versus "Meatloaf and gravy."

The result is that you wind up with egg on your face. There should be some way of identifying a file as a plot configuration file. One method of doing this is to put the words "Plot Configuration File" on the first line of the file. Then, when someone tries to give your program the wrong file, the program will print an error message.

This takes care of the wrong file problem, but what happens when you are asked to enhance the program and add optional logarithmic plotting? You could simply add another line to the configuration file, but what about all those old files? It's not reasonable to ask everyone to throw them away. The best thing to do (from a user's point of view) is to accept old format files. You can make this easier by putting a version number in the file.

A typical file now looks like:

```
Plot Configuration File V1.0
log         Logarithmic or normal plot
10.0        height (in inches)
7.0         width (in inches)
0           x lower limit
100         x upper limit
30          y lower limit
300         y upper limit
0.5         x-scale
2.0         y-scale
```

In binary files, it is common practice to put an identification number in the first four bytes of the file. This is called the *magic number*. The magic number should be different for each type of file.

One method for choosing a magic number is to start with the first four letters of the program name (e.g., *list*) and convert them to hex: 0x6c607374. Then add 0x80808080 to the number: 0xECE0F3F4.

This generates a magic number that is probably unique. The high bit is set on each byte to make the byte non-ASCII and avoid confusion between ASCII and binary files. On most Unix systems and Linux, you'll find a file called */etc/magic,* which contains information on other magic numbers used by various programs.

When reading and writing a binary file containing many different types of structures, it is easy to get lost. For example, you might read a name structure when you expected a size structure. This is usually not detected until later in the program. To locate this problem early, you can put magic numbers at the beginning of each structure. Then if the program reads the name structure and the magic number is not correct, it knows something is wrong.

Magic numbers for structures do not need to have the high bit set on each byte. Making the magic number just four ASCII characters makes it easy to pick out the beginning of structures in a file dump.

C-Style I/O Routines

C++ allows you to use the C I/O library in C++ programs. Many times this occurs because someone took a C program, translated it to C++, and didn't want to bother translating the I/O calls. In some cases, the old C library is better and easier to use than the new C++ library. For example, C string-conversion routines such as `std::sscanf` and `std::sprintf` use a far more compact formatting specification system than their C++ counterparts. (Note that it is a matter of taste whether or not compact is better.)

The declarations for the structures and functions used by the C I/O functions are stored in the standard include file `<cstdio>`.

The declaration for a file variable is:

```
std::FILE *file_variable;   /* Comment */
```

For example:

```
#include <cstdio>

std::FILE *in_file; /* File containing the input data */
```

Before a file can be used, it must be opened using the function `std::fopen`. `std::fopen` returns a pointer to the file structure for the file. The format for `std::fopen` is:

```
file_variable = std::fopen(name, mode);
```

file_variable
> A file variable.

name
> Actual name of the file ("data.txt", "temp.dat", etc.).

mode

Indicates whether the file is to be read or written. Mode is "w" for writing and "r" for reading.

The function `std::fclose` closes the file. The format of `std::fclose` is:

```
status = std::fclose(file_variable);
```

The variable `status` will be zero if the `std::fclose` was successful or nonzero for an error.

C provides three preopened files. These are listed in Table 16-8.

Table 16-8. Standard files

File	Description
stdin	Standard input (open for reading). Equivalent to C++'s `cin`.
stdout	Standard output (open for writing). Equivalent to C++'s `cout`.
stderr	Standard error (open for writing). Equivalent to C++'s `cerr`.
	(There is no C file equivalent to C++'s `clog`.)

The function `std::fgetc` reads a single character from a file. If there is no more data in the file, the function returns the constant EOF (EOF is defined in *cstdio*). Note that `std::fgetc` returns an integer, not a character. This is necessary because the EOF flag must be a noncharacter value.

Example 16-6 counts the number of characters in the file *input.txt*.

Example 16-6. copy/copy.cpp

```
#include <cstdio>
#include <cstdlib>       /* ANSI Standard C file */
#include <iostream>

const char FILE_NAME[] = "input.txt";   // Name of the input file

int main()
{
    int  count = 0;  // number of characters seen
    std::FILE *in_file;   // input file

    int ch;          // character or EOF flag from input

    in_file = std::fopen(FILE_NAME, "rb");
    if (in_file == NULL) {
        std::cerr << "Can not open " << FILE_NAME << '\n';
        exit(8);
    }

    while (true) {
        ch = std::fgetc(in_file);
        if (ch == EOF)
```

Example 16-6. copy/copy.cpp (continued)

```
            break;
        ++count;
    }
    std::cout << "Number of characters in " << FILE_NAME <<
        " is " << count << '\n';

    std::fclose(in_file);
    return (0);
}
```

A similar function, std::fputc, exists for writing a single character. Its format is:

```
    std::fputc(character, file);
```

The functions std::fgets and std::fputs work on one line at a time. The format of the std::fgets call is:

```
    line_ptr = std::fgets(line, size, file);
```

line_ptr
> Equal to line if the read was successful, or NULL if EOF or an error is detected.

line
> A character array where the function places the line.

size
> The size of the character array. std::fgets reads until it gets a line (complete with ending \n) or it reads size - 1 characters. It then ends the string with a null (\0).

For example:

```
        char    line[100];
        . . .
        std::fgets(line, sizeof(line), in_file);
```

std::fputs is similar to std::fgets except that it writes a line instead of reading one. The format of the std::fputs function is:

```
    line_ptr = std::fputs(line, file);
```

The parameters to std::fputs are similar to the ones for std::fgets. std::fputs needs no size because it gets the size of the line to write from the length of the line. (It keeps writing until it hits a null character, '\0').

> The C++ function getline reads and discards the end-of-line character ('\n'). The C std::fgets reads the entire line, including the end-of-line and stores it in the buffer. So the '\n' is put in the buffer when you use std::fgets. This can sometimes cause surprising results.

C-Style Conversion Routines

C++ uses the << operator for formatted output and the >> operator for formatted input. C has its own set of output functions (the pstd::printf family) and input conversion functions (the `std::scanf` functions). This section goes into the details of these C-style conversion routines.

The std::printf Family of Output Functions

C uses the `std::printf` function call and related functions for output. A `std::printf` call consists of two parts: a format that describes how to print the data and a list of data to print.

The general form of the `std::printf` call is:

```
std::printf(format, parameter-1, parameter-2, ...);
```

The *format* string is printed exactly. For example:

```
std::printf("Hello World\n");
```

prints:

```
Hello World
```

To print a number, you must put a % conversion in the format string. For example, when C sees %d in the format string, it takes the next parameter from the parameter list (which must be an integer) and prints it.

Figure 16-1 shows how the elements of the `std::printf` statement work to generate the final result.

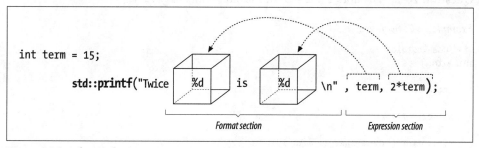

Figure 16-1. std::printf structure

The conversion %d is used for integers. Other types of parameters use different conversions. For example, if you want to print a floating-point number, you need a %f conversion. Table 16-9 lists the conversions.

Table 16-9. C-style conversions

Conversion	Variable type
%d	int
%ld	long int
%d	short int
%f	float

Table 16-9. C-style conversions (continued)

Conversion	Variable type
%lf	double
%u	unsigned int
%lu	unsigned long int
%u	unsigned short int
%s	char * (C-style string)
%c	char
%o	int (prints octal)
%x	int (prints hexadecimal)
%e	float (in the form *d.ddd*E+*dd*)

Many additional conversions also can be used in the std::printf statement. See your reference manual for details.

The std::printf function does not check for the correct number of parameters on each line. If you add too many, the extra parameters are ignored. If you add too few, C will make up values for the missing parameters. Also C does not type check parameters, so if you use a %d on a floating point number, you will get strange results.

Question 16-2: *Why does 2 + 2 = 5986? (Your results may vary.)*

Example 16-7. two/two.c

```
#include <cstdio>
int main( )
{
    int answer;

    answer = 2 + 2;

    std::printf("The answer is %d\n");
    return (0);
}
```

Question 16-3: *Why does 21 / 7 = 0? (Your results may vary.)*

Example 16-8. float3/float3.c

```
#include <cstdio>

int main( )
{
    float result;

    result = 21.0 / 7.0;
    std::printf("The result is %d\n", result);
```

Example 16-8. float3/float3.c (continued)

```
    return (0);
}
```

The function `std::fprintf` is similar to `std::printf` except that it takes one additional argument, the file to print to:

```
    std::fprintf(file, format, parameter-1, parameter-2, ...);
```

Another flavor of the `std::printf` family is the `std::sprintf` call. The first parameter of `std::sprintf` is a C-style string. The function formats the output and stores the result in the given string:

```
    std::sprintf(string, format, parameter-1, parameter-2, ...);
```

For example:

```
    char file_name[40];         /* The filename */

    /* Current file number for this segment */
    int file_number = 0;

    std::sprintf(file_name, "file.%d", file_number);
    ++file_number;
    out_file = std::fopen(file_name, "w");
```

> The return value of `std::sprintf` differs from system to system. The ANSI standard defines it as the number of characters stored in the string; however, some implementations of Unix C define it to be a pointer to the string.

The std::scanf Family of Input Functions

Reading is accomplished through the `std::scanf` family of calls. The `std::scanf` function is similar to `std::printf` in that it has sister functions: `std::fscanf` and `std::sscanf`. The `std::scanf` function reads the standard input (stdin in C terms, cin in C++ terms), parses the input, and stores the results in the parameters in the parameter list.

The format for a `scanf` function call is:

```
    number = scanf(format, &parameter1, . . .);
```

number
> Number of parameters successfully converted.

format
> Describes the data to be read.

parameter1
> First parameter to be read. Note the & in front of the parameter. These parameters must be passed by address.

If you forget to put & in front of each variable for std::scanf, the result can be a "Segmentation violation core dumped" or "Illegal memory access" error. In some cases a random variable or instruction will be modified. This is not common on Unix machines, but MS-DOS/Windows, with its lack of memory protection, cannot easily detect this problem. In MS-DOS/Windows, omitting & can cause a system crash.

There is one problem with this std::scanf: it's next to impossible to get the end-of-line handling right. However, there's a simple way to get around the limitations of std::scanf—don't use it. Instead, use std::fgets followed by the string version of std::scanf, the function std::sscanf:

```
char line[100];     // Line for data

std::fgets(line, sizeof(line), stdin);     // Read numbers
std::sscanf(line, "%d %d", &number1, &number2);
```

Finally, there is a file version of std::scanf, the function std::fscanf. It's identical to scanf except the first parameter is the file to be read. Again, this function is extremely difficult and should not be used. Use std::fgets and std::sscanf instead.

C-Style Binary I/O

Binary I/O is accomplished through two routines: std::fread and std::fwrite. The syntax for std::fread is:

```
read_size = std::fread(data_ptr, 1, size, file);
```

read_size
    Size of the data that was read. If this is less than size, an end-of-file or error occurred.

data_ptr
    Pointer to a buffer to receive the data being read.

1
    The constant 1. (For the reason behind this constant, see the sidebar.)

size
    Number of bytes to be read.

file
    Input file.

For example:

```
struct {
        int     width;
        int     height;
} rectangle;

if (std::fread(<static_cast<char *>&rectangle, 1,
```

```
            sizeof(rectangle), in_file) != sizeof(rectangle)) {
            std::fprintf(stderr, "Unable to read rectangle\n");
            exit (8);
        }
```

In this example you are reading in the structure rectangle. The & operator makes the structure into a pointer. The cast static_cast<char *> turns &rectangle into the proper parameter type, and the sizeof operator is used to determine how many bytes to read in as well as to check that the read was successful.

std::fwrite has a calling sequence similar to std::fread:

```
    write_size = std::fwrite(data_ptr, 1, size, file);
```

Question 16-4: *No matter what filename you give Example 16-9,* std::fopen *can't find it. Why?*

Example 16-9. fun-file/fun-file.cpp

```
#include <cstdio>
#include <cstdlib>

int main()
{
    char            name[100];  /* name of the file to use  */
    std::FILE         *in_file;   /* file for input */

    std::printf("Name? ");
    std::fgets(name, sizeof(name), stdin);

    in_file = std::fopen(name, "r");
    if (in_file == NULL) {
        std::fprintf(stderr, "Could not open file\n");
        exit(8);
    }
```

Example 16-9. fun-file/fun-file.cpp (continued)

```
    std::printf("File found\n");
    std::fclose(in_file);
    return (0);
}
```

C- Versus C++- Style I/O

Both C- and C++- style I/O have their own features and quirks. In this section we'll
discuss some of the differences between these two systems.

Simplicity

Let's say we want to write a simple checkbook program. We need to print an
account statement. We need some code to print each line of the account statement
(date, check number, payee, and amount).

In C the print statement looks like:

```
    std::printf("%2d/%2d/%02d %4d: %-40s %f6.2\n",
        check.date.month, check.date.day, check.date.year,
        check.number, check.payee, check.amount);
```

In C++ the print statement is:

```
    std::cout << setw(2) << check.date.month << '/' <<
                 setw(2) << check.date.day << '/' <<
                 setw(2) << setfill('0') << check.date.year << ' ' <<
                 setw(4) << check.number << ':' <<
                 setw(40) << setiosflags(std::ios::left) <<
                         check.payee <<
                 resetiosflags(std::ios::left) << ' ' <<
                 setw(6) << setprecision(2) <<
                 setiosflags(std::ios::fixed) <<
                 check.amount <<
                 setw(0) << '\n';
```

From this example we can clearly see that the C-style I/O is more compact. It is not
clear that compact is better. This author prefers the compact style of the C std::
printf functions, while many others prefer the verbosity of the C++ I/O system.
Besides if you're C++ programmers, you probably should program in C++ and not
bring legacy I/O systems into the mix.

Although it looks like C is more compact, things are not as obvious as they look. A
well-designed date class would have its own output operator. Thus we can simplify
our C++ code down to:

```
        std::cout << check.date <<
                setw(4) << check.number << ':' <<
                setw(40) << setiosflags(std::ios::left) <<
                        check.payee <<
```

```
resetiosflags(std::ios::left) << ' ' <<
setw(6) << setprecision(2) <<
setiosflags(std::ios::fixed) <<
check.amount <<
setw(0) << '\n';
```

But this assumes that only the date has an output operator. If we designed our check class correctly, it should have one as well. This means that our code now has been simplified down to:

```
std::cout << check << '\n';
```

Now this doesn't mean that complexity has gone away. It's merely been moved from outside the class to inside it.

This example serves to illustrate one of the key differences between C and C++. In C-style I/O, the information on how to manipulate the data (in this case, how to print it) is contained outside the data itself. In C++ it's possible to put the manipulation code and the data into a single class.

If we are writing out our checkbook information in only one place, the C version may be simpler and easier to work with. So for simple programs, you may want to consider using C-style I/O. But suppose that we wanted to print out the data to a number of places. If we used C-style I/O, we would have to replicate our format code all over the place or create a small function to do the printing. With C++'s classes, we can keep the printing information in one logical place. (As a person who's just had to rewrite all the C-style format statements in a rather large piece of code, I can tell you that putting the formatting information in one place, the object, has some advantages.)

Reliability

When you use C++-style I/O, the system automatically detects the type of the variable and performs the approbate conversion. It's impossible to get the types wrong.

With C-style I/O, it's easy to get the arguments to a std::printf mixed up, resulting in very strange results when you run the program. What's worse is that most compilers do not check std::printf calls and warn you if you make a mistake.

One special C I/O function you should be aware of is std::gets. This function gets a line from standard input *with no bounds-checking*. So:

```
std::gets(line);
```

is exactly like:

```
std::fgets(line, INFINITY, stdin);
```

If there are too many characters in an input line, the std::gets function will cause a buffer overflow and trash memory. This single function and its lack of bounds-checking has to be responsible for more crashes and security holes than any other single C function.* You should never use it. You can get in enough trouble with the more reliable C functions without having to play Russian roulette with this one.

Speed

I've done some benchmarks on C and C++ I/O for binary files. In general I've found the C I/O to be much faster. That's because the C I/O system is less flexible and has to deal with less overhead than the C++ system.

 I'm not talking about formatted I/O, just raw binary I/O. If you do formatted I/O in either system, you can expect your speed to go down tremendously. It's the single slowest system in the entire C and C++ library.

Which Should You Use?

Which I/O system is best? That depends on a large number of factors. First of all, any system you know is always going to be easier to use and more reliable than a system you don't know.

However, if you know both systems, C-style I/O is good for the simple stuff. If you're not doing anything fancy with classes and just want to write simple formatted reports, the C I/O system will do the job. However, for larger jobs, the C++-object oriented system with its object-oriented I/O system handles complexity and organizes complex information much better than C-style I/O.

But if you're learning I/O for the first time, I suggest that you stick with one I/O system, the C++ one. Learn C-style I/O only if you're forced to. (Say, for instance, you have to maintain some legacy code that uses the old C-style system.)

Programming Exercises

Exercise 16-1: Write a program that reads a file and counts the number of lines in it.

Exercise 16-2: Write a program to copy a file, expanding all tabs to multiple spaces. (For historical reasons—the Teletype again—almost all text files use a tab setting of 8 characters.)

Exercise 16-3: Write a program that reads a file containing a list of numbers and writes two files, one containing all the numbers divisible by 3 and another containing all the other numbers.

---

* As I am writing this, Microsoft has just released a security patch to Windows XP to fix a buffer overflow bug.

Exercise 16-4: Write a program that reads an ASCII file containing a list of numbers and writes a binary file containing the same list. Write a program that goes the other way so you can check your work.

Exercise 16-5: Write a program that copies a file and removes all characters with the high bit set (((ch & 0x80) != 0)).

Exercise 16-6: Design a file format to store a person's name, address, and other information. Write a program to read this file and produce a file containing a set of mailing labels.

Answers to Chapter Questions

Answer 16-1: The problem is that you are writing an ASCII file, but you wanted a binary file. In Unix, ASCII is the same as binary, so the program runs fine. In MS-DOS/Windows, the end-of-line issue causes problems. When you write a newline character (0x0a) to the file, a carriage return (0x0D) is added to the file. (Remember that end-of-line in MS-DOS/Windows is <carriage return><line feed>, or 0x0d, 0x0a.) Because of this editing, you get an extra carriage return (0x0d) in the output file.

To write binary data (without output editing) you need to open the file with the binary option:

```
out_file.open("test.out", std::ios::out | std::ios::binary);
```

Answer 16-2: The std::printf call does not check for the correct number of parameters. The statement:

```
std::printf("The answer is %d\n");
```

tells the std::printf to print the string "The answer is" followed by the answer. The problem is that the parameter containing the answer was omitted. When this happens, std::printf gets the answer from a random location and prints garbage.

Properly written, the std::printf statement is:

```
std::printf("The answer is %d\n", answer);
```

Answer 16-3: The std::printf call does not check the type of its parameters. You tell std::printf to print an integer number (%d) and supply it with a floating-point parameter (result). This mismatch causes unexpected results, such as printing the wrong answer.

When printing a floating-point number, you need a %f conversion. Properly written, our std::printf statement is:

```
std::printf("The answer is %f\n", result);
```

Answer 16-4: The problem is that std::fgets gets the entire line, including the newline character (\n). If you have a file named *sam*, the program reads sam\n and tries to look for a file by that name. Because there is no such file, the program reports an error.

The fix is to strip the newline character from the name:

```
name[strlen(name) - 1] = '\0';    /* Get rid of last character */
```

The error message in this case is poorly designed. True, you did not open the file, but the programmer could supply the user with more information. Are you trying to open the file for input or output? What is the name of the file you are trying to open? You don't even know whether the message you are getting is an error, a warning, or just part of the normal operation. A better error message is:

```
std::fprintf(stderr, "Error: Unable to open %s for input\n", name);
```

Notice that this message would also help us detect the programming error. When you typed in "sam", the error would be:

```
Error: Unable to open sam
for input
```

This clearly shows us that you are trying to open a file with a newline in its name.

## CHAPTER 17

Debugging and Optimization

Bloody instructions which, being learned, return to
plague the inventor.
—Shakespeare, on debugging

The hardest part of a program is not the design and writing, but the debugging phase. It is here that you find out how your program really works (instead of how you *think* it works).

As programs grow larger and larger, finding bugs becomes more and more difficult. Also, the cost of errors is growing. Software bugs and poor design decisions have cost people *billions* of dollars the last few years alone. In this chapter we'll go through techniques you can use to find and eliminate bugs.

Code Reviews

A code review is the process by which the programmer shows her code to her peers and they review it. Code reviews are the most effective way of making sure your code has a minimum number of bugs. Code reviews not only give you better code but also give you better programmers.

Producing an effective code review is an art. It requires good people-skills and management support. It takes time to get a good system in place.

Planning the Review

The first thing to consider when planning a code review is who will be on the team doing the review. Ideally you should try to have three to five people there in addition to the person who wrote the code. Fewer than three and you don't have enough people to do an effective review. More than five and you can't have an effective meeting. (In large meetings, people don't talk, they give speeches.)

At least one senior software engineer should be part of the group. He's there to make sure that the code being reviewed conforms to the overall design of the project it's written for. He also has enough experience so that he probably can spot more problems than the less experienced coders.

Ideally, you don't want management there. That's because whenever a non-technical boss shows up, you spend more time explaining things to her than reviewing code. If a manager decides she must be there, make sure she knows that her role is strictly as an observer.

One problem with code reviews is getting the team to actually attend the meetings. Bribery is one solution to this problem. Free drinks, cookies, bagels, or other eats can be used to help attendance. Lunch should also be considered.

The Review Meeting

All right: you've chosen the team, you've got a conference room, and somehow managed to get everyone into the meeting. What now?

First, you need to designate someone to take notes. This person's job is to capture all the important information generated in the meeting. This person should not be the writer of the code. The author should keep his own notes. That way, with two sets of notes, you can be sure that any changes recommended by the committee are performed.

The meeting starts with the author of the code explaining his work. How he does this is largely irrelevant. He can use the top down method, bottom up, or sideways with a left twist. As long as the other people in the room understand what he's done, he can explain his code any way he wants to.

The other people in the room should feel free to break into the conversation at any time with questions or suggestions, or when they notice a problem.

Comments should be constructive. Everything said should help make the code better. Comments such as "I think you need to check for an error return from that system call" fall into this category.

Comments like "I could have done that in half as much code" are not appropriate. This is not a competition. This is also not a design review, so don't criticize the design (unless it's flawed and will absolutely not work.)

It is important to keep the meeting on track. The purpose of the review is to make sure the code works. The meeting should be focused only on the code in front of you. Topics like new programming techniques, the latest Microsoft product, and what movie you saw last night do not belong here. They should wait until your regular gossip sessions when you and the rest of the gang hang around the copy machine to discuss the latest rumors.

Code reviews should last about one to two hours, three at the most. Any longer than that and the committee will start to skim code and skip steps just to get out of the meeting. Programmers are like a can of soda: after about three hours, they go flat and lifeless. If you need more time, break it into multiple reviews, preferably with different people doing the review each time.

If you do a review right, the result will be that you've caught a number of errors. But what's important is that those errors did not make it into the final product. Fixing something in the testing stage or, worse, after the product has shipped, is extremely costly.

There's one key advantage of code reviews that we haven't discussed yet: you not only get better programs, you get better programmers. When a mistake is caught at review time and pointed out to the programmer, she is probably not going to make that mistake again. The result is that the next program she generates will contain less errors.

One example of this occurred when I wrote the book *Practical C Programming*. I had a bad habit of using the word "that" in places where I shouldn't. The copy editor reviewed the book and crossed out about three to five "that"s per page. I got the job of editing the files and removing the approximately *2,000* extraneous uses of the word. As a result, O'Reilly and I produced a better book. But another result was that in all my subsequent books, I didn't make that mistake again.

Why People Don't Do Code Reviews

One of the main reasons that people don't do code reviews is that they are working on a tight schedule, and management has decided there isn't enough time to do them. This is a false economy. After all, is the goal to get code out on time or to get working code out on time? (If you eliminate the requirement that the code must work, you can cut down on development time tremendously.)

Code that has not been reviewed will be buggy. Hopefully these bugs are found during the testing phase where they are merely expensive to fix. Sometimes they make it into a release product where they are very expensive to fix. One of the cheapest times to fix bugs is during the coding phase, and code reviews are an excellent way to see that bugs are eliminated early. (As someone once put it, "Why is there never enough time to do things right, but always enough time to do them over?")

Metrics

Metrics are an important part of the code review process. They show how effective your review process is. With proper metrics, you can demonstrate to both the programmers and management that code reviews are effective and are saving the company money.

The metrics that should be collected for the code reviews are:

- The number of lines reviewed
- The time spent reviewing the code
- The number of defects found
- The defect density (defects per line of code)—computed
- The review rate (# lines reviewed per hour)—computed

Most review processes show a remarkable ability to find defects before the code enters the testing process. (There it costs 10–500 times as much to find defects.) Also, as you progress, you'll discover that the defect density goes down. This is because the review process not only makes for better code, but better programmers.

Serial Debugging

Before you start debugging, save the old, "working" copy of your program in a safe place. (If you are using a source control system such as SCCS, RCS, or PCVS, your last working version should be checked in.) Many times while you are searching for a problem, you may find it necessary to try out different solutions or to add temporary debugging code. Sometimes you will find you've been barking up the wrong tree and need to start over. That's when the last working copy becomes invaluable.

Once you have reproduced the problem, you must determine what caused it to happen. There are several methods for doing this.

Divide and Conquer

The divide and conquer method has already been briefly discussed in Chapter 7. It consists of putting in cout statements where you know the data is good (to make sure it really is good), where the data is bad, and several points in between. This way you can start zeroing in on the section of code that contains the error. More cout statements can further reduce the scope of the error until the bug is finally located.

The Confessional Method of Debugging

The confessional method of debugging is one by which the programmer explains his program to someone: an interested party, an uninterested party, a wall—it doesn't matter to whom he explains it as long as he talks about it.

A typical confessional session goes like this:

"Hey, Bill, could you take a look at this? My program has a bug in it. The output should be 8.0 and I'm getting –8.0. The output is computed using this formula—and I've checked out the payment value and rate and the date must be correct, unless there is something wrong with the leap-year code, which—thank you Bill, you've found my problem."

Bill never said a word.

This type of debugging is also called a *walkthrough*. Getting other people involved brings a fresh point of view to the process, and frequently other people can spot problems you have overlooked.

Debug-Only Code

The divide-and-conquer method uses temporary cout statements. They are put in as needed and taken out after they are used. The preprocessor conditional-compilation directives can be used to put in and take out debugging code. For example:

```
#ifdef DEBUG
    std::cout << "Width " << width << " Height " << height << '\n';
#endif /* DEBUG */
```

The program can be compiled with DEBUG undefined for normal use, and you can define it when debugging is needed.

Debug Command-Line Switch

Rather than using a compile-time switch to create a special version of the program, you can permanently include the debugging code and add a special program switch that will turn on debugging output. For example:

```
if (debug)
    std::cout << "Width " << width << " Height " << height << '\n';
```

where debug is a variable set if -D is present on the command line when the program is run.

Using a command-line option has the advantage that only a single version of the program exists. One of the problems with "debug-only" code is that unless the code is frequently used, it can easily become stale and out of date. Frequently a programmer tries to find a bug only to discover that the debug-only code is out of date and needs fixing.

Another advantage of the debug command-line option is that the user can turn on this switch in the field, save the output, and send it to you for analysis. The runtime option should be used in all cases instead of conditional compilation, unless there is some reason you do not want the customer to be able to get at the debugging information.

Some programs use the concept of a debug level. Level 0 outputs only minimal debugging information, level 1 more information, and on up to level 9, which outputs everything.

Another variation of this debugging technique can be seen in the Ghostscript* program by Aladdin Enterprises. This program implements the idea of debugging letters. The command option -Zxxx sets the debugging flags for each type of diagnostic output wanted. For example, f is the code for the fill algorithm, and p is the code for the path tracer. If I wanted to trace both these sections, I would specify -Zfp.

The option is implemented by code similar to this:

```
/*
 * Even though we only put 1 zero, C++ will fill in the
 * rest of the arrays with zeros
 */
char debug[128] = {0};      // The debugging flags

int main(int argc, char *argv[])
{
    while ((argc > 1) && (argv[1][0] == '-')) {
        switch (argv[1][1]) {
            /* .... normal switch .... */

            // Debug switch
            case 'Z':
                debug_ptr = &argv[1][2];
                // Loop for each letter
                while (*debug_ptr != '\0') {
                    debug[*debug_ptr] = 1;
                    ++debug_ptr;
                }
                break;
        }
        --argc;
        ++argv;
    }

    /* Rest of program */
}
```

Now that we've set the debug options, we can use them with code like the following:

```
if (debug['p'])
    std::cout << "Starting new path\n";
```

Ghostscript is a large program (some 25,000 lines) and rather difficult to debug. This form of debugging allows the user to get a great deal of information easily.

Going Through the Output

Enabling debug printout is a nice way of getting information, but many times there is so much data that the information you want can easily get lost.

---

* Ghostscript is a PostScript-like interpreter available from *http://www.ghostscript.com*.

The shell or command-line interpreter allows you to *redirect* what would normally go to the screen to a file through the use of the >file option. For example:

```
buggy -D9 >tmp.out
```

will run the program buggy with a high level of debug set and send the output to the file *tmp.out*.

The text editor on your system also makes a good file browser. You can use its search capabilities to look through the file containing the debug output for the information you want to find.

Interactive Debuggers

Most compiler manufacturers provide an interactive debugger. They give you the ability to stop the program at any point, examine and change variables, and "single-step" through the program. Because each debugger is different, a detailed discussion of each tool is not possible.

 Most compilers require that you enable debugging with a command-line option. If this option is not present, debugging information is not included in the program. If you used the compilations flags suggested in Chapter 2, your programs have been compiled with debugging enabled.

Basic Debugging Commands

However, we are going to discuss one debugger: GDB. This program is available for many Unix machines from the Free Software Foundation. Borland-C++ and Visual C++ have their own built-in debuggers. Although the exact syntax used by your debugger may be different, the principles shown here will work for all debuggers.

Basic GDB commands are the following:

run
    Start execution of a program.

break *line-number*
    Insert a breakpoint at the given line number. When a running program reaches a breakpoint, execution stops and control returns to the debugger.

break *function-name*
    Insert a breakpoint at the first line of the named function. Commonly, the command break int main is used to stop execution at the beginning of the program.

cont
    Continue execution after a breakpoint.

print *expression*
> Display the value of an expression.

step
> Execute a single line in the program. If the current statement calls a function, the function is single-stepped.

next
> Execute a single line in the program, but treat function calls as a single line. This command is used to skip over function calls.

list
> List the source program.

where
> Print the list of currently active functions.

status
> Print a list of breakpoints.

delete
> Remove a breakpoint.

Debugging a Simple Program

We have a program that should count the number of threes and sevens in a series of numbers. The problem is that it keeps getting the wrong answer for the number of sevens. Our program is shown in Example 17-1.

Example 17-1. seven/count.cpp

```
 1: #include <iostream>
 2:
 3: int seven_count;     /* number of seven's in the data */
 4: int data[5];         /* the data to count 3 and 7 in */
 5: int three_count;     /* the number of threes in the data */
 6:
 7: int main( ) {
 8:     int index;  /* index into the data */
 9:     void get_data(int data[]);
10:
11:     seven_count = 0;
12:     three_count = 0;
13:     get_data(data);
14:
15:     for (index = 1; index <= 5; ++index) {
16:         if (data[index] == 3)
17:             ++three_count;
18:         if (data[index] == 7)
19:             ++seven_count;
20:     }
21:     std::cout << "Three's " << three_count <<
22:             " Seven's " << seven_count << '\n';
```

Example 17-1. seven/count.cpp (continued)

```
23:     return (0);
24: }
25: /******************************************************
26:  * get_data -- get 5 numbers from the command line    *
27:  ******************************************************/
28: void get_data(int data[])
29: {
30:     std::cout << "Enter 5 numbers\n";
31:     std::cin >> data[1] >> data[2] >> data[3] >> data[4] >> data[5];
32: }
```

When we run this program with the data 3 7 3 0 2, the results are:

```
Threes 3 Sevens 3
```

We start by invoking the debugger (GDB) with the name of the program we are going to debug (count). The debugger initializes, outputs the prompt (gdb), and waits for a command.

```
% gdb count
GDB is free software and you are welcome to distribute copies of it
under certain conditions; type "show copying" to see the conditions.
There is absolutely no warranty for GDB; type "show warranty" for details.
GDB 4.12 (m68k-sun-sunos4.0.3),
Copyright 1994 Free Software Foundation, Inc...
(gdb)
```

We don't know where the variable is getting changed, so we'll start at the beginning and work our way through until we get an error. At every step, we'll display the variable seven_count just to make sure it's okay.

We need to stop the program at the beginning so we can single-step through it. The command break main tells GDB to set a breakpoint at the first instruction of the function main:

```
(gdb) break main
Breakpoint 1 at 0x22c2: file count.cpp, line 12.
(gdb)
```

The number 1 is used by GDB to identify the breakpoint. Now we need to start the program. The command run tells GDB to start the program, which will run until it hits the first breakpoint:

```
(gdb) run
Starting program: /usr/sdo/count/count

Breakpoint 1, main () at count.cpp:12
11          seven_count = 0;
(gdb)
```

The message Breakpoint 1, main... indicates that the program encountered a breakpoint and has now turned control over to debug.

We have reached the point where seven_count is initialized. The command next will execute a single statement, treating function calls as one statement. (The name of the command for your debugger may be different.) We go past the initialization and check to see whether it worked:

```
(gdb) next
12              three_count = 0;
(gdb) print seven_count
$1 = 0
(gdb)
```

Initialization worked. We try the next few lines, checking all the time:

```
(gdb) next
13              get_data(data);
(gdb) print seven_count
$2 = 0
(gdb) next
Enter 5 numbers
3 7 3 0 2
15              for (index = 1; index <= 5; ++index) {
(gdb) print seven_count
$3 = 2
(gdb)
```

seven_count somehow changed the value to 2. The last statement we executed was get_data(data); so something is going on in that function. We add a breakpoint at the beginning of get_data, get rid of the one at main, and start the program over with the run command:

```
(gdb) break get_data
Breakpoint 2 at 0x23b2: file count.cpp, line 30.
(gdb) info breakpoints
Num Type           Disp Enb Address      What
1   breakpoint     keep y   0x000022c2 in main at count.cpp:11
2   breakpoint     keep y   0x000023b2 in get_data(int *) at count.cpp:30
(gdb) delete 1
(gdb) run
The program being debugged has been started already.
Start it from the beginning? (y or n) Y
Starting program: /usr/sdo/count/count
Breakpoint 2, get_data (data=0x208f8) at count.cpp:30
(gdb)
```

We now start single-stepping again until we find the error:

```
Breakpoint 2, get_data (data=0x208f8) at count.cpp:30
30              std::cout << "Enter 5 numbers\n";
(gdb) print seven_count
$5 = 0
(gdb) next
31      std::cin >> data[1] >> data[2] >> data[3] >> data[4] >> data[5];
(gdb) print seven_count
$6 = 0
(gdb) next
```

```
Enter 5 numbers
3 7 3 0 2
32      }
(gdb) print seven_count
$7 = 2
(gdb) list 23
23          return (0);
24      }
25      /*****************************************************
26       * get_data -- get 5 numbers from the command line     *
27       *****************************************************/
28      void get_data(int data[])
29      {
30          std::cout << "Enter 5 numbers\n";
31      std::cin >> data[1] >> data[2] >> data[3] >> data[4] >> data[5];
32      }
```

At line 32 the data was good, but when we reached line 33, the data was bad, so the error is located at line 33 of the program, the std::cin. We've narrowed the problem down to one statement. By inspection, we can see that we are using data[5], an illegal member of the array data.

But why does seven_count go bad? Since data is only five elements long, there is no data[5]. However, the std::cin >> data[5] has to put the data someplace, so it decided to put it in a random memory location, in this case seven_count.

Debugging a Binary Search

The binary search algorithm is fairly simple. You want to see whether a given number is in an ordered list. Check your number against the one in the middle of the list. If it is the number, you were lucky—stop. If your number is bigger, you might find it in the top half of the list. Try the middle of the top half. If it is smaller, try the bottom half. Keep trying and dividing the list in half until you find the number or the list gets down to a single number.

The First Bug, a Segmentation Fault

Example 17-2 uses a binary search to see whether a number can be found in the file *numbers.dat*.

Example 17-2. search/search0.cpp

```
1: /*****************************************************
2: * search -- Search a set of numbers.               *
3: *                                                   *
4: * Usage:                                            *
5: *       search                                      *
6: *               you will be asked numbers to lookup *
7: *                                                   *
8: * Files:                                            *
```

Example 17-2. search/search0.cpp (continued)

```
 9:  *        numbers.dat -- numbers 1 per line to search    *
10:  *                         (Numbers must be ordered)       *
11:  ********************************************************/
12: #include <iostream>
13: #include <fstream>
14: #include <cstdlib>
15: #include <cstdio>
16: #include <assert.h>
17:
18: const int MAX_NUMBERS = 1000;    // Max numbers in file
19: const char *const DATA_FILE = "numbers.dat";// File with numbers
20:
21: int data[MAX_NUMBERS];   // Array of numbers to search
22: int max_count;           // Number of valid elements in data
23:
24: int main( )
25: {
26:     std::ifstream in_file;       // Input file
27:     int middle;          // Middle of our search range
28:     int low, high;       // Upper/lower bound
29:     int search;          // number to search for
30:
31:     in_file.open(DATA_FILE, std::ios::in);
32:     if (in_file.bad( )) {
33:         std::cerr << "Error:Unable to open " << DATA_FILE << '\n';
34:         exit (8);
35:     }
36:
37:     /*
38:      * Read in data
39:      */
40:
41:     max_count = 0;
42:     while (true) {
43:         char line[30];  // Line from the input file
44:
45:         if (in_file.eof( ))
46:             break;
47:
48:         in_file.getline(line, sizeof(line));
49:
50:         assert(max_count >= 0);
51:         assert(max_count < sizeof(data)/sizeof(data[0]));
52:         std::sscanf(line, "0", data[max_count]);
53:         if (data[max_count] == -1)
54:             break;
55:
56:         ++max_count;
57:     }
58:
59:     while (true) {
60:         std::cout << "Enter number to search for or -1 to quit:" ;
```

Example 17-2. search/search0.cpp (continued)

```
61:        std::cin >> search;
62:
63:        if (search == -1)
64:            break;
65:
66:        low = 0;
67:        high = max_count;
68:
69:        while (true) {
70:            middle = (low + high) / 2;
71:
72:            assert(middle >= 0);
73:            assert(middle < sizeof(data)/sizeof(data[0]));
74:            if (data[middle] == search) {
75:                std::cout << "Found at index " << middle << '\n';
76:            }
77:
78:            if (low == high) {
79:                std::cout << "Not found\n";
80:                break;
81:            }
82:
83:            assert(middle >= 0);
84:            assert(middle < sizeof(data)/sizeof(data[0]));
85:            if (data[middle] < search)
86:                low = middle;
87:            else
88:                high = middle;
89:        }
90:    }
91:    return (0);
92: }
```

Here's our data file:

File: numbers.dat

```
4
6
14
16
17
-1
```

When we run this program in Unix, the results are:

```
% search
Segmentation fault (core dumped)
```

When we run this program under Microsoft Windows, we get an application error (if we're lucky).

Either way this is not good. It means something went wrong in our program and the program tried to read memory that wasn't there. The debugger GDB can read this file and help us determine what happened:

```
% gdb search
GDB is free software and you are welcome to distribute copies of it
under certain conditions; type "show copying" to see the conditions.
There is absolutely no warranty for GDB; type "show warranty" for details.
GDB 4.12 (m68k-sun-sunos4.0.3),
Copyright 1994 Free Software Foundation, Inc...
(gdb) run
Starting program: /usr/sdo/search/search

Program received signal SIGSEGV, Segmentation fault.
0xec46320 in number ()
(gdb)
```

The debugger tells us we have been killed by a segmentation fault generated from the procedure number. But we don't have a procedure number! The routine must belong to the C++ library.

We now use the where command to find out which function called which function. This report is called a *stack trace*.

```
(gdb) where
#0  0xec46320 in number ()
#1  0xec45cc2 in _doscan ()
#2  0xec45b34 in sscanf ()
#3  0x2400 in main () at search.cpp:52
(gdb)
```

The current function is printed first, then the function that called it, and so on until we reach the outer function main. From this we see that number was called by _doscan, which was called by sscanf. We recognize sscanf as a library routine. The other functions must be subroutines called by sscanf. The last function that had control was the call of sscanf, which was made from line 52 of main.

Now we use the list command to take a look at the source for this line:

```
(gdb) list 52
45              if (in_file.eof( ))
46                  break;
47
48              in_file.getline(line, sizeof(line));
49
50              assert(max_count >= 0);
51              assert(max_count < sizeof(data)/sizeof(data[0]));
52              sscanf(line, "%d", data[max_count]);
53              if (data[max_count] == -1)
54                  break;
55
56              ++max_count;
(gdb) quit
The program is running.  Quit anyway (and kill it)? (y or n) Y
```

Line 52 caused the problem.

Another way of finding the problem is to single-step through the program until the error occurs. First list a section of the program to find a convenient place to put the breakpoint, and then start the execution and single-step process:

```
Script started on Mon Oct 31 10:07:19 1994
% gdb search
GDB is free software and you are welcome to distribute copies of it
under certain conditions; type "show copying" to see the conditions.
There is absolutely no warranty for GDB; type "show warranty" for details.
GDB 4.12 (m68k-sun-sunos4.0.3),
Copyright 1994 Free Software Foundation, Inc...
(gdb) list main
20        const char *const DATA_FILE = "numbers.dat"; // File with nums
21
22      int data[MAX_NUMBERS];  // Array of numbers to search
23      int max_count;          // Number of valid elements in data
24      int main()
25      {
26          std::ifstream in_file;    // Input file
27          int middle;          // Middle of our search range
28          int low, high;       // Upper/lower bound
29          int search;          // Number to search for
(gdb) break main
Breakpoint 1 at 0x2318: file search.cpp, line 25.
(gdb) run
Starting program: /usr/sdo/search/search

Breakpoint 1, main () at search.cpp:25
26          ifstream in_file;   // Input file
(gdb) step
31          in_file.open(DATA_FILE, ios::in);
(gdb) step
32          if (in_file.bad()) {
(gdb) step
41          max_count = 0;
(gdb) step
45              if (in_file.eof())
(gdb) step
48              in_file.getline(line, sizeof(line));
(gdb) step
50              assert(max_count >= 0);
(gdb) step
51              assert(max_count < sizeof(data)/sizeof(data[0]));
(gdb) step
52              sscanf(line, "%d", data[max_count]);
(gdb) step

Program received signal SIGSEGV, Segmentation fault.
0xec46320 in number ()
(gdb) quit
The program is running.  Quit anyway (and kill it)? (y or n) y
```

This method, too, points at line 52 as the culprit. On inspection we notice that we forgot to put an ampersand (&) in front of the third parameter for std::sscanf. So we change line 52 from:

```
std::sscanf(line, "%d", data[max_count]);
```

to:

```
std::sscanf(line, "%d", &data[max_count]);
```

and try again.

 You might wonder why we use the function sscanf when the line:

```
in_file >> data[max_count];
```

performs the same function.

The answer is simple. We used sscanf to cause problems. Without the pointer error, we would have nothing to debug. The in_file statement is more reliable, and reliable code has no place in a chapter on debugging.

The Unintended Infinite Loop

Rather than fix the std::scanf call, we've decided to enter the 21st century and use C++ style I/O calls. The first number in our list is 4, so we try it. This time our output looks like:

```
Enter number to search for or -1 to quit: 4
Found at index 0
Found at index 0
Not found
Enter number to search for or -1 to quit: ^C
```

The program should find the number, let us know it's at index 0, and then ask for another number. Instead we get two found messages and one not found message. We know that everything is running smoothly up to the time we get the first found message. After that things go downhill.

Getting back into the debugger, we use the list command to locate the found message and put a breakpoint there:

```
% gdb search
GDB is free software and you are welcome to distribute copies of it
under certain conditions; type "show copying" to see the conditions.
There is absolutely no warranty for GDB; type "show warranty" for details.
GDB 4.12 (m68k-sun-sunos4.0.3),
Copyright 1994 Free Software Foundation, Inc...
(gdb) list 69,81
69              while (true) {
70                  middle = (low + high) / 2;
71
72                  assert(middle >= 0);
73                  assert(middle <sizeof(data)/sizeof(data[0]));
```

```
74                  if (data[middle] == search) {
75                      std::cout << "Found at index " << middle << '\n';
76                  }
77
78                  if (low == high) {
79                      std::cout << "Not found\n";
80                      break;
81                  }
(gdb) break 75
Breakpoint 1 at 0x249e: file search.cpp, line 71.
(gdb) run
Starting program: /usr/sdo/search/search
Enter number to search for or -1 to quit: 4

Breakpoint 1, main () at search.cpp:71
75                      std::cout << "Found at index " << middle << '\n';
(gdb) step
Found at index 0
78                  if (low == high) {
(gdb) step
83              assert(middle >= 0);
(gdb) step
84              assert(middle <sizeof(data)/sizeof(data[0]));
(gdb) step
85              if (data[middle] < search)
(gdb) step
88                  high = middle;
(gdb) step
70              middle = (low + high) / 2;
(gdb) step
72              assert(middle >= 0);
(gdb) step
73              assert(middle <sizeof(data)/sizeof(data[0]));
(gdb) step
74                  if (data[middle] == search) {
(gdb) step
75                      std::cout << "Found at index " << middle << '\n';
(gdb) step
Found at index 0
78                  if (low == high) {
(gdb) quit
The program is running.  Quit anyway (and kill it)? (y or n) y
```

The program doesn't exit the loop. Instead it continues with the search. Because the number has already been found, this search results in strange behavior. We are missing a break after the cout.

We need to change:

```
if (data[middle] == search) {
    std::cout << "Found at index " << middle << '\n';
}
```

to:

```
    if (data[middle] == search) {
        std::cout << "Found at index " << middle << '\n';
        break;
    }
```

Making this fix, we try the program again:

```
% search
Enter number to search for or -1 to quit: 4
Found at index 0
Enter number to search for or -1 to quit: 6
Found at index 1
Enter number to search for or -1 to quit: 3
Not found
Enter number to search for or -1 to quit: 5
program runs forever (or until we abort it)
```

We have a runaway program. This time, instead of setting a breakpoint, we just start running the program. After a few seconds pass and we believe that we are stuck in the infinite loop, we stop the program with a control-C (^C). Normally this would abort the program and return us to the shell prompt. Since we are running with the debugger, it returns control to GDB:

```
% gdb search
GDB is free software and you are welcome to distribute copies of it
under certain conditions; type "show copying" to see the conditions.
There is absolutely no warranty for GDB; type "show warranty" for details.
GDB 4.12 (m68k-sun-sunos4.0.3),
Copyright 1994 Free Software Foundation, Inc...
(gdb) run
Starting program: /usr/sdo/search/search
Enter number to search for or -1 to quit: 5
^C
Program received signal SIGINT, Interrupt.
0x2500 in main () at search.cpp:79
79                      if (data[middle] < search)
```

Now we can use the single-step command to step through the infinite loop, looking at key values along the way.

```
87                      if (data[middle] < search)
(gdb) print middle
$1 = 0
(gdb) print data[middle]
$2 = 4
(gdb) print search
$3 = 5
(gdb) step
88                      low = middle;
(gdb) step
71                      middle = (low + high) / 2;
(gdb) step
73                      assert(middle >= 0);
(gdb) step
74                      assert(middle <sizeof(data)/sizeof(data[0]));
```

```
(gdb) step
75                      if (data[middle] == search) {
(gdb) step
80                      if (low == high) {
(gdb) step
85                      assert(middle >= 0);
(gdb) step
86                      assert(middle <sizeof(data)/sizeof(data[0]));
(gdb) step
87                      if (data[middle] < search)
(gdb) step
88                          low = middle;
(gdb) step
71                      middle = (low + high) / 2;
(gdb) step
73                      assert(middle >= 0);
(gdb) step
74                      assert(middle <sizeof(data)/sizeof(data[0]));
(gdb) step
75                      if (data[middle] == search) {
(gdb) step
80                      if (low == high) {
(gdb) step
85                      assert(middle >= 0);
(gdb) step
86                      assert(middle <sizeof(data)/sizeof(data[0]));
(gdb) step
87                      if (data[middle] < search)
(gdb) step
88                          low = middle;
(gdb) step
71                      middle = (low + high) / 2;
(gdb) step
73                      assert(middle >= 0);
(gdb) step
74                      assert(middle <sizeof(data)/sizeof(data[0]));
(gdb) step
75                      if (data[middle] == search) {
(gdb) step
80                      if (low == high) {
(gdb) step
85                      assert(middle >= 0);
(gdb) step
86                      assert(middle <sizeof(data)/sizeof(data[0]));
(gdb) step
87                      if (data[middle] < search)
(gdb) step
88                          low = middle;
(gdb) step
71                      middle = (low + high) / 2;
(gdb) step
73                      assert(middle >= 0);
(gdb) step
74                      assert(middle <sizeof(data)/sizeof(data[0]));
```

```
(gdb) step
75                      if (data[middle] == search) {
(gdb) print low
$5 = 0
(gdb) print middle
$6 = 0
(gdb) print high
$7 = 1
(gdb) print search
$8 = 5
(gdb) print data[0]
$9 = 4
(gdb) print data[1]
$10 = 6
(gdb) quit
The program is running.  Quit anyway (and kill it)? (y or n) y
```

The problem is that we have reached a point where the following is true:

```
low = 0  middle = 0  high = 1
```

The item we are searching for falls exactly between elements 0 and 1. Our algorithm has an off-by-one error. Obviously the middle element does not match. If it did, we'd exit with a found at message. So there is no point including the middle element in our new search range. Our code to adjust the interval is:

```
if (data[middle] < search)
    low = middle;
else
    high = middle;
```

It should be:

```
if (data[middle] < search)
    low = middle + 1;
else
    high = middle - 1;
```

The full version of the corrected program is shown in Example 17-3.

Example 17-3. search/search4.cpp

```
 1: /*******************************************************
 2:  * search -- Search a set of numbers.                  *
 3:  *                                                     *
 4:  * Usage:                                              *
 5:  *      search                                         *
 6:  *              you will be asked numbers to lookup    *
 7:  *                                                     *
 8:  * Files:                                              *
 9:  *      numbers.dat -- numbers 1 per line to search    *
10:  *                      (Numbers must be ordered)      *
11:  *******************************************************/
12: #include <iostream>
13: #include <fstream>
14: #include <cstdlib>
```

Example 17-3. search/search4.cpp (continued)

```cpp
15: #include <cstdio>
16: #include <assert.h>
17:
18: const int MAX_NUMBERS = 1000;    // Max numbers in file
19: const char *const DATA_FILE = "numbers.dat";// File with numbers
20:
21: int data[MAX_NUMBERS];   // Array of numbers to search
22: int max_count;           // Number of valid elements in data
23: int main()
24: {
25:     std::ifstream in_file;      // Input file
26:     int middle;             // Middle of our search range
27:     int low, high;          // Upper/lower bound
28:     int search;             // number to search for
29:
30:     in_file.open(DATA_FILE, std::ios::in);
31:     if (in_file.bad()) {
32:         std::cerr << "Error:Unable to open " << DATA_FILE << '\n';
33:         exit (8);
34:     }
35:
36:     /*
37:      * Read in data
38:      */
39:
40:     max_count = 0;
41:
42:     while (true) {
43:         char line[30];   // Line from the input file
44:
45:         if (in_file.eof())
46:             break;
47:
48:         in_file.getline(line, sizeof(line));
49:
50:         assert(max_count >= 0);
51:         assert(max_count < sizeof(data)/sizeof(data[0]));
52:         std::sscanf(line, "0", &data[max_count]);
53:         if (data[max_count] == -1)
54:             break;
55:
56:         ++max_count;
57:     }
58:
59:     while (true) {
60:         std::cout << "Enter number to search for or -1 to quit:" ;
61:         std::cin >> search;
62:
63:         if (search == -1)
64:             break;
65:
66:         low = 0;
```

Example 17-3. search/search4.cpp (continued)

```
67:            high = max_count;
68:
69:            while (true) {
70:                if (low >= high) {
71:                    std::cout << "Not found\n";
72:                    break;
73:                }
74:                middle = (low + high) / 2;
75:
76:                assert(middle >= 0);
77:                assert(middle < sizeof(data)/sizeof(data[0]));
78:                if (data[middle] == search) {
79:                    std::cout << "Found at index " << middle << '\n';
80:                    break;
81:                }
82:
83:                assert(middle >= 0);
84:                assert(middle < sizeof(data)/sizeof(data[0]));
85:                if (data[middle] < search)
86:                    low = middle +1;
87:                else
88:                    high = middle -1;
89:            }
90:        }
91:    return (0);
92: }
```

Interactive Debugging Tips and Tricks

Interactive debuggers work well for most programs, but sometimes they need a little help. Consider Example 17-4. We try to debug it and find it fails when point_number is 735. Why it fails on call 735 to lookup we don't know, but the first 734 calls work and the next one doesn't. All we know is that we call float_point_color 800 times, it calls lookup 800 times, and something goes wrong at 735.

We want to put a breakpoint before the calculation is made. When the debugger inserts a breakpoint into a program, the program will execute normally until it hits the breakpoint, then control will return to the debugger. This allows the user to examine and change variables, as well as perform other debugging commands. When a cont command is typed, the program will continue execution as though nothing happened. The problem is that there are 734 points before the one we want, and we don't want to stop for each of them.

Example 17-4. debug/cstop.cpp

```
float point_color(int point_number)
{
    float correction;          // color correction factor
    extern float red,green,blue;// current colors
```

Example 17-4. debug/cstop.cpp (continued)

```
    // Lookup color correction
    extern lookup(int point_number);

    correction = lookup(point_number);
    return (red*correction * 100.0 +
            blue*correction * 10.0 +
            green*correction);
}
```

How do we force the debugger to stop only when point_number == 735? We can do this by adding the following temporary code:

```
48:     if (point_number == 735)  /* ### Temp code ### */
49:         point_number = point_number;   /* ### Line to stop on ### */
```

Line 49 does nothing useful except serve as a line that the debugger can stop on. We can put a breakpoint on that line with the command break 49. The program will process the first 734 points, then execute line 49, hitting the breakpoint. (Some debuggers have a conditional breakpoint. The advanced GDB command break 49 if point_number == 735 would also work; however, your debugger may not have such advanced features.)

Runtime Errors

Runtime errors are usually the easiest to fix. Following are some types of runtime errors:

Segmentation violation

This error indicates that the program tried to dereference a pointer containing a bad value.

Stack overflow

The program tried to use too many temporary variables. Sometimes this means the program is too big or using too many big temporary arrays, but most of the time this is due to infinite recursion problems. Almost all Unix systems automatically check for this error. Borland-C++ will check for stack overflow only if the compile-time option -N is used.

Divide by zero

Divide by zero is an obvious error. Unix masks the problem by reporting an integer divide by zero with the error message Floating exception (core dumped).

In all cases, program execution will be stopped. In Unix, an image of the running program, called a core file, is written out. This file can be analyzed by the debugger to determine why the program died. Our first run of Example 17-4 resulted in a core dump. (One of the problems with core dumps is that the core files are very big and can fill up a disk quickly.)

One problem with runtime errors is that when they occur, program execution stops immediately. The buffers for buffered files are not flushed. This can lead to some unexpected surprises. Consider Example 17-5.

Example 17-5. debug/flush.cpp

```
#include <iostream>
int main( )
{
    int i,j;    /* two random integers */

    i = 1;
    j = 0;
    std::cout << "Starting\n";
    std::cout << "Before divide...";
    i = i / j;  // divide by zero error
    std::cout << "After\n";
    return(0);
}
```

When run, this program outputs:

```
Starting
Floating exception (core dumped)
```

This might lead you to think the divide had never started, when in fact it had. What happened to the message "Before divide..."? The cout statement executed and put the message in a buffer; then the program died. The buffer never got a chance to be emptied.

By putting explicit flush-buffer commands inside the code, we get a truer picture of what is happening, as shown in Example 17-6.

Example 17-6. debug/flush2.cpp

```
#include <iostream>
int main( )
{
    int i,j;    /* two random integers */

    i = 1;
    j = 0;
    std::cout << "Starting\n";
    std::cout.flush( );
    std::cout << "Before divide...";
    std::cout.flush( );
    i = i / j;  // divide by zero error
    std::cout << "After\n";
    std::cout.flush( );
    return(0);
}
```

The flush statement makes the I/O less efficient, but more current.

Optimization

And now a word on optimization: *don't*. Most programs do not need to be optimized. They run fast enough. Who cares whether an interactive program takes 0.5 seconds to start up instead of 0.2?

To be fair, there are a lot of slow programs out there that can be sped up. This is usually done not by the simple optimization steps shown in this chapter, but by replacing poorly designed core algorithms with more efficient ones.

For a well-written program, the simplest way to get your program to run faster is to get a faster computer. Many times it is cheaper to buy a more powerful machine than it is to optimize a program, because you may introduce new errors into your code. Don't expect miracles from optimization. Usually most programs can be sped up only 10 percent to 20 percent.

Profiling

In general you'll find that your program spends 90% of its time in 10% of your code. That means that optimizing that code will give the greatest results. Most compilers come with a profile that lets you instrument your code and identify which sections are taking up the most time. Unfortunately each tool is different and a discussion of all of the is not possible in this book.

Analyzing and Optimizing code

Example 17-7 initializes a matrix (two-dimensional array). Let's take a look at this code and see if there's any way of making it faster

Example 17-7. matrix/matrix1.cpp

```
#include <assert.h>
const int X_SIZE = 60;
const int Y_SIZE = 30;

int matrix[X_SIZE][Y_SIZE];

void init_matrix()
{
    int x,y;     // current element to initialize

    for (x = 0; x < X_SIZE; ++x) {
        for (y = 0; y < Y_SIZE; ++y) {
            assert((x >= 0) && (x < X_SIZE));
            assert((y >= 0) && (y < Y_SIZE));
            matrix[x][y] = -1;
        }
    }
}
```

Register Declarations

How can this function be optimized? First we notice we are using two local variables. By using the qualifier register on these variables, we tell the compiler that they are frequently used and should be placed in fast registers instead of relatively slow main memory. The number of registers varies from computer to computer. Slow machines like the PC have 2, most Unix systems have about 11, and supercomputers can have as many as 128. It is possible to declare more register variables than you have registers. C++ will put the extra variables in main memory.

 The register form of optimization has been overtaken by compiler technology. Most compilers do a better job of register allocation than you can by manually adding register hints, and they ignore any user register modifiers. However, this technique is still valid for older compilers.

The program now looks like Example 17-8.

Example 17-8. matrix/matrix2.cpp

```
#include <assert.h>
const int X_SIZE = 60;
const int Y_SIZE = 30;

int matrix[X_SIZE][Y_SIZE];

void init_matrix()
{
    register int x,y;    // current element to initialize

    for (x = 0; x < X_SIZE; ++x) {
        for (y = 0; y < Y_SIZE; ++y) {
            assert((x >= 0) && (x < X_SIZE));
            assert((y >= 0) && (y < Y_SIZE));
            matrix[x][y] = -1;
        }
    }
}
```

Loop ordering

The outer loop is executed 60 times. This means the overhead associated with starting the inner loop is executed 60 times. If we reverse the order of the loops, we will have to deal with the inner loop only 30 times.

In general, loops should be ordered so the innermost loop is the most complex and the outermost loop is the simplest. Example 17-9 contains the init_matrix function with the loops reordered.

Example 17-9. matrix/matrix3.cpp

```cpp
#include <assert.h>
const int X_SIZE = 60;
const int Y_SIZE = 30;

int matrix[X_SIZE][Y_SIZE];

void init_matrix()
{
    register int x,y;      // current element to initialize

    for (y = 0; y < Y_SIZE; ++y) {
        for (x = 0; x < X_SIZE; ++x) {
            assert((x >= 0) && (x < X_SIZE));
            assert((y >= 0) && (y < Y_SIZE));
            matrix[x][y] = -1;
        }
    }
}
```

The power of powers of 2

Indexing an array requires a multiplication operation. For example, to execute the line:

```cpp
matrix[x][y] = -1;
```

the program must compute the location where we want to put the −1. To do this, the program must perform the following steps:

1. Get the address of the matrix.

2. Compute x * Y_SIZE.

3. Compute y.

4. Add up all three parts to form the address. In C++ this code looks like:

```cpp
*(matrix + (x * Y_SIZE) + y) = -1;
```

However, you typically won't write matrix accesses this way because C++ handles the details. But being aware of the details can help you generate more efficient code.

Almost all C++ compilers will convert multiplication by a power of 2 (2, 4, 8, ...) into shifts, thus taking an expensive operation (multiply) and changing it into an inexpensive operation (shift).

For example:

```cpp
i = 32 * j;
```

is compiled as:

```cpp
i = j << 5; /* 2**5 == 32 */
```

In Example 17-9 we define Y_SIZE as 30, which is not a power of 2. By increasing Y_SIZE to 32, we waste some memory but get a faster program.

Example 17-10 shows how we can take advantage of a power of 2.

Example 17-10. matrix/matrix4.cpp

```
#include <assert.h>
const int X_SIZE = 60;
const int Y_SIZE = 32;

int matrix[X_SIZE][Y_SIZE];

void init_matrix()
{
    register int x,y;     // current element to initialize

    for (y = 0; y < Y_SIZE; ++y) {
        for (x = 0; x < X_SIZE; ++x) {
            assert((x >= 0) && (x < X_SIZE));
            assert((y >= 0) && (y < Y_SIZE));
            matrix[x][y] = -1;
        }
    }
}
```

Making use of pointers

Since we are initializing consecutive memory locations, we can optimize the program even further. We can initialize the matrix by starting at the first location and storing a −1 in the next X_SIZE * Y_SIZE elements. Using this method, we cut the number of loops down to one. The indexing of the matrix has changed from a standard index (matrix[x][y]), requiring a shift and add, into a pointer dereference (*matrix_ptr) and an increment (++matrix_ptr). In Example 17-11, we've turned our arrays into pointers.

Example 17-11. matrix/matrix5.cpp

```
const int X_SIZE = 60;
const int Y_SIZE = 30;

int matrix[X_SIZE][Y_SIZE];

void init_matrix()
{
    register int index;        // element counter
    register int *matrix_ptr;  // Current element

    matrix_ptr = &matrix[0][0];
    for (index = 0; index < X_SIZE * Y_SIZE; ++index) {
        *matrix_ptr = -1;
        ++matrix_ptr;
    }
}
```

But why have both a loop counter and a matrix_ptr? Couldn't we combine the two? In fact we can. In Example 17-12 we've successfully eliminated the loop counter by combining it with the array pointer.

Example 17-12. matrix/matrix6.cpp

```
const int X_SIZE = 60;
const int Y_SIZE = 30;

int matrix[X_SIZE][Y_SIZE];

void init_matrix()
{
    register int *matrix_ptr;    // Current element

    for (matrix_ptr = &matrix[0][0];
            matrix_ptr <= &matrix[X_SIZE-1][Y_SIZE-1];
            ++matrix_ptr) {

        *matrix_ptr = -1;
    }
}
```

The function is now well optimized. The only way we could make it better is to manually code it into assembly language. This might make it faster; however, assembly language is highly nonportable and very error-prone. But in this case, someone else has written a highly optimized assembly-language (usually) function that we can use to do the job, and it's a part of the standard C++ library.

Using the System Library

The library routine memset can be used to fill a matrix or array with a single character value. We can use it to initialize the matrix in this program. Frequently used library subroutines such as memset are often coded into assembly language and may make use of special processor-dependent tricks to do the job faster than could be done in C++. In Example 17-13 we let the function memset do the work.

Example 17-13. matrix/matrix7.cpp

```
#include <cstring>

const int X_SIZE = 60;
const int Y_SIZE = 30;

int matrix[X_SIZE][Y_SIZE];

void init_matrix()
{
    std::memset(matrix, -1, sizeof(matrix));
}
```

Now our function consists of only a single function call. It seems a shame to have to call a function just to call another function. We have to pay for the overhead of two function calls. It would be better if we called memset from the main function. Why don't we rewrite all the functions that call init_matrix so they use memset? Because it has several hundred init_matrix calls, and we don't want to do all that editing.

So how do we get rid of the overhead of a function call? By making the function inline. Our final version of the function uses inline to eliminate all the call overhead. It can be seen in Example 17-14.

Example 17-14. matrix/matrix8.cpp

```cpp
#include <cstring>

const int X_SIZE = 60;
const int Y_SIZE = 30;

int matrix[X_SIZE][Y_SIZE];

inline void init_matrix()
{
    std::memset(matrix, -1, sizeof(matrix));
}
```

Why does memset successfully initialize the matrix to −1, but when we try to use it to set every element to 1, we fail?

```cpp
#include <cstring>

const int X_SIZE = 60;
const int Y_SIZE = 30;

int matrix[X_SIZE][Y_SIZE];

inline void init_matrix() {
    memset(matrix, 1, sizeof(matrix));
}
```

How to Optimize

Our matrix initialization function illustrates several optimizing strategies. These are:

Removing invariant code
Code that does not need to be put inside a loop should be put outside the loop. For example:

```cpp
for (i = 0; i < 10; ++i)
    matrix[i] = i + j * 10;
```

can be written as:

```cpp
j_times_10 = j * 10;
for (i = 0; i < 10; ++i)
    matrix[i] = i + j_times_10;
for (i = 0; i < 10; ++i)
```

Most good optimizing compilers will do this work for you if possible.

Loop ordering

Nested loops should be ordered with the simplest loop outermost and the most complex loops innermost.

Reference parameters

Use constant reference parameters (const *type&*) instead of constant parameters for structures, unions, and classes.

Powers of two

Use a power of two when doing integer multiply or divide. Most compilers will substitute a shift for the operation.

Pointers

Using pointers to go through an array is generally faster using an index, but pointers are more tricky to use.

Inline functions

Using inline functions eliminates the overhead associated with a function call. It also can make the code bigger and a little more difficult to debug. (See the case study below.)

Reduction in strength

This is a fancy way of saying use cheap operations instead of expensive ones. Table 17-1 lists the relative cost of common operations.

Table 17-1. Relative cost of operations

Operation	Relative cost
File input and output (<< and >>), including the C functions printf and scanf	1,000
new and delete	800
Trigonometric functions (sin, cos, ...)	500
Floating point (any operation)	100
Integer divide	30
Integer multiply	20
Function call	10
assert[a]	8
Simple array index	6
Shifts	5
Add/subtract	5
Pointer dereference	2
Bitwise AND, OR, NOT	1
Logical AND, OR, NOT	1

[a] The assert statement can be removed by using the compile time option -DNDEBUG. However, these statements should be removed with care, as they provide insurance against bad things happening in your program. Sometimes the fastest way is not the best.

The C++ I/O system and the C formatting functions called using `std::scanf`, `std::printf`, and `std::sscanf` are extremely costly because they have to go through the format string one character at a time looking for a format conversion character (%). They then have to do a costly conversion between a character string and a number. These functions should be avoided in time-critical sections of code.

Case Study: Inline Functions Versus Normal Functions

I once worked on writing a word-processing program for a large computer manufacturer. We had a function `next_char` that was used to get the next character from the current file. It was used in thousands of places throughout the program. When we first tested the program with `next_char` written as a function, the program was unacceptably slow. Analyzing our program, we found that 90 percent of the time was spent in `next_char`. So we changed it to an inline function. The speed doubled; however, our code size went up 40 percent and required a memory expansion card to work. So the speed was all right, but the size was unacceptable. We finally had to write the routine as a function in hand-optimized assembly language to get both the size and the speed to acceptable levels.

Case Study: Optimizing a Color-Rendering Algorithm

I once was asked to optimize a program that did color rendering for a large picture. The problem was that the program took eight hours to process a single picture. This limited us to doing one picture a day.

The first thing I did was run the program on a machine with a floating-point accelerator. This brought the time down to about six hours. Next I got permission to use a high-speed RISC computer that belonged to another project but was currently sitting idle. That reduced the time to two hours.

I saved six hours solely by using faster machines. No code had changed yet.

Two fairly simple functions were being called only once from the innermost loop. Rewriting these functions as macros saved about 15 minutes.

Next I changed all the floating-point operations I could from floating-point to integer. The savings amounted to 30 minutes out of a 1:45 run.

Then I noticed the program was spending about 5 minutes reading an ASCII file containing a long list of floating-point numbers used in the conversion process. Knowing that scanf is an extremely expensive function, I cut the initialization process down to almost nothing by making the file binary. Total runtime was now down to 1:10.

By carefully inspecting the code and using every trick I knew, I saved another 5 minutes, leaving me 5 minutes short of my goal of an hour per run. At this point my project was refocused and the program put in mothballs for use at some future date.

Programming Exercises

Exercise 17-1: Take one of your previous programs and run it using the interactive debugger to examine several intermediate values.

Exercise 17-2: Write a matrix-multiply function. Create a test program that not only tests the function, but times it as well. Optimize the program using pointers and determine the time savings.

Exercise 17-3: Write a program to sum the elements in an array. Optimize it.

Exercise 17-4: Write a program that counts the number of bits in a character array. Optimize it through the use of register-integer variables. Time it on several different arrays of different sizes. How much time do you save?

Exercise 17-5: Write your own version of the library function memcpy. Optimize it. Most implementations of memcpy are written in assembly language and take advantage of all the quirks and tricks of the processor. How does your memcpy compare to theirs?

Answers to Chapter Questions

Answer 17-1: The problem is that memset is a character-fill routine. An integer consists of 2 or 4 bytes (characters). Each byte is assigned the value 1. So a 2-byte integer will receive the value:

```
integer = 0x0101;
```

The 1-byte hex value for −1 is 0xFF. The 2-byte hex value of −1 is 0xFFFF. So we can take two single-byte −1 values, put them together, and come out with −1. This works for zero also. Any other number will produce the wrong answer. For example, 1 is 0x01. Two bytes of this is 0x0101, or 257.

## CHAPTER 18

Operator Overloading

Overloaded, undermanned, meant to founder, we
Euchred God Almighty's storm, bluffed the Eternal
Sea!
—Kipling

C++ is very good at giving you the tools to organize and use information in a way that's most natural to you. Operator overloading is one of the features that facilitates this. It allows you to define functions to be called when ordinary C++ operators are used on the classes you've defined. For example, you can use operator overloading to tell C++ how to combine two boxes (a_box + b_box). (This assumes that you have a definition of what it means to add two boxes and that it makes sense to do so.) In this chapter we will go step by step through the creation of a fixed-point class and all the operators for it.

Creating a Simple Fixed-Point Class

In this section we define a fixed-point number class. Unlike floating-point numbers where the decimal point can move from place to place (0.1, 30.34, 0.0008) fixed-point numbers have a set number of digits after the decimal point.

Fixed-point numbers are very useful in applications in which speed is essential but you don't need a lot of accuracy. For example, I've used fixed-point functions for color computations in the printing of color pictures. The logic had to decide which color to select for each pixel. For example, the logic had to determine whether or not to put a red dot on the paper. If the color value was more than half red, a dot was printed. So 0.95 was red and 0.23 was not. We didn't need the extra precision of floating point because we didn't care about the extra decimal places. (0.95 was red. 0.9500034 was still red.)

Since floating-point operations cost a lot more than the integer calculations used to implement fixed point, our use of fixed point sped up the processing considerably.

Fixed Point Basics

In our fixed-point class, all numbers have two digits after the decimal point. No more, no less. That's because we've fixed our decimal point at the second position. Here are some examples of the types of numbers we are dealing with:

    12.34   0.01   5.00   853.82   68.10

Internally the numbers are stored as a **long int**. Table 18-1 shows the external representation of some numbers and their internal form.

Table 18-1. External and internal number formats

External representation	Internal representation
12.34	1234
0.00	0
0.01	1
68.10	6810

To add two fixed-point numbers together, just add their values:

	External representation	Internal representation
	12.34	1234
+	56.78	5678
=	69.12	6192

As you can see, addition is a simple, straightforward process. Also, since we are using integers instead of floating-point numbers, it is a fast process. For subtraction, the values are just subtracted.

Multiplication is a little tricker. It requires that you multiple by the values and then divide by a correction factor. (The correction factor is 10^{digits}, where *digits* is the number of digits after the decimal point.) For example:

	External representation	Internal representation
	1.01	101
*	20.0	2000
Before correction	----	202000
= (corrected)	20.20	2020

Division is accomplished in a similar manner, but the correction is multiplied, not divided.

Creating the fixed_pt Class

Externally, our fixed-point number looks much like a floating-point number but the decimal point is always in the same place. Internally we store the number as a **long int**, so the definition for our fixed_pt class begins with a declaration of the internal data:

```
namespace fixed_pt {

class fixed_pt
{
    private:
        long int value; // Value of our fixed point number
```

Next we define several member functions. These include the usual constructors and destructors:

```
public:
    // Default constructor, zero everything
    fixed_pt(): value(0) { }

    // Copy constructor
    fixed_pt(const fixed_pt& other_fixed_pt) :
        value(other_fixed_pt.value)
    { }

    // Destructor does nothing
    ~fixed_pt() {}
```

Now we define a conversion constructor that lets you initialize a fixed-point number using a **double**:

```
// Construct a fixed_pt out of a double
fixed_pt(const double init_real) :
    value(static_cast<long int>(
        init_real * static_cast<double>(fixed_exp)))
{}
```

It should be noted that all we are really doing is setting the value to init_real * fixed_exp, but we want to do our calculations in floating point so we must cast fixed_exp do a **double**. Also, the result is a **long int**, so we must add another cast to change the result into the right type. So when all the details are added, a simple statement becomes a little messy.

Notice that we did not declare the constructor as an **explicit** constructor. That means that it can be used in implied conversions. So the following two statements are both valid:

```
fixed_pt::fixed_pt p1(1.23); // Explict does not matter
fixed_pt::fixed_pt = 4.56;   // Constructor must not be explicit
```

If we declared the constructor **explicit**, the implied conversion of 4.56 to a fixed-point number would not be allowed by the compiler.

We've decided to truncate floating-point numbers when converting them to fixed point. For example, 4.563 becomes fixed-point 4.56. Also 8.999 becomes 8.99. But there is a problem: the floating-point number 1.23 becomes fixed-point 1.22.

How can this happen? The conversion is obvious. It may be obvious to you and me, but not to the computer. The internal format used to store most floating-point numbers does not have an exact way of storing 1.23. Instead, the computer approximates the number as best it can. The result is that the number stored is 1.229999999999999982. This truncates to 1.22.

So how do we get around this problem? The answer is to fudge things a little and add in a fudge factor to help make the answer come out the way we want it to.

So our full constructor is:

```
// Construct a fixed_pt out of a double
fixed_pt(const double init_real) :
    value(static_cast<long int>(
        init_real * static_cast<double>(fixed_exp) +
        fudge_factor))
{}
```

Actually, as we were writing the code for our fixed-point class, we noticed that we convert a double to a fixed-point number a lot of times. So to avoid redundant code, we moved the conversion from the constructor into its own function. Thus, the final version of the conversion constructor (and support routine) looks like:

```
private:
    static long int double_to_fp(const double the_double) {
        return (
            static_cast<long int>(
                the_double *
                static_cast<double>(fixed_exp) +
                fixed_fudge_factor));
    }
public:
    // Construct a fixed_pt out of a double
    fixed_pt(const double init_real) :
        value(double_to_fp(init_real))
    {}
```

Finally we add some simple access functions to get and set the value of the number.

```
// Function to set the number
void set(const double real) {
    value = double_to_fp(real);

}

// Function to return the value
double get() const {
    return (static_cast<double>(value) / fixed_exp);
}
```

As you may recall, the const appearing after the get function was discussed in Chapter 14.

Now we want to use our fixed numbers. Declaring variables is simple. Even initializing them with numbers such as 3.45 is easy:

```
fixed_pt::fixed_pt start;      // Starting point for the graph
fixed_pt::fixed_pt end(3.45);    // Ending point
```

But what happens when we want to add two fixed numbers? We need to define a function to do it:

```
namespace fixed_pt {

// Version 1 of the fixed point add function
inline fixed_pt add(const fixed_pt& oper1, const fixed_pt& oper2)
{
    fixed_pt result.value = oper1.value + oper2.value;
    return (result);
}
```

A few things should be noted about this function. First, we defined it to take two fixed-point numbers and return a fixed-point number. That way we group additions:

```
// Add three fixed point numbers
answer = add(first, add(second, third));
```

Constant reference parameters are used (const fixed_pt&) for our two arguments. This is one of the most efficient ways of passing structures into a function. Finally, because it is such a small function, we've defined it as an inline function for efficiency.

In our add function, we explicitly declare a result and return it. We can do both in one step:

```
// Version 2 of the fixed_pt add function
inline fixed_pt add(const fixed_pt& oper1, const fixed_pt& oper2)
{
    return (fixed_pt(oper1.value + oper2.value);
}
```

Although it is a little harder to understand, it is more efficient.

There's some bookkeeping required to support this function. First, we need a constructor that will create a fixed-point number from an integer. Since this is not used outside of functions that deal with the internals of the fixed-point class, we declare it private:

```
private:
    // Used for internal conversions for our friends
    fixed_pt(const long int i_value) : value(i_value){}
```

Since our add function needs access to this constructor, we must declare the function as a friend to our fixed-point class.

```
friend fixed_pt add(const fixed_pt& oper1, const fixed_pt& oper2)
```

It is important to understand what C++ does behind your back. Even such a simple statement as:

```
answer = add(first, second);
```

calls a constructor, an assignment operator, and a destructor—all in that little piece of code.

In version 1 of the add function, we explicitly allocated a variable for the result. In version 2, C++ automatically creates a temporary variable for the result. This variable has no name and doesn't really exist outside the return statement.

Creating the temporary variable causes the constructor to be called. The temporary variable is then assigned to answer; thus we have a call to the assignment function. After the assignment, C++ no longer has any use for the temporary variable and throws it away by calling the destructor.

Operator Functions

Using the add function for fixed-point numbers is a little awkward. It would be nice to be able to convince C++ to automatically call this function whenever we try to add two fixed numbers together with the + operator. That's where operator overloading comes in. All we have to do is to turn the add function into a function named operator + (technically you can't have a space in a function name, but this is a special case):

```
inline fixed_pt operator + (const fixed_pt& oper1,
                            const fixed_pt& oper2)
{
  return fixed_pt(oper1.value + oper2.value);
}
```

When C++ sees that the fixed_pt class has a member function named operator + it automatically generates code that calls it when two fixed-point objects are added.

The operator overloading functions should be used carefully. You should try to design them so they follow common-sense rules. That is, + should have something to do with addition; –, with subtraction; and so on. The C++ I/O streams break this rule by defining the shift operators (<< and >>) as input and output operators. This can lead to some confusion, such as:

```
std::cout << 8 << 2;
```

Does this output "8" followed by "2," or does it output the value of the expression (8 << 2)? Unless you're an expert, you can't tell. In this case, the numbers "8" and "2" will be output.

You've seen how you can overload the + operator. Now let's explore what other operators you can use.

Binary Arithmetic Operators

Binary operators take two arguments, one on each side of the operator. For example, multiplication and division are binary operators:

```
x * y;
a / b;
```

Unary operators take a single parameter. Unary operators include unary – and the address-of (&) operator:

```
-x
&y
```

The binary arithmetic operator functions take two constant parameters and produce a result. One of the parameters must be a class or structure object. The result can be anything. For example, the following functions are legal for binary addition:

```
fixed_pt operator +(const fixed_pt& v1, const fixed_pt& v2);
fixed_pt operator +(const fixed_pt& v1, const float v2);
fixed_pt operator +(const float v1,     const fixed_pt& v2);

fixed_pt operator +(float v1,    float v2);              // Illegal
// You can't overload a basic C++ operator such as adding two floating
// point numbers.
```

It makes sense to add real (float) and fixed-point numbers together. The result is that we've had to define a lot of different functions just to support the addition for our fixed-point class. Such variation of the definition is typical when overloading operators.

Table 18-2 lists the binary operators that can be overloaded.

Table 18-2. Binary operators that can be overloaded

Operator	Meaning
+	Addition
-	Subtraction
*	Multiplication
/	Division
%	Modulus
^	Bitwise exclusive OR
&	Bitwise AND
|	Bitwise OR
<<	Left shift
>>	Right shift

Relational Operators

The relational operators include such operators as equal (==) and not equal (!=). Normally they take two constant objects and return either true or false. (Actually they can return anything, but that would violate the spirit of relational operators.)

The equality operator for our fixed-point class is:

```
inline bool operator == (const fixed_pt& oper1, const fixed_pt& oper2)
{
    return (oper1.value == oper2.value);
}
```

Table 18-3 lists the relational operators.

Table 18-3. Relational operators

Operator	Meaning
==	Equality
!=	Inequality
<	Less than
>	Greater than
<=	Less than or equal to
>=	Greater than or equal to

Unary Operators

Unary operators, such as negative (–), take a single parameter. The negative operator for our fixed-point type is:

```
inline fixed_pt operator - (const fixed_pt& oper1, const double oper2)
{
    return fixed_pt(oper1.value - fixed_pt::double_to_fp(oper2));
}
```

Table 18-4 lists the unary operators.

Table 18-4. Unary operators

Operator	Meaning
+	Positive
-	Negative
*	Dereference
&	Address of
~	Ones complement

Shortcut Operators

Operators such as += and −= are shortcuts for more complicated operators. But what are the return values of += and −=? A very close examination of the C++ standard reveals that these operators return the value of the variable after the increase or decrease. For example:

```
i = 5;
j = i += 2;    // Don't code like this
```

assigns j the value 7. The += function for our fixed-point class is:

```
inline fixed_pt& operator += (fixed_pt& oper1,
                        const fixed_pt& oper2)
{
    oper1.value += oper2.value;
    return (oper1);
}
```

Note that unlike the other operator functions we've defined, the first parameter is not a constant. Also, we return a reference to the first variable, not a new variable or a copy of the first.

Table 18-5 lists the shortcut operators.

Table 18-5. Simple shortcut operators

Operator	Meaning
+=	Increase
−=	Decrease
*=	Multiply by
/=	Divide by
%=	Remainder
^=	Exclusive OR into
&=	AND into
|=	OR into
<<=	Shift left
>>=	Shift right

Increment and Decrement Operators

The increment and decrement operators have two forms: prefix and postfix. For example:

```
i = 5;
j = i++;    // j = 5
i = 5;
j = ++i;    // j = 6
```

Both these operators use a function named operator ++. So how do you tell them apart? The C++ language contains a hack to handle this case. The prefix form of the operator takes one argument, the item to be incremented. The postfix takes two, the item to be incremented and an integer. The actual integer used is meaningless; it's just a position holder to differentiate the two forms of the operation.

Our functions to handle the two forms of ++ are:

```
// Prefix      x = ++f
inline fixed_pt& operator ++(fixed_pt& oper)
{
    oper.value += fixed_exp;
    return (oper);
}

// Postfix     x = f++
inline fixed_pt operator ++(fixed_pt oper, int)
{
    fixed_pt result(oper);   // Result before we incremented
    oper.value += fixed_exp;
    return (result);
}
```

This is messy. C++ has reduced us to using cute tricks: the unused integer parameter. In actual practice, I never use the postfix version of increment and always put the prefix version on a line by itself. That way, I can avoid most of these problems.

The choice, prefix versus postfix, was decided by looking at the code for the two versions. As you can see, the prefix version is much simpler than the postfix version. Restricting yourself to the prefix version not only simplifies your code, but it also makes the compiler's job a little easier.

Table 18-6 lists the increment and decrement operators.

Table 18-6. Increment and decrement operators

Operator	Meaning
++	Increment
--	Decrement

Logical Operators

Logical operators include AND (&&), OR (||), and NOT (!). They can be overloaded, but just because you *can* do it doesn't mean you should. In theory, logical operators work only on bool values. In practice, because numbers can be converted to the bool type (0 is false, nonzero is true), these operators work for any number. But don't confuse the issue more by overloading them.

Table 18-7 lists the logical operators.

Table 18-7. Logical operators

Operation	Meaning
||	Logical OR
&&	Logical AND
!	Logical NOT

I/O Operators

You've been using the operators << and >> for input and output. Actually these operators are overloaded versions of the shift operators. This has the advantage of making I/O fairly simple, at the cost of some minor confusion.

We would like to be able to output our fixed-point numbers just like any other data type. To do this we need to define a << operator for it.

We are sending our data to the output stream class std::ostream. The data itself is fixed_pt. So our output function is:

```
inline std::ostream& operator << (std::ostream& out_file,
                                  const fixed_pt& number)
{
    long int before_dp = number.value / fixed_exp;
    long int after_dp1 = abs(number.value % fixed_exp);
    long int after_dp2 = after_dp1 % 10;
    after_dp1 /= 10;

    out_file << before_dp << '.' << after_dp1 << after_dp2;
    return (out_file);
}
```

The function returns a reference to the output file. This enables the caller to string a series of << operations together, such as:

```
fixed_pt a_fixed_pt(1.2);
std::cout << "The answer is " << a_fixed_pt << '\n';
```

The result of this code is:

```
The answer is 1.20
```

Normally the << operator takes two constant arguments. In this case, the first parameter is a nonconstant std::ostream. This is because the << operator, when used for output, has side effects, the major one being that the data goes to the output stream. In general, however, it's not a good idea to add side effects to an operator that doesn't already have them.

Input should be just as simple as output. You might think all we have to do is read the numbers (and the related extra characters):

```
// Simple-minded input operation
inline istream& operator >> (istream& in_file, fixed_pt& number) {
    int before_dp;      // Part before the decimal point
```

```
        char dot;              // The decimal point
        char after_dp1;        // After decimal point (first digit)
        char after_dp2;        // After decimal point (second digit)

        in_file >> before_dp >> dot >> after_dp1 >> after_dp2;
        number.value = before_dp * fixed_exp +
                       after_dp1 - '0' * 10 +
                       after_dp2 - '0';
        return (in_file);
    }
```

In practice, it's not so simple. Something might go wrong. For example, the user may type in 1x23 instead of 1.23. What do we do then?

The answer is that we would fail gracefully. In our new reading routine, the first thing we do is set the value of our number to 0.00. That way, if we do fail, there is a known value in the number:

```
    inline std::istream& operator >> (std::istream& in_file,
                                      fixed_pt& number)
    {
        number.value = 0;
```

Next we create a `std::istream::sentry` variable. This variable protects the `std::istream` in case of failure:

```
    std::istream::sentry the_sentry(in_file, true);
```

The second parameter tells the sentry to skip any leading whitespace. (It's optional. The default value is false, which tells the sentry to not skip the whitespace.)

Now we need to check to see if everything went well when the sentry was constructed:

```
    if (the_sentry) {
        // Everything is OK, do the read
        ....
    } else {
        in_file.setstate(std::ios::failbit); // Indicate failure
    }
```

The function `setstate` is used to set a flag indicating that the input operation found a problem. This allows the caller to test to see whether the input worked by calling the `bad` function. (This function can also cause an exception to be thrown. See Chapter 22 for more information.)

Let's assume that everything is OK. We've skipped the whitespace at the beginning of the number, so we should now be pointing to the digits in front of the decimal point. Let's grab them. Of course we check for errors afterwards:

```
    in_file >> before_dp;   // Get number before the decimal point
    if (in_file.bad()) return (in_file);
```

The next step is to read the decimal point, make sure that nothing went wrong, and that we got the decimal point:

```
in_file >> ch;   // Get first character after number

if (in_file.bad()) return (in_file);

// Expect a decimal point
if (ch != '.') {
    in_file.setstate(std::ios::failbit);
    return (in_file);
}
```

Now we get the two characters after the decimal point and check for errors:

```
in_file >> after_dp1 >> after_dp2;
if (in_file.bad()) return (in_file);
```

Both characters should be digits (we're not very flexible in our input format—that's a feature, not a bug). To make sure that the correct characters are read, we use the standard library function isdigit to check each of them to make sure they are digits. (See your library documentation for information on isdigit and related functions.)

```
// Check result for validity
if ((!isdigit(after_dp1)) || (!isdigit(after_dp2))) {
    in_file.setstate(std::ios::failbit);
    return (in_file);
}
```

Everything is OK at this point, so we set the number and we're done:

```
// Todo make after db two digits exact
number.value = before_dp * fixed_exp +
    (after_dp1 - '0') * 10 +
    (after_dp2 - '0');
```

The complete version of the fixed-point number reader appears in Example 18-1.

Example 18-1. fixed_pt/fixed_pt.read

```
/*********************************************************
 * istream >> fixed_pt -- read a fixed_pt number         *
 *                                                       *
 * Parameters                                            *
 *      in_file -- file to read                          *
 *      number -- place to put the number                *
 *                                                       *
 * Returns                                               *
 *      reference to the input file                      *
 *********************************************************/
std::istream& operator >> (std::istream& in_file, fixed_pt& number)
{
    long int before_dp;  // Part before decimal point (dp)
    char after_dp1, after_dp2;  // Part after decimal point (dp)
    char ch;             // Random character used to verify input

    number = 0.0;        // Initialize the number (just in case)

    // We only work for 2 digit fixed point numbers
```

Example 18-1. fixed_pt/fixed_pt.read (continued)

```
    assert(fixed_exp == 100);

    // Sentry to protect the I/O
    std::istream::sentry the_sentry(in_file, true);

    if (the_sentry)
    {
        if (in_file.bad()) return (in_file);

        // Get the number that follows the whitespace
        in_file >> before_dp;

        if (in_file.bad()) return (in_file);

        in_file >> ch;  // Get first character after number

        if (in_file.bad()) return (in_file);

        // Expect a decimal point
        if (ch != '.') {
            in_file.setstate(std::ios::failbit);
            return (in_file);
        }

        in_file >> after_dp1 >> after_dp2;
        if (in_file.bad()) return (in_file);

        // Check result for validity
        if ((!isdigit(after_dp1)) || (!isdigit(after_dp2))) {
            in_file.setstate(std::ios::failbit);
            return (in_file);
        }

        // Todo make after db two digits exact
        number.value = before_dp * fixed_exp +
            (after_dp1 - '0') * 10 +
            (after_dp2 - '0');

    }
    else
    {
        in_file.setstate(std::ios::failbit);
    }
    return (in_file);
}
```

Index Operator "[ ]"

The operator [ ] is used by C++ to index arrays. As you will see in Chapter 20, this operator is very useful when defining a class that mimics an array. Normally, this function takes two arguments, a class that simulates an array and an index, and returns a reference to an item in the array:

```
double& operator[](array_class& array, int index)
```

We cover the [] operator in more detail in Chapter 23.

new and delete

We'll say very little about overloading the global operators new and delete at this time. First of all, they aren't introduced until Chapter 20, so you don't know what they do. Second, when you know what they do, you won't want to override them.

I've seen only one program where the new and delete operators (or at least their C equivalents) were overridden. That program was written by a very clever programmer who liked to do everything a little strangely. The result was code that was a nightmare to debug.

So unless you are a very clever programmer, leave new and delete alone. And if you are a clever programmer, please leave new and delete alone anyway. Some day I might have to debug your code.

Exotic Operators

C++ contains a very rich set of operators. Some of these are rarely, if ever, used. These include:

( ) Allows you to define a default function for a class.

, Comma operator. Allows two expressions to be concatenated. It is rarely used and probably should not be overloaded.

->* Pointer to member. Rarely used.

-> Class member.

All of these operators are discussed in Chapter 29.

Operator Member Functions

So far we've been using operator overloading functions just like ordinary functions. They can also be defined as member functions. The only difference is that as member functions the first argument, the class itself, is implied. For example, you can write the operator += as an ordinary function or as a member function. Here's the ordinary version that you've already seen:

```
inline fixed_pt& operator +=(fixed_pt& oper1, const fixed_pt& oper2)
{
    oper1.value += oper2.value;
    return (oper1);
}
```

Here's the member function:

```
class fixed_pt {
    // .....
    public:
        inline fixed_pt& operator +=(const fixed_pt& oper2)
        {
            value += oper2.value;
            return (*this);
        }
```

The only trick used in this function is the keyword this. This is a predefined variable that refers to the current object. For example, you can access the data member value using the statement:

```
value += oper2.value;
```

The same statement can be written as:

```
this->value += oper2.value;
```

In most cases, you don't need to use this. In a few cases, however, such as with the += operator, it comes in handy.

Which flavor of the operator overloading functions should you use? The one that makes your program the clearest and easiest to read. In general, I use the standard functions for the simple operators, such as +, −, *, and /, while I use member functions for the shortcut and unary operators, such as +=, −=, ++, and unary −.

Some overloaded functions work only as member functions. These include the casting operators and class-specific versions of new and delete.

All overload operator functions that have the class type as the left argument should be member functions. This helps keep everything in one well-designed class.

Casting

Finally we come to the cast operators. Casting is a way of changing one type to another, such as when we cast our fixed_pt type to a long int (truncating the two digits after the decimal point). We can define a cast operator for this function as:

```
class fixed_pt {
    public:
        // (We didn't really put this in our fixed_point class)
        operator double() {return (value / fixed_exp);}
```

C++ automatically calls this function whenever it wants to turn a fixed_pt into a long int.

The trouble is that by defining a cast, you give C++ something else that it can call behind your back. Personally, I like to know whenever C++ calls something, so I avoid creating cast operators. Unless you have a very good reason to define one, don't create a cast operator function.

Warts

The fixed_pt class described in this chapter has been simplified a bit to make it easy to understand and to best teach operator overloading. There are some limitations to this code that you should be aware of, however.

First, although the number of digits after the decimal point is controlled by the constant fixed_exp, in reality the code is limited to two digits after the decimal point. That's because the input and output functions have this limit hardcoded in. (They should be made general.)

Also, with C++ templates (see Chapter 24) there is no reason to hardcode the location of the decimal point at all. You can create a general-purpose template that lets you specify the fixed point when you declare the class. More on this later.

In spite of these problems, this class does serve as a good illustration of how to perform operator overloading in C++.

Full Definition of the Fixed-Point Class

Examples 18-2 and 18-3 list the entire fixed-point class. The beginning of the header file summarizes all the functions that are defined. In creating this class, I discovered that it consisted of many (29 to be exact) little one- and two-line functions. Commenting each of these with a full-function comment block would obscure the code. In other words, this is one of the few cases (the *very* few) where adding comments would cause confusion, so most of the small functions have no comments.

When creating this class, I noticed that a lot of the functions have a similar structure. For example, += looks a lot like –= and so on. As a matter of fact, I created the –= operator by copying the += functions and editing a little. C++ contains a rich operator set that causes this sort of repetition to happen when you're trying to define a complete set of operators for a class.

Finally, the simple operations are defined in the file *fixed_pt.h* (Example 18-2) while the longer functions are left in the file *fixed_pt.cpp* (Example 18-3). Finally, we've included a limited unit test in *fixed_test.cpp* (Example 18-4).

Example 18-2. fixed_pt/fixed_pt.h

```
#ifndef __fixed_pt_h__   // Avoid double includes
#define __fixed_pt_h__   // Prevent double include

#include <iostream>
#include <assert.h>
#include <stdlib.h>

namespace fixed_pt {
```

Example 18-2. fixed_pt/fixed_pt.h (continued)

```
/* Note: This should be made into a template so that multiple
 * fixed points may be used, but the purpose of this class
 * is to teach operator overloading and templates would be a
 * needless complication.
 */

const int fixed_exp = 100;      // 10**fixed_point */

/* Fudge factor to make doubles into fixed point numbers */
const double fixed_fudge_factor = 0.0001;


/*********************************************************
 * Fixed point class                                    *
 *                                                      *
 * Members defined                                      *
 *      fixed_pt()              // Default constructor   *
 *      fixed_pt(double)        // Specifiy an inital    *
 *                              // value                *
 *      fixed_pt(fixed_pt)      // Copy constructor      *
 *                                                      *
 *      set(double)            // Set the value         *
 *      double get();          // Return the value       *
 *                              // as a double           *
 *                                                      *
 * Operator member functions                            *
 *                    f -- a fixed_pt number            *
 *                    s -- a scalar (double)            *
 *      f = f                                            *
 *      f += f;                                          *
 *      f += s;                                          *
 *      f -= f;                                          *
 *      f -= s;                                          *
 *      f /= f;                                          *
 *      f /= s;                                          *
 *      f *= f;                                          *
 *      f *= s;                                          *
 *      f++                                              *
 *      ++f                                              *
 *      f--                                              *
 *      --f                                              *
 *                                                      *
 * Arithmetic operators defined                         *
 *      f = f + f;                                       *
 *      f = s + f;                                       *
 *      f = f + s;                                       *
 *      f = f - f;                                       *
 *      f = s - f;                                       *
 *      f = f - s;                                       *
 *      f = f * f;                                       *
 *      f = s * f;                                       *
 *      f = f * s;                                       *
```

Example 18-2. fixed_pt/fixed_pt.h (continued)

```
 *        f = f / f;                                         *
 *        f = s / f;                                         *
 *        f = f / s;                                         *
 *        -f                                                 *
 *        +f                                                 *
 *        ostream << f     // Output function                *
 *        istream >> f     // Input function                 *
 ********************************************************/
class fixed_pt
{
    private:
        long int value; // Value of our fixed point number

        static long int double_to_fp(const double the_double) {
            return (
                static_cast<long int>(
                    the_double *
                    static_cast<double>(fixed_exp) +
                    fixed_fudge_factor));
        }


    public:
        // Default constructor, zero everything
        fixed_pt(): value(0) { }

        // Copy constructor
        fixed_pt(const fixed_pt& other_fixed_pt) :
            value(other_fixed_pt.value)
        { }

        // Construct a fixed_pt out of a double
        fixed_pt(const double init_real) :
            value(double_to_fp(init_real))
        {}

        // Destructor does nothing
        ~fixed_pt() {}

        // Function to set the number
        void set(const double real) {
            value = double_to_fp(real);

        }

        // Function to return the value
        double get() const {
            return (static_cast<double>(value) / fixed_exp);
        }

        // Note: Because of the way we store internal data
        // we do not have to check for self assignment
```

Example 18-2. fixed_pt/fixed_pt.h (continued)

```
    fixed_pt operator = (const fixed_pt& oper2) {
        value = oper2.value;
        return (*this);
    }


    fixed_pt& operator += (const fixed_pt& oper2) {
        value += oper2.value;
        return (*this);
    }


    fixed_pt& operator += (double oper2) {
        value += double_to_fp(oper2);
        return (*this);
    }


    fixed_pt& operator -= (const fixed_pt& oper2) {
        value -= oper2.value;
        return (*this);
    }


    fixed_pt& operator -= (double oper2) {
        value -= double_to_fp(oper2);
        return (*this);
    }


    fixed_pt& operator *= (const fixed_pt& oper2) {
        value *= oper2.value;
        value /= fixed_exp;
        return *this;
    }

    fixed_pt& operator *= (double oper2) {
        value *= double_to_fp(oper2);
        value /= fixed_exp;
        return (*this);
    }

    fixed_pt& operator /= (const fixed_pt& oper2) {
        assert(oper2.value != 0.0);
        value /= oper2.value;
        value *= fixed_exp;
    }

    fixed_pt& operator /= (double oper2) {
        assert(double_to_fp(oper2) != 0.0);
        value /= double_to_fp(oper2);
        value *= fixed_exp;
        return (*this);
    }

    // f++
    fixed_pt operator ++(int) {
```

Example 18-2. fixed_pt/fixed_pt.h (continued)

```
            fixed_pt result(*this);
            value += fixed_exp;
            return (result);
        }

        // ++f
        fixed_pt& operator ++() {
            value += fixed_exp;
            return (*this);
        }

        // f--
        fixed_pt operator --(int) {
            fixed_pt result(*this);
            value -= fixed_exp;
            return (result);
        }

        // --f
        fixed_pt& operator --() {
            value -= fixed_exp;
            return (*this);
        }

    private:
        // Used for internal conversions for our friends
        fixed_pt(const long int i_value) : value(i_value){}

    friend fixed_pt operator + (const fixed_pt& oper1, const fixed_pt& oper2);
    friend fixed_pt operator + (const fixed_pt& oper1, const double oper2);
    friend fixed_pt operator + (const double oper1, const fixed_pt& oper2);

    friend fixed_pt operator - (const fixed_pt& oper1, const fixed_pt& oper2);
    friend fixed_pt operator - (const fixed_pt& oper1, const double oper2);
    friend fixed_pt operator - (double oper1, const fixed_pt& oper2);

    friend fixed_pt operator * (const fixed_pt& oper1, const fixed_pt& oper2);
    friend fixed_pt operator * (const fixed_pt& oper1, const double oper2);
    friend fixed_pt operator * (double oper1, const fixed_pt& oper2);

    friend fixed_pt operator / (const fixed_pt& oper1, const fixed_pt& oper2);
    friend fixed_pt operator / (const fixed_pt& oper1, const double oper2);
    friend fixed_pt operator / (const double& oper1, const fixed_pt& oper2);

    friend bool operator == (const fixed_pt& oper1, const fixed_pt& oper2);
    friend fixed_pt operator - (const fixed_pt& oper1);
    friend std::ostream& operator << (std::ostream& out_file, const fixed_pt& number);
    friend std::istream& operator >> (std::istream& in_file, fixed_pt& number);
};

inline fixed_pt operator + (const fixed_pt& oper1, const fixed_pt& oper2)
{
```

Example 18-2. fixed_pt/fixed_pt.h (continued)

```
    return fixed_pt(oper1.value + oper2.value);
}

inline fixed_pt operator + (const fixed_pt& oper1, const double oper2)
{
    return fixed_pt(oper1.value + fixed_pt::double_to_fp(oper2));
}

inline fixed_pt operator + (double oper1, const fixed_pt& oper2)
{
    return fixed_pt(fixed_pt::double_to_fp(oper1) + oper2.value);
}

inline fixed_pt operator - (const fixed_pt& oper1, const fixed_pt& oper2)
{
    return fixed_pt(oper1.value - oper2.value);
}

inline fixed_pt operator - (const fixed_pt& oper1, const double oper2)
{
    return fixed_pt(oper1.value - fixed_pt::double_to_fp(oper2));
}

inline fixed_pt operator - (double oper1, const fixed_pt& oper2)
{
    return fixed_pt(fixed_pt::double_to_fp(oper1) - oper2.value);
}

inline fixed_pt operator * (const fixed_pt& oper1, const fixed_pt& oper2)
{
    return fixed_pt(oper1.value * oper2.value / fixed_exp);
}

inline fixed_pt operator * (const fixed_pt& oper1, const double oper2)
{
    return fixed_pt(oper1.value * fixed_pt::double_to_fp(oper2) / fixed_exp);
}

inline fixed_pt operator * (const double oper1, const fixed_pt& oper2)
{
    return fixed_pt(fixed_pt::double_to_fp(oper1) * oper2.value / fixed_exp);
}

inline fixed_pt operator / (const fixed_pt& oper1, const fixed_pt& oper2)
{
    assert(oper2.value != 0);
    return fixed_pt((oper1.value * fixed_exp) / oper2.value);
}


inline fixed_pt operator / (const double& oper1, const fixed_pt& oper2)
{
```

Example 18-2. fixed_pt/fixed_pt.h (continued)

```
        assert(oper2.value != 0);
        return fixed_pt((fixed_pt::double_to_fp(oper1) * fixed_exp) / oper2.value);
}

inline fixed_pt operator / (const fixed_pt& oper1, const double oper2)
{
        assert(oper2 != 0);
        return fixed_pt((oper1.value  * fixed_exp) / fixed_pt::double_to_fp(oper2));
}

inline bool operator == (const fixed_pt& oper1, const fixed_pt& oper2)
{
        return (oper1.value == oper2.value);
}

inline bool operator != (const fixed_pt& oper1, const fixed_pt& oper2)
{
        return (!(oper1 == oper2));
}

inline fixed_pt operator - (const fixed_pt& oper1)
{
        return fixed_pt(-oper1.value);
}

inline fixed_pt operator + (const fixed_pt& oper1)
{
        return fixed_pt(oper1);
}

inline std::ostream& operator << (std::ostream& out_file, const fixed_pt& number)
{
        long int before_dp = number.value / fixed_exp;
        long int after_dp1  = abs(number.value % fixed_exp);
        long int after_dp2  = after_dp1 % 10;
        after_dp1 /= 10;

        out_file << before_dp << '.' << after_dp1 << after_dp2;
        return (out_file);
}

extern std::istream& operator >> (std::istream& in_file, fixed_pt& number);


}
#endif /* __fixed_pt_h__ */      // Avoid double includes
```

Example 18-3. fixed_pt/fixed_pt.cpp

```
#include <iostream>

#include "fixed_pt.h"
```

Example 18-3. fixed_pt/fixed_pt.cpp (continued)

```cpp
#include "ctype.h"

namespace fixed_pt {

/********************************************************
 * istream >> fixed_pt -- read a fixed_pt number       *
 *                                                     *
 * Parameters                                          *
 *      in_file -- file to read                        *
 *      number -- place to put the number              *
 *                                                     *
 * Returns                                             *
 *      reference to the input file                    *
 ********************************************************/
std::istream& operator >> (std::istream& in_file, fixed_pt& number)
{
    long int before_dp; // Part before decimal point (dp)
    char after_dp1, after_dp2;  // Part after decimal point (dp)
    char ch;                // Random character used to verify input

    number = 0.0;           // Initialize the number (just in case)

    // We only work for 2 digit fixed point numbers
    assert(fixed_exp == 100);

    // Sentry to protect the I/O
    std::istream::sentry the_sentry(in_file, true);

    if (the_sentry)
    {
        if (in_file.bad()) return (in_file);

        // Get the number that follows the whitespace
        in_file >> before_dp;

        if (in_file.bad()) return (in_file);

        in_file >> ch;  // Get first character after number

        if (in_file.bad()) return (in_file);

        // Expect a decimal point
        if (ch != '.') {
            in_file.setstate(std::ios::failbit);
            return (in_file);
        }

        in_file >> after_dp1 >> after_dp2;
        if (in_file.bad()) return (in_file);

        // Check result for validity
        if ((!isdigit(after_dp1)) || (!isdigit(after_dp2))) {
```

Example 18-3. fixed_pt/fixed_pt.cpp (continued)

```
        in_file.setstate(std::ios::failbit);
        return (in_file);
    }

    // Todo make after db two digits exact
    number.value = before_dp * fixed_exp +
        (after_dp1 - '0') * 10 +
        (after_dp2 - '0');

    }
    else
    {
        in_file.setstate(std::ios::failbit);
    }
    return (in_file);
}

}
```

Example 18-4. fixed_pt/fixed_test.cpp

```
#include <iostream>
#include "fixed_pt.h"


int main()
{
    std::cout << "Expect 1.23 " << fixed_pt::fixed_pt(1.23) << std::endl;
    std::cout << "Expect 1.00 " << fixed_pt::fixed_pt(1.00) << std::endl;
    std::cout << "Expect 1.02 " << fixed_pt::fixed_pt(1.02) << std::endl;
    std::cout << "Expect 1.20 " << fixed_pt::fixed_pt(1.20) << std::endl;
    fixed_pt::fixed_pt f3 = 1.23;
    std::cout << "Expect 1.23 " << f3 << std::endl;

    fixed_pt::fixed_pt f1(1.23 + 0.005);
    fixed_pt::fixed_pt f2(4.56 + 0.005);

    std::cout << f1 << " + " << f2 << " = " << f1 + f2 << std::endl;
    std::cout << f1 << " - " << f2 << " = " << f1 - f2 << std::endl;
    std::cout << f1 << " * " << f2 << " = " << f1 * f2 << std::endl;
    std::cout << f1 << " / " << f2 << " = " << f1 / f2 << std::endl;

    return (0);
}
```

Question 18-1: *Why does Example 18-5 fail? When run it prints out:*

```
Copy constructor called
Copy constructor called
```

over and over. Hint: Review the section "Copy Constructor" in Chapter 13. Thanks to Jeff Hewett for this problem.

Example 18-5. equal/equal.cpp

```
#include <iostream>

class trouble {
    public:
        int data;

        trouble();
        trouble(const trouble& old);
        trouble operator = (const trouble old_trouble);
};

trouble::trouble() {
    data = 0;
}

trouble::trouble(const trouble& old) {
    std::cout << "Copy constructor called\n";
    *this = old;
}

trouble trouble::operator = (const trouble old_trouble) {
    std::cout << "Operator = called\n";
    data = old_trouble.data;
    return (*this);
}

int main()
{
    trouble trouble1;
    trouble trouble2(trouble1);

    return (0);
}
```

Programming Exercises

Exercise 18-1: Write a class to handle fractions such as "1/3." Define addition, subtraction, multiplication, and division operators for these fractions.

For example: 1/3 + 1/2 = 5/6.

Exercise 18-2: Write a fixed-point number class to handle numbers. All numbers are of the form DDDDD.D. In other words, all numbers have only a single digit to the right of the decimal point. Use integers to implement this class.

Exercise 18-3: Write a class to implement a sparse integer array. This is much like a simple integer array:

```
int simple_array[100];
```

But unlike a simple array, the indices can go from 0 to 1,000,000. That's the bad news. The good news is that at most 100 elements will be set at any time. The rest of the elements will be zero.

Exercise 18-4: Write a time class. Implement functions to add, subtract, read, and print times.

Exercise 18-5: Write a date class that allows you to add, subtract, read, and print simple dates of the form MM/DD. Assume year is not a leap year.

Exercise 18-6: (Advanced) Write a full-date class that allows you to add, subtract, read, and print dates of the form MM/DD/YY.

Answers to Chapter Questions

Answer 18-1: The copy constructor calls the operator = function. The parameter list to this function is:

```
trouble trouble::operator = (trouble old_trouble) {
```

The parameter to this function is being passed as a call-by-value parameter. When C++ sees this type of parameter it calls the copy constructor to put the parameter on the stack.

```
trouble trouble::operator = (trouble old_trouble) {
    std::cout << "Operator = called\n";
    data = old_trouble.data;
    return (*this);
}
```

```
trouble::trouble(
        const trouble& old) called
```

So we have an infinite loop. The copy constructor calls the operator = function. C++ sees the call-by-value parameter and calls the copy constructor, which calls operator = and causes the copy constructor to be called. This keeps up until the system runs out of stack space or the user gets disgusted and aborts the program.

The solution is to pass the parameter to operator = as a reference. This not only is more efficient, but also works:

```
trouble trouble::operator = (const trouble& old_trouble) {
```

Unfortunately, this only solves part of the problem. Now, we don't call the copy constructor going into the operator = function. But when we return (*this), the return value has to be copied, so we still call the copy constructor. The solution is to return a reference to the class instead of a copy of the class. Thus, our declaration of the operator = function should be:

```
trouble& trouble::operator = (const trouble& old_trouble) {
```

## CHAPTER 19

Floating Point

1 is equal to 2 for sufficiently large values of 1.
—Anonymous

Computers handle integers very well. The arithmetic is simple, exact, and fast. Floating point is the opposite. Computers do floating-point arithmetic only with great difficulty.

This chapter discusses some of the problems that can occur with floating point. To address the principles involved in floating-point arithmetic, we have defined a simple decimal floating-point format. We suggest you put aside your computer and work through these problems using pencil and paper so you can see firsthand the problems and pitfalls that occur.

The format used by computers is very similar to the one defined in this chapter, except that instead of using base 10, computers use base 2, 8, or 16. However, all the problems demonstrated here on paper can occur in a computer.

Floating-Point Format

Floating-point numbers consist of three parts: a sign, a fraction, and an exponent. Our fraction is expressed as a four-digit decimal. The exponent is a single-decimal digit. So our format is:

$$\pm f.fff \times 10^{\pm e}$$

where:

$\pm$ is the sign (plus or minus).

f.fff is the four-digit fraction.

$\pm e$ is the single-digit exponent.

Zero is $+0.000 \times 10^{+0}$. We represent these numbers in "E" format: $\pm f.fffE\pm e$. This format is similar to the floating-point format used in many computers. The IEEE has defined a floating-point standard (#742), but not all machines use it.

Table 19-1 shows some typical floating-point numbers.

Table 19-1. Floating-point examples

Notation	Number
+1.000E+0	1.0
+3.300E+5	330000.0
−8.223E−3	−0.008223
+0.000E+0	0.0

The floating-point operations defined in this chapter follow a rigid set of rules. To minimize errors we make use of a *guard digit*. That is an extra digit added to the end of the fraction during computation. Many computers use a guard digit in their floating-point units.

Floating Addition/Subtraction

To add two numbers, such as 2.0 and 0.3, the computer must perform the following steps:

1. Start with the numbers.

   +2.000E+0 The number is 2.0.
   +3.000E−1 The number is 0.3.

2. Add guard digits to both numbers.

   +2.0000E+0 The number is 2.0.
   +3.0000E−1 The number is 0.3.

3. Shift the number with the smallest exponent to the right one digit and increment its exponent. Continue until the exponents of the two numbers match.

   +2.0000E+0 The number is 2.0.
   +0.3000E−0 The number is 0.3.

4. Add the two fractions. The result has the same exponent as the two numbers.

   +2.0000E+0 The number is 2.0.
   +0.3000E−0 The number is 0.3.

   +2.3000E+0 The result is 2.3.

5. Normalize the number by shifting it left or right until there is just one nonzero digit to the left of the decimal point. Adjust the exponent accordingly. A number like +0.1234E+0 would be normalized to +1.2340E−1. Because the number +2.3000E+0 is already normalized, we do nothing.

6. Finally, if the guard digit is greater than or equal to 5, round the next digit up. Otherwise, truncate the number.

+2.3000E+0   Round last digit.
+2.300E+0   The result is 2.3.

To subtract a number:

1. Change the sign of the second operand.
2. Add.

Multiplication and Division

When we want to multiply two numbers, such as 0.12 × 11.0, the following rules apply:

1. Start with the numbers:

   +1.200E–1   The number is 0.12.
   +1.100E+1   The number is 11.0.

2. Add the guard digit.

   +1.2000E–1   The number is 0.12.
   +1.1000E+1   The number is 11.0.

3. Multiply the two fractions and add the exponents (1.2 × 1.1 = 1.32, –1 + 1 = 0).

   +1.2000E–1   The number is 0.12.
   +1.1000E+1   The number is 11.0.
   _____
   +1.320E+0   The result is 1.32.

4. Normalize the result.

   +1.32000E+0   The number is 1.32.

5. If the guard digit is greater than or equal to 5, round the next digit up. Otherwise, truncate the number.

   +1.3200E+0   The number is 1.32

Notice that in multiply, you didn't have to go through all that shifting. The rules for multiplication are a lot shorter than those for add as far as the computer hardware designers are concerned. Integer multiplication is a lot slower than integer addition. In floating point, multiplication speed is a lot closer to that of addition.

To divide numbers like 100.0 by 30.0, we must perform the following steps:

1. Start with the numbers.

   +1.000E+2   The number is 100.0.
   +3.000E+1   The number is 30.0.

2. Add the guard digit.

+1.0000E+2   The number is 100.0.
+3.0000E+1   The number is 30.0.

3. Divide the fractions, and subtract the exponents.

+1.0000E+2   The number is 100.0.
+3.0000E+1   The number is 30.0.
_____

+0.3333E+1   The result is 3.333.

4. Normalize the result.

+3.3330E+0   The result is 3.333.

5. If the guard digit is less than or equal to 5, round the next digit up. Otherwise, truncate the number.

+3.333E+0   The result is 3.333.

Overflow and Underflow

There are limits to the size of the number a computer can handle. What is the result of the following calculation?

$$9.000E+9 \times 9.000E+9$$

Multiplying it out, we get:

$$8.1 \times 10^{19}$$

However, we are limited to a single-digit exponent, too small to hold 19. This is an example of *overflow* (sometimes called exponent overflow). Some computers generate a trap when this occurs, thus interrupting the program and causing an error message to be printed. Others are not so nice and generate a wrong answer (like 8.100E+9). Computers that follow the IEEE floating-point standard generate a special value called +Infinity.

Underflow occurs when the numbers become too small for the computer to handle. Example:

$$1.000E-9 \times 1.000E-9$$

The result is:

$$1.0 \times 10^{-18}$$

Because −18 is too small to fit into one digit, we have underflow. Again, like overflow, the results of underflow are system-dependent.

Roundoff Error

Floating point is not exact. Everyone knows that 1 + 1 is 2, but did you know that ⅓ + ⅓ does not = ⅔? This can be shown by the following floating-point calculations:

⅔ as floating point is 6.667E–1

⅓ as floating point is 3.333E–1

```
+3.333E–1
+3.333E–1
```
_____

```
+6.666E–1, or 0.6666
```

which is not:

```
+6.667E–1
```

Every computer has a similar problem with doing floating-point calculations. For example, the number 0.2 has no exact representation in binary floating point.

Floating point should never be used for money. Because we are used to dealing with dollars and cents, it is tempting to define the amount $1.98 as:

```
float amount = 1.98;
```

However, the more calculations you do with floating point, the bigger the roundoff error. Banks, credit cards, and the IRS tend to be very fussy about money. Giving the IRS a check that's almost right is not going to make them happy. Money should be stored as an integer number of pennies.

Accuracy

How many digits of the fraction are accurate? At first glance you might be tempted to say all four digits. Those of you who have read the previous section on roundoff error might be tempted to change your answer to three.

The answer is: the accuracy depends on the calculation. Certain operations, such as subtracting two numbers that are close to each other, generate inexact results. Consider the following equation:

$$1 - \tfrac{1}{3} - \tfrac{1}{3} - \tfrac{1}{3}$$

In floating-point notation this is:

```
 1.000E+0
–0.333E–0
–0.333E–0
–0.333E–0
```
_____

```
 0.0010E+0, or 1.000E–3
```

The correct answer is 0.000E+0 and we got 1.000E–3. The very first digit of the fraction is wrong. This is an example of the problem called roundoff error that can occur during floating-point operations.

Minimizing Roundoff Error

There are many techniques for minimizing roundoff error. Guard digits have already been discussed. Another trick is to use **double** instead of **float**. This gives you approximately twice the accuracy as well as twice the range. It also pushes away the minimization problem twice as far. But roundoff errors still can creep in.

Advanced techniques for limiting the problems caused by floating point can be found in books on numerical analysis. They are beyond the scope of this text. The purpose of this chapter is to give you some idea of what sort of problems can be encountered.

Floating point by its very nature is not exact. People tend to think of computers as very accurate machines. They can be, but they also can give wildly wrong results. You should be aware of the places where errors can slip into your program.

Determining Accuracy

There is a simple way of determining how accurate your floating point is (for simple calculations). The method used in the following program is to add 1.0 + 0.1, 1.0 + 0.01, 1.0 + 0.001, and so on until the second number gets so small that it makes no difference in the result.

The old C language specified that all floating-point numbers were to be done in **double**. C++ removed that restriction, but because many C++ compilers are really front-ends to a C compiler, frequently C++ arithmetic is done in **double**. This means that if number1 and number2 are declared as float, the expression:

```
while (number1 + number2 != number1)
```

is equivalent to:

```
while (double(number1) + double(number2) != double(number1))
```

If you use the 1 + 0.001 trick, the automatic conversion of **float** to **double** may give a distorted picture of the accuracy of your machine. (In one case, 84 bits of accuracy were reported for a 32-bit format.) Example 19-1 computes the accuracy of both floating point as used in equations and floating point as stored in memory. Note the trick used to determine the accuracy of the floating-point numbers in storage.

Example 19-1. float/float.cpp

```
#include <iostream>
#include <iomanip>

int main()
{
    // two number to work with
    float number1, number2;
    float result;           // result of calculation
    int   counter;          // loop counter and accuracy check
```

Example 19-1. float/float.cpp (continued)

```
    number1 = 1.0;
    number2 = 1.0;
    counter = 0;

    while (number1 + number2 != number1) {
        ++counter;
        number2 = number2 / 10.0;
    }
    std::cout << std::setw(2) << counter <<
        " digits accuracy in calculations\n";

    number2 = 1.0;
    counter = 0;

    while (true) {
        result = number1 + number2;
        if (result == number1)
            break;
        ++counter;
        number2 = number2 / 10.0;
    }
    std::cout << std::setw(2) << counter <<
        " digits accuracy in storage\n";
    return (0);
}
```

The results are as follows:

```
20 digits accuracy in calculations
8 digits accuracy in storage
```

This program gives only an approximation of the floating-point precision arithmetic. A more accurate definition can be found in the standard include file *float.h*.

Precision and Speed

A variable of type **double** has about twice the precision of a normal **float** variable. Most people assume that double-precision arithmetic takes longer than single-precision. This is not always the case. Let's assume we have one of the older compilers that does everything in **double**.

For the equation:

```
float answer, number1, number2;
```

```
answer = number1 + number2;
```

C++ must perform the following steps:

1. Convert number1 from single to double precision.

2. Convert `number2` from single to double precision.

3. Double-precision add.

4. Convert result into single precision.

5. Store the result in `answer`.

If the variables were of type **double**, C++ would have to perform only the following steps:

1. Double-precision add.

2. Store result in `answer`.

As you can see, the second form is a lot simpler, requiring three fewer conversions. In some cases, converting a program from single precision to double precision makes it run *faster*.

 Because C++ specifies that floating point can be done in **double** or **float**, you can't be sure of anything. Changing all **floats** into **doubles** may make the program run faster, slower, or the same. The only thing you can be sure of when using floating point is that the results are unpredictable.

Many computers, including the PC and Sun/3 series machines, have a special chip called a floating-point processor that does all the floating-point arithmetic. Actual tests using the Motorola 68881 floating-point chip (which is used in the Sun/3) and floating point on the PC show that single precision and double precision run at the same speed.

Power Series

Many trigonometry functions are computed using a *power series*. For example, the series for sine is:

$$\sin(x) = x - \frac{x^3}{3!} + \frac{x^5}{5!} - \frac{x^7}{7!} + \ldots$$

The question is, how many terms do we need to get four-digit accuracy? Table 19-2 contains the terms for $\sin(\pi/2)$.

Table 19-2. Terms for $\sin(\pi/2)$

	Term	Value	Total
1	x	1.571E+0	
2	$\frac{x^3}{3!}$	6.462E−1	9.248E−1
3	$\frac{x^5}{5!}$	7.974E−2	1.005E+0

Table 19-2. Terms for sin(π/2) (continued)

	Term	Value	Total
4	$\dfrac{x^7}{7!}$	4.686E−3	9.998E−1
5	$\dfrac{x^9}{9!}$	1.606E−4	1.000E+0
6	$\dfrac{x^{11}}{11!}$	3.604E−6	1.000E+0

From this we conclude that five terms are needed. However, if we try to compute sin(π), we get Table 19-3.

Table 19-3. Terms for sin(p)

	Term	Value	Total
1	x	3.142E+0	
2	$\dfrac{x^3}{3!}$	5.170E+0	−2.028E+0
3	$\dfrac{x^5}{5!}$	2.552E−0	5.241E−1
4	$\dfrac{x^7}{7!}$	5.998E−1	−7.570E−2
5	$\dfrac{x^9}{9!}$	8.224E−2	6.542E−3
6	$\dfrac{x^{11}}{11!}$	7.381E−3	−8.388E−4
7	$\dfrac{x^{13}}{13!}$	4.671E−4	−3.717E−4
8	$\dfrac{x^{15}}{15!}$	2.196E−5	−3.937E−4
9	$\dfrac{x^{17}}{17!}$	7.970E−7	−3.929E−4
10	$\dfrac{x^{19}}{19!}$	2.300E−8	−3.929E−4

π needs nine terms; so different angles require a different number of terms. (A program for computing the sine to four-digit accuracy showing intermediate terms is included in Appendix D.)

Compiler designers have a dilemma when it comes to designing a sine function. If they know ahead of time the number of terms to use, they can optimize their algorithms for that number of terms. However, they lose accuracy for some angles. So a compromise must be struck between speed and accuracy.

Don't assume that because the number came from the computer, it is accurate. The library functions can generate bad answers—especially when working with excessively large or small values. Most of the time you will not have any problems with these functions, but you should be aware of their limitations.

Finally, there is the question of what is sin(1,000,000)? Our floating-point format is good for only four digits. The sine function is cyclical. That is, sin(0) = sin(2π) = sin(4π). Therefore, sin(1,000,000) is the same as sin(1,000,000 mod 2π).

Because our floating-point format is good to only four digits, sin(1,000,000) is actually sin(1,000,*xxx*), where *xxx* represents unknown digits. But the sin function is periodic with a period 2π, which means it goes through its full range in a space of 2π. Because the range of unknown (1,000) is bigger than 2π, the error renders meaningless the result of the sine.

Insignificant Figures

I attended a physics class at Cal Tech taught by two professors. One was giving a lecture on the sun when he said, "... and the mean temperature of the inside of the sun is 13,000,000 to 25,000,000 degrees." At this point the other instructor broke in and asked, "Is that Celsius or Kelvin?" (absolute zero on the Kelvin scale = degrees Celsius −273)

The first lecturer turned to the board for a minute and then said, "What's the difference?" The moral of the story is that when your calculations have a possible error of 12,000,000, a difference of 273 doesn't mean very much.

Programming Exercises

Exercise 19-1: Write a class that uses strings to represent floating-point numbers in the format used in this chapter. The class should have functions to read, write, add, subtract, multiply, and divide floating-point numbers.

Exercise 19-2: Create a class to handle fixed-point numbers. A fixed-point number has a constant (fixed) number of digits to the right of the decimal point.

## CHAPTER 20

Advanced Pointers

A race that binds
Its body in chains and calls them Liberty,
And calls each fresh link progress.
—Robert Buchanan

One of the more useful and complex features of C++ is its use of pointers. With pointers you can create complex data structures such as linked lists and trees. Figure 20-1 illustrates some of these data structures.

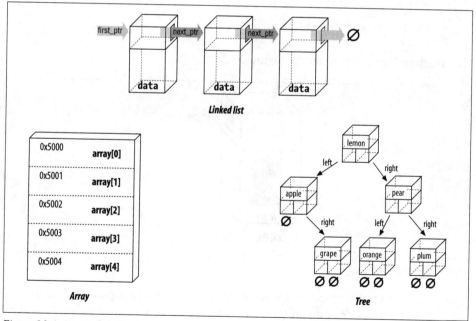

Figure 20-1. Examples of pointer use

Up to now all your data structures have been allocated by the compiler as either permanent or temporary variables. With pointers you can create and allocate *dynamic data structures*, which can grow or shrink as needed. In this chapter you will learn how to use some of the more common dynamic data structures.

It should be noted that C++ has something called the Standard Template Library (STL), which implements the data structures presented in this chapter. These STL classes are much more reliable and flexible when it comes to managing dynamic memory. Thus, in practice, people rarely explicitly use the data structures described below.

We will study them anyway, however, because by examining them we'll learn a lot about the basics of dynamic memory management. The linked list and tree are classic dynamic memory management tools and understanding them will give you the skills to create more complex, real world, data structures.

Pointers, Structures, and Classes

Structures and classes may contain pointers, or even a pointer to another instance of the same structure. In the following example:

```
class item {
    public:
        int value;
        item *next_ptr;
};
```

the structure item is illustrated by Figure 20-2.

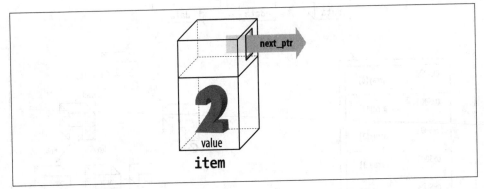

Figure 20-2. Item

The operator **new** allocates storage for a variable and returns a pointer. It is used to create new things out of thin air (actually out of an area of memory called the heap). Up to now we've used pointers solely to point to named variables. So if we used a statement like:

```
int data;
```

```
    int *number_ptr;

    number_ptr = &data;
```

the thing we are pointing to has a name (data). The operator **new** creates a new, unnamed variable and returns a pointer to it. The "things" created by new can only be referenced through pointers, never by name.

In the following example, we use **new** to allocate an integer from the heap. The variable element_ptr will point to our new integer.

```
    int *element_ptr;          // Pointer to an integer
    element_ptr = new int;     // Get an integer from the heap
```

The operator **new** takes a single argument: the type of the item to be allocated. According to the C++ standard, if **new** runs out of memory, it throws an exception that normally aborts the program. (See Chapter 22 for information on how to handle this and avoid aborting.) On older C++ systems, when **new** runs out of memory, it returns a null pointer.

Suppose we are working on a complex record list that contains (among other things) a mailing list. We want to keep our storage use to a minimum, so we only want to allocate memory for a person if he or she exists. Creating an array of class person would allocate the data statically and use up too much space. So we will allocate space as needed. Our structure for a person is:

```
    class person {
        public:
            std::string  name;         // Name of the person
            std::string  address;      // Where he lives
            std::string  city_state_zip;// Part 2 of address
            int      age;              // His age
            float    height;           // His height in inches
    }
```

We want to allocate space for this person. Later the pointer to this record will be put in the record list.

To create a new person, we use the following:

```
    struct person *new_ptr;

    new_ptr = new person;
```

The operator **new** can also allocate more complex data types such as arrays. Example 20-1 allocates storage for a integer array 80 elements long. The variable data_ptr points to this storage.

Example 20-1. new_array/new_array.cpp

```
int main( )
{
    int *data_ptr;

    data_ptr = new int[80];
```

All we've done is substitute a simple type (such as person) with an array specification (int[80]).

delete Operator

The operator **new** gets memory from the heap. To return the memory to the heap you use the operator **delete**. The general form of the **delete** operator is:

```
delete pointer;      // Where pointer is a pointer to a simple object
pointer = NULL;
```

where pointer is a pointer previously allocated by **new**. If the **new** operator allocated an array, you must use the form:

```
delete[] pointer;      // Where pointer is a pointer to an array
pointer = NULL;
```

There are two forms of the **delete** operator because there is no way for C++ to tell the difference between a pointer to an object and a pointer to an array of objects. The **delete** operator relies on the programmer using "[]" to tell the two apart.

If you accidently omit the "[]" when deleting an array, C++ will think you are giving delete a pointer to a single object and will delete only that object.

Strictly speaking, the line:

```
pointer = NULL;
```

is unnecessary. However, it is a good idea to "null out" pointers after they are deleted. That way, you don't try use a pointer to deleted memory, and you also help prevent any attempts to delete the same memory twice.

The following is an example using **new** to get storage and **delete** to dispose of it:

```
const DATA_SIZE = (16 * 1024);

void copy()
{
    char *data_ptr;      // Pointer to large data buffer

    data_ptr = new char[DATA_SIZE];      // Get the buffer

    /*
     * Use the data buffer to copy a file
     */
    delete[] data_ptr;
    data_ptr = NULL;
}
```

But what happens if we forget to free the memory? The buffer becomes dead. That is, the memory management system thinks it's being used, but no one is using it. (The technical term for this is a "memory leak.") If the **delete** statement is removed from the function copy, each successive call eats up another 16K of memory.

The other problem that can occur is using memory that has been freed. When **delete** is used, the memory is returned to the memory pool and can be reused. Using a pointer after a **delete** call is similar to an array index out-of-bounds error. You are using memory that belongs to someone else. This can cause unexpected results or program crashes.

Linked Lists

Suppose you are writing a program to send a list of names to another computer using a communications line. The operator types in the names during the day, and after work you dial up the other computer and send the names. The problem is, you don't know ahead of time how many names are going to be typed. By using a *linked-list* data structure, you can create a list of names that can grow as more names are entered. With a linked list you can also easily insert names into the middle of the list (which would be slow and difficult with an array). Also, as you will see later, linked lists can be combined with other data structures to handle extremely complex data.

A linked list is a chain of items in which each item points to the next item in the chain. Think about the treasure hunt games you played when you were a kid. You were given a note that said, "Look in the mailbox." You raced to the mailbox and found the next clue, "Look in the big tree in the back yard," and so on until you found your treasure (or you got lost). In a treasure hunt each clue points to the next one.

Figure 20-3 graphically illustrates a linked list.

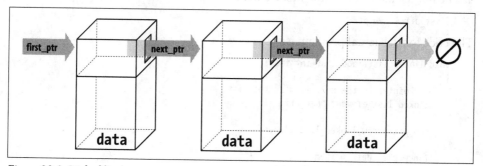

Figure 20-3. Linked list

The class declarations for a linked list are:

```
class linked_list {
    public:
```

```
class linked_list_element {
    public:
        int     data;              // Data in this element
    private:
        // Pointer to next element
        linked_list_element *next_ptr;
    friend class linked_list;
};

public:
    linked_list_element *first_ptr;   // First element in the list

    // Initialize the linked list
    linked_list( ) {first_ptr = NULL;}

    // ... Other member functions
};
```

The variable first_ptr points to the first element of the list. In the beginning, before we insert any elements into the list (it is empty), this variable is initialized to NULL.

Figure 20-4 illustrates how a new element can be added to the beginning of a linked list. Now all we have to do is translate this into C++ code.

To do this in C++, we execute the following steps:

1. Create the item we are going to add.

```
new_ptr = new linked_list_element;
```

2. Store the item in the new element.

```
(*new_ptr).data = item;
```

3. Make the first element of the list point to the new element.

```
(*new_ptr).next_ptr = first_ptr;
```

4. The new element is now the first element.

```
first_ptr = new_ptr;
```

The code for the actual program is:

```
void linked_list::add_list(int item)
{
    // Pointer to the next item in the list
    linked_list_element *new_ptr;

    new_ptr = new linked_list_element;

    (*new.ptr).data = item
    (*new_ptr).next_ptr = first_ptr;
    first_ptr = new_ptr;
}
```

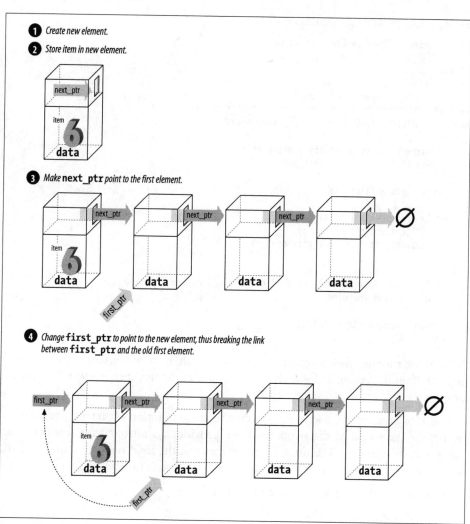

1 *Create new element.*

2 *Store item in new element.*

3 *Make* **next_ptr** *point to the first element.*

4 *Change* **first_ptr** *to point to the new element, thus breaking the link between* **first_ptr** *and the old first element.*

Figure 20-4. New element

Now that we can put things in a list, let's use that ability. We'll now write a short function to search the list until we find a key item or we run out of data. Example 20-2 contains the new find function.

Example 20-2. find/find.cpp

```cpp
#include <iostream>
#include <string>
#include "linked.h"
/*******************************************************
 * find -- look for a data item in the list            *
 *                                                     *
 * Parameters                                          *
```

Example 20-2. find/find.cpp (continued)

```
 *      name -- name to look for in the list          *
 *                                                      *
 *                                                      *
 * Returns                                              *
 *      true if name is found                           *
 *      false if name is not found                      *
 **********************************************************/
bool linked_list::find(const std::string& name)
{
    /* current structure we are looking at */
    linked_list_element *current_ptr;

    current_ptr = first_ptr;

    while ((current_ptr->data != name != 0) &&
           (current_ptr != NULL))
        current_ptr = current_ptr->next_ptr;

    /*
     * If current_ptr is null, we fell off the end of the list and
     * didn't find the name
     */
    return (current_ptr != NULL);
}
```

Why does running this program sometimes result in a bus error? Other times it reports "found" (return 1) for an item that is not in the list. (See Answer 20-1 for the answer.)

In our find program we had to use the cumbersome notation (*current_ptr).data to access the data field of the structure. C++ provides a shorthand for this construct using the -> operator. The dot (.) operator means the field of a structure, and the structure pointer operator (->) indicates the field of a structure pointer.

The following two expressions are equivalent:

```
(*current_ptr).data = value;
current_ptr->data = value;
```

Ordered Linked Lists

So far we have only added new elements to the head of a linked list. Suppose we want to add elements in order. Figure 20-5 is an example of an ordered linked list.

Figure 20-6 shows the steps necessary to add a new element, "53", to the list.

The following member function implements this algorithm. The first step is to locate the insertion point. The first_ptr points to the first element of the list. The program moves the variable before_ptr along the list until it finds the proper place for the insertion. The variable after_ptr is set to point to the next value. The new element will be inserted between these elements.

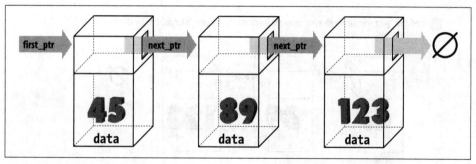

Figure 20-5. Ordered list

```
void linked_list::enter(int item):
{
    linked_list_item *before_ptr; // Insert after this element
    linked_list_item *after_ptr;  // Insert before this element

    /*
     * Warning: This routine does not take
     *   care of the case where the element is
     *   inserted at the head of the list
     */

    before_ptr = first_ptr;
    while (true) {
        before_ptr = after_ptr;
        after_ptr = after_ptr->next_ptr;

        // Did we hit the end of the list?
        if (after_ptr == NULL)
            break;

        // Did we find the place?
        if (item >= after_ptr->data)
            break;
    }
}
```

Now we know where to insert the new element. All we must do is insert it. We start at the element before the new one (before_ptr). This element should point to the new element, so:

```
before_ptr->next_ptr = new_ptr;
```

Next is the new element (new_ptr). It needs to point to the element after it, or after_ptr. This is accomplished with the code:

```
new_ptr->next_ptr = after_ptr;
```

The element after_ptr needs to point to the rest of the chain. Because it already does, we leave it alone. The full code for inserting the new element is:

```
// Create new item
new_ptr = new linked_list_item;
```

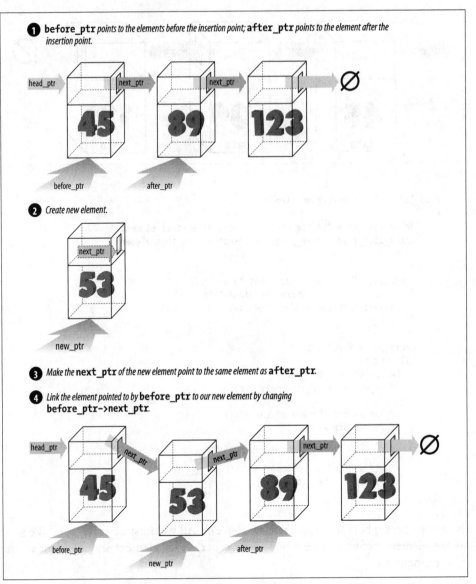

1 **before_ptr** *points to the elements before the insertion point;* **after_ptr** *points to the element after the insertion point.*

2 *Create new element.*

3 *Make the* **next_ptr** *of the new element point to the same element as* **after_ptr**.

4 *Link the element pointed to by* **before_ptr** *to our new element by changing* **before_ptr->next_ptr**.

Figure 20-6. Adding element "53" to an ordered list

```
new_ptr->data = item;

// Link in the new item
before_ptr->next_ptr = new_ptr;
new_ptr->next_ptr = after_ptr;
}
```

Doubly Linked Lists

An element in a doubly linked list contains two links. One link points forward to the next element; the other points backward to the previous element. Doubly linked lists are useful where the program needs to go through the list both forward and backward.

The classes for a doubly linked list are:

```
class double_list {
    private:
        class double_list_element {
            public:
                int data;                       // Data item
            private:
                double_list_element *next_ptr;      // Forward link
                double_list_element *previous_ptr;// Backward link
            friend class double_list;
        };
    public:
        double_list_element *head_ptr;   // Head of the list

        double_list() {head_ptr = NULL;}

        // ... Other member functions
```

This is shown graphically in Figure 20-7.

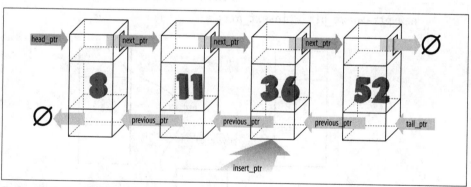

Figure 20-7. Doubly linked list

To insert an item into the list, we first locate the insertion point:

```
void double_list::enter(int item)
{
    double_list_element *insert_ptr; // Insert before this element

    /*
     * Warning: This routine does not take
     *   care of the case where the element is
     *   inserted at the head of the list
     *   or the end of the list
     */
```

```
    insert_ptr = head_ptr;
    while (true) {
        insert_ptr = insert_ptr->next;

        // Have we reached the end?
        if (insert_ptr == NULL)
            break;

        // Have we reached the right place?
        if (item >= insert_ptr->data)
            break;
    }
```

Notice that we do not have to keep track of the variable before_ptr. The pointer insert_ptr->previous_ptr is used to locate the previous element. To insert a new element, we must adjust two sets of pointers. First we create the new element:

```
// Create new element
new_ptr = new double_list_element;
```

Next we set up the forward pointer for the new item:

```
new_ptr->next_ptr = insert_ptr;
```

Graphically this is represented by Figure 20-8.

Next we connect the link to the previous element using the following code:

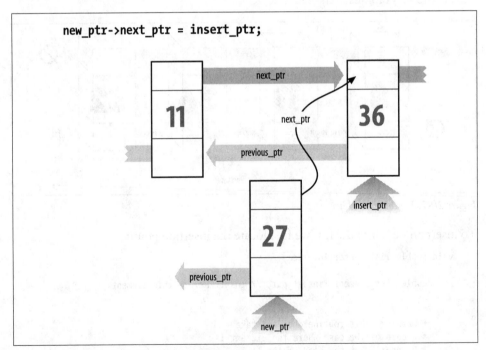

Figure 20-8. Doubly linked list insert, part 1

```
new_ptr->previous_ptr = insert_ptr->previous_ptr;
```

Graphically, this is represented in Figure 20-9.

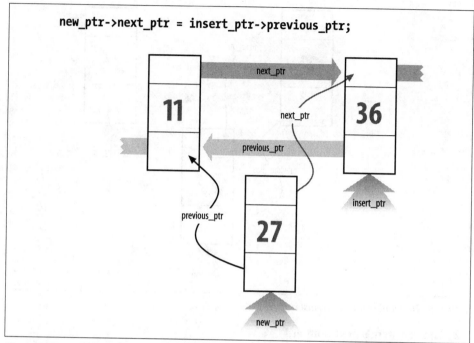

Figure 20-9. Doubly linked list insert, part 2

The links are set up for the new element. Now all we have to do is break the old links between items 11 and 36 and connect them to the new item (27).

Getting to item 11 is a bit of a trick. We only have a pointer to item 36 (insert_ptr). However, if we follow the previous link back (insert_ptr->previous_ptr), we get the item (11) that we want. Now all we have to do is fix the next_ptr for this item.

The C++ code for this is surprisingly simple:

```
insert_ptr->previous_ptr->next_ptr = new_ptr;
```

You can see this operation represented graphically in Figure 20-9.

We have only one remaining link to fix: the previous_ptr of the insert_ptr. In C++ the code looks like this:

```
insert_ptr->previous_ptr = new_ptr;
```

This operation is represented graphically by Figure 20-10.

In summary, to insert a new item in a doubly linked list, you must set four links:

1. The new item's previous pointer:

```
new_ptr->previous_ptr = insert_ptr->previous_ptr;
```

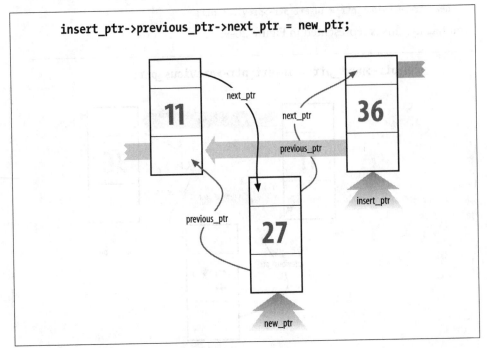

```
insert_ptr->previous_ptr->next_ptr = new_ptr;
```

Figure 20-10. Doubly linked list insert, part 3

2. The new item's next pointer:

```
new_ptr->next_ptr = insert_ptr;
```

3. The previous pointer of the item that will follow the new item:

```
insert_ptr->previous_ptr->next_ptr = new_ptr;
```

4. The next pointer of the item that will precede the new item:

```
insert_ptr->previous_ptr = new_ptr;
```

The final results are illustrated in Figure 20-11.

Trees

Suppose we want to create an alphabetized list of the words that appear in a file. We could use a linked list, but searching a linked list is slow because we must check each element until we find the correct insertion point. By using a data type called a *tree,* we can reduce the number of comparisons tremendously. A *binary tree structure* looks like Figure 20-12. Each box is called a *node* of the tree. The box at the top is the *root* and the boxes at the bottom are the *leaves.** Each node contains two pointers: a left pointer and a right pointer, which point to the left and right subtrees.

---

* Programming trees are written with the root at the top and the leaves at the bottom. Common sense tells you that this is upside down. In case you haven't noticed, common sense has very little to do with programming.

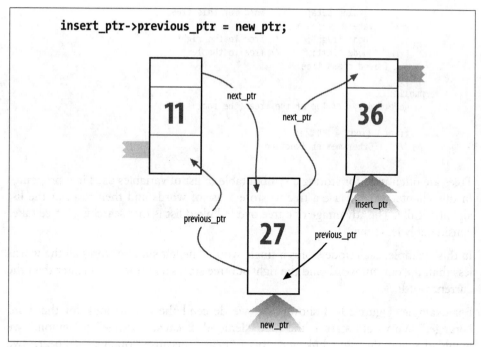

Figure 20-11. Doubly linked list insert, part 4

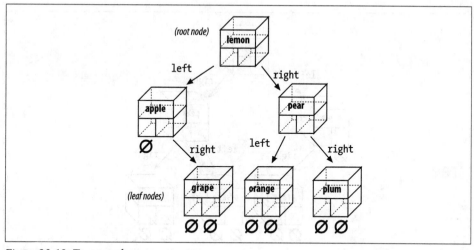

Figure 20-12. Tree search

The structure for a tree is:

```
class tree {
    private:
        class node {
            public:
```

```
        string data;     // Word for this tree
    private:
        node *right;     // Tree to the right
        node *left;      // Tree to the left
    friend class tree;
};
public:
    node *root;  // Top of the tree (the root)

    tree() {root = NULL;};
    // ... Other member function
};
```

Trees are often used for storing a symbol table (a list of variables used in a program). In this chapter we will use a tree to store a list of words and then to print the list alphabetically. The advantage of a tree over a linked list is that searching a tree takes considerably less time.

In this example, each node stores a single word. The left subtree stores all the words less than the current word, and the right subtree stores all the words greater than the current word.

For example, Figure 20-13 shows how we descend the tree to look for the word "orange." We would start at the root, "lemon." Because "orange" > "lemon," we would descend the right link and go to "pear." Because "orange" < "pear," we descend the left link, where we find "orange."

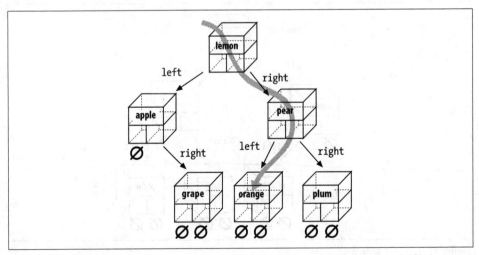

Figure 20-13. Tree

Recursion is extremely useful with trees. Our rules for recursion are 1) the function must make things simpler and 2) there must be some endpoint.

The algorithm for inserting a word in a tree is:

1. If this is a null tree (or subtree), create a one-node tree with this word.
2. If this node contains the word, do nothing.
3. Otherwise, enter the word in the left or right subtree, depending on the value of the word.

Does this algorithm satisfy our recursion rules? The function has two definite end-points:

- A match is found.
- We have a null node.

Otherwise, we enter the word into a subtree (which is simpler than the whole tree).

To see how this works, consider what happens when we insert the word "fig" into the tree. First we check the word "fig" against "lemon." "Fig" is smaller, so we go to "apple." Because "fig" is bigger, we go to "grape." Because "fig" is smaller than "grape," we try the left link. It is NULL, so we create a new node.

The function to enter a value into a tree is:

```
void tree::enter_one(node *&tree_node, const string& word)
{
    int  result;         // Result of strcmp

    // See if we have reached the end
    if (tree_node == NULL) {
        tree_node = new node;

        tree_node->left = NULL;
        tree_node->right = NULL;
        tree_node->word = word;
    }
    if (tree_node->data == word)
        return;

    if (tree_node->data < word)
        enter_one(tree_node->right, word);
    else
        enter_one(tree_node->left, word);
}
```

The function to start this process is:

```
void tree::enter(char *word) {
    enter_one(root, word);
};
```

This function passes a pointer to the root of the tree to enter_one. If the root is NULL, enter_one creates the node. Because we are changing the value of a pointer, we must pass a reference to the pointer.

Printing a Tree

Despite the complex nature of a tree structure, it is easy to print. Again we use recursion. The printing algorithm is:

1. For the null tree, print nothing.
2. Print the data that comes before this node (left tree).
3. Print this node.
4. Print the data that comes after this node (right tree).

The code for printing the tree is:

```
void tree::print_one(node *top)
{
    if (top == NULL)
        return;                 // Short tree

    print_one(top->left);
    std::cout << top->word << '\n';
    print_one(top->right);
}
void tree::print( ) {
    print_one(root);
}
```

The Rest of the Program

Now that we have the data structure defined, all we need to complete the program is a few more functions. The main function checks for the correct number of arguments and then calls the scanner and the print_one routine.

The scan function reads the file and breaks it into words. It uses the standard macro isalpha. The macro returns 1 if its argument is a letter and 0 otherwise. It is defined in the standard include file cctype. After a word is found, the function enter is called to put the word in the tree.

Example 20-3 is the listing of *words.cpp*.

Example 20-3. words/words.cpp

```
/*****************************************************
 * words -- scan a file and print out a list of words  *
 *              in ASCII order.                         *
 *                                                      *
 * Usage:                                               *
 *      words <file>                                    *
 *****************************************************/
#include <iostream>
#include <fstream>
#include <cctype>
```

Example 20-3. words/words.cpp (continued)

```cpp
#include <string>
#include <cstdlib>

class tree {
    private:
        // The basic node of a tree
        class node {
            private:
                node    *right;     // tree to the right
                node    *left;      // tree to the left
            public:
                std::string  word;  // word for this tree

                friend class tree;
        };

        // the top of the tree
        node *root;

        // Enter a new node into a tree or sub-tree
        void enter_one(node *&node, const std::string& word);

        // Print a single node
        void print_one(node *top);
    public:
        tree() { root = NULL;}

        // Add a new word to our tree
        void enter(std::string& word) {
            enter_one(root, word);
        }

        // Print the tree
        void print() {
            print_one(root);
        }
};

static tree words;      // List of words we are looking for

/******************************************************
 * scan -- scan the file for words                    *
 *                                                    *
 * Parameters                                         *
 *      name -- name of the file to scan              *
 ******************************************************/
void scan(const char *const name)
{
    std::string new_word;   // word we are working on
    int  ch;                // current character
    std::ifstream in_file;  // input file
```

Example 20-3. words/words.cpp (continued)

```cpp
    in_file.open(name, std::ios::in);
    if (in_file.bad()) {
        std::cerr << "Error:Unable to open " << name << '\n';
        exit(8);
    }
    while (true) {
        // scan past the whitespace
        while (true) {
            ch = in_file.get();

            if (std::isalpha(ch) || (ch == EOF))
                break;
        }

        if (ch == EOF)
            break;

        new_word = ch;
        while (true)
        {
            ch = in_file.get();
            if (!std::isalpha(ch))
                break;
            new_word += ch;
        }
        words.enter(new_word);
    }
}


int main(int argc, char *argv[])
{
    if (argc != 2) {
        std::cerr <<  "Error:Wrong number of parameters\n";
        std::cerr << "       on the command line\n";
        std::cerr << "Usage is:\n";
        std::cerr << "    words 'file'\n";
        exit(8);
    }
    scan(argv[1]);
    words.print();
    return (0);
}

/********************************************************
 * tree::enter_one -- enter a word into the tree        *
 *                                                      *
 * Parameters                                           *
 *     new_node -- current node we are looking at       *
 *     word -- word to enter                            *
 ********************************************************/
void tree::enter_one(node *&new_node, const std::string& word)
```

Example 20-3. words/words.cpp (continued)

```cpp
{
    // see if we have reached the end
    if (new_node == NULL) {
        new_node = new node;

        new_node->left = NULL;
        new_node->right = NULL;
        new_node->word = word;
    }
    if (new_node->word == word)
        return;

    if (new_node->word < word)
        enter_one(new_node->right, word);
    else
        enter_one(new_node->left, word);
}

/********************************************************
 * tree::print_one -- print out the words in a tree    *
 *                                                      *
 * Parameters                                           *
 *       top -- the root of the tree to print           *
 ********************************************************/
void tree::print_one(node *top)
{
    if (top == NULL)
        return;                    // short tree

    print_one(top->left);
    std::cout << top->word << '\n';
    print_one(top->right);
}
```

I once made a program that read the dictionary into memory using a tree structure and then used it in a program that searched for misspelled words. Although trees are supposed to be fast, this program was so slow you would think I had used a linked list. Why?

Hint: *Graphically construct a tree using the words "able," "baker," "cook," "delta," and "easy" and look at the result.*

Data Structures for a Chess Program

A classic problem in artificial intelligence is the game of chess. We are going to design a data structure for a chess-playing program. In chess there are several moves you can make. Your opponent has many responses, to which you have many answers, and so on, back and forth for several levels of moves.

Our data structure is beginning to look like a tree. But this is not a binary tree, because we have more than two branches for each node (Figure 20-14).

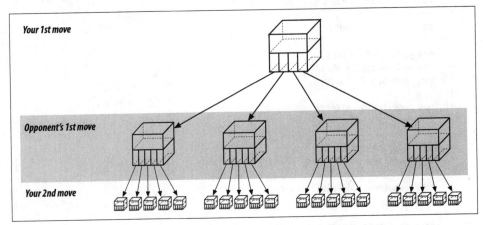

Figure 20-14. Chess tree

We are tempted to use the following data structure:

```
class chess {
    public:
        class board_class board; // Current board position
        class next_class {
            class move_class move;        // Our next move
            class chess *chess_ptr; // Pointer to the resulting position
        } next[MAX_MOVES];
};
```

The problem is that the number of moves from any given position varies dramatically. For example, in the beginning you have lots of pieces running around.* Pieces such as rooks, queens, and bishops can move any number of squares in a straight line. When you reach the end game (in an evenly matched game), each side probably has only a few pawns and one major piece. The number of possible moves has been greatly reduced.

We want to be as efficient as possible in our storage because a chess program stresses the limits of our machine. We can reduce storage requirements by changing the next-move array to a linked list. The resulting structure is:

```
class next_class {
    class move_class move;        // Our next move
    class next_class *chess_ptr;  // Pointer to the resulting position
};
```

---

* Trivia question: what are the 21 moves you can make in chess from the starting position? You can move each pawn up one (8 moves) or two (8 more), and the knights can move out to the left and right (4 more) (8+8+4=20). What's the 21st move?

```
struct chess {
    class board_class board;        // Current board position
    class next_class *list_ptr;     // List of moves we can make from here
    class next_class this_move;     // The move we are making
};
```

Graphically, this looks like Figure 20-15.

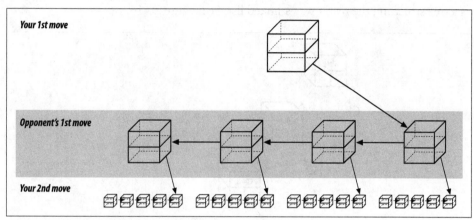

Figure 20-15. Revised chess structure

The new version adds a little complexity, but it saves a great deal of storage. That's because instead of having to allocate an array that contains all possible moves (whether used or not), we use a list to allocate only as many moves as we need to.

Programming Exercises

Exercise 20-1: Write a cross-reference program.

Exercise 20-2: Write a function to delete an element of a linked list.

Exercise 20-3: Write a function to delete an element of a doubly linked list.

Exercise 20-4: Write a function to delete an element of a tree.

Answers to Chapter Questions

Answer 20-1: The problem is with the statement:

```
while ((current_ptr->data != value) &&
       (current_ptr != NULL))
```

current_ptr->data is checked *before* we check to see whether current_ptr is a valid pointer (!= NULL). If it is NULL, we can easily check a random memory location that could contain anything. The solution is to check current_ptr before checking what it is pointing to:

```
while (current_ptr != NULL) {
    if (current_ptr->data == value)
        break;
```

Answer 20-2: The problem was as follows: because the first word in the dictionary was the smallest, every other word used the right-hand link. In fact, because the entire list was ordered, only the right-hand link was used. Although this was defined as a tree structure, the result was a linked list. See Figure 20-16.

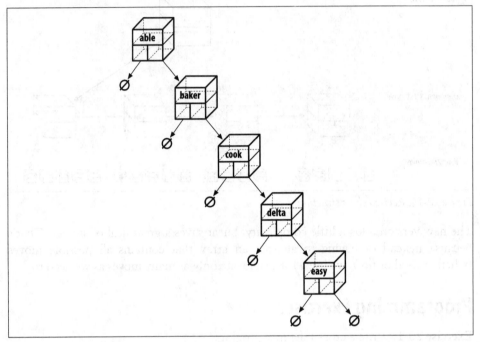

Figure 20-16. Dictionary tree

Some of the more advanced books on data structures, such as Wirth's *Algorithms + Data Structures = Programs*, discuss ways of preventing this by balancing a binary tree.

Trivia Answer: You give up. That's right, the 21st move is to resign.

## CHAPTER 21

Advanced Classes

*The ruling ideas of each age have ever
been the ideas of its ruling class.*
—Karl Marx
Manifesto of the Communist Party

This chapter discusses derived classes, virtual functions, and virtual classes.

Derived Classes

Suppose we want a stack that allows us to push on three items at a time in addition to performing all usual operations of a stack.* If we parse this statement in C++ terms, we discover something significant. We want a stack that:

1. Does all the operations of a typical stack. (In C++ this is called a base class.)

2. Expands on this by allowing us to do something more: specifically, push things on in groups of threes. (C++ calls this a *derived class*.)

Our basic stack is defined in Example 13-1.

We need to define a new expanded stack, which allows us to push multiple items. We call this an m_stack. This new stack does everything a simple stack does but also lets you push three items on at once. C++ allows you to build new classes on old ones. In this case we will be building our multiple-push stack (m_stack) on the existing simple stack (stack). Technically we will be using the class stack as a *base class* to create a new *derived class*, the multiple-push stack.

We start by telling C++ that we are creating m_stack out of stack:

```
class m_stack: public stack {
```

---

* This example is a little artificial because we wanted to keep things simple. But the techniques presented here apply to more complex objects.

The keyword **public** tells C++ to make all the public members of stack accessible to the outside world. If we declared stack as **private**, the **public** and **protected** members of stack would be accessible only inside m_stack.

This declaration tells C++ that we are going to use stack as a base for m_stack. Figure 21-1 shows how C++ views this combination.

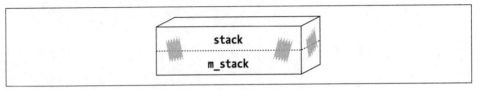

Figure 21-1. Derived class m_stack and base class stack

Now we need to define the member function that pushes three items on the stack (push_three). The code for this function looks like:

```
inline void m_stack::push_three(
    const int item1,
    const int item3,
    const int item3)
{
    // This calls push in the stack class
    push(item1);
    push(item2);
    push(item3);
}
```

We have been very careful in selecting the name of this member function. It is called push_three instead of push for a reason. If we called it push, the code:

```
inline void m_stack::push(
    const int item1,
    const int item3,
    const int item3)
{
    // This calls push in the m_stack class
    push(item1);
    push(item2);
    push(item3);
}
```

would call the member function push in the class m_stack, *not* stack's push as we want. The result is that we call m_stack's push, which calls push three times. This push belongs to m_stack, so we call push again, and so on. The result is that push will call itself over and over until the system runs out of memory.

This is not want we want. We need to tell C++ that we want to call the push in stack. This can be accomplished by using the scope operator ::. The new version of m_stack::push looks like this:

```
inline void m_stack::push(
    const int item1,
    const int item3,
    const int item3)
{
    // This calls push in the m_stack class
    stck::push(item1);
    stck::push(item2);
    stck::push(item3);
}
```

This code assumes that we need to use the name push for both the stack and m_stack classes. We don't: the name push_three is more descriptive for the m_stack member function, so we'll use that. The full definition for both the stack and m_stack classes is shown in Example 21-1.

Example 21-1. stack_c/stack_d1.cpp

```
/********************************************************
 * Stack                                               *
 *        A file implementing a simple stack class     *
 ********************************************************/
#include <cstdlib>
#include <iostream>

const int STACK_SIZE = 100;      // Maximum size of a stack

/********************************************************
 * Stack class                                         *
 *                                                     *
 * Member functions                                    *
 *        stack -- initialize the stack.               *
 *        push -- put an item on the stack.            *
 *        pop -- remove an item from the stack.        *
 ********************************************************/
// The stack itself
class stack {
    protected:
        int count;               // Number of items in the stack
        int data[STACK_SIZE];    // The items themselves
    public:
        // Initialize the stack
        stack();
        // ~stack() -- default destructor
        // copy constructor defaults

        // Push an item on the stack
        void push(const int item);

        // Pop an item from the stack
        int pop();
};

/********************************************************
```

Example 21-1. stack_c/stack_d1.cpp (continued)

```
 * stack::stack -- initialize the stack.                 *
 ******************************************************/
inline stack::stack( )
{
    count = 0;   // Zero the stack
}
/******************************************************
 * stack::push -- push an item on the stack.           *
 *                                                     *
 * Warning: We do not check for overflow.              *
 *                                                     *
 * Parameters                                          *
 *       item -- item to put in the stack              *
 ******************************************************/
inline void stack::push(const int item)
{
    assert((count >= 0) &&
           (count < sizeof(data)/sizeof(data[0])));

    data[count] = item;
    ++count;
}
/******************************************************
 * stack::pop -- get an item off the stack.            *
 *                                                     *
 * Warning: We do not check for stack underflow.       *
 *                                                     *
 * Returns                                             *
 *       The top item from the stack.                  *
 ******************************************************/
inline int stack::pop( )
{
    // Stack goes down by one
    --count;

    assert((count >= 0) &&
           (count < sizeof(data)/sizeof(data[0])));

    // Then we return the top value
    return (data[count]);
}


/******************************************************
 * m_stack -- Stack on which we can push multiple items *
 *                                                     *
 * Member function                                     *
 *       push_many -- push an item on the stack        *
 ******************************************************/
class m_stack: public stack {
    public:
        // m_stack -- default constructor
        // ~m_stack -- default destructor
```

Example 21-1. stack_c/stack_d1.cpp (continued)

```
        // copy constructor defaults

        // Push three items on the stack
        void push_three(const int item1,
                const int item2,
                const int item3);

        // Sum the elements
        int sum( );
};
/**********************************************************
 * m_stack::push_three -- push an item on the stack.      *
 *                                                        *
 * Parameters                                             *
 *      item1, item2, item3 --                            *
 *              items to put in the stack                 *
 **********************************************************/
inline void m_stack::push_three(const int item1,
                const int item2, const int item3)
{
    stack::push(item1);
    stack::push(item2);
    stack::push(item3);
}
/**********************************************************
 * m_stack::sum -- Sum the elements in the stack          *
 *                                                        *
 * Returns:                                               *
 *      The elements in the stack.                        *
 **********************************************************/
inline int m_stack::sum( ) {
    int index;              // Index into the array
    int total = 0;          // Running sum

    for (index = 0; index < count; ++index) {
        assert(index >= 0);
        assert(index < sizeof(data)/sizeof(data[0]));

        total += data[index];
    }
    return (total);
}
```

You may have noticed that we've added a member function called sum. This function
returns the total of all the elements in the stack. Our sum function needs access to the
array named data in the class stack to work. Normally this variable would be
declared private to prevent outsiders from messing with it. But in this case we would
like for no one but m_stack to be able to access this variable. The C++ keyword
protected gives us the access we want. It tells C++ that any derived class that uses
this class as a base class can access this data, but outsiders are locked out.

So the three protection keywords are:

`private`

Access is limited to the class only.

`protected`

The class and any derived class that use the class as a base class can access the member.

`public`

Anyone can access the member.

Also, because `m_stack` is derived from `stack`, you can use an `m_stack` type variable wherever a `stack` type variable is used. In the following example, we create an `m_stack` named `multi_stack` that is used as a parameter to the function `push_things`, which takes a normal, unbounded stack as a parameter:

```
void push_things(stack& a_stack) {
    a_stack.push(1);
    a_stack.push(2);
}

// ...
m_stack multi_stack; // A random stack
// ....
push_things(bounded_stack);
```

The function `push_things` takes a stack as a parameter. Even though the variable `multi_stack` is an `m_stack` type variable, C++ turns it into a `stack` when `push_things` is called.

One way to explain this is that although `multi_stack` is of type `m_stack`, when it is used by `push_things`, the function is looking through a peephole that allows it to see only the stack part of the variable, as shown in Figure 21-2.

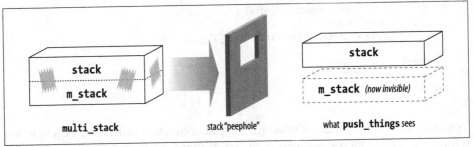

Figure 21-2. How push_things sees an m_stack

Let's improve the basic stack so that instead of always allocating a fixed-size stack, we allocate the stack dynamically. The new stack starts with:

```
class stack {
    private:
```

```
        int *data;      // Pointer to the data in the stack
    protected:
        int count;      // Current item on the stack
    public:
        stack(const unsigned int size) {
            data = new int[size];
            count = 0;
        };
        virtual ~stack() {
            delete []data;
            data = NULL;
        }
    // ...
```

(We discuss the keyword **virtual** later in this chapter.)

This stack is more flexible. To use the new stack, we must give it a size when we declare the stack variable. For example:

```
    stack big_stack(1000);
    stack small_stack(10);
    stack bad_stack; // Illegal, size required
```

Back to the m_stack class: somehow we need to call the base class constructor (stack) with a parameter.

The way we do this is to put the base-constructor initialization just after the declaration of the constructor for the derived class.

But this flexibility creates some problems for the m_stack: the constructor for stack contains a parameter. How is the m_stack to initialize the simple stack?

The solution is to use a syntax similar to initializing a constant data member:

```
    class m_stack: public stack {
        private:
            const unsigned int stack_size;   // Size of the simple stack
        public:
            m_stack(const unsigned int size) : stack(size),
                                               stack_size(size) {
            }
```

So expression stack(size) calls the constructor for stack while stack_size(size) initializes the constant data member stack_size. (Or if you've got a warped mind, you can think of stack_size(size) as calling the constructor for the integer constant stack_size.)

Because the new version of stack uses dynamic memory (**new** and **delete**), it is *vital* that we define the "big four" member functions: the constructor, destructor, copy constructor, and assignment operator (=). When we use simple member variables to store our data, the default destructor would automatically reclaim all the memory we used. But now that we are using the heap, we must use delete to free the memory and that needs to be done in the destructor.

Virtual Functions

Today there are many different ways of sending a letter. We can mail it by the United States Postal Service, send it via Federal Express, or even fax it. All these methods get the letter to the person to whom you're sending it (most of the time), but they differ in cost and speed.

Let's define a class called `mail` to handle the sending of a letter. We start by defining an address class and then use this class to define addresses for the sender and the receiver. (The definition of the address class is "just a simple matter of programming" and is left to the reader.)

Our `mail` class looks like this:

```
class mail {
    public:
        address sender;   // Who's sending the mail (return address)?
        address receiver; // Who's getting the mail?

        // Send the letter
        void send_it() {
        // ... Some magic happens here
        };
};
```

There is, however, one little problem with this class: we're depending on "magic" to get our letters sent. The process for sending a letter is different depending on which service we are using. One way to handle this is to have `send_it` call the appropriate routine depending on what service we are using:

```
void mail::send_it() {
    switch (service) {
        case POST_OFFICE:
            put_in_local_mailbox();
            break;
        case FEDERAL_EXPRESS:
            fill_out_waybill();
            call_federal_for_pickup();
            break;
        case UPS:
            put_out_ups_yes_sign();
            give_package_to_driver();
            break;
        //... and so on for every service in the universe
```

This solution is a bit clunky. Our mail class must know about all the mailing services in the world. Also consider what happens when we add another function to the class:

```
class mail {
    public:
        // Returns the cost of mailing in cents
        int cost() {
```

```
                // ... more magic
        }
```

Do we create another big switch statement? If we do, we'll have two of them to worry about. What's worse, the sending instructions and cost for each service are now spread out over two functions. It would be nice if we could group all the functions for the Postal Service in one class, all of Federal Express in another class, and so on.

For example, a class for the Postal Service might be:

```
class post_office: public mail{
    public:
        // Send the letter
        void send_it() {
            put_in_local_mailbox();
        };
        // Cost returns cost of sending a letter in cents
        int cost() {
            // Costs 37 cents to mail a letter
            return (37);    // WARNING: This can easily become dated
        }
};
```

Now we have the information for each single service in a single class. The information is stored in a format that is easy to understand. The problem is that it is not easy to use. For example, let's write a routine to send a letter:

```
void get_address_and_send(mail& letter)
{
    letter.from = my_address;
    letter.to = get_to_address();
    letter.send_it();
}
//...
    class post_office simple_letter;
    get_address_and_send(simple_letter);
```

The trouble is that letter is a mail class, so when we call letter.send_it(), we call the send_it of the base class mail. What we need is a way of telling C++, "Please call the send function of the derived class instead of the base class."

The **virtual** keyword identifies a member function that can be overridden by a member function in the derived class. If we are using a derived class, C++ will look for members in the derived class and then in the base class, in that order. If we are using a base class variable (even if the actual instance is a derived class), C++ will search only the base class for the member function. The exception is when the base class defines a **virtual** function. In this case, the derived class is searched and then the base class.

Table 21-1 illustrates the various search algorithms.

Table 21-1. Member function search order

Class type	Member function type	Search order
Derived	Normal	Derived, then base
Base	Normal	Base
Base	Virtual	Derived, then base

Example 21-2 illustrates the use of **virtual** functions.

Example 21-2. virt/virt.cpp

```
// Illustrates the use of virtual functions
#include <iostream>

class base {
    public:
        void a() { std::cout << "base::a called\n"; }
        virtual void b() { std::cout << "base::b called\n"; }
        virtual void c() { std::cout << "base::c called\n"; }
};

class derived: public base {
    public:
        void a() { std::cout << "derived::a called\n"; }
        void b() { std::cout << "derived::b called\n"; }
};

void do_base(base& a_base)
{
    std::cout << "Call functions in the base class\n";

    a_base.a();
    a_base.b();
    a_base.c();
}

int main()
{
    derived a_derived;

    std::cout << "Calling functions in the derived class\n";

    a_derived.a();
    a_derived.b();
    a_derived.c();

    do_base(a_derived);
    return (0);
}
```

The derived class contains three member functions. Two are self-defined: a and b. The third, c, is inherited from the base class. When we call a, C++ looks at the derived class to see whether that class defines the function. In this case it does, so the line:

```
a_derived.a( );
```

outputs:

```
derived::a called
```

When b is called the same thing happens, and we get:

```
derived::b called
```

It doesn't matter whether the base class defines a and b or not. C++ calls the derived class and goes no further.

However, the derived class doesn't contain a member function named c. So when we reach the line:

```
a_derived.c( );
```

C++ tries to find c in the derived class and fails. Then it tries to find the member function in the base class. In this case it succeeds and we get:

```
base::c called
```

Now let's move on to the function do_base. Because it takes a base class as its argument, C++ restricts its search for member functions to the base class. So the line:

```
a_base.a( );
```

outputs:

```
base::a called
```

But what happens when the member function b is called? This is a **virtual** function. That tells C++ that the search rules are changed. C++ first checks whether there is a b member function in the derived class; then C++ checks the base class. In the case of b, there is a b in the derived class, so the line:

```
a_base.b( );
```

outputs:

```
derived::b called
```

The member function c is also a **virtual** function. Therefore, C++ starts by looking for the function in the derived class. In this case, the function is not defined there, so C++ then looks in the base class. The function is defined there, so we get:

```
base::c called
```

Now getting back to our mail. We need a simple base class that describes the basic mailing functions for each different type of service:

```
class mail {
    public:
        address sender; // Who is sending the mail (return address)?
        address receiver; // Who is getting the mail?
```

```
        // Send the letter
        virtual void send_it() {
            std::cout <<
                    "Error: send_it not defined in derived class.\n"
            exit (8);
        };
        // Cost of sending a letter in pennies
        virtual int cost() {
            std::cout << "Error: cost not defined in derived class.\n"
            exit (8);
        };
};
```

We can define a derived class for each different type of service. For example:

```
class post_office: public mail {
    public:
        void send_it() {
            put_letter_in_box();
        }
        int cost() {
            return (29);
        }
};
```

Now we can write a routine to send a letter and not have to worry about the details. All we have to do is call send_it and let the **virtual** function do the work.

The mail class is an abstraction that describes a generalized mailer. To associate a real mailing service, we need to use it as the base for a derived class. But what happens if the programmer forgets to put the right member functions in the derived class? For example:

```
class federal_express: public mail {
    public:
        void send_it() {
            put_letter_in_box();
        }
        // Something is missing
};
```

When we try to find the cost of sending a letter via Federal Express, C++ will notice that there's no cost function in federal_express and call the one in mail. The cost function in mail knows that it should never be called, so it spits out an error message and aborts the program. Getting an error message is nice, but getting it at compilation rather than during the run would be better.

C++ allows you to specify **virtual** functions that *must* be overridden in a derived class. For this example, the new, improved, abstract mailer is:

```
class mail {
    public:
        address sender;     // Who is sending the mail (return address)?
        address receiver;   // Who is getting the mail?
```

```
        // Send the letter
        virtual void send_it( ) = 0;
        // Cost of sending a letter in pennies
        virtual int cost( ) = 0;
    };
```

The = 0 tells C++ that these member functions are *pure virtual functions*. That is, they can never be called directly. Any class containing one or more pure virtual functions is called an *abstract class*. If you tried to use an abstract class as an ordinary type, such as:

```
    void send_package( ) {
        mail a_mailer;   // Attempt to use an abstract class
```

you would get a compile-time error.

Virtual Classes

Let's take a look at an auto repair shop. Our shop consists of two rooms. The first is the garage where they repair the cars, and the second is the office where all the paper work is done. Let's design C++ classes for this situation.

Both the garage and the office are rooms, so we have a base class of room and derived classes of garage and office. In C++ our class definitions would be as follows:

```
    class room {
        // .....
    };

    class garage : public room {
        // ....
    };

    class office : public room {
        // ....
    };
```

The two classes garage and office when combined make up the business. The C++ class for this is:

```
    class repair_shop: public garage, office {
        // ...
    }
```

Figure 21-3 illustrates this class structure.

This works well for most repair shops. But what about the small guy that doesn't have enough space for two rooms and must put a desk in the garage and use it as part of his office? In his case, he has one room which is part garage and part office.

Ideally our class diagram should look like Figure 21-4. But we need some way of telling C++, "Don't generate two rooms because we have one room with two uses." This is done by declaring the base class **virtual**. This keyword tells C++ that the class has multiple uses depending on which part we are taking about.

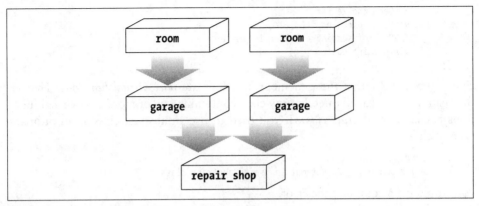

Figure 21-3. Two-room repair shop

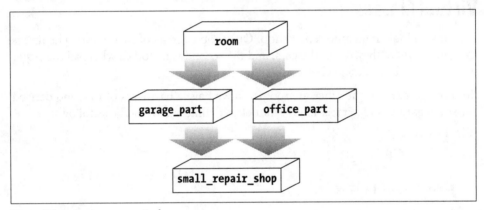

Figure 21-4. One-room repair shop

```
class room {
    // ....
};

class garage_part : virtual public room {
    // ....
};

class office_part : virtual public room {
    // ....
};

public small_repair_shop: public office_part, garage_part {
    // ...
};
```

It should be noted that the classes for the garage section of the business and the office section have to know if they are occupying a room or part of a room.

The class room is used as the base for two derived classes; derived classes cause their base class's constructor to be called to initialize the class. Does this mean that the constructor for room will be called twice? The answer is no. C++ is smart enough to know that room is used twice and to ignore the second initialization.

Function Hiding in Derived Classes

Example 21-3 defines a base class with the overloaded function do_it, which comes in both integer and floating-point versions. The program also defines a derived class that contains the single integer function do_it.

Example 21-3. doit/doit.cpp

```
class simple {
    public:
        int do_it(int i, int j) { return (i*j); }
        float do_it(float f) { return (f*2);}
};
class derived: public simple {
    public:
        int do_it(int i, int j) { return (i+j); }
};
```

Clearly, when we are using the derived class and we call the integer version of do_it, we are calling the one in the derived class. But what happens if we call the floating-point version? The derived class has no floating-point do_it. Normally, if we don't have a member function in the derived class, C++ will look to the base class.

However, since a version of do_it is defined in the derived class, C++ will look to the derived class for *all* flavors of do_it. In other words, if one form of do_it is defined in the derived class, that locks out all forms of the function:

```
int main( ) {
    derived test;        // Define a class for our testing
    int i;               // Test variable
    float f;             // Test variable

    i = test.do_it(1, 3);   // Legal; returns 4 (1 + 3)
    f = test.do_it(4.0);    // Illegal; "do_it(float)" not defined in
                            // the class "derived"
```

Constructors and Destructors in Derived Classes

Constructors and destructors behave differently from normal member functions, especially when used with derived classes. When a derived-class variable is created, the constructor for the base class is called first, followed by the constructor for the derived class.

Example 21-4 defines a simple base class and uses it to create a derived class.

Example 21-4. cons/class.cpp

```
#include <iostream>

class base_class {
    public:
        base_class() {
            std::cout << "base_class constructor called\n";
        }
        ~base_class() {
            std::cout << "base_class destructor called\n";
        }
};
class derived_class:public base_class {
    public:
        derived_class() {
            std::cout << "derived_class constructor called\n";
        }
        ~derived_class() {
            std::cout << "derived_class destructor called\n";
        }
};
```

Now when we execute the code:

```
    derived_class *sample_ptr = new derived_class;
```

the program prints:

```
    base_class constructor called
    derived_class constructor called
```

After the variable is destroyed, the destructors are called. The destructor for the derived class is called first, followed by the destructor for the base class. So when we destroy the variable with the statement:

```
    delete sample_ptr;
    sample_ptr = NULL;
```

we get:

```
    derived_class destructor called
    base_class destructor called
```

But C++ has a surprise lurking for us. Remember that derived-class objects can operate as base-class objects. For example:

```
    base_class *base_ptr = new derived_class;
```

is perfectly legal. However, there is a problem when the variable is deleted:

```
    delete base_ptr;
    base_ptr = NULL;
```

You see, base_ptr is a pointer to a base class. At this point, all the code can see is the base class. There is no way for C++ to know that there is a derived class out there. So when the variable is deleted, C++ fails to call the derived class destructor.

The output of the **delete** statement is:

```
base_class destructor called
```

We have just tricked C++ into deleting a class without calling the proper destructor.

We need some way to tell C++, "Hey, there is a derived class out there and you might want to call its destructor." The way we do this is to make the destructor for the base class a virtual function:

```cpp
class base_class {
    public:
        base_class() {
            std::cout << "base_class constructor called\n";
        }
        virtual ~base_class() {
            std::cout << "base_class destructor called\n";
        }
};
```

The keyword **virtual** normally means, "Call the function in the derived class instead of the one in the base class." For the destructor, it has a slightly different meaning. When C++ sees a virtual destructor, it will call the destructor of the derived class and then call the destructor of the base class.

So with the **virtual** destructor in place, we can safely delete the base_class variable, and the program will output the proper information:

```
derived_class destructor called
base_class destructor called
```

Question 21-1: *Why does Example 21-1 fail when we delete the variable list_ptr? The program seems to get upset when it tries to call* clear *at line 21.*

Example 21-5. blow/blow.cpp

```cpp
#include <iostream>
#include <cstdlib>

class list {
    private:
        int item;        // Current item number

    public:
        virtual void clear() = 0;

        void next_item() {
            ++item;
        }
```

Example 21-5. blow/blow.cpp (continued)

```
        list() {
            item = 0;
        }

        virtual ~list() {
            clear();
        }
};

class list_of_integers : public list {
    public:
        int array[100];    // Place to store the items

        void clear() {
            int i;        // Array index

            for (i = 0; i < 100; ++i)
                array[i] = 0;
        }
};

int main()
{
    list_of_integers *list_ptr = new list_of_integers;

    // Cause problems
    delete list_ptr;
    list_ptr = NULL;
    return (0);
}
```

The dynamic_cast Operator

The dynamic_cast operator can be used to change a pointer or reference to a base class to that of the derived class and vice versa. This conversion is done in a safe manner. If you attempt to do an incorrect conversion, an exception is thrown. By default this aborts the program. (See Chapter 22 for information on exceptions.)

For example:

```
    class room { ... };
    class office: public class room { ... }
    class garage: public class room { ... }

    void funct(room *ptr)
    {
        // Correct and safe conversion -- no problem
        office *office_ptr = dynamic_cast<office *>(ptr);
```

```
        // Incorrect conversion -- throws an exception
        garage *other_ptr = dynamic_cast<office *>(ptr);
    ...
    }

    int main()
    {
        office the_office;

        funct(&the_office);
```

The call to funct changes a pointer to a derived class (office) into a pointer to the base class (room). This is done automatically by C++.

The first dynamic_cast converts the pointer back to a pointer to the correct derrived class. The second tries to convert the object into a garage. Since the actual object is an office, the conversion fails and an exception is thrown.

Summary

Since programming began, programmers have been trying to find ways of building reusable code. C++, through the use of derived classes, allows you to build classes on top of existing code. This provides a great deal of flexibility and makes the code easier to organize and maintain.

Programming Exercises

Exercise 21-1: Combine the checkbook class of Exercise 13-2 with the queue class of Exercise 13-3 to implement a checkbook class that can print out the last ten entries of your checkbook.

Exercise 21-2: Define a "string-match" base class.

```
class string_matcher {
    public:
        // Returns true if string matches, false if not
        int match(const char *const match);
    ...
```

Define derived classes that match words, numbers, and blank strings.

Exercise 21-3: Define a base class shape that can describe any simple shape, such as a square, circle, or equilateral triangle. The size of all these shapes can be reduced to a single dimension.

Define derived classes for each of the three shapes.

Create a virtual function in the base class that returns the area of each shape.

Note that you will need to more precisely define what dimensions are stored in the base class. (Is the size in the base class for circle the radius of the circle or the diameter?)

Exercise 21-4: Write a base class called pet that describes any common household pet. Define two derived classes called fish and dog with items specific to that type of animal. Write pure virtual functions in the base class for operations that are common to both types of animals yet are handled in different ways by each of them.

Exercise 21-5: Write a base class number that holds a single integer value and contains one member function, print_it. Define three derived classes to print the value in hex, octal, and decimal.

Answers to Chapter Questions

Answer 21-1: Remember that destructors are called in the order derived class first, then base class. In this case, the destructor for the derived class, list_of_integers, is called to destroy the class. The class is gone.

Next, the destructor for the base class list is called. It calls the function clear. This is a pure virtual function, so C++ must call the clear function in the derived class. But the derived class is gone. There is no clear function. This makes C++ very upset and it aborts the program. (Actually, only good compilers will cause a program to abort. Others may do something really strange to your program.)

You should never call pure virtual functions from a destructor. Actually, be very careful when you call virtual functions of any type in a destructor.

## PART V

Other Language Features

## CHAPTER 22

Exceptions

How glorious it is—and also how painful—to be an
exception.
—Alfred de Musset

Airplanes fly from one place to another and 99.9% of the time there's no trouble. But when there is trouble, such as a stuck wheel or an engine fire, pilots are trained to handle the emergency.

Let's examine in detail what happens during an airborne emergency such as an engine catching fire. This is an exception to normal flight. First, a fire alarm goes off in the cockpit. The alarm catches the pilots' attention, and they start going through the fire-emergency procedure. This is an extensive list of things to do in case of fire. The airline prepared this list ahead of time, and the pilots have the list memorized. The pilots do what's necessary to handle the exception: activate the fire extinguisher, shut down the engine, land very quickly, etc.

Let's translate this procedure into C++ pseudocode. When the pilots take off they are going to try to fly the plane from one point to another without problems. The C++ "code" for this is:

```
try {
    fly_from_point_a_to_point_b();
}
```

The **try** keyword indicates that we are going to attempt an operation that may cause an exception.

But what happens when we get an exception? We need to handle it. The C++ code for this is:

```
catch (fire_emergency& fire_info) {
    active_extinguisher(fire_info.engine);
    turn_off(fire_info.engine);
    land_at_next_airport();
}
```

The keyword **catch** indicates that this section of code handles an exception. In this case the exception handled is a fire_emergency. This is the *type* of emergency. It could be a fire in engine number 1, engine number 2, or engine number 3 (assuming a three-engine plane). Which engine is on fire is stored in the variable fire_info.

The fire_emergency class describes what type of fire occurred. Its definition is:

```
class fire_emergency {
    public:
        int engine;    // Which engine is on fire
        // Other information about the fire
};
```

We've covered everything but the actual detection of the fire. Buried within each engine is a fire sensor. The code for this sensor is:

```
// Watch for fire in engine #2
void sensor_2( ) {
    while (engine_running( )) {
        if (engine_on_fire( )) {
            fire_emergency fire_info;

            fire_info.engine = 2;
            throw(fire_info);
        }
    }
}
```

When this code senses a fire, it puts the information in a fire_emergency variable named fire_info and triggers an exception with the **throw** statement.

When the **throw** statement is executed, normal processing is stopped. After all, when a fire occurs, normal flying is stopped. Execution is transferred to the **catch** statement for the fire_emergency.

To summarize, *exception handling* consists of:

- A description of a possible problem, in this case the fire_emergency class.
- A section of code in which the exception may occur, which is enclosed in a **try** statement. In this case, the statement is fly_from_point_a_to_point_b( ).
- Something that causes an exception and triggers the emergency procedures through a **throw** statement.
- Exception-handling code inside a **catch** block.

Adding Exceptions to the Stack Class

In Chapter 13, we defined a simple stack. The push and pop functions perform bounds checking on the current stack location using assert statements. For example:

```
inline void stack::push(const int item)
{
```

```
    assert((count >= 0) &&
           (count < sizeof(data)/sizeof(data[0])));
    data[count] = item;
    ++count;
}
```

The assert statement aborts the program when count is out of range. This is a rather drastic way of handling the problem. A nicer way of doing things is to throw an exception. This gives the program a chance to catch the error instead of aborting. Think of how the pilots would feel if the plane displayed an error message and shut down every time there was a fire.

Now we'll leave the plane world and take a look at real-world exceptions and see how to add exception handling to our stack class.

Creating an Exception

The first thing we need to do is decide what type of exceptions we are going to handle and describe them as classes. In our stack example, the only exception we expect is an out-of-bounds error. We'll describe this error with a simple string. The class for an out-of-bounds error is:

```
class bound_err {
    public:
        const string what;     // What caused the error

        // Initialize the bound error with a message
        bound_err(const std::string& i_what): what(i_what) {}
        // bound_err&  operator = -- defaults
        // bound_err(bound_err) -- default copy constructor
        // ~bound_err -- default destructor
};
```

Using a Try Block for Normal Execution

Exception checking starts with the keyword **try**. This tells C++ that exceptions may be generated in the section of code that follows and that they will be handled immediately after the **try** block. For example, if we are trying to perform a big stack operation, the code might look like this:

```
try {
    do_big_stack_operation();
};
```

Immediately after the **try** block, we need to use a **catch** statement to tell C++ what problems we will handle. The syntax for this statement is:

```
catch (problem_type& parameter) {
    statements;
}
```

The *problem_type* is the class that describes what happened. For the out-of-bounds error, the **catch** statement looks like:

```
catch (bound_err& what_happened) {
    std::cerr << "Error: Bounds exceeded\n";
    std::cerr << "Reason: " << what_happened.what << '\n';
}
```

Several **catch** statements may be used to catch different types of exceptions. If an exception is not caught, it is considered an *unexpected exception* and will cause a call to the unexpected-exception handler, which aborts the program by default. If you want to catch all exceptions, use "..." for the exception type. For example:

```
catch (bound_err& what_happened) {
    // .... Body of catch
}
catch (...) {
    std::cerr << "Something strange happened\n";
}
```

Throwing an Exception

Now we need to update our old stack program and replace all the "error-message-and-abort" code with **throw** statements. The new procedure for push now looks like this:

```
inline void stack::push(const int item)
{
    if ((count < 0) ||
        (count >= sizeof(data)/sizeof(data[0]))) {
        bound_err overflow("Push overflows stack");
        throw overflow;
    }
    data[count] = item;
    ++count;
}
```

Actually we don't need a special variable for overflow. The code can be consolidated. In the previous example, I used two statements to show explicitly what is going on. The following code performs the same operation:

```
inline void stack::push(const int item)
{
    if ((count < 0) ||
        (count >= sizeof(data)/sizeof(data[0]))) {
        throw bound_err("Push overflows stack");
    }
    data[count] = item;
    ++count;
}
```

The basic function definition we've been using so far tells C++, "Expect any exception to be thrown at any time." The push function can only throw a *bound_err* exception. C++ allows you to list all the possible exceptions in a function by putting a **throw** directive at the end of the function declaration:

```
inline void stack::push(const int item) throw(bound_err) {
```

But what happens if we throw an exception that's not in the list of exceptions? C++ turns this into a call to the function unexpected(). This normally causes the program to terminate.

Example 22-1 contains a stack that uses exceptions when something goes wrong.

Example 22-1. stack_c/stack_e1.cpp

```
/*********************************************************
 * Stack                                                 *
 *      A file implementing a simple stack class         *
 *********************************************************/
#include <cstdlib>
#include <iostream>
#include <assert.h>

const int STACK_SIZE = 100;      // Maximum size of a stack

/*********************************************************
 * bound_err -- a class used to handle out of bounds     *
 *              execeptions.                              *
 *********************************************************/
class bound_err {
    public:
        const string what;       // What caused the error

        // Initialize the bound error with a message
        bound_err(const string& i_what) what(i_what) {}
        // Assignment operator defaults
        // bound_err(bound_err) -- default copy constructor
        // ~ bound_err -- default destructor
};

/*********************************************************
 * Stack class                                           *
 *                                                       *
 * Member functions                                      *
 *      init -- initialize the stack.                    *
 *      push -- put an item on the stack.                *
 *      pop -- remove an item from the stack.            *
 *********************************************************/
// The stack itself
class stack {
    private:
        int count;               // Number of items in the stack
        int data[STACK_SIZE];    // The items themselves
    public:
        // Initialize the stack
        stack(): count(0) {};
```

Example 22-1. stack_c/stack_e1.cpp (continued)

```
        // Copy constructor defaults
        // Assignment operator defaults

        // Push an item on the stack
        void push(const int item) throw(bound_err);

        // Pop an item from the stack
        int pop( ) throw(bound_err);
};
/****************************************************
 * stack::push -- push an item on the stack.      *
 *                                                *
 * Warning: We do not check for overflow.         *
 *                                                *
 * Parameters                                     *
 *      item -- item to put in the stack          *
 ****************************************************/
inline void stack::push(const int item) throw(bound_err)
{
    if ((count < 0) &&
            (count >= sizeof(data)/sizeof(data[0]))) {
        throw("Push overflows stack");
    }
    data[count] = item;
    ++count;
}
/****************************************************
 * stack::pop -- get an item off the stack.       *
 *                                                *
 * Warning: We do not check for stack underflow.  *
 *                                                *
 * Returns                                        *
 *      The top item from the stack.              *
 ****************************************************/
inline int stack::pop( ) throw(bound_err)
{
    // Stack goes down by one
    --count;

    if ((count < 0) &&
            (count >= sizeof(data)/sizeof(data[0]))) {
        throw("Pop underflows stack");
    }
    // Then we return the top value
    return (data[count]);
}
static stack test_stack;         // Define a stack for our bounds checking

/****************************************************
 * push_a_lot -- Push too much on to the stack    *
 ****************************************************/
static void push_a_lot() {
```

Example 22-1. stack_c/stack_e1.cpp (continued)

```
    int i;          // Push counter

    for (i = 0; i < 5000; i++) {
        test_stack.push(i);
    }
}

int main()
{
    try {
        push_a_lot();
    }
    catch (bound_err& err) {
        cerr << "Error: Bounds exceeded\n";
        cerr << "Reason: " << err.what << '\n';
        exit (8);
    }
    catch (...) {
        cerr << "Error: Unexpected exception occurred\n";
        exit (8);
    }
    return (0);
}
```

Exceptions and Destructors

Let's say we want to make sure that the stack is empty when it's destroyed. So we write a destructor for our stack class:

```
// This is not a good idea
inline stack::~stack() {
    if (count != 0)
        throw(bound_err("Stack is not empty"));
}
```

This sort of code contains a hidden trap waiting to be sprung. Let's suppose that we push a few items on the stack and then execute some unrelated code that causes an exception to be thrown. The sequence of events is:

1. Create a stack variable.

2. Push items on it.

3. Execute unrelated code.

4. Throw an exception.

5. The exception is not handled in the current procedure, so the exception logic destroys all the variables declared in the current procedure. This includes the stack variable.

6. The destructor for the stack variable is called by the exception code. This causes a second exception to be thrown.

So what happens when an exception is thrown inside an exception? The answer is that the program terminates, so it's not a good idea to throw an exception in a destructor.

Exceptions Versus assert

When a problem occurs, the assert statement prints out an error message and aborts the program. This error message contains the condition that failed, as well as the file name and line number where the problem occurred. This is very useful to a maintenance programmer, but not that useful to an end user.

asserts can also be compiled out of "production" code by using the -DNDEBUG option.

The assert statement is useful for checking for conditions that should never happen. The purpose of the assert is to abort the program as soon as a problem is detected.

Exceptions, on the other hand, are designed to handle conditions that are rare, but expected to occur. These occasional problems can then be handled by the program in a nice way. For example, if we attempt to push too much information on the stack, the program can simply abort that operation and continue with the next step, instead of aborting the entire program.

In general, if you don't know what to do with the error, check it with an assert. If you think that someone may want to handle it, throw an exception.

Programming Exercises

Exercise 22-1: Add code to the queue class of Exercise 13-3 that will trigger an exception when too many items are put in the queue.

Exercise 22-2: Take the fraction class from Exercise 1-3 and add code to generate an exception when a divide-by-zero occurs. In addition, add code to generate an exception when a bad number is read.

Exercise 22-3: Update the checkbook class of Exercise 13-2 so it generates an exception when your balance goes below zero.

Exercise 22-4: Write a function count_letter that takes a single character. This function will count the number of consonants and vowels. If a nonletter is given to the function, it generates an exception.

## CHAPTER 23

Modular Programming

Many hands make light work.
—John Heywood

So far, we have been dealing with small programs. As programs grow larger and larger, they should be split into sections, or *modules*. C++ allows programs to be split into multiple files, compiled separately, and then combined (linked) to form a single program.

In this chapter, we go through a programming example, discussing the C++ techniques needed to create good modules. You also are shown how to use make to put these modules together to form a program.

Modules

A module is a collection of functions or classes that perform related functions. For example, there could be a module to handle database functions such as lookup, enter, and sort. Another module could handle complex numbers, and so on.

Also, as programming problems get big, more and more programmers are needed to finish them. An efficient way of splitting up a large project is to assign each programmer a different module. That way each programmer only has to worry about the internal details of her own code.

In this chapter, we discuss a module to handle *infinite arrays*. The functions in this package allow the user to store data in an array without worrying about the array's size. The infinite array grows as needed (limited only by the amount of memory in the computer). The infinite array will be used to store data for a histogram, but it can also be used to store things such as line numbers from a cross-reference program or other types of data.

Public and Private

Modules are divided into two parts, *public* and *private*. The public part tells the user how to call the functions in the module and contains the definitions of data structures and functions that are to be used from outside the module. The public definitions are put in a header file, which is included in the user's program. In the infinite array example, we have put the public declarations in the file *ia.h* (see listing in Example 23-2).

Anything internal to the module is private. Everything that is not directly usable by the outside world should be kept private.

The extern Storage Class

The **extern** storage class is used to indicate that a variable or function is defined outside the current file but is used in this file. Example 23-1 illustrates a simple use of the **extern** modifier.

Example 23-1. tf/main.cpp

```
#include <iostream>

/* number of times through the loop */
extern int counter;

/* routine to increment the counter */
extern void inc_counter();

int main()
{
    int   index; /* loop index */

    for (index = 0; index < 10; ++index)
        inc_counter();
    std::cout << "Counter is " << counter << '\n';
    return (0);
}
```

Example 23-2. File: tf/count.cpp

```
/* number of times through the loop */
int counter = 0;

/* trivial example */
void inc_counter()
{
    ++counter;
}
```

The function main uses the variable counter. Because counter is not defined in main, it is defined in the file *count.cpp*. The **extern** declaration is used by *main.cpp* to indicate that counter is declared somewhere else, in this case the file *count.cpp*. The modifier **extern** is not used in this file, because this is the "real" declaration of the variable.

Actually, three storage class identifiers can be used to indicate the files in which a variable is defined, as shown in Table 23-1.

Table 23-1. Storage class identification

Modifier	Meaning
extern	Variable/function is defined in another file. (The variable can also be defined in the current file.)
<blank>	Variable/function is defined in this file (public) and can be used in other files.
static	Variable/function is local to this file (private).

Notice that the keyword **static** has two meanings. (It is the most overworked keyword in the C++ language. For a complete list of the meanings of **static** see Table 14-1.) For data defined globally, static means "private to this file." For data defined inside a function, it means "variable is allocated from static memory (instead of the temporary stack)."

C++ is very liberal in its use of the rules for **static, extern,** and <blank> storage classes. It is possible to declare a variable as **extern** at the beginning of a program and later define it as <blank>.

```
extern sam;
int sam = 1;    // This is legal
```

This ability is useful when you have all your external variables defined in a header file. The program includes the header file (and defines the variables as **extern**), and then defines the variable for real.

Another problem concerns declaring a variable in two different files.

File: main.cpp

```
int     flag  = 0;     // Flag is off

int main( )
{
    std::cout << "Flag is " << flag << '\n';
}
```
File: sub.cpp
```
int     flag = 1;       // Flag is on
```

What happens in this case? There are several possibilities:

- flag could be initialized to 0 because *main.cpp* is loaded first.

- `flag` could be initialized to 1 because the entry in *sub.cpp* overwrites the one in *main.cpp*.
- I don't know, but whatever it is, it's probably bad.

In this case, there is only one global variable called `flag`. It will be initialized to either 1 or 0 depending on the whims of the compiler. (The good ones generate an error.) It is entirely possible for the program `main` to print out:

```
flag is 1
```

even though we initialized it to 0. To avoid the problem of hidden initializations, use the keyword **static** to limit the scope of variables to the file in which they are declared.

Say we wrote the following:

```
File: main.cpp
static int      flag  = 0;      // Flag is off

int main()
{
        std::cout << "Flag is " << flag << '\n';
}
File: sub.cpp
static int      flag = 1;       // Flag is on
```

In this case, `flag` in *main.cpp* is an entirely different variable from `flag` in *sub.cpp*. However, you should still give the variables different names to avoid confusion.

Headers

Information that is shared between modules should be put in a header file. By convention, all header filenames end with ".h". In the infinite array example, we use the file *ia.h*.

The header should contain all the public information, such as:

- A comment section describing clearly what the module does and what is available to the user
- Public class declarations
- Common constants
- Public structures
- Prototypes of all the public functions
- **extern** declarations for public variables

In the infinite array example, more than half the file *ia.h* is devoted to comments. This commenting is not excessive; the real guts of the coding is hidden in the program file *ia.cpp*. The *ia.h* file serves both as a program file and as documentation to the outside world.

Notice that there is no mention in the *ia.h* comments about how the infinite array is implemented. At this level, we don't care how something is done, just what functions are available.

Example 23-3. ia/ia.h

```
/**********************************************************
 * definitions for the infinite array (ia) class         *
 *                                                        *
 * An infinite array is an array whose size can grow      *
 * as needed.  Adding more elements to the array          *
 * will just cause it to grow.                            *
 *--------------------------------------------------------*
 * class infinite_array                                   *
 *     Member functions                                   *
 *         infinite_array( )  -- default constructor      *
 *         ~infinite_array( ) -- destructor               *
 *         int& operator [](int index)                    *
 *                   gets an element of the infinite array *
 **********************************************************/
#include <string.h>

// number of elements to store in each cell of the infinite array
const unsigned int BLOCK_SIZE = 10;

class infinite_array {
    private:
        // the data for this block
        int    data[BLOCK_SIZE];

        // pointer to the next array
        class infinite_array *next;
    public:
        // Default constructor
        infinite_array( )
        {
            next = NULL;
            memset(data, '\0', sizeof(data));
        }

        // Default destructor
        ~infinite_array( );

        // Return a reference to an element of the array
        int& operator[] (const unsigned int index);
};
```

A few things should be noted about this file. Everything in the file is a constant definition, a data structure declaration, or an external declaration. Any code that is defined is inline. No actual code or storage is defined in the header file.

The Body of the Module

The body of the module contains all the functions and data for that module. Private functions that are not to be called from outside the module should be declared **static**. Variables declared outside of a function that are not used outside the module are declared **static**.

A Program to Use Infinite Arrays

The infinite array structure is shown in Figure 23-1. The program uses a simple linked list to store the elements of the array. A linked list can grow longer as needed (until you run out of memory). Each list element, or bucket, can store 10 numbers. To find element 38, the program starts at the beginning, skips past the first three buckets, and extracts element 8 from the data in the current bucket.

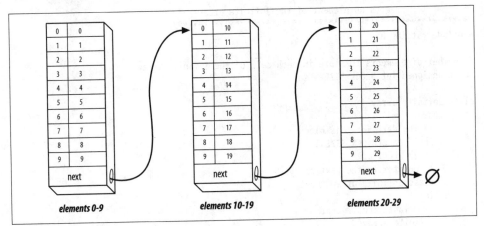

Figure 23-1. Infinite array structure

Example 23-4 contains the code for module *ia.cpp*.

Example 23-4. ia/ia.cpp

```
/********************************************************
 * infinite-array -- routines to handle infinite arrays *
 *                                                       *
 * An infinite array is an array that grows as needed.   *
 * There is no index too large for an infinite array     *
 * (unless we run out of memory).                        *
 ********************************************************/
#include <iostream>
#include <cstdlib>
#include <assert.h>

#include "ia.h"                    // get common definitions
```

Example 23-4. ia/ia.cpp (continued)

```
/********************************************************
 * operator [] -- find an element of an infinite array  *
 *                                                       *
 * Parameters                                            *
 *       index    -- index into the array                *
 *                                                       *
 * Returns                                               *
 *       Reference to the element in the array           *
 ********************************************************/
int& infinite_array::operator [] (const unsigned int index)
{
    // pointer to the current bucket
    class infinite_array *current_ptr;

    unsigned int current_index; // Index we are working with

    current_ptr = this;
    current_index = index;

    while (current_index >= BLOCK_SIZE) {
        if (current_ptr->next == NULL) {
            current_ptr->next = new infinite_array;
            if (current_ptr->next == NULL) {
                std::cerr << "Error:Out of memory\n";
                exit(8);
            }
        }
        current_ptr = current_ptr->next;
        current_index -= BLOCK_SIZE;
    }
    assert(current_index >= 0);
    assert(current_index <
            sizeof(current_ptr->data)/sizeof(current_ptr->data[0]));
    return (current_ptr->data[current_index]);
}

/********************************************************
 * ~infinite_array -- Destroy the infinite array        *
 ********************************************************/
infinite_array::~infinite_array()
{
    /*
     * Note: We use a cute trick here.
     *
     * Because each bucket in the infinite array is
     * an infinite array itself, when we destroy
     * next, it will destroy all that bucket's "next"s
     * and so on recusively clearing the entire array.
     */
    if (next != NULL) {
        delete next;
```

Example 23-4. ia/ia.cpp (continued)

```
        next = NULL;
    }
}
```

The Makefile for Multiple Files

The utility make is designed to aid the programmer in compiling and linking programs. Before make, the programmer had to type compile commands explicitly each time there was a change in the program:

```
g++ -Wall -g -ohello hello.cpp
```

 In this chapter we use the commands for the GNU g++ compiler. The C++ compiler on your system may have a different name and a slightly different syntax.

As programs grow, the number of commands needed to create them grows. Typing in a series of 10 or 20 commands is tiresome and error-prone, so programmers started writing *shell scripts* (or, in MS-DOS, *.BAT files*). Then all the programmer had to type was do-it and the computer would compile everything. This was overkill, however, because all the files were recompiled regardless of need.

As the number of files in a project grew, this recompiling became a significant problem. Changing one small file, starting the compilation, and then having to wait until the next day while the computer executed several hundred compile commands was frustrating—especially when only one compile was really needed.

The program make was created to do *intelligent compiles*. Its purpose is to first decide what commands need to be executed and then execute them.

The file *Makefile* (upper/lowercase is important in Unix) contains the rules used by make to decide how to build the program. The *Makefile* contains the following sections:

- Comments
- Macros
- Explicit rules
- Default rules

Any line beginning with a # is a comment.

A macro has the format:

> *name = data*

Name is any valid identifier. *Data* is the text that will be substituted whenever make sees $(*name*).

Here's an example:

```
#
# Very simple Makefile
#
MACRO = Doing All

all:
        echo $(MACRO)
```

Explicit rules tell make what commands are needed to create the program. These rules can take several forms. The most common is:

```
target: source [source2] [source3]
    command
    [command]
    [command]
    . . .
```

Target is the name of a file to create. It is "made," or created, out of the source file *source*. If the *target* is created out of several files, they are all listed.

The command used to create the target is listed on the next line. Sometimes it takes more than one command to create the target. Commands are listed one per line. Each is indented by a tab.

For example, the rule:

```
hello: hello.cpp
        g++ -Wall -g -o hello hello.cpp
```

tells make to create the file *hello* from the file *hello.cpp* using the command:

```
g++ -Wall -g -o hello hello.cpp
```

make will create *hello* only if necessary. The files used in the creation of *hello*, arranged in chronological order (by modification time), are shown in Table 23-2.

Table 23-2. File modification times

Unix	MS-DOS/Windows	Modification time
hello.cpp	HELLO.CPP	Oldest
hello.o	HELLO.OBJ	Old
hello	HELLO.EXE	Newest

If the programmer changes the source file *hello.cpp*, the file's modification time will be out of date with respect to the other files. make will sense this and re-create the other files.

Another form of the explicit rule is:

source:
    command
    [*command*]

In this case, the commands are executed each time make is run, unconditionally.

If the commands are omitted from an explicit rule, make uses a set of built-in rules to determine what command to execute.

For example, the rule:

```
hist.o: ia.h hist.cpp
```

tells make to create *hist.o* from *hist.cpp* and *ia.h*, using the standard rule for making *<file>.o* from *<file>.cpp*. This rule is:

```
g++ $(CFLAGS) -c file.cpp
```

(make predefines the macro $(CFLAGS).)

We are going to create a main program *hist.cpp* that calls the module *ia.cpp*. Both files include the header *ia.h*, so they depend on it. The Unix *Makefile* that creates the program *hist* from *hist.cpp* and *ia.cpp* is listed in Example 23-5.

Example 23-5. ia/makefile.unx

```
#
# Makefile for many Unix compilers using the
# "standard" command name CC
#
CC=CC
CFLAGS=-g
SRC=ia.cpp hist.cc
OBJ=ia.o  hist.o

all: hist

hist: $(OBJ)
        $(CC) $(CFLAGS) -o hist $(OBJ)

hist.o: ia.h hist.cpp
        $(CC) $(CFLAGS) -c hist.cpp

ia.o: ia.h ia.cpp
        $(CC) $(CFLAGS) -c ia.cpp

clean:
        rm hist io.o hist.o
```

The macro SRC is a list of all the C++ files. OBJ is a list of all the object (*.o*) files. The lines:

```
hist: $(OBJ)
        g++ $(CFLAGS) -o hist $(OBJ)
```

tell make to create *hist* from the object files. If any of the object files are out of date, make will re-create them.

The line:

```
hist.o:ia.h
```

tells make to create *hist.o* from *ia.h* and *hist.cpp* (*hist.cpp* is implied). Because no command is specified, the default is used.

Example 23-6 shows the Makefile for MS-DOS/Windows, using Borland-C++.

Example 23-6. ia/makefile.bcc

```
#
# Makefile for Borland's Borland-C++ compiler
#
CC=bcc32
#
# Flags
#        -N  -- Check for stack overflow
#        -v  -- Enable debugging
#        -w  -- Turn on all warnings
#        -tWC -- Console application
#
CFLAGS=-N -v -w -tWC
SRC=ia.cpp hist.cpp
OBJ=ia.obj hist.obj

all: hist.exe

hist.exe: $(OBJ)
        $(CC) $(CFLAGS) -ehist $(OBJ)

hist.obj: ia.h hist.cpp
        $(CC) $(CFLAGS) -c hist.cpp

ia.obj: ia.h ia.cpp
        $(CC) $(CFLAGS) -c ia.cpp

clean:
        erase hist.exe io.obj hist.obj
```

There is one big drawback with make. It only checks to see whether the files have changed, not the rules. If you have compiled your entire program with CFLAGS = -g for debugging and need to produce the production version (CFLAGS = -O), make will *not* recompile.

The Unix command touch changes the modification date of a file. (It doesn't change the file; it just makes the operating system think it did.) If you touch a source file such as *hello.cpp* and then run make, the program will be re-created. This is useful if you have changed the compile-time flags and want to force a recompilation.

Make provides a rich set of commands for creating programs. Only a few have been discussed here.[*]

Using the Infinite Array

The histogram program (hist) is designed to use the infinite array package. It takes one file as its argument. The file contains a list of numbers between 0 and 99. Any number of entries may be used. The program prints a histogram showing how many times each number appears. (A histogram is a graphic representation of the frequency of data.)

This file contains a number of interesting programming techniques.

The first one technique is to let the computer do the work whenever possible. For example, don't program like this:

```
const int LENGTH_X = 300;    // Width of the box in dots
const int LENGTH_Y = 400;    // Height of the box in dots
const int AREA = 12000;      // Total box area in dots
```

In this case, the programmer has decided to multiply 300 by 400 to compute the area. He would be better served by letting the computer do the multiplying:

```
const int LENGTH_X = 300;    // Width of the box in dots
const int LENGTH_Y = 400;    // Height of the box in dots

const int AREA = (LENGTH_X * LENGTH_Y);  // Total box area in dots
```

That way, if either LENGTH_X or LENGTH_Y is changed, AREA changes automatically. Also, the computer is more accurate in its computations. (If you noticed, the programmer made an error: his AREA is too small by a factor of 10.)

In the histogram program, the number of data points in each output line is computed by the following definition:

```
const float FACTOR =
    ((HIGH_BOUND - LOW_BOUND) / (float)(NUMBER_OF_LINES));
```

The user should be helped whenever possible. In the hist program, if the user does not type the correct number of parameters on the command line, a message appears telling what is wrong and how to correct it.

The program uses the library routine memset to initialize the counters array. This routine is highly efficient for setting all values of an array to zero. The line:

```
memset(counters, '\0', sizeof(counters));
```

---

[*] If you are going to create programs that require more than 10 or 20 source files, it is suggested you read the book *Managing Projects with make* (O'Reilly & Associates, Inc.).

zeros the entire array counters. sizeof(counters) makes sure the entire array is zeroed. Example 23-7 contains a program that uses the infinite array for storing data used to produce a histogram.

Example 23-7. ia/hist.cpp

```cpp
/********************************************************
 * hist -- generate a histogram of an array of numbers  *
 *                                                       *
 * Usage                                                 *
 *      hist <file>                                      *
 *                                                       *
 * Where                                                 *
 *      file is the name of the file to work on          *
 ********************************************************/
#include <iostream>
#include <fstream>
#include <iomanip>
#include <cstdlib>
#include <assert.h>

#include "ia.h"

/*
 * the following definitions define the histogram
 */
const int NUMBER_OF_LINES = 50; // # Lines in the result
const int LOW_BOUND       = 0;  // Lowest number we record
const int HIGH_BOUND      = 99; // Highest number we record
/*
 * if we have NUMBER_OF_LINES data to
 * output then each item must use
 * the following factor
 */
const int FACTOR =
  ((HIGH_BOUND - LOW_BOUND +1) / NUMBER_OF_LINES);

// number of characters wide to make the histogram
const int WIDTH = 60;

// Array to store the data in
static infinite_array data_array;
// Number if items in the array
static int data_items;

int main(int argc, char *argv[])
{
    void  read_data(const char *const name);// get the data into the array
    void  print_histogram();// print the data

    if (argc != 2) {
        std::cerr << "Error:Wrong number of arguments\n";
        std::cerr << "Usage is:\n";
```

Example 23-7. ia/hist.cpp (continued)

```cpp
        std::cerr << " hist <data-file>\n";
        exit(8);
    }
    data_items = 0;

    read_data(argv[1]);
    print_histogram();
    return (0);
}
/********************************************************
 * read_data -- read data from the input file into     *
 *              the data_array.                         *
 *                                                      *
 * Parameters                                           *
 *      name -- the name of the file to read            *
 ********************************************************/
void  read_data(const char *const name)
{
    std::ifstream in_file(name); // input file
    int data;                    // data from input

    if (in_file.bad()) {
        std::cerr << "Error:Unable to open " << name << '\n';
        exit(8);
    }
    while (!in_file.eof()) {
        in_file >> data;

        // If we get an eof we ran out of data in last read
        if (in_file.eof())
            break;

        // No assert needed becuase data_array is an ia
        data_array[data_items] = data;
        ++data_items;
    }
}
/********************************************************
 * print_histogram -- print the histogram output.      *
 ********************************************************/
void  print_histogram()
{
    // upper bound for printout
    int   counters[NUMBER_OF_LINES];
    int low;              // lower bound for printout
    int   out_of_range = 0;// number of items out of bounds
    int   max_count = 0;// biggest counter
    float scale;          // scale for outputting dots
    int   index;          // index into the data

    memset(counters, '\0', sizeof(counters));
```

Example 23-7. ia/hist.cpp (continued)

```
    for (index = 0; index < data_items; ++index) {
        int data;// data for this point

        data = data_array[index];

        if ((data < LOW_BOUND) || (data > HIGH_BOUND))
            ++out_of_range;
        else {
            // index into counters array
            int    count_index;

            count_index = static_cast<int>(
                    static_cast<float>(data - LOW_BOUND) / FACTOR);

            assert(count_index >= 0);
            assert(count_index < sizeof(counters)/sizeof(counters[0]));
            ++counters[count_index];
            if (counters[count_index] > max_count)
                max_count = counters[count_index];
        }
    }

    scale = float(max_count) / float(WIDTH);

    low = LOW_BOUND;

    for (index = 0; index < NUMBER_OF_LINES; ++index) {
        // index for outputting the dots
        int    char_index;
        int    number_of_dots;   // number of * to output

        std::cout << std::setw(2) << index << ' ' <<
                std::setw(3) << low << "-" <<
                std::setw(3) << (low + FACTOR -1) << " (" <<
                std::setw(4) << counters[index] << "): ";

        number_of_dots = int(float(counters[index]) / scale);
        for (char_index = 0; char_index < number_of_dots;
            ++char_index)
            std::cout << '*';
        std::cout << '\n';
        low += FACTOR;
    }
    std::cout << out_of_range << " items out of range\n";
}
```

A sample run of this program produces the following output:

```
%   hist   test
0:  0-  2 ( 100): **********************
1:  2-  4 ( 200): ******************************************
```

```
 2:  4-  6 ( 100): ************************
 3:  6-  8 ( 100): ***********************
 4:  8- 10 (   0):
 5: 10- 12 ( 100): ************************
 6: 12- 14 (  50): ************
 7: 14- 16 ( 150): ***********************************
 8: 16- 18 (  50): ************
 9: 18- 20 (  50): ************
10: 20- 22 ( 100): ************************
11: 22- 24 ( 100): ************************
12: 24- 26 (  50): ************
13: 26- 28 ( 100): ************************
14: 28- 30 (  50): ************
15: 30- 32 ( 100): ************************
16: 32- 34 (  50): ************
17: 34- 36 (   0):
18: 36- 38 ( 100): ************************
19: 38- 40 (   1):
20: 40- 42 ( 150): ***********************************
21: 42- 44 (  50): ************
22: 44- 46 ( 250): **********************************************************
23: 46- 48 ( 100): ************************
24: 48- 51 ( 150): ***********************************
25: 51- 53 ( 100): ************************
26: 53- 55 (  50): ************
27: 55- 57 ( 200): ***********************************************
28: 57- 59 (  50): ************
29: 59- 61 (  50): ************
30: 61- 63 (  50): ************
31: 63- 65 ( 150): ***********************************
32: 65- 67 ( 100): ************************
33: 67- 69 (   0):
34: 69- 71 ( 199): ***********************************************
35: 71- 73 ( 200): ***********************************************
36: 73- 75 ( 100): ************************
37: 75- 77 (  50): ************
38: 77- 79 ( 100): ************************
39: 79- 81 ( 100): ************************
40: 81- 83 ( 200): ***********************************************
41: 83- 85 ( 100): ************************
42: 85- 87 (   0):
43: 87- 89 (   0):
44: 89- 91 (  50): ************
45: 91- 93 ( 150): ***********************************
46: 93- 95 ( 100): ************************
47: 95- 97 (  50): ************
48: 97- 99 ( 100): ************************
49: 99-101 (   0):
500 items out of range
```

Dividing a Task into Modules

Unfortunately, computer programming is more of an art than a science. There are no hard and fast rules that tell you how to divide a task into modules. Knowing what makes a good module and what doesn't comes with experience and practice.

This section describes some general rules for module division and how they can be applied to real-world programs. The techniques described here have worked well for me. You should use whatever works for you.

Information is a vital part of any program. The key to a program is your decision about what information you want to use and what processing you want to perform on it. Be sure to analyze the information flow before you begin the design.

Design the modules to minimize the amount of information that has to pass between them. If you look at the organization of the Army, for example, you'll see that it is divided up into modules. There is the infantry, artillery, tank corps, and so on. The amount of information that passes between these modules is minimized. For example, if an infantry sergeant wants the artillery to bombard an enemy position, he calls up artillery command and says, "There's a pillbox at location Y-94. Get rid of it." The artillery command handles all the details of deciding which battery to use, how much firepower to allocate based on the requirements of other fire missions, maintaining supplies, and many more details.[*]

Programs should be organized the same way. Information that can be kept inside a module should be. Minimizing the amount of intermodule communication cuts down on communication errors and limits maintenance problems that occur when a module is upgraded.

Module Design Guidelines

Although there are no strict rules when it comes to laying out the modules for a program, here are some general guidelines:

- The number of public functions in a module should be small.
- The information passed between modules should be small.
- All the functions in a module should perform related jobs.
- Modules should contain no more than 1,500 lines. With more lines, they become difficult to edit, print, and understand.

---

[*] This is a very general diagram of the division of an ideal army. The system used by the United States Army is more complex and so highly classified that even the generals don't know how it works.

Programming Exercises

Exercise 23-1: Write a class that handles page formatting. It should contain the following functions:

```
open_file(char *name)
```
Opens the print file.

```
define_header(char *heading)
```
Defines heading text.

```
print_line(char *line)
```
Sends a line to the file.

```
page( )
```
Starts a new page.

```
close_file( )
```
Closes the print file.

Exercise 23-2: Write a module called search_open that receives an array of filenames, searches the array until it finds one that exists, and opens that file.

Exercise 23-3: Write a symbol table class containing the following functions:

```
void enter(const std::string& name)
```
Enters a name into the symbol table.

```
int lookup(const std::string& name)
```
Returns 1 if the name is in the table; returns 0 otherwise.

```
void remove(const std::string& name)
```
Removes a name from the symbol table.

Exercise 23-4: Take the words program from Chapter 20, and combine it with the infinite array module to create a cross-reference program. (As an added bonus, teach it about C++ comments and strings to create a C++ cross-referencer.)

## CHAPTER 24

Templates

Thou cunning'st pattern of excelling nature.
—Shakespeare
Othello, Act V

What Is a Template?

Templates are a relatively new addition to C++. They allow you to write generic classes and functions that work for several different data types. The result is that you can write generic code once and then use it over and over again for many different uses. In fact, C++ comes with something called the Standard Template Library (STL), which makes extensive use of templates to provide powerful data-processing tools to the C++ user.

There are some problems with templates, however. Working out the implementation details was very difficult for the people on the C++ Standards Committee. There was a lot of hard fighting involving tanks, motors, and heavy artillery (or the academic equivalent, which is a tartly worded memo). As a result, template implementation details were one of the last items in the C++ Standard to be agreed upon. Later in this chapter, we'll discuss some of the implementation problems with templates.

Templates: The Hard Way

Suppose we want to define a function max to return the maximum of two items. Actually, we don't want to define just one max function, but a family of functions: one to find the maximum of two **int**s, one for **float**s, one for **char**s, and so on.

We start by defining a parameterized macro to generate the code for the function. This is called the *definition stage*. The macro looks like this:

```
#define define_max(type) type max(type d1, type d2) { \
    if (d1 > d2)                                       \
        return (d1);                                   \
```

```
    return (d2);                                    \
}
```

 Each line except the last one ends in a backslash (\). A **#define** macro
spans a single line, so the backslash turns our five lines into one. By
putting the backslashes in the same column, we can easily tell if we
miss one.

This macro generates no code. It merely provides the definition that is used in the
next phase to generate the functions we want. This is called the *generation phase*.
The following three statements use the define_max macro to generate three versions
of the max function:

```
define_max(int);
define_max(float);
define_max(char);
```

Finally, somewhere in the code we use the functions we've just defined. (This is
called the *use phase*, of course.)

```
int main( ) {
    float f = max(3.5, 8.7);
    int   i = max(100, 800);
    char ch = max('A', 'Q');
```

Figure 24-1 shows the source code for the **#define** style templates and the code generated by them.

This method works adequately for simple functions like max. It doesn't work well for
larger functions. One drawback to this system is that we must invoke the macro
define_max for each data type we want to use. It would be nice if C++ called define_max
automatically.

Templates: The C++ Way

Templates allow you to define a generic function. C++ then uses this template to
generate a specific *instance* of the function as needed. For example, to define the
function max as a template, we write:

```
template<typename kind>
kind max(kind d1, kind d2) {
    if (d1 > d2)
        return (d1);
    return (d2);
}
```

 The construct <typename kind> tells C++ that the word kind can be
replaced by any type.

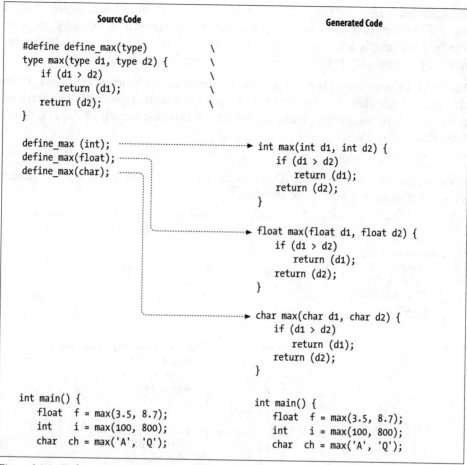

```
                Source Code                                    Generated Code

#define define_max(type)            \
type max(type d1, type d2) {        \
    if (d1 > d2)                    \
        return (d1);                \
    return (d2);                    \
}

define_max (int); ·············        ······▶  int max(int d1, int d2) {
define_max(float); ········                          if (d1 > d2)
define_max(char); ·······                                return (d1);
                                                     return (d2);
                                                 }

                                       ·······▶  float max(float d1, float d2) {
                                                     if (d1 > d2)
                                                         return (d1);
                                                     return (d2);
                                                 }

                                       ·······▶  char max(char d1, char d2) {
                                                     if (d1 > d2)
                                                         return (d1);
                                                     return (d2);
                                                 }

int main() {                                     int main() {
    float  f = max(3.5, 8.7);                        float  f = max(3.5, 8.7);
    int    i = max(100, 800);                        int    i = max(100, 800);
    char  ch = max('A', 'Q');                        char  ch = max('A', 'Q');
```

Figure 24-1. Code generated by #define style templates

This **template** declaration corresponds to the definition of the parameterized macro. Like the parameterized macro, it generates no code; it merely provides a definition for the next phase.

Now we can use the template much like we used the functions defined by the parameterized macro:

```
int main( ) {
    float f = max(3.5, 8.7);
    int   i = max(100, 800);
    char ch = max('A', 'Q');
    int  i2 = max(600, 200);
```

You may have noticed that we skipped the generation phase. That's because C++ automatically performs the generation for us. In other words, C++ looks at the line:

```
float f = max(3.5, 8.7);
```

and sees that it uses the function max (float, float). It then checks to see whether the code for this function has been generated and generates it if necessary. In other words, everything is automatic. (There are practical limits to what can be done automatically, as you will see in the implementation details section.)

Figure 24-2 shows the code generated by the **template** implementation of max. From this you can see that the first time max is used for a **float** it generates the floating-point version of max. Next we use max for **int**, and the **int** version of max is created. Note that the last line:

```
int  i2 = max(600, 200);
```

does not generate any function. This is because we've already generated the integer version max and don't need to do so again.

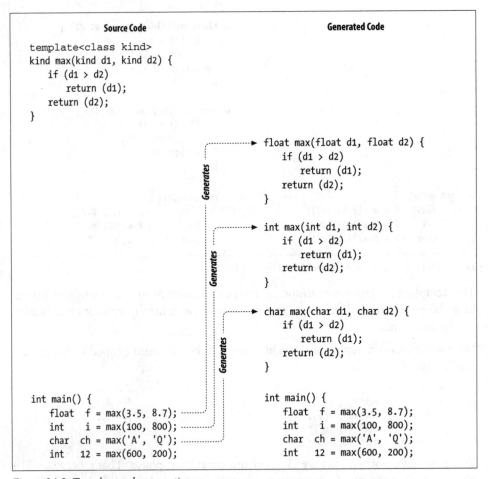

Figure 24-2. Template code generation

Function Specialization

Templates go a bit further than simple code generation. They can handle special cases as well. Suppose we want to use the function max to compare C style strings as well:

```
const char *name1 = "Able";
const char *name2 = "Baker";

std::cout << max(name1, name2) << '\n';
```

We have a problem, because C Style strings are represented by a character pointer (char *). The comparison:

```
if (d1 > d2)
```

compares the value of the *pointers*, not the data that's pointed to. What we want to do is tell C++: "Use the normal comparison except when the data type is a C style string, and then use strcmp."

This is done through a process called *specialization*. We declare a special version of the max function just for strings:

```
char *max(const char *const d1, const char *const d2) {
    if (std::strcmp(d1, d2) > 0)
        return (d1);
    return (d2);
}
```

When C++ first sees the use of the function max, it looks through the list of simple functions before it looks through its list of templates. Thus when we have:

```
std::cout << max(name1, name2) << '\n';
```

C++ will find the simple function:

```
max(const char *const, const char *const)
```

before trying to expand the template max(kind d1, kind d2).

Example 24-1 illustrates the use of template functions.

Example 24-1. max-t/max.cpp

```
#include <iostream>
#include <cstring>

// A template for the "max" function

template<typename kind>
kind max(kind d1, kind d2) {
    if (d1 > d2)
        return (d1);
    return (d2);
}
```

Example 24-1. max-t/max.cpp (continued)

```
// A specialization for the "max" function
//    because we handle char * a little differently
const char *const max(const char *const d1, const char *const d2) {
    if (std::strcmp(d1, d2) > 0)
        return (d1);
    return (d2);
}

int main( )
{
    // Let's test out max
    std::cout << "max(1,2) " << max(1,2) << '\n';
    std::cout << "max(2,1) " << max(2,1) << '\n';

    std::cout << "max(\"able\", \"baker\") " <<
                  max("able", "baker") << '\n';

    std::cout << "max(\"baker\", \"able\") " <<
                  max("baker", "able") << '\n';
    return (0);
}
```

Class Templates

Class templates are a little more complex than function templates. Declaring them is easy; they are defined just like function templates. Example 24-2 shows the stack class from Chapter 13, written as a template.

Example 24-2. max-t/stack1.cpp

```
#include <cstdlib>
#include <iostream>
#include <assert.h>

const int STACK_SIZE = 100;     // Maximum size of a stack

/********************************************************
 * Stack class                                          *
 *                                                      *
 * Member functions                                     *
 *      stack -- initalize the stack.                   *
 *      push -- put an item on the stack.               *
 *      pop -- remove an item from the stack.           *
 ********************************************************/
// The stack itself
template<typename kind>
class stack {
    private:
        int count;                 // Number of items in the stack
        kind data[STACK_SIZE];     // The items themselves
```

Example 24-2. max-t/stack1.cpp (continued)

```
public:
    // Initialize the stack
    stack() {
        count = 0;  // Zero the stack
    }

    // Push an item on the stack
    void push(const kind item) {
        assert(count >= 0);
        assert(count < sizeof(data)/sizeof(data[0]));

        data[count] = item;
        ++count;
    }

    // Pop an item from the stack
    kind pop() {
        // Stack goes down by one
        --count;

        assert(count >= 0);
        assert(count < sizeof(data)/sizeof(data[0]));

        // Then we return the top value
        return (data[count]);
    }
};
```

There is a problem, however. To use this class we need to declare an instance of it. In the past, we've been able to declare a stack with the statement:

```
stack a_stack;    // This won't work
```

The problem is that stack is now a generic template. The stack can now contain anything. When C++ sees this declaration, it's going to ask, "A stack of what?" We must specify the type of data we are storing. The new declaration is:

```
stack<int> a_stack;    // A stack of integers
```

The <int> tells C++ to use int for kind throughout the stack. We can now use the new class variable:

```
a_stack.push(1);
x = a_stack.pop();
```

In the stack class, we defined all the member functions inside the class definition. We could just as well have specified the procedures outside the class. To do so, we must put the template clause template<class kind> in front of each procedure and put the template parameter (<kind>) in the name of the class. For example, the push routine would look like this:

```
/*********************************************************
 * stack::push -- push an item on the stack             *
 *                                                       *
 * Warning: We do not check for overflow                 *
 *                                                       *
 * Parameters                                            *
 *        item -- item to put on the stack               *
 *********************************************************/
template<typename kind>
inline void stack<kind>::push(const kind item)
{
    assert(count >= 0);
    assert(count < sizeof(data)/sizeof(data[0]));

    data[count] = item;
    ++count;
}
```

Class Specialization

You can think of a class template such as this:

```
template <typename kind>stack { ...
```

as instructions that tell C++ how to generate a set of classes named stack<int>, stack<double>, stack<float>, and so on. C++ will also generate automatically the member functions: stack<int>::push, stack<double>::push, and stack<float>::push.

However, if you explicitly declare a member function yourself, C++ will use your definition before generating its own. Suppose we want to have a stack store C-style strings (char *). We don't want to store the pointers; we want to store the actual strings. To do this, we need a special version of the push function that duplicates the string before pushing it onto the stack:

```
inline void stack<char *>::push(const char *const item)
{
    data[count] = std::strdup(item);
    ++count;
}
```

Note that we didn't use template<typename kind> at the beginning of the function. The **template** keyword tells C++, "This is a generic class. Generate specific versions from it." With no **template**, we are telling C++, "This is the real thing. Use it directly."

Implementation Details

Now we come to a problem that has vexed most compiler makers, the details of the compilation process. Consider the files that make up Example 24-3. The program defines the following files listed in Examples 24-3 through 24-6.

integer.h
>   Defines a simple integer class.

square.h
>   Defines the prototype for the template function square.

square.cpp
>   Defines the body of the template function square.

main.cpp
>   Uses the template function square with the class integer.

Example 24-3. template/integer.h

```
class integer
{
    public:
        int value;

        integer(int i_value): value(i_value) {};

        integer operator * (const integer i2)
        {
            integer result(value * i2.value);
            return (result);
        }
};
```

Example 24-4. File: template/square.h

```
template<class integer> extern integer square(const integer value);
```

Example 24-5. File: template/main.cpp

```
#include "square.h"
#include "integer.h"

int main( )
{
    integer test(5);

    integer test2 = square(test);
    return (0);
}
```

Example 24-6. File: template/square.cpp

```
#include "square.h"

export
template<class integer> integer square(const integer i)
{
    return (i.value * i.value);
}
```

Now consider what must happen when we compile these files. We'll start with file *main.cpp*. When this file is compiled, the compiler sees that the template function square is used with the class integer. Normally, this would cause it to generate the code for square<integer>. But there is a problem: the body of this function is defined in the file *square.cpp*, which we are not compiling at this time. The result is that the compiler doesn't have enough information to generate the template.

But when we compile *square.cpp*, the compiler knows nothing about the class integer, so it can't generate the code for square<integer> either.

The C++ Standard has a solution to this problem. The solution is to put the keyword export in front of the definition of the function square in the file *square.cpp*. This tells the C++ compiler, "This template definition may be used in other files so keep its code around to be expanded in later compilations."

So the first thing we do is to compile *square.cpp*. The export directive tells the compiler to save a definition of the function somewhere. Next we compile *main.cpp*. The compiler sees that we want to generate code for square<integer>, goes to its library of exported templates, looks for the definition square, and uses it to generate the code.

Real-World Templates

Unfortunately, the standards for handling templates were one of the last things to be defined in the process of creating the C++ Standard. As a result, many compilers cannot compile standard code.

Most compilers force you to define all the data types you're going to use with a template before you define the body of a template. In our example, this means that we must include the line:

```
#include "integer.h"
```

in the *square.cpp* file. We also must tell C++ that we want to generate a function for square<integer> through the use of the statement:

```
template integer square<integer>(const integer value);
```

So our updated *square.cpp* would look like this:

Example 24-7. template/square2.cpp

```
#include "square.h"
#include "integer.h"

template integer square<integer>(const integer i);

template<class number> number square(const number i)
{
    return (i.value * i.value);
}
```

When to Generate Code

Suppose we have 20 files, all of which use the template function max<int>. On some compilers, this means that the body of the function is generated for every file in which it is used (in this case, the function is generated 20 times). That also means that the code for the function body is loaded 20 times in our program. That's 19 times too many.

Some compilers are smart enough to detect multiple loading of the same function and delete the extras. Some are not, and the result can be very large object files.

To solve this problem, some compiler makers force you to provide hints in your code to tell them when to generate a template and when not to. The actual syntax for the hints varies from compiler to compiler, so check your compiler documentation.

Writing Portable Templates

How can you write a portable template? One way to create a truly portable template is to write all your templates as inline functions and put all your functions in a single header file. As far as I can tell, this method works for every compiler that has templates. It may not be the most efficient way of doing things, but it is the most portable.

Advanced Features

There are a few advanced template features that are beyond the scope of this book. These include default parameters and partial specialization.

Default Parameters

Let's suppose that we wish to create a class to hold an address list. There are several different classes that hold addresses. There's one for a local addresses and one for international addresses. Since the two will never be mixed, let's use a template for our address list that handles everything:

```
// Half designed
template<class address> class address_list { ... }
```

But there's another design feature we must consider. Some lists are short (0–1000 names) and some are long (1,000–10,000,000 names). The short ones we can keep in memory; the long ones need to be put on disk.

There are two classes for the storing of list data, the in_memory_list and the on_disk_list. We can augment our template to include a provision for how the list is implemented:

```
// Closer
template<class address, class list> class address_list { .... }
```

But 99% of the time we want to use the in_memory_list implementation. We can tell C++ to use this as the default in our template specification:

```
// Closer
template<class address, class list = in_memory_class>
class address_list { .... }
```

Now if we don't specify an implementation for our list, C++ will use the in_memory_ list. So the following two statements are equivalent:

```
template<local_address, in_memory_class> small_local_addresses;
template<local_address> small_local_addresses;
```

Partial Specialization

When we defined our template for the function max we had to define a specialization for the case when a character pointer (char *) was used. Let's suppose we have a template that takes two types:

```
// Template definition
template<typename container, typename item> class store {...};
```

The first type is an ordered container, such as a queue or stack, and the second type is what to put in the container.

But C-style strings are a problem. They don't handle their own memory allocation, so they can be a bit tricky. What we'd like to do is to turn the C-style strings into C++ strings whenever they are used for the item.

For that we need to create a specialization of the template. But the template takes two parameters, a container and an item. If we wanted to use full specializations, we would have to create one every possible container type.

A solution is to create a partial specialization, where we specialize only the parts of the template that we need. The partial specialization for our store class looks like this:

```
// Partial specilization
template<typename container> class store<container, char *> {...}
```

The second definition tells C++ that whenever the second parameter is a C-style sting, it should use this definition for the template. For all other types, the first definition is used.

There are a number of tricky ways partial specialization can be used. Let's look at the template:

```
template<typename T1, typename T2> class example {....};
```

We can have a specialization for when the two types are the same:

```
template<typename T1> class example<T1, T1> {....};
```

We can also have a different specialization for when the first parameter is a pointer:

```
template<typename T1, typename T2> class example<T1*, T2> {....};
```

And so on.

Template specifications should be written with the most general first and the most specific last. That's because the compiler goes through the various forms of the template from the last declared to the first declared to see if it can find one that matches the parameters presented.

Templates are an extremely powerful programming tool. Careful planning and design is essential to using partial specialization properly. (Don't use it to patch up a bad design.)

Summary

Templates provide a convenient way of writing generic classes and functions. Many compiler makers have not completely implemented this feature, however. As a result, you'll probably have to play with the compilation switches and some **#pragma** directives to get things to work.

When you do get templates working, the result can be some very powerful code. An example of this is the Standard Template Library (see Chapter 25).

Programming Exercises

Exercise 24-1: Write a template min that returns the minimum of two values. Make sure you handle C-style strings correctly.

Exercise 24-2: Write a template class to implement an array with bounds checking.

Exercise 24-3: Define a template class that implements a set. The class allows you to set, clear, and test elements. (An integer version of this class was presented in Exercise 13-4.)

CHAPTER 25

Standard Template Library

Goodness and evil never share the same road, just as
ice and charcoal never share the same container.
—Chinese proverb

As people began to develop code, they noticed that they were coding the same things over and over again. For example, in every large C program, you'll probably find an implementation of a linked list. Since it's better to reuse than to rewrite, the designers of C++ have added a library of common containers (lists, arrays, and others) to the language. This library is known as the Standard Template Library or STL.

These containers are designed as templates so that they can hold almost anything. The library provides not only the containers but also iterators that make access to the contents of a container easier.

Finally, there are the algorithms that perform common functions on a container, such as sorting, merging two containers, locating elements, and other such functions.

STL Basics

In this section we take a look at the basic concepts that went into the design of the STL and how all these design elements come together to provide a very robust and flexible way of handling items.

Containers

The core of the STL is the container. We're already familiar with a couple of STL container types, the vector (a single-dimension array) and the stack.

The STL divides containers into sequences, which store their elements in order, and associative containers, in which elements are accessed using a key value.

The basic STL containers are:

vector

> A random-access sequential container. This looks pretty much like a C++ array, but you can expand it by inserting elements into it. You can also delete elements from a vector.

deque

> Similar to a vector, but it's faster at inserting and deleting elements in the middle of the container.

list

> A doubly linked list. Does not allow for random access.

set

> A set of items. Items in the set are ordered and unique.

multiset

> A set that permits multiple items with the same value to be stored in it.

map

> Also known as associative array. This is a container whose values can be looked up by a key. Because this is a template, the key and value can be almost anything. Only one value is stored for each key.

multimap

> A map that allows multiple values to be stored for each key.

These containers give you a way of storing most data in almost any way you want to. Now that we've got our data stored, we need access to it.

Iterators

Iterators allow you to go through a container and access the data inside. One form of this is the forward iterator, which allows you to access each element from first to last. There is a reverse iterator that allows you to go the other way and a bidirectional iterator, which goes both ways. Finally, there is the random access iterator, which allows you to access any element randomly.

Not all containers support all iterator types. For example, the vector supports random access iterators, while the list container does not.

We'll see how to use iterators in the class program described later in this chapter.

Algorithms

We have containers to hold the data and iterators so we can access it. For example, the sort algorithm can be used to sort an ordered container such as a vector. Some of the other algorithms include:

find

> Finds an item in a container

count
: Counts the number of items in a container

equal
: Tests to see if containers are equal

for_each
: Runs each element of a container through a given function

copy
: Copies a container

reverse
: Reverses the elements of an ordered container

These three elements—containers, iterators, and algorithms—make up the STL. Now that we know the basics, let's see how to use this library in the real world.

Class List—A Set of Students

Suppose we are working on a school scheduling program. We need to keep track of the number of students in each class. In STL terms, we need a container to hold the students. The type of container we need is a set.

A set is a container that holds an ordered list of items. In this case our items are student names (which are represented by strings). To define our class list, we use the following declarations:

```
#include <set>
#include <string>

std::set<std::string> class_set;     // A list of students in the class
```

The statement #include <set> is used to get the definition of the set template. We then use this template to define a set of strings named class_set. (The term "set" is used instead of the more common "list" to avoid confusion with the STL type list, which is discussed later in this chapter.)

We can now add names to our set of students:

```
while (! in_file.eof()) {
    std::string student;

    in_file >> student;
    class_set.insert(student);
}
```

This code uses the member function insert to add new students to our set.

Iterating Through a Set

Now we need to print out the class roster. To do so, we need to write some code to go through the set of students and print out each student's name. The STL has a concept called an *iterator* to help us do just that. You can think of an iterator as a pointer to an item in a set (or any other STL container). Actually, an iterator is much more complex than a pointer, but the STL tries to hide that complexity from you and make an iterator look as much like a pointer as possible.

Our iterator for the printing of students is declared as follows:

```
std::set<std::string>::const_iterator cur_student;
```

We are using const_iterator because we will not be changing the values of the items as we go through them.

Now for the actual stepping through the set. The first element of the set is called class_set.begin( ); the empty space past the last element is called class_set.end( ). To step through all the elements of the set, we use the following code:

```
for (cur_student = class_set.begin( );
     cur_student != class_set.end( );
    ++cur_student)
{
    std::cout << (*cur_student) << '\n';
}
```

Notice that to end the loop we used the condition:

```
cur_student != class_set.end( );
```

instead of:

```
cur_student < class_set.end( );      // Wrong!
```

That's because the elements of a set are unordered, which means that you cannot compare two iterators for anything except equality. They either point to the same element or they don't. It's meaningless to say that one element comes before another.

Using std::foreach to Write Out the Set

Iterating through an entire container is a common operation. In fact, there's an STL library function to do just that. Rather than write our own code, we can use the STL foreach algorithm to output our list:

```
#include <algorithem>
//......
static void write_student(set<string>::const_iterator& cur_student) {
    std::cout << *cur_student << '\n';
}
//......
    foreach(class_set.begin(), class_set.end( ), write_student);
```

The include file *algorithm* brings in the STL algorithm functions. In this case, the algorithm we are interested in is foreach. The function, write_student, merely writes out a student's name.

The heart of the code is the foreach function call. The first argument is the place to start; the second argument is one after the place to stop. (Note that this one-past-stopping is a key concept used in many STL functions.) Finally, we have a function to be called for each student.

Multisets

One of the problems* with sets is that each item in a set must be unique. So what happens if two students named John Smith enroll in the same class? When we try to do our insert, the set code will see that we've already got John Smith in the set and refuse to add another one.

A set of objects that can contain duplicates is called a std::multiset. Except for the way in which it handles duplicates, a std::multiset is just like a set. So we really need to declare our class using this new container:

```
std::multiset<string> class_set;      // A list of students in the class
```

Creating a Waiting List with the STL List

Suppose we have more students who want to take a class than we have places to put them. In that case we'll have to start a waiting list for those people who want to get in if space opens up.

We can't use a set as a waiting list, because a set stores the elements in order and we want to make our list first come, first served. For that we need the STL container std::list. A std::list is an ordered list of elements that allows us to add students on the back end and remove them from the front end.

Our waiting list declaration is:

```
#include <list>

std::list<std::string> waiting_list; // Waiting list for the class
```

When we want to add a student to the back of the list, we use the code:

```
waiting_list.push_back(student);
```

To remove a student from the front, we need two statements:

```
student = waiting_list.top();
waiting_list.pop_front();
```

---

* I've been told this is a feature, not a problem.

Iterating through a list is just like iterating through a set. That's because they are both containers, and the STL is designed so that all containers act the same whenever possible.

Storing Grades in a STL Map

Let's change our class roster so that we record not only the name of each student, but also the student's grade as well. We do this using something called a map. To define our class map, we use the following declaration:

```
#include <map>

// Map key=name(string), value = grade(char)
template map<string, char> student_roster;
```

Inserting an item into a map is a little trickier that inserting one into a set because we are inserting a pair of items. The STL handles this nicely by providing a pair class that takes two elements and turns them into an item that a map can handle. For example, if John Smith is in the class and got an A, we would write:

```
student_roster(pair(string("John Smith"), 'A'));
```

Suppose we want to find out what Mr. Smith's grade is. We can search for his record using the find function call. It takes three parameters: a place to start the search, a place to end the search, and something to look for. It returns an iterator pointing to the item found or, if nothing is found, the value returned by the end function. To look for Mr. Smith's grade, we use the code:

```
map<string, char>::const_iterator record_loc;

record_loc = find(student_roster.begin(), student_roster.end();
                   string("John Smith"));
```

Now let's check to see if we found the student:

```
if (record_loc == student_roster.end())
    std::cerr << "John Smith not found in the class\n";
```

The iterator points to a pair consisting of the student's name and grade. The fields of a pair are named first and second. To print John's record, we use the statement:

```
std::cout << "Student: " << record_loc->first << " Grade:" <<
    record_loc->second << '\n';
```

Putting It All Together

Now let's use our knowledge of the STL to create a class to handle a simple class roster and waiting list. The class class_stuff will contain member functions to perform the following tasks:

- Add a student to a class. If the class is full, the student will be added to the waiting list.
- Remove a student from a class. If the waiting list has a student in it, the first student on the waiting list gets put in the class.
- Record a grade for each assignment.
- Print a class roster including grades.

Let's start by defining the class. We'll record information about students in the class in a map. The key is the student's name, and the value is a vector containing the grades.

A vector is very similar to a list. However, it allows indexed access to its elements much the same way an array does. We will use the function size to determine the number of elements in the vector and resize to increase the size if needed.

The start of our class_stuff definition looks like this:

```
class class_stuff {
    public:
        typedef std::vector<int> grades;       // A set of grades

        std::map<std::string, grades> roster;  // Roster of current class
        std::list<std::string> waiting_list;   // People waiting on the list
```

Now we need to define the member functions. The first one adds a student to a class:

```
void class_stuff::add_student(
    const string& name  // Name of the student to add
)
{
```

We first check to see if the student is already in the class; if she is, we don't add her again:

```
if (roster.find(name) != roster.end())
    return; // Already in the class, don't reuse
```

Next we check to see if the number of students currently in the class has reached the limit. If there is room, we add the student to the class using the new_student function described below. If there is not room in the class, the student goes on the end of the waiting list:

```
if (roster.size() < MAX_STUDENTS) {
    // Class has room, add to class
    new_student(name);
} else {
    // No room, put on waiting list
    waiting_list.push_back(name);
}
}
```

The new_student function is responsible for adding a student to the roster. It creates an empty set of grades, then inserts the student into the class:

```
// Insert a student into the class
void class_stuff::new_student(
    const string& name  // Student to add to the class
)
{
    grades no_grades;   // Empty grade vector
    roster.insert(pair<string, grades>(name, no_grades));
}
};
```

The code to drop a student first checks to see if the student is actually in the class; he can't be dropped if he's not enrolled:

```
void class_stuff::drop_student(
    const string& name  // Name of the student to drop
)
{
    // The student we are probably going to drop
    map<string, grades>::iterator the_student =
        roster.find(name);

    if (the_student == roster.end())
        return; // Student is not in the class
```

Next we remove the student from the class. The erase member function eliminates an element from the map:

```
    roster.erase(name);
```

Finally we check the waiting list and add one student from it if there's someone available:

```
    // Add a person from the waiting_list if
    // there's anyone waiting
    if (waiting_list.size() > 0) {
        string wait_name = waiting_list.front();
        waiting_list.pop_front();
        new_student(wait_name);
    }
}
```

To record a grade, we first find the student's record:

```
void class_stuff::record_grade(
    const string& name,         // Name of the student
    const int grade,            // Grade of this assignment
                                // Assignment number
    const unsigned int assignment_number
)
{
    map<string, grades>::iterator the_student =
        roster.find(name);

    if (the_student == roster.end())
    {
        std::cerr << "ERROR: No such student " << name << '\n';
```

```
        return;
    }
```

Then we adjust the size of the grade vector so that it has enough entries to contain the assignment:

```
// Resize the grade list if there's not enough room
if (the_student->second.size( ) <= assignment_number)
    the_student->second.resize(assignment_number+1);
```

Finally, we store the value of the grade:

```
    the_student->second[assignment_number] = grade;
}
```

Our last function prints the grades for all the students in a class. To do this we need a sorted list of names. We start by copying the names from the roster into a container (storted_names) that can be sorted:

```
void class_stuff::print_grades( )
{
    std::vector<std::string> sorted_names;          // Student names sorted

    // The student we are inserting into the storted_names list
    map<string, grades>::iterator cur_student;

    for (cur_student = roster.begin( );
         cur_student != roster.end( );
         ++cur_student)
    {
        sorted_names.push_back(cur_student->first);
    }
```

The std::sort function is one of the algorithms supplied by the STL. You give it a range of items to sort and it sorts them. In this case, we want to sort the entire std::vector from beginning to end:

```
    sort(sorted_names.begin( ), sorted_names.end( ));
```

Now it's simply a matter of stepping through the sorted name list and printing the data. About the only new thing in this section of code is the use of [] to access elements of the roster. Remember that roster is a mapping of key to value. One way to find out the value associated with a particular key is to use the [] as follows:

```
    value = a_map[key];
```

The rest of the code for printing the grades is pretty straightforward:

```
    // The current student to print
    std::vector<std::string>::const_iterator cur_print;

    for (cur_print = sorted_names.begin( );
         cur_print != sorted_names.end( );
         ++cur_print)
    {
        std::cout << *cur_print << '\t';
```

```
            // The grade we are printing now
            grades::const_iterator cur_grade;

            for (cur_grade = roster[*cur_print].begin( );
                 cur_grade != roster[*cur_print].end( );
                 ++cur_grade)
            {
                std::cout << *cur_grade << ' ';
            }
            std::cout << '\n';
        }
    }
```

Example 25-1 shows the full code for our class_stuff object, as well as some test
code.

Example 25-1. class/class.cpp

```
/*****************************************************
 * class_stuff -- A simple class to handle students  *
 * and grades.                                        *
 *****************************************************/
#include <iostream>

#include <string>
#include <vector>
#include <map>
#include <list>

#include <algorithm>

const unsigned int MAX_STUDENTS = 5;    // Max number of students per class
// Set low for testing

class class_stuff {
    public:
        typedef std::vector<int> grades;// A set of grades

        std::map<std::string, grades> roster;   // Roster of current class
        std::list<std::string> waiting_list;    // People waiting on the list
    public:
        // Constructor defaults
        // Destructor defaults
        // Copy constructor defaults
        // Assignment operator
    public:
        void add_student(const std::string& name);
        void drop_student(const std::string& name);
        void record_grade(const std::string& name,
                const int grade,
```

Example 25-1. class/class.cpp (continued)

```
                const unsigned int assignment_number
        );
        void print_grades( );
    private:
        // Insert a student into the class
        void new_student(
            const std::string& name     // Student to add to the class
        )
        {
            grades no_grades;    // Empty grade vector
            roster.insert(
                std::pair<std::string, grades>(name, no_grades));
        }
};

/******************************************************
 * class_stuff::add_student -- Add a student to a class *
 *     If the class if full, add him to the waiting     *
 *     list.                                            *
 ******************************************************/
void class_stuff::add_student(
    const std::string& name       // Name of the student to add
)
{
    if (roster.find(name) != roster.end( ))
        return; // Already in the class, don't reuse

    if (roster.size( ) < MAX_STUDENTS) {
        // Class has room, add to class
        new_student(name);
    } else {
        // No room, put on waiting list
        waiting_list.push_back(name);
    }
}
/******************************************************
 * class_stuff::drop_student -- Remove student from     *
 * a class.  If there's a waiting list his place is     *
 * filled by the first student on the list.             *
 ******************************************************/
void class_stuff::drop_student(
    const std::string& name       // Name of the student to drop
)
{
    // The student we are probably going to drop
    std::map<std::string, grades>::iterator the_student =
        roster.find(name);

    if (the_student == roster.end( ))
        return; // Student is not in the class

    roster.erase(name);
```

Example 25-1. class/class.cpp (continued)

```cpp
        // Add a person from the waiting_list if
        // there's anyone waiting
        if (waiting_list.size( ) > 0) {
            std::string wait_name = waiting_list.front( );
            waiting_list.pop_front( );
            new_student(wait_name);
        }
    }

/*****************************************************
 * class_stuff::record_grade -- Record a grade for   *
 *      a student.                                    *
 *****************************************************/
void class_stuff::record_grade(
    const std::string& name,        // Name of the student
    const int grade,                // Grade of this assignment
                                    // Assignment number
    const unsigned int assignment_number
)
{
    std::map<std::string, grades>::iterator the_student =
        roster.find(name);

    if (the_student == roster.end( ))
    {
        std::cerr << "ERROR: No such student " << name << '\n';
        return;
    }
    // Resize the grade list if there's not enough room
    if (the_student->second.size( ) <= assignment_number)
        the_student->second.resize(assignment_number+1);

    the_student->second[assignment_number] = grade;
}

/*****************************************************
 * class_stuff::print_grades -- Print the students   *
 * and their grades.                                 *
 *****************************************************/
void class_stuff::print_grades( )
{
    std::vector<std::string> sorted_names;          // Student names sorted

    // The student we are inserting into the storted_names list
    std::map<std::string, grades>::iterator cur_student;

    for (cur_student = roster.begin( );
         cur_student != roster.end( );
         ++cur_student)
    {
        sorted_names.push_back(cur_student->first);
    }
```

Example 25-1. class/class.cpp (continued)

```cpp
    std::sort(sorted_names.begin( ), sorted_names.end( ));

    // The current student to print
    std::vector<std::string>::const_iterator cur_print;

    for (cur_print = sorted_names.begin( );
         cur_print != sorted_names.end( );
         ++cur_print)
    {
        std::cout << *cur_print << '\t';

        // The grade we are printing now
        grades::const_iterator cur_grade;

        for (cur_grade = roster[*cur_print].begin( );
             cur_grade != roster[*cur_print].end( );
             ++cur_grade)
        {
            std::cout << *cur_grade << ' ';
        }
        std::cout << '\n';
    }
}


int main( )
{
    // A class for testing
    class_stuff test_class;

    test_class.add_student("Able, Sam");
    test_class.add_student("Baker, Mary");
    test_class.add_student("Johnson, Robin");
    test_class.add_student("Smith, Joe");
    test_class.add_student("Mouse, Micky");

    test_class.add_student("Gadot, Waiting");
    test_class.add_student("Congreve, William");

    std::cout << "Before drop " << std::endl;
    test_class.print_grades( );
    std::cout << "\n";

    test_class.drop_student("Johnson, Robin");

    std::cout << "After drop " << std::endl;
    test_class.print_grades( );
    std::cout << "\n";

    int i;

    for (i = 0; i < 5; ++i)
```

Example 25-1. class/class.cpp (continued)

```
{
    test_class.record_grade("Able, Sam",     i*10+50, i);
    test_class.record_grade("Baker, Mary",    i*10+50, i);
    test_class.record_grade("Smith, Joe",     i*10+50, i);
    test_class.record_grade("Mouse, Micky",   i*10+50, i);
    test_class.record_grade("Gadot, Waiting", i*10+50, i);
}

std::cout << "Final " << std::endl;
test_class.print_grades();
std::cout << "\n";

return (0);
}
```

Practical Considerations When Using the STL

The containers and related functions of the STL do a good job of making your life easier. However, because the STL is so flexible and powerful, it can sometimes be difficult to get things right. In this section we'll explore a few techniques that can make your life much easier.

Getting the Types Right

One of the big problems with using STL containers is remembering the types of the variables and parameters being used. It's very easy to use the wrong type. You'll encounter this problem with the STL more than with most other code in part due to the flexibility of the system coupled with the large number types used in the definition of containers and the functions that work on them.

One way to make things clearer is through the use of typedef statements. For example:

```
typedef std::map<std::string, grades> class_roster;
```

Definitions like this tend to cut down on the clutter because class_roster is much clearer (and a little shorter) than map<string, grades>. It also makes maintenance easier because the definition of your type is in one place.

 We did not make extensive use of the typedef statement in this chapter because the purpose of the chapter is to teach you about the underlying STL templates. It would have been clearer (but not as instructive) if we had used them.

Error Messages

One of the problems with templates is that compiler parser technology is not yet up to speed when it comes to issuing error messages. The following example is *one* line of a multiline error message coming out of a broken program:

```
classx.cpp:78: no matching function for call to `map< basic_string< char, string_
char_traits< char>, __default_alloc_template< true, 0> >, vector< int, __default_
alloc_template< true, 0> >, less< basic_string< char, string_char_traits< char>, __
default_alloc_template< true, 0> > >, __default_alloc_template< true, 0> >::find (__
rb_tree_iterator< pair< const basic_string< char, string_char_traits< char>, __
default_alloc_template< true, 0> >, vector< int, __default_alloc_template< true, 0> >
>, pair< const basic_string< char, string_char_traits< char>, __default_alloc_
template< true, 0> >, vector< int, __default_alloc_template< true, 0> > > &, pair<
const basic_string< char, string_char_traits< char>, __default_alloc_template< true,
0> >, vector< int, __default_alloc_template< true, 0> > > *>, __rb_tree_iterator<
pair< const basic_string< char, string_char_traits< char>, __default_alloc_template<
true, 0> >, vector< int, __default_alloc_template< true, 0> > >, pair< const basic_
string< char, string_char_traits< char>, __default_alloc_template< true, 0> >,
vector< int, __default_alloc_template< true, 0> > > &, pair< const basic_string<
char, string_char_traits< char>, __default_alloc_template< true, 0> >, vector< int, _
_default_alloc_template< true, 0> > > *>, map< basic_string< char, string_char_
traits< char>, __default_alloc_template< true, 0> >, vector< int, __default_alloc_
template< true, 0> >, less< basic_string< char, string_char_traits< char>, __default_
alloc_template< true, 0> > >, __default_alloc_template< true, 0> > &)'
```

From this we can see that something went wrong on line 78, but it's difficult to tell what. (Turns out that this is a type-related problem.) Unfortunately, because of the clutter, it's next to impossible to tell what's wrong other than it's near line 78 and it has something to do with the STL.

The STL pushes the limits of C++ technology, and sometimes the limits push back.

Getting More Information

There is a good reference for the STL at *http://www.sgi.com/tech/stl/index.html*. Please note that this reference is for a slightly more advanced version of the STL than the one used in the C++ standard.Another STL reference can be found at *http://www.cs. rpi.edu/projects/STL/htdocs/stl.html*.

Exercises

Exercise 25-1: In Chapter 1 we defined a histogram program that used our home-grown infinite array. Rewrite the program to use the STL.

Exercise 25-2: Write a program that produces an index for a book. The input file is a set of page numbers and index information of the form:

```
<page-number>    <index entry>
```

There may be more than one record for each index entry. The output should be a sorted list of index entries such as:

```
alpha 10, 20, 30
beta 5, 6, 18
.....
```

Exercise 25-3: Change the cross-reference program you wrote for Exercise 1-1 to use the STL.

Exercise 25-4: Write a program that does a frequency count of each word in a document.

CHAPTER 26

Program Design

If carpenters made houses the way programmers
design programs, the first woodpecker to come along
would destroy all of civilization.
—Traditional computer proverb

Now that you've got the mechanics of programming down, we'll take a look at how to design good code. Creating a well-designed program is both a science and an art form. There is lot of science involved in the techniques and rules used to produce a good design. Your artistic side comes in to play when you use these rules to lay out a well-designed and beautiful program.

Design Goals

Before we decide how to make a well-designed program, we need to define what we mean by well designed. Different people value different things. But in most cases, people tend to value the same attributes. So let's explore what people value in a program:

Reliability
> People want a program that works. Crashes are extremely frustrating. They cost people time, cause data loss, and in extreme cases can cost people's lives. So reliability is extremely important.

Economy
> Most people, especially managers, don't like to spend money. They want the cheapest software possible.

Ease of use
> No program is useful if people can't use it. This may sound a bit obvious, but lots of programmers suffer from the "added feature disease" where they want to cram as many features as possible into their code. The result is something overly complex and difficult to use: in other words, a badly designed program.

Design Factors

Now that we know what we want in a design, let's see what we need to get there. As the science of programming has developed, people have discovered several factors that go into a good program design. You don't have to create a program with these factors in mind, but most programs that do a good job of satisfying the design goals listed above are designed with these factors in mind:

Simplicity

The simplest code that does the job is usually the best. It's the most reliable because it has the fewest things that can go wrong. Doing as little as possible also means that the code is cost-efficient to produce.

There are other benefits as well. Simple code is easy to maintain and enhance, so future programming costs are reduced, too.

Finally, the less you give a user to do, the less he can screw up. That generally means that the simplest software is the easiest to use.

Information hiding

A good design provides a minimal interface to the user and hides as many of the details as possible.

Expandability

Can the program be quickly and easily expanded? For example, suppose you are writing a word processor. How difficult would it be to use a different character set, such as Spanish or Korean? Better yet, how difficult would it be to adapt it to a more complex character set, such as Hebrew or Chinese?

Remember when PCs first came out: the maximum amount of memory you could have was 640K, and the early MS-DOS filesystem (FAT12) couldn't handle a disk bigger than 16MB. Both these limits have proven to be terribly inadequate.

Testable

If your program can be tested and tested easily, it will be tested. Testing leads to reliability. (Note that extensive testing should never be used as a substitute for a good design. Testing can only show the presence of defects, not their absence.)

But programs have a life of their own. They don't stop with version 1.0. There are a few design attributes that are appreciated by the people who have to maintain and enhance your code.

Reusability/generality

Writing code takes a lot of time and effort. Using already written code (assuming it does the job) takes very little time and effort. Good code design calls for your code to be reusable whenever possible.

For example, the linked list structure is extremely useful. In C everyone tends to create her own linked list package (a linked list of names, a list of messages, a list of events, etc.). The result is a lot of redundant code.

C++ has the STL, which contains a container class (std::list) that gives you all the features of a linked list. (Most of the time it's implemented as a linked list, but you don't have to know about the implementation details.) Because this container is generic, C++ programmers don't have to keep re-creating the same code over and over again.

A good design makes maximum use of reusable code and at the same time is itself designed so that it can be reused.

Different circumstances require different design criteria. I know of one oil company that spends lots and lots of money on making sure that their software is correct and extremely accurate. This software has one job: simulating how one pipe threads on to another. I asked them why they had a whole department devoted to pipe threads and they told me, "When a thread fails, we generally lose about fifty million dollars and a dozen lives."

Their design values accuracy and verifiability. They want to be really sure that their numbers are right. Lives depend on them.

On the other hand, I wrote a program to replace the standard Unix command *vacation* because the existing Unix command wouldn't work with our security system. The command was released with minimal testing and other reliability checks. After all, the existing command didn't work, and if the new command didn't work, the users didn't really lose anything.

Design Principles

There are a couple of basic design principles you should keep in mind when creating your design. They will help you create a design that not only works, but is robust and elegant.

The first is "Think, then code." Far too many people, when given an assignment, can't wait to start coding. But the good programmers spend some time understanding the problem and studying all aspects of it before they start coding. After all, if you are driving from San Diego to Chicago, do you jump in the car and head northeast, hoping you'll get there, or do you get out a map and plan your route? It's a lot less trouble if you plan things before you start doing.

The other design principle is "be lazy" (a.k.a efficient). The easiest code you'll ever have to implement and debug is the code that you designed out of existence. The less you do, the less that can go wrong. You'll also find that your programs are much simpler and more reliable.

Design Guideline: Think about a problem before you try to solve it.

Design Guideline: Be as efficient and economical as possible.

Coding

We're going to start our discussion at the bottom and work our way up. The smallest unit of code that we design is the procedure. Procedures are then used to build up more complex units, such as modules and objects. By starting simple and making sure our foundation is good, we can easily add on to create more complex, yet robust programs.

Procedure Design

A procedure in C++ is like a paragraph in a book. It is used to express a single, coherent thought. Just as a paragraph deals with a single subject, a procedure should perform a single operation. Ideally you should be able to express what a procedure does in a single simple sentence. For example:

This procedure takes a number and returns its square.

A badly designed procedure tries to do multiple jobs. For example:

Depending on what values are passed in, this function will

1. allocate a new block of memory on the heap,
2. delete a block of memory from the heap, or
3. change the size of a heap block.

It's the body of the procedure that does the actual work. A procedure should do its job simply and coherently. In general, programmers design and work on an entire procedure at a time, so the procedure should be small enough that the whole procedure can fit in a programmer's brain at one time. In practice this means that a procedure should be only one or two pages long, three at the most.

Design Guideline: Procedures should be no more than two or three pages long.

Procedure interface

The public part of a procedure is its prototype. The prototype defines all the information needed by the compiler to generate code that calls the procedure. With proper commenting and documentation, the prototype also tells the programmer using the procedure everything he needs to know. In other words, the prototype defines everything that goes into and out of the procedure.

Global variables

All the variables used by a procedure are either local to the procedure or parameters *except* for global variables. (The word "except" is an extremely nasty word. Frequently it indicates a complication or extra rule. Thing were probably simple before the "except" came into the picture.)

The use of a single global variable inside a procedure makes the whole procedure much more complex. For example, suppose you want to know what a procedure does for a given call. If that procedure uses no global variables, all you have to do is look at the parameters to that procedure to figure out what is going to happen.

You can determine what the parameters are by looking at a single line in the caller. All the other variables are local to the procedure. That's only three pages long, so you probably can figure out what happens to them.

But now let's throw in a global variable. That means that the input to the procedure is not only the parameters, but the global variable. So who sets it? Because the variable is global, it can be set from just about anywhere in your program. Thus, to determine the input to a procedure, you must analyze not only the caller, but also all the code in the entire program. I've seen people do string searches through tens of thousands of files trying to find out who's setting a global variable.

Figure 26-1 shows the information flow into and out of a procedure and how this is affected by global variables

One way people try to get around this problem is to require that all programmers list the global variables used by their procedures in the heading comments to the function. There are a couple of problems with this. First of all, 99.9% of the programmers don't do it and the other 0.1% don't keep the list up to date, so it's totally useless. In addition, knowing that a procedure uses a global variable doesn't solve the problems caused by not knowing when and how it is used by the outside code.

Design Guideline: Use global variables as little as possible.

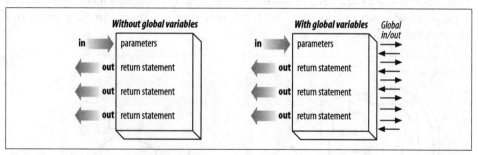

Figure 26-1. Procedure inputs and outputs

Information hiding

A well-designed procedure makes good use of a key principle of good design: information hiding. All the user of a procedure should see is the prototype for the procedure and some documentation explaining what it does. The rest is hidden from him. He doesn't need to know the details of how the procedure does its job. All he needs to know is what the procedure does and how to call it. The rest is irrelevant detail, and hiding irrelevant details is the key to proper information hiding.

Or as one of my clients said, "Tell me what I have to know and shut up about the other stuff."

Coding details

There are some coding rules for procedures that have been developed over time; if used consistently, they make things easier and more reliable:

1. For every C++ program file (e.g., *the_code.cpp),* there should be a corresponding header file (e.g., *the_code.h)* containing the prototypes for all the public procedures in the C++ file. This header file should contain only the procedures for the corresponding C++ file. Don't put functions from multiple program files in a single header file.

2. The C++ program file and the header file should have the same name with different extensions, for example, *the_code.cpp* and *the_code.h.*

3. The C++ program file should include its own header file. This lets the C++ compiler check to make sure that the function prototype is consistent with the function implementation.

Modules and Structured Programming

A collection of closely related procedures in a single file is called a *module.* Modules are put together to form a program. The proper organization of modules is a key aspect of program design.

First, your module organization should be as simple as possible. Figure 26-1A shows a program with seven modules. With no organization, there are 42 connections between the modules.

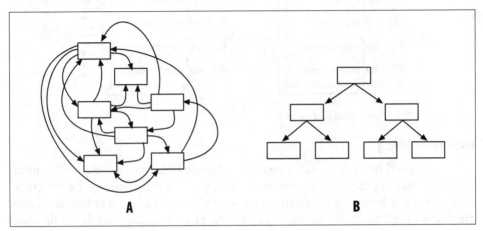

Figure 26-2. Module interactions

A programmer who is debugging a module must make sure that the other six modules he deals with work. Any problems in them are her problem. Testing such a system is a problem as well. To test one module, you need to bring in the other six. Unit testing of a single module is not possible.

Now consider the organization in Figure 26-1B. This system uses a hierarchical module organization. Consider the benefits of this organization. The modules at the bottom level call no one, so they can be tested in isolation. After these modules pass their unit tests, they can be used by the other modules.

People working on the middle-level modules have to contend with only two submodules to make sure their module works. They have some assurance their modules work—after all, they did pass the unit test—so the middle-level programmers can concentrate on dealing with their own modules.

The same thing holds true for the person dealing with the top-level modules.

By organizing things into a hierarchical structure, we've added order to the program and limited problems.

Design Guideline: Arrange modules into a organized structure whenever possible.

Interconnections

Although Figure 26-2 indicates that one module calls another, it doesn't show the number of calls that are being made. If we've done a good job hiding information, that number is minimal.

Let's first take a look at an example of what not do to. We have a module that writes data to a file. Some of the procedures are:

```
store_char -- Stores a character in the buffer
n_char -- Returns the number of characters in the buffer
flush_buffer -- Writes the buffer out to disk
```

When we want to write a character to the file, all we have to do is put the character in the buffer, check to see if the buffer is full, and, if it is, flush it to disk. The code looks something like this:

```
store_char(io_ptr, ch);
if (n_char(io_ptr) >= MAX_BUFFER)*
    flush_buffer(io_ptr);
```

This is an extremely bad design for a number of reasons. First, to write a single character to a file, the calling function must interact with the I/O module four times. Four? There are only three procedure calls. The fourth interaction is the constant MAX_BUFFER. So we have four connections where one would do.

One of the biggest problems with the code is the poor effort at information hiding. For this program, what does the caller need to know to use the I/O package?

- The caller must know that the I/O module is buffered.
- The caller must know the sequence of functions to call to send out a single character.
- The caller knows that the I/O package uses fixed size buffers. (The fact that MAX_BUFFER is a constant tells us that.)

All of this is information the caller should not need to know. Let's look at an alternative interface:

```
write_char(io_ptr, ch) -- Sends a character to a file.
```

This function may buffer the character, but it may not. All the caller needs to know is that it works. How it works is irrelevant. In other words, the system may be buffered, unbuffered, or use a hardware assist. We don't know and we don't care. The character gets to the file. That's all we care about.

Back to our original three-function call interface. Let's see what problems can occur with it. First, the caller must call the proper functions in the proper sequence each time. This is a needless duplication of code.

There is also a maintainability problem. Suppose we decided that fixed-size buffers are bad and wish to use dynamic buffers. We'll add a function call get_max_buffer to our module. But what about all the modules out there that have MAX_BUFFER hard-

---

* The greater than or equal comparison (>=) is used instead of equal (==). as a bit of defensive programming. If somehow we overflow the buffer (n_char(io_ptr) > MAX_BUFFER), we'll flush the buffer and the program will continue safely.

coded in them? Those will have to be changed. Because we have used poor information-hiding techniques, we have created a maintenance nightmare for ourselves.

One final note: a better design would encapsulate the io_ptr data structure and all the functions that manipulate it in a single C++ class, as we will see later on in this chapter.

Real-Life Module Organization

Let's see how a set of modules can be organized in real life. In this case we are dealing with a computer-controlled cutter designed to cut out tennis shoes. The major components of this device are:

- A computer that controls the machine. This computer is also used to store the patterns for the various shoes.
- A positioning device for the cutting head.
- An operator control panel (lots of buttons and indicators).

The basic design results in five major modules:

1. The workflow module. This module is responsible for scheduling the various cutting jobs that come up (e.g., do ten batches for size 9, then twelve of size 11, and so on).
2. The positioning control system, which is responsible for moving the cutting head around and doing the actual cutting.
3. A hardware-monitoring system. Its job is to check all the status indicators and make sure that all the equipment is functioning correctly. (There's a lot of little stuff, such as oil filters, blowers, air filters, air supply, and so on, that all needs to work or we can't cut.)
4. The control panel input module. This module is responsible for handling any buttons that the operator pushes.
5. The control panel output module. All the blinking lights are run from this module.

A diagram of the major pieces can be seen in Figure 26-3.

This organization, although not quite hierarchical, is quite simple. Each module has a well-defined job to do. The modules provide a small, simple interface to the other modules.

The other thing about the modules is that they are designed to be independently tested. For example, when the project started, the machine didn't exist. What we had was a computer, a pile of parts, and a lot of stuff on back order. Since the workflow manager didn't require any hardware, it was developed first. The other modules were faked with test routines. The fake routines used the same interface (header files) as the real ones. They just didn't do any real work.

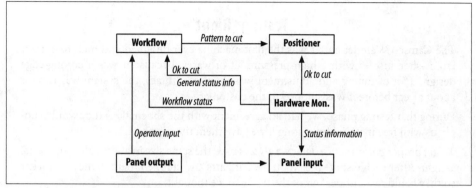

Figure 26-3. Cutting system, module design

It is interesting to note that the unit tests were used to test not only the software but the hardware. The unit test for the positioner module consisted of a front-end that sent various goto commands to the system. The first few tests were a little hairy because the limit switches had not been installed on the hardware, and there was nothing to prevent us from running the cutting head past the end and damaging the carriage. (Actually, the limits were rigorously enforced by a nervous mechanical engineer who held his hand inches above the emergency power off for the entire test. He wasn't about to let our software damage his hard work.)

This module structure let us create something that was not only simple, but testable. The result is increased reliability and decreased integration and maintenance costs.

Module Summary

So far we've learned a lot about how to design and organize our code. But programming deals with data as well as code. In the next few sections, we'll see how to include data in our design through the use of object-oriented design techniques.

Objects

So far our discussion has been focused on procedures. That's because procedures are one of the basic building blocks of a program. The other major piece of the puzzle is data structures. Combine the two and you have an object.

The design guidelines for a simple object are much like the ones for a module. You want to create a simple interface, hide as much information as possible, and keep the interconnects between objects to a minimum.

But objects give us one big advantage over the simple data structure/module design. With simple modules, your view of the data is limited. You either see the whole structure or you don't. Thus it's not possible (without getting very tricky) to write a procedure that accesses the common elements of several different types of data structures.

Perhaps an example will explain this better. On the weekends, I'm a real engineer at the Poway-Midland Railroad. There are three major types of locomotives: steam, diesel, and electric. They have some attributes in common; they all pull trains, for example. But there are some attributes unique to each locomotive. For example, only a steam engine requires lots of water to operate.

Using simple data structures, it's impossible to design a single data structure that encompasses all three locomotive types without wasting space. For example, the following structure describes all three types of locomotives—not well, but it does describe them:*

```
struct locomotive {
    bool running;    // Is the locomotive running
    int speed;       // Speed in MPH
    int num_cars;    // Number of cars it can pull

    int water;       // Water consuption in gallons / hour
                     // [Steam engine only]
```

---

* I know that there are steam locomotives that burn things other than coal, but for the purposes of this example, I'm simplifying the universe and steam engines burn only coal.

```
        int coal;      // Coal used in tons / hour
                       // [Steam only]
        int diesel_oil;  // Oil consumed in gallons / hour
                       // [Diesel only]

        // .. rest of the data
    };
```

Arranging data in this way is neither simple nor efficient. Objects let you arrange data in a new way by letting you create a general base object and derive more complex objects from it.

For example:

```
    class generic_locomotive {
        public:
            bool running;      // Is the locomotive running
            int speed;         // Speed in MPH
            int num_cars;      // Number of cars it can pull

            // ... rest of the data
    };

    class steam_engine: public generic_locomotive {
        public:
            int water;  // Water consuption in gallons / hour
                        // [Steam engine only]
            int coal;   // Coal used in tons / hour
                        // [Steam only]
     };

    class diesel_locomotive: public generic_locomotive {
        public:
            int diesel_oil;      // Oil consumed in gallons / hour
                                 // [Diesel only]

            // .. rest of the data
    };

    class electrice_motor : public generic_locomotive {
        public:
            // Electric Locomotives aren't that complex

            // .. rest of the data
    };
```

This data organization gives us tremendous flexibility. We are no longer constrained to writing procedures that deal with data structures as whole. Instead, procedures that want to deal with a generic locomotive can deal with the data type class locomotive. Other procedures that are locomotive-type-dependent can deal with their type of locomotive.

So our procedures can deal with the data at different levels. Thus with derived objects we've created different views into our data.

This is a good example of information hiding. Functions that deal with generic locomotives don't have to know about the specifics of each engine. They deal only with the generics. Figure 26-4 shows this information layering technique.

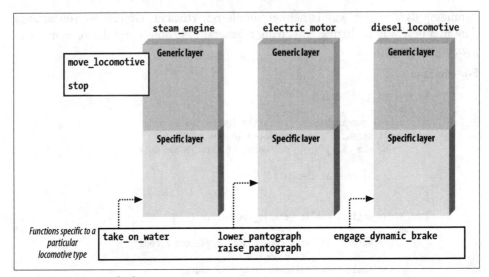

Figure 26-4. Layers of information

One of the nice things about virtual member functions is that they aid in information hiding. They provide an interface that is seen in the base class, but whose specifics reside in the derived class.

Interfaces and C++ Classes

Ideally, when you publish an interface you want to publish only the public data. In C++, to publish the interface for a class, you include the class definition in a header file. There is a problem, however; the class definition includes both public and private data.

This can cause problems.

Let's go back to our machine tool example. We had a hardware support module; it's a published interface (header file). For testing, we replaced it with a hardware simulation module that used the same published interface (the exact same header file).

When the interface is a class, you can't do that. That's because your hardware support class will probably have different private members than the simulation support class. Thus you need to keep two header files around, one for the hardware module and one for the simulation.

The public information in these header files must be duplicated, and thus you have all the problems associated with trying to keep two different files up to date and synchronized.

Unfortunately, C++ is not perfect, and the fact that private information must be published is one of its big problems.

In any design, the architect must make a number of trade-offs and compromises. In the case of C++, it was designed to be mostly compatible with the older C language. The designer, Bjarne Stroustrup, also wanted something that could be compiled using the technology of the time (early 1980s).

It was these factors that led him to design classes the way they are. Unfortunately, as a side effect of this design, interface and implementation information were both forced into the class definition.

But given the circumstances under which he worked, Mr. Stroustrup did a brilliant job of creating a new language, in spite of any rough spots which may appear.

Real-World Design Techniques

Over the years, people have developed a number of clever design techniques to help organize their programs. This section will discuss some of the more useful ones.

The Linked List Problem

The linked list problem is actually a C problem, but the various solutions and its ultimate solution in C++ provide a good understanding of the various techniques that can be used to solve a problem.

The code I'm working on now has several linked lists:

- Pending message list
- Running process list
- Keyboard event list
- Idle process list
- Registered connection list
- ... and so on.

There is an insert and delete function for each type of list:

```
insert_msg / remove_msg
insert_run / remove_run
insert_kbd / remove_kbd
insert_idle / remove_idle
insert_connect / remove_connect
... and so on
```

This is a needless duplication of code. There has to be a better way. In C, one solution is to play games with the data. The trick is to define a common linked-list structure:

```
/* C Code */
struct list_head {
    struct list_head *next, *prev;
};
```

This structure is put at the start of each data structure that may be used in a linked list:

```
/* C Code */
struct pending_message_node {
    struct list_head list;      /* List info.  Must be first */
    struct message the_message;/* The stored message */
};
```

Now we can take advantage of the fact that each mode in our pending message list begins with a list_head, use casting to turn our pending_message_node into a generic node, and use the generic linked list procedures on it:

```
/* C "solution" to a difficult code resue problem */
struct pending_message_node *pending_messages = NULL;
struct pending_message_node *a_new_message;

/* Fill in node */
add_node_to_list(
    (struct list_head *)pending_messages,
    (struct list_head *)a_new_message);
/* Note the C style casts.  This is C code */
```

This technique depends on the fact that the compiler lays out the memory for a structure with the first field (in this case list) first. This sort of layout is not required by the standard, but almost all compilers do it. (And those that don't cause people who depend on this feature a lot of headaches. They'll be forced to rewrite their code so it doesn't depend on compiler-dependent features.)

The C solution to this problem is pretty good given the limitation of the C language. But the C++ language gives us many more techniques for solving this problem.

The use of C casts is just the poor man's way of doing base and derived classes. The C++ equivalent is:

```
/* Not a good solution.  See below */
class list {
    private:
        list *next;
        list *prev;
    public:
        // Rest of the stuff
};

class pending_message_node: public list {
```

```
        // .... message data
    };
```

But there is a problem with this organization. The list and the message have nothing in common. A list is not a refinement of a message, and a message is not a refinement of a list.

Code that wants to process a message and doesn't want to deal with a list item can't deal with a pending_message_node. We could write it as:

```
/* Not a good solution still */
class list {
    // ...
};
class pending_message {
    // ...
}
class pending_message_node: public list, public pending_message {
    // Nothing needed here
};
```

This "structure" merely rearranges a badly designed data structure into one that's even more silly.

Ideally we want to organize our information like this:

```
class pending_message {
    // ...
};

class pending_message_list {
    // List stuff
    public:
        class pending_message message;
};
```

But now we're back to the problem that started this discussion. We're going to have to create a list for every type of object:

```
class msg_list ....
class keypress_list ...
class event_list ...
class free_block_list ...
```

This means that to properly design our data, we're going to have a lot of almost identical classes. This would be a lot of duplication of effort, except for one thing: templates. The result is that we can write all these classes using one template:

```
template class list<typename data> {
    // List stuff
    public:
        data node;
};
```

One last note: it's a little easier that this. We don't have to write the list class ourselves. It's already part of the Standard Template Library (STL):

```
#include <list>

class msg { /* .... */ };
std::list<msg> message_list;

class keypress { /* ..... */};
std::list<keypress> keypress_list;
```

Thus we've taken the long way round to discover that all you need to solve the "list problem" is to use the STL. But it's interesting how the problem can be solved using a language with limited features (C), as well as seeing a number of designs to avoid.

Callbacks

Let's suppose you are writing a text editor. There are three main modules to this program:

- A keyboard module that reads and decodes input
- A buffer/file module that keeps track of the text being edited
- A set of command modules that provide commands that change the text

One of the keyboard module's jobs is to read the keyboard input and call the appropriate command function. The mapping of keys to commands is accomplished through the use of a configuration file (also under control of the keyboard module).

So to do its job, the keyboard module needs to know the names of all the commands and what function to call to execute them.

One way to organize this information is to create a table containing this information and give it to the keyboard processor:

```
struct cmd_info {
    const char *command;
    void (*function)();
}[] cmd_table = {
    {"delete", do_delete},
    {"search", do_search},
    {"exit",   do_exit},
    ....
```

But this means that the module containing the table must know every command in the system. This way of doing things causes two major problems. First, we have discarded our module hierarchy and invalidated some of the information hiding we have so carefully built up. Now, one module, the command table module, needs to know everything. Second, we have to maintain the thing. Any time any one of the command modules changes, the file containing the command table must change as well.

Figure 26-5 shows our module layout.

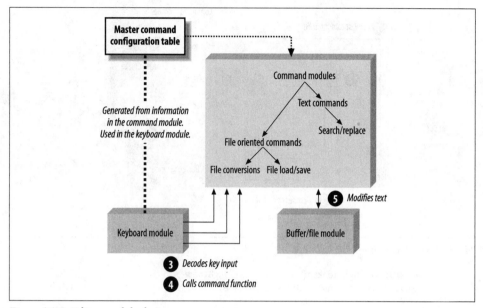

Figure 26-5. Editor module design

A better solution is to build this table at run time. During initialization time, the top command module is told to register all the user-level commands. For example, it may register the "exit" command:

```
keyboard_module::register_command("exit", &do_exit);
```

The top-level command module knows about its submodules and tells them to register their commands. They in turn call the subsubmodules, and so on.

The result is that the command table is built up at run time. Thus, we let the computer keep track of all the commands instead of doing it manually. This is more reliable and easier to do.

Figure 26-6 shows these module interactions.

Thus callbacks let us organize things so that the program configures itself automatically.

Decoupling the Interface and Implementation

Let's suppose we wish to create a simple database. In it we will store a person's name and phone number. A class to handle this might look like the following:

```
class phone_book {
    public:
        void store(const std::string& name, const std::string& number);
```

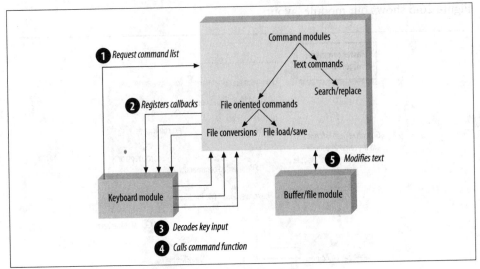

Figure 26-6. New Editor module design

```
        std::string& lookup(const std::string& name);
        void remove(const std::string& name);
        // .. additional member functions
    private:
        // Implementation dependent stuff
};
```

This class definition is then stuck in a header file for all to use.

The problem is that we are forced by C++ to put implementation-dependent stuff in the header file. This means that the user knows implementation details that are none of her business. It also means that we cannot provide more than one implementation of our phone book class. (We could play some games with derived classes, but that just moves the problem down a level to the derived class.)

Let's change our definition slightly and write our class as follows:

```
    class phone_book_implementation;

    class phone_book {
        public:
            void store(const std::string& name, const std::string& number);
            std::string& lookup(const std::string& name);
            void remove(const std::string& name);
            // .. additional member functions
        private:
            phone_book_implementation *the_implementation;
    };
```

Note that we did not define what the phone_book_implementation actually is. C++ is perfectly happy to create a pointer to it without knowing anything about it (other than that it is a class of some sort).

It is the job of the phone_book constructor to connect the implementation with the interface. In this example, we use a array-based phone book implementation:

```
phone_book::phone_book( ) {
    the_implementation = new phone_book_array_implementatation;
}
```

But there is nothing to prevent us from using a hash-based implementation:

```
phone_book::phone_book( ) {
    the_implementation = new phone_book_hash_implementatation;
}
```

Using this system, we've decoupled the implementation from the interface. This is a good thing (mostly). In this case the caller does not know which implementation was selected.

For example, we could use array-based implementations if we have, say, 1–100 names, a hash for 100–10,000, a small database such as MySQL for 10,000 to 10,000,000, and a commercial database for more than 10,000,000.

What's more, it is possible to switch implementations at run time. For example:

```
phone_book::store(const std::string& name, const std::string& number) {
    number_of_entries++;
    if (need_to_switch_from_hash_to_mysql_database( )) {
        phone_book_implementation *new_implementation =
            new phone_book_msql_impelemntation;
        copy_database(new_implementation, the_implementation);
        delete(the_implementation);
        the_impelementation = new_implementation;
    }
    // .. rest of the function
};
```

As you can see, this design has certain advantages. By decoupling the implementation from the interface, we've gained tremendous flexibility in choosing an implementation.

The design also has some drawbacks, the biggest of which is that it adds an extra layer between the phone_book user and the implementation. In most simple programs, this layer is not needed. Also, the use of derived classes in such a situation is no longer a simple matter of C++; instead, it requires some tricky coding. But this does serve to show what you can do with C++ to solve problems creatively.

Conclusion

The best single piece of advice I can give you concerning a program design is:

Do One!

Amazingly, there are a lot of people out there who start coding without thinking about what they are doing beforehand. If you think, then code, the result is much better code. A tenfold improvement can easily be achieved.

Second, show your design to your peers and get them to review it. Experience is one of the best design tools; you have the experience of others.

(The design of this chapter was reviewed by an editor. Its implementation was reviewed by the editor and a set of technical reviewers, one of whom thinks nothing of issuing forth with loud, harsh criticism whenever I do something stupid.)

Finally, C++ gives you a number of tools and techniques for designing your programs. These give you the ability to create a design that is clear, simple, and does the job. A well-designed program is a thing of beauty, so go out there and make the world a more beautiful place.

## CHAPTER 27

Putting It All Together

For there isn't a job on the top of the earth
the beggar don't know, nor do.
—Kipling

In this chapter we create a complete program. Every step of the process is covered, from setting forth the requirements to testing the result.

Requirements

Before we start, we need to decide what we are going to do. This is a very important step and is left out of far too many programming cycles.

This chapter's program must fulfill several requirements. First, it must be long enough to demonstrate modular programming, but at the same time short enough to fit inside a single chapter. Second, it must be complex enough to demonstrate a wide range of C++ features, but simple enough for a novice C++ programmer to understand.

Finally, it must be useful. This is not so simple to define. What's useful to one person might not be useful to another. We decided to refine this requirement and restate it as "It must be useful to C++ programmers." The program we have selected reads C++ source files and generates simple statistics on the nesting of parentheses and the ratio of comments to code lines.

The specification for our statistics program is:

Preliminary Specification for a C++ Statistics Gathering Program
Steve Oualline
February 10, 2002

The program stat gathers statistics about C++ source files and prints them. The command line is:

    stat *files*

where files is a list of source files. Example 27-1 shows the output of the program on a short test file.

Example 27-1. stat/stat.out

```
 1 ( 0 { 0 #include <iostream>
 2 ( 0 { 0
 3 ( 0 { 0 int    result;    // the result of the calculations
 4 ( 0 { 0 char   oper_char; // operator the user specified
 5 ( 0 { 0 int    value;     // value specified after the operator
 6 ( 0 { 0
 7 ( 0 { 0 int main()
 8 ( 0 { 1 {
 9 ( 0 { 1     result = 0; // initialize the result
10 ( 0 { 1
11 ( 0 { 1     // loop forever (or until break reached)
12 ( 0 { 2     while (true) {
13 ( 0 { 2       std::cout << "Result: " << result << '\n';
14 ( 0 { 2       std::cout << "Enter operator and number: ";
15 ( 0 { 2
16 ( 0 { 2       std::cin >> oper_char >> value;
17 ( 0 { 2
18 ( 0 { 2          if ((oper_char == 'q') || (oper_char == 'Q'))
19 ( 0 { 2             break;
20 ( 0 { 2
21 ( 0 { 3          if (oper_char == '+') {
22 ( 0 { 3              result += value;
23 ( 0 { 3          } else if (oper_char == '-') {
24 ( 0 { 3              result -= value;
25 ( 0 { 3          } else if (oper_char == '*') {
26 ( 0 { 3              result *= value;
27 ( 0 { 3          } else if (oper_char == '/') {
28 ( 0 { 4             if (value == 0) {
29 ( 0 { 4           std::cout << "Error:Divide by zero\n";
30 ( 0 { 4           std::cout << "   operation ignored\n";
31 ( 0 { 3             } else
32 ( 0 { 3                 result /= value;
33 ( 0 { 3          } else {
34 ( 0 { 3           std::cout << "Unknown operator " << oper_char << '\n';
35 ( 0 { 2          }
36 ( 0 { 1     }
37 ( 0 { 1     return (0);
38 ( 0 { 0 }
Total number of lines: 38
Maximum nesting of () : 2
Maximum nesting of {} : 4
Number of blank lines ................6
Number of comment only lines ..........1
Number of code only lines ............27
Number of lines with code and comments 4
Comment to code ratio 16.1%
```

Code Design

There are several schools of code design. In structured programming, you divide the code into modules, the module into submodules, the submodules into subsubmodules, and so on. This is also known as procedure-oriented programming. In object-oriented programming, you try to think of the problem as a collection of data that you manipulate through member functions.

There are also other approaches, such as state tables and transition diagrams. All of these have the same basic principle at heart: "Arrange the program's information in the clearest and simplest way possible and try to turn it into C++ code."

Our program breaks down into several logical modules. First, there is a token scanner, which reads raw C++ code and turns it into tokens. Actually, this function subdivides into two smaller modules. The first reads the input stream and determines what type of character we have. The second takes in character-type information and uses it to assemble tokens. The other module contains the statistics gathering and a small main program.

Token Module

Our program scans C++ source code and uses the tokens to generate statistics. A token is a group of characters that form a single word, number, or symbol. For example, the line:

```
answer = (123 + 456) / 89;  // Compute some sort of result
```

consists of the tokens:

```
T_ID           The word "answer"
T_OPERATOR     The character "="
T_L_PAREN      Left parenthesis
T_NUMBER       The number 123
T_OPERATOR     The character "+"
T_NUMBER       The number 456
T_R_PAREN      Right parenthesis
T_OPERATOR     The divide operator
T_NUMBER       The number 89
T_OPERATOR     The semicolon
T_COMMENT      The // comment
T_NEW_LINE     The end-of-line character
```

Our token module needs to identify groups of characters. For example, an identifier is defined as a letter or underscore, followed by any number of letters or digits. Our tokenizer thus needs to contain the pseudocode:

```
If the current character is a letter then
        scan until we get a character that's not a letter or digit
```

As you can see from the pseudocode, our tokenizer depends a great deal on character types, so we need a module to help us with the type information.

Character-Type Module

The purpose of the character-type module is to read characters and decode their types. Some types overlap. For example, C_ALPHA_NUMERIC includes the C_NUMERIC character set. This module stores most of the type information in an array and requires only a little logic to handle the special types like C_ALPHA_NUMERIC.

Statistics Class

In this program, a statistic is an object that consumes tokens and outputs statistics. We start by defining an abstract class for our statistics. This class is used as the basis for the statistics we are collecting. The class diagram can be seen in Figure 27-1.

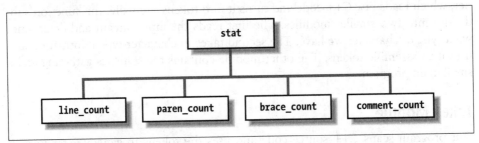

Figure 27-1. Statistics class hierarchy

Our definition of a statistic is "something that uses tokens to collect statistics." These statistics may be printed at the beginning of each line or at the end of the file.

Our four statistics are more specific. For example, the class paren_counter counts the nesting of parentheses as well as the maximum nesting. The current nesting is printed at the beginning of each line (the "(" number). The maximum nesting level is written out at the end of the file.

The other classes are defined in a similar manner. The only trick used here is that we've made the line numbering a statistic. It counts the number of T_NEW_LINE tokens and outputs that count at the start of each line.

Coding

The coding process was fairly simple. The only problem that came up was getting the end-of-line correct.

Functional Description

This section describes all the classes and major functions in our program. For a more complete and detailed description, take a look at the listings at the end of this chapter.

char_type Class

The char_type class sets the type of a character. For the most part, this is done through a table named type_info. Some types, such as C_ALPHA_NUMERIC, include two different types of characters, C_ALPHA and C_DIGIT. Therefore, in addition to our table, we need a little code for the special cases.

input_file Class

This class reads data from the input file one character at a time. It buffers a line and on command writes the line to the output.

token Class

We want an input stream of tokens. We have an input stream consisting of characters. The main function of this class, next_token, turns characters into tokens. Actually, our tokenizer is rather simple, because we don't have to deal with most of the details that a full C++ tokenizer must handle.

The coding for this function is fairly straightforward, except for the fact that it breaks up multiline comments into a series of T_COMMENT and T_NEW_LINE tokens.

One clever trick is used in this section. The TOKEN_LIST macro is used to generate an enumerated list of token types and a string array containing the names of each of the tokens. Let's examine how this is done in more detail.

The definition of the TOKEN_LIST class is:

```
#define TOKEN_LIST \
    T(T_NUMBER),      /* Simple number (floating point or integer) */ \
    T(T_STRING),      /* String or character constant */         \
    T(T_COMMENT),     /* Comment */                              \
    T(T_NEWLINE),     /* Newline character */                    \
    T(T_OPERATOR),    /* Arithmetic operator */                  \
    T(T_L_PAREN),     /* Character "(" */                        \
    T(T_R_PAREN),     /* Character ")" */                        \
    T(T_L_CURLY),     /* Character "{" */                        \
    T(T_R_CURLY),     /* Character "}" */                        \
    T(T_ID),          /* Identifier */                           \
    T(T_EOF)          /* End of File */
```

When invoked, this macro will generate the code:

```
T(T_NUMBER),
T(T_STRING),
// .. and so on
```

If we define a T macro, it will be expanded when the TOKEN_LIST macro is expanded. We would like to use the TOKEN_LIST macro to generate a list of names, so we define the T macro as:

```
#define T(x) x       // Define T() as the name
```

Now, our TOKEN_LIST macro will generate:

```
T_NUMBER,
T_STRING,
// .. and so on
```

Putting all this together with a little more code, we get a way to generate a TOKEN_TYPE enum list:

```
#define T(x) x          // Define T() as the name
enum TOKEN_TYPE {
    TOKEN_LIST
};
#undef T                // Remove old temporary macro
```

Later we redefine T so it generates a string:

```
#define T(x) #x         // Define x as a string
```

This allows us to use TOKEN_LIST to generate a list of strings containing the names of the tokens:

```
#define T(x) #x          // Define x as a string
const char *const TOKEN_NAMES[] = {
    TOKEN_LIST
};
#undef T                 // Remove old temporary macro
```

When expanded, this macro generates:

```
const char *const TOKEN_NAMES[] = {
    "T_NUMBER",
    "T_STRING",
    //....
```

Using tricks like this is acceptable in limited cases. However, such tricks should be extensively commented so the maintenance programmer who has to fix your code can understand what you did.

stat Class

stat class is an abstract class that is used as a basis for the four real statistics we are collecting. It starts with a member function to consume tokens. This function is a pure virtual function, which means that any derived classes must define the function take_token:

```
class stat {
    public:
        virtual void take_token(TOKEN_TYPE token) = 0;
```

The function take_token generates statistics from tokens. We need some way of printing them in two places. The first is at the beginning of each line, and the second is at the end of the file. Our abstract class contains two virtual functions to handle these two cases:

```
            virtual void line_start() {};
            virtual void eof() {};
    };
```

Unlike take_token, these functions have default bodies—empty bodies, but bodies just the same. What does this mean? Our derived classes *must* define take_token. They don't have to define line_start or eof.

line_counter Class

The simplest statistic we collect is a count of the number of lines processed so far. This counting is done through the line_counter class. The only token it cares about is T_NEW_LINE. At the beginning of each line it outputs the line number (the current count of the T_NEW_LINE tokens). At the end of file, this class outputs nothing. As a matter of fact, the line_counter class doesn't even define an eof function. Instead, we let the default in the base class (stat) do the "work."

brace_counter Class

This class keeps track of the nesting level of the curly braces { }. We feed the class a stream of tokens through the take_token member function. This function keeps track of the left and right curly braces and ignores everything else:

```
// Consume tokens,  count the nesting of {}
void brace_counter::take_token(TOKEN_TYPE token) {
    switch (token) {
        case T_L_CURLY:
            ++cur_level;
            if (cur_level > max_level)
                max_level = cur_level;
            break;
        case T_R_CURLY:
            --cur_level;
            break;
        default:
            // Ignore
            break;
    }
}
```

The results of this statistic are printed in two places. The first is at the beginning of each line. The second is at the end-of-file. We define two member functions to print these statistics:

```
// Output start of line statistics
// namely the current line number
void brace_counter::line_start() {
    std::cout.setf(ios::left);
    std::cout.width(2);
```

```
        std::cout << '{' <<  cur_level << ' ';

        std::cout.unsetf(std::ios::left);
        std::cout.width();
    }

    // Output eof statistics
    // namely the total number of lines
    void brace_counter::eof() {
        std::cout << "Maximum nesting of {} : " << max_level << '\n';
    }
```

paren_counter Class

This class is very similar to the brace_counter class. As a matter of fact, it was created by copying the brace_counter class and performing a few simple edits.

We probably should combine the paren_counter class and the brace_counter class into one class that uses a parameter to tell it what to count. Oh well, something for the next version.

comment_counter Class

In this class, we keep track of lines with comments in them, lines with code in them, lines with both comments and code, and lines with none. The results are printed at the end of file.

do_file Procedure

The do_file procedure reads each file one token at a time, and sends them to the take_token routine for every statistic class. But how does it know what statistics classes to use? There is a list:

```
    static line_counter line_count;         // Counter of lines
    static paren_counter paren_count;       // Counter of () levels
    static brace_counter brace_count;       // Counter of {} levels
    static comment_counter comment_count;   // Counter of comment info

    // A list of the statistics we are collecting
    static stat *stat_list[] = {
        &line_count,
        &paren_count,
        &brace_count,
        &comment_count,
        NULL
    };
```

A couple of things should be noted about this list: although line_count, paren_count, brace_count, and comment_count are all different types, they are all based on the type stat. This means that we can put them in an array called stat_list. This design also makes it easy to add another statistic to the list. All we have to do is define a new class and put a new entry in the stat_list.

Testing

To test this program, we came up with a small C++ program that contains every different type of possible token. The results are shown in Example 27-2.

Example 27-2. stat/test.cpp

```
/******************************************************
 * This is a mult-line comment                        *
 *      T_COMMENT, T_NEWLINE                           *
 ******************************************************/
const int LINE_MAX = 500;        // T_ID, T_OPERATOR, T_NUMBER

// T_L_PAREN, T_R_PAREN
static void do_file( const char *const name)
{
    // T_L_CURLY
    char *name = "Test"          // T_STRING

    // T_R_CURLY
}
// T_EOF
```

Revisions

As it stands, the program collects a very limited set of statistics. It might be nice to add things like average identifier size, per-procedure statistics, and pre-class statistics. One thing we kept in mind when we designed our program is the need for expandability.

We stopped our statistics collection at four types of statistics because we had fulfilled our mission to demonstrate a reasonable, advanced set of C++ constructs. We didn't add more because it would make the program too complex to fit in the chapter. On the whole, the program does its job well.

A Final Warning

Just because you can generate a statistic doesn't mean it's useful.

Program Files

The following examples contain the complete listing of our program, by file. They are listed here for reference:

Example	File
27-3	The ch_type.h file
27-4	The ch_type.cpp file
27-5	The token.h file
27-6	The token.cpp file
27-7	*The stat.cpp file*
27-8	Unix Makefile for CC (Generic Unix)
27-9	Unix *Makefile for g++*
27-10	Borland-C++ Makefile
27-11	Microsoft Visual C++ Makefile

Example 27-3. stat/ch_type.h

```
/*********************************************************
 * char_type -- Character type class                    *
 *                                                       *
 * Member functions:                                     *
 *     type -- returns the type of a character.          *
 *             (Limited to simple types)                 *
 *     is(ch, char_type) -- check to see if ch is        *
 *             a member of the given type.               *
 *             (Works for derrived types as well.)       *
 *********************************************************/
class char_type {
    public:
        enum CHAR_TYPE {
            C_EOF,                // End of file character
            C_WHITE,     // Whitespace or control character
            C_NEWLINE,   // A newline character
            C_ALPHA,     // A Letter (includes _)
            C_DIGIT,     // A Number
            C_OPERATOR,  // Random operator
            C_SLASH,     // The character '/'
            C_L_PAREN,   // The character '('
            C_R_PAREN,   // The character ')'
            C_L_CURLY,   // The character '{'
            C_R_CURLY,   // The character '}'
            C_SINGLE,    // The character '\''
            C_DOUBLE,    // The character '"'
            // End of simple types, more complex, derrived types follow
            C_HEX_DIGIT,// Hexidecimal digit
            C_ALPHA_NUMERIC    // Alpha numeric
        };
    private:
        static enum CHAR_TYPE type_info[256];   // Information on each character

        // Fill in a range of type info stuff
        void fill_range(int start, int end, CHAR_TYPE type);
    public:
        char_type();    // Initialize the data
```

Example 27-3. stat/ch_type.h (continued)

```
        // ~char_type    -- default destructor

        // Returns true if character is a given type
        int is(int ch, CHAR_TYPE kind);

        CHAR_TYPE type(int ch);
};
```

Example 27-4. stat/ch_type.cpp

```
/********************************************************
 * ch_type package                                     *
 *                                                      *
 * The class ch_type is used to tell the type of       *
 * various characters.                                 *
 *                                                      *
 * The main member functions are:                      *
 *      is -- True if the character is the indicated    *
 *                type.                                 *
 *      type -- Return type of character.               *
 ********************************************************/
#include <iostream>
#include <assert.h>

#include "ch_type.h"

// Define the type information array
char_type::CHAR_TYPE char_type::type_info[256];
/********************************************************
 * fill_range -- fill in a range of types for the      *
 *      character type class                           *
 *                                                      *
 * Parameters                                           *
 *      start, end -- range of items to fill in         *
 *      type -- type to use for filling                 *
 ********************************************************/
void char_type::fill_range(int start, int end, CHAR_TYPE type)
{
    int cur_ch;

    for (cur_ch = start; cur_ch <= end; ++cur_ch) {
        assert(cur_ch >= 0);
        assert(cur_ch < sizeof(type_info)/sizeof(type_info[0]));
        type_info[cur_ch] = type;
    }
}


/********************************************************
 * char_type::char_type -- initialize the char type table*
 ********************************************************/
char_type::char_type()
{
```

Example 27-4. stat/ch_type.cpp (continued)

```
    fill_range(0, 255, C_WHITE);

    fill_range('A', 'Z', C_ALPHA);
    fill_range('a', 'z', C_ALPHA);
    type_info['_'] = C_ALPHA;

    fill_range('0', '9', C_DIGIT);

    type_info['!'] = C_OPERATOR;
    type_info['#'] = C_OPERATOR;
    type_info['$'] = C_OPERATOR;
    type_info['%'] = C_OPERATOR;
    type_info['^'] = C_OPERATOR;
    type_info['&'] = C_OPERATOR;
    type_info['*'] = C_OPERATOR;
    type_info['-'] = C_OPERATOR;
    type_info['+'] = C_OPERATOR;
    type_info['='] = C_OPERATOR;
    type_info['|'] = C_OPERATOR;
    type_info['~'] = C_OPERATOR;
    type_info[','] = C_OPERATOR;
    type_info[':'] = C_OPERATOR;
    type_info['?'] = C_OPERATOR;
    type_info['.'] = C_OPERATOR;
    type_info['<'] = C_OPERATOR;
    type_info['>'] = C_OPERATOR;

    type_info['/'] = C_SLASH;
    type_info['\n'] = C_NEWLINE;

    type_info['('] = C_L_PAREN;
    type_info[')'] = C_R_PAREN;

    type_info['{'] = C_L_CURLY;
    type_info['}'] = C_R_CURLY;

    type_info['"'] = C_DOUBLE;
    type_info['\''] = C_SINGLE;
}

int char_type::is(int ch, CHAR_TYPE kind)
{
    if (ch == EOF) return (kind == C_EOF);

    switch (kind) {
        case C_HEX_DIGIT:

            assert(ch >= 0);
            assert(ch < sizeof(type_info)/sizeof(type_info[0]));

            if (type_info[ch] == C_DIGIT)
                return (1);
```

Example 27-4. stat/ch_type.cpp (continued)

```
            if ((ch >= 'A') && (ch <= 'F'))
                return (1);
            if ((ch >= 'a') && (ch <= 'f'))
                return (1);
            return (0);
        case C_ALPHA_NUMERIC:
            assert(ch >= 0);
            assert(ch < sizeof(type_info)/sizeof(type_info[0]));

            return ((type_info[ch] == C_ALPHA) ||
                    (type_info[ch] == C_DIGIT));
        default:
            assert(ch >= 0);
            assert(ch < sizeof(type_info)/sizeof(type_info[0]));

            return (type_info[ch] == kind);
    }
};

char_type::CHAR_TYPE char_type::type(const int ch) {
    if (ch == EOF) return (C_EOF);

    assert(ch >= 0);
    assert(ch < sizeof(type_info)/sizeof(type_info[0]));

    return (type_info[ch]);
}
```

Example 27-5. stat/token.h

```
#include <string>
#include <iostream>
/*******************************************************
 * token -- token handling module                      *
 *                                                      *
 * Functions:                                           *
 *      next_token -- get the next token from the input *
 *******************************************************/

/*
 * A list of tokens
 *      Note, how this list is used depends on defining the macro T.
 *      This macro is used for defining the tokens types themselves
 *      as well as the string version of the tokens.
 */
#define TOKEN_LIST \
    T(T_NUMBER),        /* Simple number (floating point or integer) */ \
    T(T_STRING),        /* String or character constant */             \
    T(T_COMMENT),       /* Comment */                                  \
    T(T_NEWLINE),       /* Newline character */                        \
    T(T_OPERATOR),      /* Arithmetic operator */                      \
    T(T_L_PAREN),       /* Character "(" */                            \
```

Example 27-5. stat/token.h (continued)

```
    T(T_R_PAREN),          /* Character ")" */               \
    T(T_L_CURLY),          /* Character "{" */               \
    T(T_R_CURLY),          /* Character "}" */               \
    T(T_ID),               /* Identifier */                  \
    T(T_EOF)               /* End of File */

/*
 * Define the enumerated list of tokens.
 *     This makes use of a trick using the T macro
 *     and our TOKEN_LIST
 */
#define T(x) x            // Define T( ) as the name
enum TOKEN_TYPE {
    TOKEN_LIST
};
#undef T                  // Remove old temporary macro

// A list of the names of the tokens
extern const char *const TOKEN_NAMES[];

/*********************************************************
 * input_file -- data from the input file                *
 *                                                       *
 * The current two characters are store in               *
 *     cur_char and next_char                            *
 *                                                       *
 * The member function read_char moves eveyone up        *
 * one character.                                        *
 *                                                       *
 * The line is buffered and output everytime a newline   *
 * is passed.                                            *
 *********************************************************/
class input_file: public std::ifstream {
    private:
        std::string line;        // Current line
    public:
        int cur_char;   // Current character (can be EOF)
        int next_char;  // Next character (can be EOF)

        /*
         * Initialize the input file and read the first 2
         * characters.
         */
        input_file(const char *const name) :
            std::ifstream(name),
            line("")
        {
            if (bad( ))
                return;
            cur_char = get( );
            next_char = get( );
        }
```

Example 27-5. stat/token.h (continued)

```cpp
        /*
         * Write the line to the screen
         */
        void flush_line() {
            std::cout << line;
            std::cout.flush();
            line = "";
        }
        /*
         * Advance one character
         */
        void read_char() {
            line += cur_char;

            cur_char = next_char;
            next_char = get();
        }
};


/******************************************************
 * token class                                        *
 *                                                    *
 *      Reads the next token in the input stream      *
 *      and returns its type.                         *
 ******************************************************/
class token {
    private:
        // True if we are in the middle of a comment
        int in_comment;

        // True if we need to read a character
        // (This hack is designed to get the new lines right)
        int need_to_read_one;

        // Read a /* */ style comment
        TOKEN_TYPE read_comment(input_file& in_file);
    public:
        token() {
            in_comment = false;
            need_to_read_one = 0;
        }

        // Return the next token in the stream
        TOKEN_TYPE next_token(input_file& in_file);
};
```

Example 27-6. stat/token.cpp

```cpp
/******************************************************
 * token -- token handling module                     *
 *                                                    *
```

Example 27-6. stat/token.cpp (continued)

```
 * Functions:                                          *
 *      next_token -- get the next token from the input *
 ********************************************************/
#include <fstream>
#include <cstdlib>

#include "ch_type.h"
#include "token.h"

/*
 * Define the token name list
 *      This makes use of a trick using the T macro
 *      and our TOKEN_LIST
 */
#define T(x) #x         // Define x as a string
const char *const TOKEN_NAMES[] = {
    TOKEN_LIST
};
#undef T                    // Remove old temporary macro

static char_type char_type;     // Character type information
/********************************************************
 * read_comment -- read in a comment                   *
 *                                                      *
 * Parameters                                           *
 *      in_file -- file to read                         *
 *                                                      *
 * Returns                                              *
 *      Token read.  Can be a T_COMMENT or T_NEW_LINE   *
 *      depending on what we read.                      *
 *                                                      *
 *      Multi-line comments are split into multiple     *
 *      tokens.                                          *
 ********************************************************/
TOKEN_TYPE token::read_comment(input_file& in_file)
{
    if (in_file.cur_char == '\n') {
        in_file.read_char();
        return (T_NEWLINE);
    }
    while (true) {
        in_comment = true;
        if (in_file.cur_char == EOF) {
            std::cerr << "Error: EOF inside comment\n";
            return (T_EOF);
        }
        if (in_file.cur_char == '\n')
            return (T_COMMENT);
        if ((in_file.cur_char == '*') &&
            (in_file.next_char == '/')) {
            in_comment = false;
            // Skip past the ending */
```

Example 27-6. stat/token.cpp (continued)

```
                in_file.read_char( );
                in_file.read_char( );
                return (T_COMMENT);
            }
            in_file.read_char( );
        }
}
/*******************************************************
 * next_token -- read the next token in an input stream *
 *                                                       *
 * Parameters                                            *
 *      in_file -- file to read                          *
 *                                                       *
 * Returns                                               *
 *      next token                                       *
 *******************************************************/
TOKEN_TYPE token::next_token(input_file& in_file)
{

    if (need_to_read_one)
        in_file.read_char( );

    need_to_read_one = 0;

    if (in_comment)
        return (read_comment(in_file));

    while (char_type.is(in_file.cur_char, char_type::C_WHITE)) {
        in_file.read_char( );
    }
    if (in_file.cur_char == EOF)
        return (T_EOF);

    switch (char_type.type(in_file.cur_char)) {
        case char_type::C_NEWLINE:
            in_file.read_char( );
            return (T_NEWLINE);
        case char_type::C_ALPHA:
            while (char_type.is(in_file.cur_char,
                                char_type::C_ALPHA_NUMERIC))
                in_file.read_char( );
            return (T_ID);
        case char_type::C_DIGIT:
            in_file.read_char( );
            if ((in_file.cur_char == 'X') || (in_file.cur_char == 'x')) {
                in_file.read_char( );
                while (char_type.is(in_file.cur_char,
                                    char_type::C_HEX_DIGIT)) {

                    in_file.read_char( );
                }
                return (T_NUMBER);
```

Example 27-6. stat/token.cpp (continued)

```
        }
        while (char_type.is(in_file.cur_char, char_type::C_DIGIT))
            in_file.read_char();
        return (T_NUMBER);
    case char_type::C_SLASH:
        // Check for  /* characters
        if (in_file.next_char == '*') {
            return (read_comment(in_file));
        }
        // Now check for double slash comments
        if (in_file.next_char == '/') {
            while (true) {
                // Comment starting with // and ending with EOF is legal
                if (in_file.cur_char == EOF)
                    return (T_COMMENT);
                if (in_file.cur_char == '\n')
                    return (T_COMMENT);
                in_file.read_char();
            }
        }
        // Fall through
    case char_type::C_OPERATOR:
        in_file.read_char();
        return (T_OPERATOR);
    case char_type::C_L_PAREN:
        in_file.read_char();
        return (T_L_PAREN);
    case char_type::C_R_PAREN:
        in_file.read_char();
        return (T_R_PAREN);
    case char_type::C_L_CURLY:
        in_file.read_char();
        return (T_L_CURLY);
    case char_type::C_R_CURLY:
        in_file.read_char();
        return (T_R_CURLY);
    case char_type::C_DOUBLE:
        while (true) {
            in_file.read_char();
            // Check for end of string
            if (in_file.cur_char == '"')
                break;

            // Escape character, then skip the next character
            if (in_file.cur_char == '\\')
                in_file.read_char();
        }
        in_file.read_char();
        return (T_STRING);
    case char_type::C_SINGLE:
        while (true) {
            in_file.read_char();
```

Example 27-6. stat/token.cpp (continued)

```cpp
                // Check for end of character
                if (in_file.cur_char == '\'')
                    break;

                // Escape character, then skip the next character
                if (in_file.cur_char == '\\')
                    in_file.read_char();
            }
            in_file.read_char();
            return (T_STRING);
        default:
            assert("Internal error: Very strange character" != 0);
    }
    assert("Internal error: We should never get here" != 0);
    return (T_EOF);      // Should never get here either
}
```

Example 27-7. stat/stat.cpp

```cpp
/********************************************************
 * stat                                                 *
 *       Produce statistics about a program             *
 *                                                      *
 * Usage:                                               *
 *       stat [options] <file-list>                     *
 *                                                      *
 ********************************************************/
#include <iostream>
#include <fstream>
#include <iomanip>
#include <cstdlib>
#include <cstring>
#include <assert.h>

#include "ch_type.h"
#include "token.h"


/********************************************************
 * stat -- general purpose statistic                    *
 *                                                      *
 * Member functions:                                    *
 *       take_token -- receives token and uses it to     *
 *                          compute statistic           *
 *       line_start -- output stat at the beginning of   *
 *                          a line.                     *
 *       eof       -- output stat at the end of the file *
 ********************************************************/
class a_stat {
    public:
        virtual void take_token(TOKEN_TYPE token) = 0;
        virtual void line_start() {};
        virtual void eof() {};
```

Example 27-7. stat/stat.cpp (continued)

```
        // Default constructor
        // Default destructor
        // Copy constructor defaults as well (probably not used)
};

/**********************************************************
 * line_counter -- handle line number / line count        *
 *               stat.                                     *
 *                                                         *
 * Counts the number of T_NEW_LINE tokens seen and         *
 * output the current line number at the beginning         *
 * of the line.                                            *
 *                                                         *
 * At EOF it will output the total number of lines         *
 **********************************************************/
class line_counter: public a_stat {
    private:
        int cur_line;   // Line number for the current line
    public:
        // Initialize the line counter -- to zero
        line_counter() {
            cur_line = 0;
        };
        // Default destrctor
        // Default copy constructor (probably never called)

        // Consume tokens,  count the number of new line tokens
        void take_token(TOKEN_TYPE token) {
            if (token == T_NEWLINE)
                ++cur_line;
        }

        // Output start of line statistics
        // namely the current line number
        void line_start() {
            std::cout << std::setw(4) << cur_line << ' ' << std::setw(0);
        }

        // Output eof statistics
        // namely the total number of lines
        void eof() {
            std::cout << "Total number of lines: " << cur_line << '\n';
        }
};

/**********************************************************
 * paren_count -- count the nesting level of ()           *
 *                                                         *
 * Counts the number of T_L_PAREN vs T_R_PAREN tokens      *
 * and writes the current nesting level at the beginning   *
 * of each line.                                           *
 *                                                         *
```

Example 27-7. stat/stat.cpp (continued)

```
 * Also keeps track of the maximum nesting level.            *
 ********************************************************/
class paren_counter: public a_stat {
    private:
        int cur_level;          // Current nesting level
        int max_level;          // Maximum nesting level
    public:
        // Initialize the counter
        paren_counter() {
            cur_level = 0;
            max_level = 0;
        };
        // Default destructor
        // Default copy constructor (probably never called)

        // Consume tokens,  count the nesting of ()
        void take_token(TOKEN_TYPE token) {
            switch (token) {
                case T_L_PAREN:
                    ++cur_level;
                    if (cur_level > max_level)
                        max_level = cur_level;
                    break;
                case T_R_PAREN:
                    --cur_level;
                    break;
                default:
                    // Ignore
                    break;
            }
        }

        // Output start of line statistics
        // namely the current line number
        void line_start() {
            std::cout.setf(std::ios::left);
            std::cout.width(2);

            std::cout << '(' <<  cur_level << ' ';

            std::cout.unsetf(std::ios::left);
            std::cout.width();
        }

        // Output eof statistics
        // namely the total number of lines
        void eof() {
            std::cout << "Maximum nesting of () : " << max_level << '\n';
        }
};

/********************************************************
```

Example 27-7. stat/stat.cpp (continued)

```
 * brace_counter -- count the nesting level of {}        *
 *                                                       *
 * Counts the number of T_L_CURLY vs T_R_CURLY tokens    *
 * and writes the current nesting level at the beginning *
 * of each line.                                         *
 *                                                       *
 * Also keeps track of the maximum nesting level.        *
 *                                                       *
 * Note: brace_counter and paren_counter should          *
 * probably be combined.                                 *
 ********************************************************/
class brace_counter: public a_stat {
    private:
        int cur_level;          // Current nesting level
        int max_level;          // Maximum nesting level
    public:
        // Initialize the counter
        brace_counter() {
            cur_level = 0;
            max_level = 0;
        };
        // Default destructor
        // Default copy constructor (probably never called)

        // Consume tokens,  count the nesting of ()
        void take_token(TOKEN_TYPE token) {
            switch (token) {
                case T_L_CURLY:
                    ++cur_level;
                    if (cur_level > max_level)
                        max_level = cur_level;
                    break;
                case T_R_CURLY:
                    --cur_level;
                    break;
                default:
                    // Ignore
                    break;
            }
        }

        // Output start of line statistics
        // namely the current line number
        void line_start() {
            std::cout.setf(std::ios::left);
            std::cout.width(2);

            std::cout << '{' <<  cur_level << ' ';

            std::cout.unsetf(std::ios::left);
            std::cout.width();
        }
```

Example 27-7. stat/stat.cpp (continued)

```cpp
            // Output eof statistics
            // namely the total number of lines
            void eof() {
                std::cout << "Maximum nesting of {} : " << max_level << '\n';
            }
};


/**********************************************************
 * comment_counter -- count the number of lines           *
 *      with and without comments.                         *
 *                                                         *
 * Outputs nothing at the beginning of each line, but      *
 * will output a ratio at the end of file                  *
 *                                                         *
 * Note: This class makes use of two bits:                 *
 *      CF_COMMENT  -- a comment was seen                   *
 *      CF_CODE     -- code was seen                        *
 * to collect statistics.                                  *
 *                                                         *
 * These are combined to form an index into the counter    *
 * array so the value of these two bits is very            *
 * important.                                              *
 **********************************************************/
static const int CF_COMMENT = (1<<0);   // Line contains comment
static const int CF_CODE    = (1<<1);   // Line contains code
// These bits are combined to form the statistics
//
//      0                     -- [0] Blank line
//      CF_COMMENT            -- [1] Comment only line
//      CF_CODE               -- [2] Code only line
//      CF_COMMENT|CF_CODE -- [3] Comments and code on this line

class comment_counter: public a_stat {
    private:
        int counters[4];        // Count of various types of stats.
        int flags;              // Flags for the current line
    public:
        // Initialize the counters
        comment_counter() {
            memset(counters, '\0', sizeof(counters));
            flags = 0;
        };
        // Default destructor
        // Default copy constructor (probably never called)

        // Consume tokens,  count the nesting of ()
        void take_token(TOKEN_TYPE token) {
            switch (token) {
                case T_COMMENT:
                    flags |= CF_COMMENT;
                    break;
```

Example 27-7. stat/stat.cpp (continued)

```
                default:
                    flags |= CF_CODE;
                    break;
                case T_NEWLINE:
                    assert(flags >= 0);
                    assert(flags < sizeof(counters)/sizeof(counters[0]));
                    ++counters[flags];
                    flags = 0;
                    break;
            }
        }

        // void line_start() -- defaults to base

        // Output eof statistics
        // namely the total number of lines
        void eof() {
            std::cout << "Number of blank lines ................." <<
                    counters[0] << '\n';
            std::cout << "Number of comment only lines .........." <<
                    counters[1] << '\n';
            std::cout << "Number of code only lines ............." <<
                    counters[2] << '\n';
            std::cout << "Number of lines with code and comments " <<
                    counters[3] << '\n';
            std::cout.setf(std::ios::fixed);
            std::cout.precision(1);
            std::cout << "Comment to code ratio " <<
                float(counters[1] + counters[3]) /
                float(counters[2] + counters[3]) * 100.0 << "%\n";
        }
};


static line_counter line_count;          // Counter of lines
static paren_counter paren_count;        // Counter of () levels
static brace_counter brace_count;        // Counter of {} levels
static comment_counter comment_count;    // Counter of comment info

// A list of the statistics we are collecting
static a_stat *stat_list[] = {
    &line_count,
    &paren_count,
    &brace_count,
    &comment_count,
    NULL
};


/******************************************************
 * do_file -- process a single file                   *
 *                                                    *
```

Example 27-7. stat/stat.cpp (continued)

```
 * Parameters                                          *
 *       name -- the name of the file to process       *
 *******************************************************/
static void do_file(const char *const name)
{
    input_file in_file(name);    // File to read
    token token;                 // Token reader/parser
    TOKEN_TYPE cur_token;        // Current token type
    class a_stat **cur_stat;     // Pointer to stat for collection/writing

    if (in_file.bad()) {
        std::cerr << "Error: Could not open file " <<
                name << " for reading\n";
        return;
    }
    while (true) {
        cur_token = token.next_token(in_file);
        for (cur_stat = stat_list; *cur_stat != NULL; ++cur_stat)
            (*cur_stat)->take_token(cur_token);
#ifdef DEBUG
        assert(cur_token >= 0);
        assert(cur_token < sizeof(TOKEN_NAMES)/sizeof(TOKEN_NAMES[0]));
        std::cout << "   " << TOKEN_NAMES[cur_token] << '\n';
#endif /* DEBUG */

        switch (cur_token) {
            case T_NEWLINE:
                for (cur_stat = stat_list; *cur_stat != NULL; ++cur_stat)
                    (*cur_stat)->line_start();
                in_file.flush_line();
                break;
            case T_EOF:
                for (cur_stat = stat_list; *cur_stat != NULL; ++cur_stat)
                    (*cur_stat)->eof();
                return;
            default:
                // Do nothing
                break;
        }
    }
}

int main(int argc, char *argv[])
{
    char *prog_name = argv[0];  // Name of the program

    if (argc == 1) {
        std::cerr << "Usage is " << prog_name << "[options] <file-list>\n";
        exit (8);
    }

    for (/* argc set */; argc > 1; --argc) {
```

Example 27-7. stat/stat.cpp (continued)

```
        do_file(argv[1]);
        ++argv;
    }
    return (0);
}
```

Example 27-8. stat/makefile.unx

```
#
# Makefile for many Unix compilers using the
# "standard" command name CC
#
CC=CC
CFLAGS=-g
OBJS= stat.o ch_type.o token.o

all: stat.out stat

stat.out: stat
        stat ../calc3/calc3.cpp >stat.out

stat: $(OBJS)
        $(CC) $(CCFLAGS) -o stat $(OBJS)

stat.o: stat.cpp token.h
        $(CC) $(CCFLAGS) -c stat.cpp

ch_type.o: ch_type.cpp ch_type.h
        $(CC) $(CCFLAGS) -c ch_type.cpp

token.o: token.cpp token.h ch_type.h
        $(CC) $(CCFLAGS) -c token.cpp


clean:
        rm stat stat.o ch_type.o token.o
```

Example 27-9. stat/makefile.gnu

```
#
# Makefile for the Free Software Foundations g++ compiler
#
CC=g++
CCFLAGS=-g -Wall
OBJS= stat.o ch_type.o token.o

all: stat.out stat

stat.out: stat
        stat ../calc3/calc3.cpp >stat.out

stat: $(OBJS)
```

Example 27-9. stat/makefile.gnu (continued)

```
        $(CC) $(CCFLAGS) -o stat $(OBJS)

stat.o: stat.cpp token.h
        $(CC) $(CCFLAGS) -c stat.cpp

ch_type.o: ch_type.cpp ch_type.h
        $(CC) $(CCFLAGS) -c ch_type.cpp

token.o: token.cpp token.h ch_type.h
        $(CC) $(CCFLAGS) -c token.cpp

clean:
        rm stat stat.o ch_type.o token.o
```

Example 27-10. stat/makefile.bcc

```
#
# Makefile for Borland's Borland-C++ compiler
#
CC=bcc32
#
# Flags
#
#       -N -- Check for stack overflow
#       -v -- Enable debugging
#       -w -- Turn on all warnings
#       -tWC -- Console application
#
CFLAGS=-N -v -w -tWC
OBJS= stat.obj ch_type.obj token.obj

all: stat.out stat.exe

stat.out: stat.exe
        stat ..\calc3\calc3.cpp >stat.out

stat.exe: $(OBJS)
        $(CC) $(CCFLAGS) -estat $(OBJS)

stat.obj: stat.cpp token.h
        $(CC) $(CCFLAGS) -c stat.cpp

ch_type.obj: ch_type.cpp ch_type.h
        $(CC) $(CCFLAGS) -c ch_type.cpp

token.obj: token.cpp token.h ch_type.h
        $(CC) $(CCFLAGS) -c token.cpp


clean:
        erase stat.exe stat.obj ch_type.obj token.obj
```

Example 27-11. stat/makefile.msc

```
#
# Makefile for Microsoft Visual C++
#
CC=cl
#
# Flags
#       AL -- Compile for large model
#       Zi -- Enable debugging
#       W1 -- Turn on warnings
#
CFLAGS=/AL /Zi /W1
OBJS= stat.obj ch_type.obj token.obj

all: stat.out stat.exe

stat.out: stat.exe
        stat ..\calc3\calc3.cpp >stat.out

stat.exe: $(OBJS)
        $(CC) $(CCFLAGS)  $(OBJS)

stat.obj: stat.cpp token.h
        $(CC) $(CCFLAGS) -c stat.cpp

ch_type.obj: ch_type.cpp ch_type.h
        $(CC) $(CCFLAGS) -c ch_type.cpp

token.obj: token.cpp token.h ch_type.h
        $(CC) $(CCFLAGS) -c token.cpp


clean:
        erase stat.exe stat.obj ch_type.obj token.obj
```

Programming Exercises

Exercise 27-1: Write a program that checks a text file for doubled words.

Exercise 27-2: Write a program that removes vulgar words from a file and replaces them with more acceptable equivalents.

Exercise 27-3: Write a mailing-list program. This program will read, write, sort and print mailing labels.

Exercise 27-4: Update the statistics program presented in this chapter to add a cross-reference capability.

Exercise 27-5: Write a program that takes a text file and splits each long line into two smaller lines. The split point should be at the end of a sentence if possible, or at the end of a word if a sentence is too long.

## CHAPTER 28

From C to C++

No distinction so little excites envy as that which is
derived from ancestors by a long descent.
—François de Salignac de la Mothe Fénelon

C++ was built on the older language C, and there's a lot of C code still around. That's both a blessing and a curse. It's a curse because you'll probably have to deal with a lot of ancient code. On the other hand, there will always be work for you. This chapter describes some of the differences between C and C++, as well as how to migrate from one to the other.

K&R-Style Functions

Classic C (also called K&R C after its authors, Brian Kernighan and Dennis Ritchie) uses a function header that's different from the one used in C++. In C++ the parameter types and names are included inside the () defining the function. In Classic C, only the names appear. Type information comes later. The following code shows the same function twice, first as defined in C++, followed by its K&R definition:

```
int do_it(char *name, int function)    // C++ function definition
{
    // Body of the function

int do_it(name, function)              // Classic C definition
char *name;
int function;
{
    // Body of the function
```

When C++ came along, the ANSI C committee decided it would be a good idea if C used the new function definitions. However, because there was a lot of code out there using the old method, C accepts both types of functions. C++ does not.

Prototypes

Classic C does not require prototypes. In many cases, prototypes are missing from C programs. A function that does not have a prototype has an implied prototype of:

```
int funct();    // Default prototype for Classic C functions
```

The () in C does not denote an empty argument list. Instead it denotes a variable length argument list with no type checking of the parameters. Also, Classic C prototypes have no parameter lists. The only "prototype" you'll see consists merely of "()", such as:

```
int do_it();    // Classic C function prototype
```

This tells C that do_it returns an **int** and takes any number of parameters. C does not type-check parameters, so the following are legal calls to do_it:

```
i = do_it();
i = do_it(1, 2, 3);
i = do_it("Test", 'a');
```

C++ requires function prototypes, so you have to put them in. There are tools out there such as the GNU *prototize* utility that help you by reading your code and generating function prototypes. Otherwise, you will have to do it manually.

struct

In C++, when you declare a **struct**, you can use the structure as a type name. For example:

```
struct sample {
    int i, j;    // Data for the sample
};
sample sample_var;   // Last sample seen
```

C is more strict. You must put the keyword **struct** before each variable declaration:

```
struct sample sample_var;  // Legal in C
sample sample_var;         // Illegal in C
```

malloc and free

In C++, you use the **new** operator to get memory from the heap and use **delete** to return the memory. C has no built-in memory-handling operations. Instead, it makes use of two library routines: malloc and free.

The C malloc function

The function malloc takes a single parameter—the number of bytes to allocate—and returns a pointer to them (as a char * or void *). But how do we know how big a structure is? That's where the sizeof operator comes in. It returns the number of bytes in a structure. To allocate a new variable of type struct foo in C, we use the code:

```
foo_ptr = (struct foo *)malloc(sizeof(struct foo));
```

Note that we must use a cast to turn the pointer returned by malloc into something useful. The C++ syntax for the same operation is much cleaner:

```
foo_ptr = new foo;
```

Suppose we want to allocate an array of three structures. We need to multiply our allocation size by three, resulting in the following C code:

```
foo_ptr = (struct foo *)malloc(sizeof(struct foo) * 3);
```

The much simpler C++ equivalent is:

```
foo_ptr = new foo[3];
```

The calloc Function

The function calloc is similar to malloc except that it takes two parameters: the number of elements in the array of objects and the size of a single element. Using our array of three foos example, we get:

```
foo_var = (struct foo*)calloc(3, sizeof(foo));
```

The other difference is that calloc initializes the structure to zero. Thus, the C++ equivalent is:

```
foo_var = new foo[3];
memset(foo_var, '\0', sizeof(foo) * 3);
```

Programs can freely mix C-style malloc and C++ **new** calls. The C memory allocators are messy, however, and should be converted to their C++ version whenever possible.

There are a number of traps concerning C-style memory allocation. Suppose we take our structure foo and turn it into a class. We can, but shouldn't, use the C memory routines to allocate space for the class:

```
class foo {...};
foo_var = (struct foo *)malloc(sizeof(struct foo)); // Don't code like this
```

Because C++ treats struct as a special form of class, most compilers won't complain about this code. The problem is that our malloc statement allocates space for foo and *that's all*. No constructor is called, so it's quite possible that the class will not get set up correctly. The C++ new operator not only allocates the memory, but also calls the constructor so that the class is properly initialized.

The C free function

C uses the function free to return memory to the heap. The function free takes a single character pointer as a parameter (thus making a lot of casting necessary):

```
free((char *)foo_var);
foo_var = NULL;
```

In C++ you delete a foo_var that points to a simple value this way:

```
delete foo_var;
foo_var = NULL;
```

If foo_array is an pointer to an array, you delete it with the code:

```
delete []foo_array;
foo_array = NULL;
```

Again, you must be careful when turning foo into a class. The free function just returns the memory to the heap. It does not call the destructor for foo, while the delete operator calls the destructor and then deletes the class's memory.

C-style memory allocation is messy and risky. When converting code to C++ you probably should get rid of all malloc, calloc, and free calls whenever possible.

 According to the ANSI C standard, memory allocated by malloc must be deallocated by free. Similarly, memory allocated by **new** must be deallocated by **delete**. However, most of the compilers I've seen implement **new** as a call to malloc and **delete** as a call to free. In other words, mixing **new**/free or malloc/**free** calls will *usually* work. To avoid errors, you should follow the rules and avoid mixing C and C++ operations.

Turning Structures into Classes

Frequently when examining C code you may find a number of defined struct statements that look like they should be objects defined as C++ classes. Actually, a structure is really just a data-only class with all the members public.

C programmers frequently take advantage of the fact that a structure contains only data. One example of this is reading and writing a structure to a binary file. For example:

```
a_struct struct_var;   // A structure variable

// Perform a raw read to read in the structure
read_size = read(fd, (char *)&struct_var, sizeof(struct_var));

// Perform a raw write to send the data to a file
write_size = write(fd, (char *)&struct_var, sizeof(struct_var));
```

Turning a structure like this into a class can cause problems. C++ keeps extra information, such as virtual function pointers, in a class. When you write the class to disk using a raw write, you are outputting all that information. What's worse, when you read the class in, you overwrite this bookkeeping data.

For example, suppose we have the class:

```
class sample {
    public:
        const int sample_size;      // Number of samples
        int cur_sample;             // Current sample number
        sample() : sample_size(100) {} // Set up class
        virtual void get_sample(); // Routine to get a sample
};
```

Internally, this class consists of *three* member variables: a constant, sample_size (which C++ won't allow you to change); a simple variable, cur_sample; and a pointer to the real function to be used when get_sample is called. All three of these are written to disk by the call:

```
sample a_sample;
// ...
write_size = write(fd, (char *)&a_sample, sizeof(a_sample));
```

When this class is read, *all three members* are changed. That includes the constant (which we aren't supposed to change) and the function pointer (which now probably points to something strange).

C programmers also make use of the memset function to set all the members of a structure to zero. For example:

```
struct a_struct { ... }
a_struct struct_var;
// ...
memset(&struct_var, '\0', sizeof(struct_var));
```

Be careful when turning a structure into a class. If we had used the class a_sample in the previous example instead of the structure struct_var, we would have zeroed the constant sample_size as well as the virtual function pointer. The result would probably be a crash if we ever tried to call get_sample.

setjmp and longjmp

C has its own way of handling exceptions through the use of setjmp and longjmp. The setjmp function marks a place in a program. The longjmp function jumps to the place marked by setjmp.

Normally setjmp returns a zero. This tells the program to execute normal code. When an exception occurs, the longjmp call returns to the location of the setjmp function. The only difference the program can see between a real setjmp call and a fake setjmp call caused by a longjmp is that normally setjmp returns a zero. When setjmp is "called" by longjmp, the return value is controlled by a parameter to longjmp.

The definition of the setjmp function is:

```
#include <setjmp.h>

int setjmp(jmp_buf env);
```

where env is the place where setjmp saves the current environment for later use by longjmp.

The setjmp function return values are as follows:

0
> Normal call

Nonzero
> Non-zero return codes are the result of a longjmp call.

The definition of the longjmp call is:

```
void longjmp(jmp_buf env, int return_code);
```

where env is the environment initialized by a previous setjmp call, and return_code is the return code that will be returned by the setjmp call.

Figure 28-1 illustrates the control flow when using setjmp and longjmp.

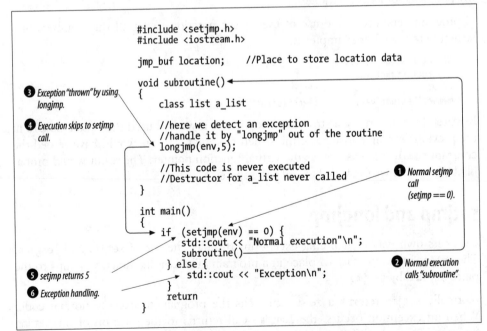

Figure 28-1. setjmp/longjmp control flow

There is one problem here, however. The longjmp call returns control to the corresponding setjmp. *It does not call the destructors of any classes that are "destroyed" in the process.*

In Figure 28-1 we can see that in the subroutine we define a class named a_list. Normally we would call the destructor for a_list at the end of the function or at a **return** statement. However, in this case we use longjmp to exit the function. Since longjmp is a C function, it knows nothing about classes and destructors and does not call the destructor for a_list. So we now have a situation where a variable has disappeared but the destructor has not been called. The technical name for this situation is a "foul-up."

When converting C to C++, change all setjmp/longjmp combinations into exceptions.

Mixing C and C++ Code

It is possible for C++ code to call a C function. The trick is that you need to tell C++ that the function you are calling is written in C and not C++. This is accomplished by declaring the function prototypes inside an extern "C" block. For example:

```
extern "C" {
    extern int the_c_function(int arg);
}
```

Summary

What you must do to get C to compile with a C++ compiler:

- Change K&R-style function headers into standard C++ headers.
- Add prototypes.
- Rename any functions or variables that are C++ keywords.
- Change setjmp/longjmp calls into **catch/throw** operations.

Once you've done these tasks, you have a C+$\frac{1}{2}$ program. It works, but it's really a C program in C++'s clothing. To convert it to a real C++ program, you also need to do the following:

- Change malloc to **new**.
- Change free to **delete** or **delete** [] calls.
- Turn printf and scanf calls into cout and cin.
- When turning **struct** declarations into **class** variables, be careful of read, write, and memset functions that use the entire structure or class.

Programming Exercise

Exercise 28-1: There are a lot of C programs out there. Turn one into C++.

CHAPTER 29

C++'s Dustier Corners

There be of them that have left
a name behind them.
—Ecclesiasticus XLIV, 1

This chapter describes the few remaining features of C++ that are not described in any of the previous chapters. It is titled *"C++'s Dustier Corners"* because these statements are hardly ever used in real programming.

do/while

The **do/while** statement has the following syntax:

```
do {
        statement;
        statement;
} while    (expression);
```

The program loops, tests the expression, and stops if the expression is false (0).

 This construct always executes at least once.

do/while is not frequently used in C++ because most programmers prefer to use a **while/break** combination.

goto

All the sample programs in this book were coded without using a single **goto**. In actual practice I find I use a **goto** statement about once every other year. For those rare times that a **goto** is necessary, its syntax is:

```
goto label;
```

where *label* is a statement label. Statement labels follow the same naming convention as variable names. Labeling a statement is done as follows:

```
label: statement;
```

For example:

```
for (x = 0; x < X_LIMIT; ++x) {
    for (y = 0; y < Y_LIMIT; ++y) {
        assert((x >= 0) && (x < X_LIMIT));
        assert((y >= 0) && (y < Y_LIMIT));
        if (data[x][y] == 0)
            goto found;
    }
}
std::cout << "Not found\n";
exit(8);

found:
    std::cout << "Found at (" << x << ',' << y << ")\n";
```

One of the things you don't want to do is to use a **goto** statement to skip over initialization code. For example:

```
{
    goto skip_start;

    {
        int first = 1;

skip_start:
        printf("First is %d\n", first);
    }
}
```

This confuses the compiler and should be avoided.

Question 29-1: *Why does Example 29-1 not print an error message when an incorrect command is entered? Hint: There is a reason I put this in the* **goto** *section.*

Example 29-1. def/def.cpp

```
#include <iostream>
#include <cstdlib>

int main()
{
    char line[10];

    while (true) {
        std::cout << "Enter add(a), delete(d), quit(q): ";
        std::cin.getline(line, sizeof(line));

        switch (line[0]) {
        case 'a':
```

Example 29-1. def/def.cpp (continued)

```
                std::cout << "Add\n";
                break;
            case 'd':
                std::cout << "Delete\n";
                break;
            case 'q':
                std::cout << "Quit\n";
                exit(0);
            defualt:
                std::cout << "Error:Bad command " << line[0] << '\n';
                break;
        }
    }
    return (0);
}
```

The ?: Construct

The **?** and **:** operators work much the same as **if/then/else**. Unlike **if/then/else**, the **?:** operators can be used inside of an expression. The general form of **?:** is:

```
(expression) ? expr1 : expr2;
```

For example, the following assigns to amount_owed the value of the balance or zero, depending on the amount of the balance:

```
amount_owed = (balance < 0) ? 0 : balance;
```

The following macro returns the minimum of its two arguments:

```
#define min(x, y) ((x) < (y) ? (x) : (y))
```

 The C++ library has a perfectly good min function so you don't have to define it yourself. Use the template for safety and efficiency.

The Comma Operator

The comma operator (,) can be used to group statements. For example:

```
if (total < 0) {
    std::cout << "You owe nothing\n";
    total = 0;
}
```

can be written as:

```
if (total < 0)
    std::cout << "You owe nothing\n", total = 0;
```

In most cases, {} should be used instead of a comma. About the only place the comma operator is useful is in a **for** statement. The following **for** loop increments two counters, two and three, by 2 and 3:

```
for (two = 0, three = 0;
    two < 10;
    two += 2, three += 3)
        std::cout << two << ' ' << three << '\n';
```

Overloading the ( ) Operator

The ( ) operator can be overloaded for a class to give the class a "default" function. For example:

```
class example {
    public:
        int operator () (int i) {
            return (i * 2);
        }
};
// ....
        example example_var;

        j = example_var(3);    // j is assigned the value 6 (3 * 2)
```

Overloading the ( ) operator is rarely done. Normal member functions can easily be used for the same purpose but have the advantage of providing the user with a function name.

Pointers to Members

The operator ::* is used to point to a member of a class. For example, in the following code we declare data_ptr as a "pointer to an integer in sample":

```
class sample {
    public:
        int i;    // A couple of member variables
        int j;
};
```

```
int sample::* data_ptr;
```

Now data_ptr can point to either the i or the j member of sample. (After all, they are the only integer members of sample.)

Let's set data_ptr so it points to the member i:

```
data_ptr = &sample::i;
```

An ordinary pointer identifies a single item. A member pointer identifies a member but does not identify an individual variable. All we've done is set data_ptr to a member of sample. data_ptr does not point to a particular integer.

To use data_ptr you need to tell it which object you want:

```
sample a_sample; // A typical sample
sample b_sample;

std::cout << a_sample.*data_ptr << '\n';
std::cout << b_sample.*data_ptr << '\n';
```

The line:

```
std::cout << a_sample.*data_ptr << '\n';
```

tells C++ that we want to print an element of the variable a_sample. The variable data_ptr points to an integer member of sample. (The members i and j are our only two integer members.)

There is a shorthand notation for use with class pointers as well:

```
sample *sample_ptr = &sample1;

std::cout << sample_ptr->*data_ptr << '\n';
```

The syntax for pointers to members is a little convoluted and not terribly useful. I've only seen it used once by an *extremely* clever programmer. (The first maintenance programmer who got the code immediately ripped it out anyway.)

The asm Statement

Sometimes there are things that you just can't do in C++. In those rare cases, the asm statement comes to the rescue. It lets you specify assembly code directly. The general form of this statement is:

```
asm("assembly statement")
```

Needless to say, this statement is highly nonportable.

The mutable Qualifier

Normally you can't modify the members of a constant object. If a member is declared mutable, it can be modified. For example:

```
class sample {
    public:
        int i1;
        mutable float f1;
// ...
};

const sample a_sample;

a_sample.i1 = 1;    // Illegal, attempt to modify a constant
a_sample.f1 = 1.0;  // Legal. f1 is mutable.
```

Run Time Type Identification

The typeid function returns information about the type of an expression. The result is of type std::type_info. This class contains the member function name() and returns the name of the type.

For example:

```
type_info info = typeid(1.0 + 2);

std::cout << "Result is of type " << info.name() << endl;
```

Trigraphs

C++ has a number of trigraphs designed for people whose keyboard is missing some of the special characters found on most computer keyboards. For example, ??= can be used instead of #.

Answers to Chapter Questions

Answer 29-1: The compiler didn't see our default line because we misspelled "default" as "defualt." This was not flagged as an error because "defualt" is a valid **goto** label. That's why when we compile the program we get the following warning:

```
def.c(26): warning: defualt unused in function main
```

This means we defined a label for a **goto**, but never used it.

CHAPTER 30
Programming Adages

Second thoughts are ever wiser.
—Euripides

This chapter consists of guidelines and rules for practical programming.

General

- Comment, comment, comment. Put a lot of comments in your program. They tell other programmers what you did, and they also tell you what you did.
- Use the "KISS" principle (Keep It Simple, Stupid). Clear and simple is better than complex and wonderful.
- Avoid side effects. Use ++ and -- on lines by themselves.
- Never put an assignment inside a conditional. Never put an assignment inside any other statement.
- Know the difference between = and ==. Using = for == is a very common mistake and is difficult to find.
- Never do "nothing" silently:

    ```
    // Don't program like this
    for (index = 0; data[index] < key; ++index);
    // Did you see the semicolon at the end of the last line?
    ```

    Always put in a comment:

    ```
    for (index = 0; data[index] < key; ++index)
            /* Do nothing */;
    ```

- Practice coding. Practice is crucial for people involved in almost every other profession that requires a significant level of skill and creativity (e.g., artists, athletes). Help others learn to program. It's good practice for you to go over what you already know, or think you know.

Design

- If you come to a choice between a relatively "quick hack" or a somewhat more involved but more flexible solution, always go for the more flexible solution. You're more likely to reuse it or learn from it. You're also more likely to be thankful later on when requirements shift a little and your code is ready for it.
- Never trust any user input to be what you expect. What would your program do at any given point if a cat walked across the keyboard, several times?
- Watch out for signed unsigned conversions and overflow/underflow conditions.

Declarations

- Put variable declarations one per line and comment them.
- Make variable names long enough to be easily understood, but not so long that they are difficult to type in. (Two or three words is usually enough.)
- Never use default return declarations. If a function returns an integer, declare it as type **int**.

switch Statement

- Always put a default case in a switch statement. Even if it does nothing, put it in:

```
switch (expression) {
    default:
        /* Do nothing */;
        break;
}
```

- Every case in a switch should end with a **break** or a /* fall through */ statement.

Preprocessor

- Always put parentheses, (), around each constant expression defined by a preprocessor #**define** directive:

```
#define BOX_SIZE (3 * 10) /* Size of the box in pixels */
```

- Put () around each argument of a parameterized macro:

```
#define SQUARE(x) ((x) * (x))
```

- Surround macros that contain complete statements with curly braces:

```
// A fatal error has occurred.  Tell user and abort
#define DIE(msg) {printf(msg);exit(8);}
```

- When using the **#ifdef/#endif** construct for conditional compilation, put the **#define** and **#undef** statements near the top of the program and comment them.
- Whenever possible, use **const** instead of **#define**.
- The use of **inline** functions is preferred over the use of parameterized macros.

Style

- A single block of code enclosed in { } should not span more than a couple of pages. Split up any bigger blocks into several smaller, simpler procedures.
- When your code starts to run into the right margin, it's time to split the procedure into several smaller, simpler procedures.
- Always define a constructor, destructor, and copy constructor for a class. If using the C++ defaults, "define" these routines with a comment such as:

```
class example {
    public:
        // Example -- default constructor
```

Compiling

- Always create a *Makefile* so others will know how to compile your program.
- When compiling, turn on all the warning flags. You never know what the compiler might find.

The Ten Commandments for C++ Programmers

These commandments were written by Phin Straite.

1. Thou shalt not rely on the compiler default methods for construction, destruction, copy construction, or assignment for any but the simplest of classes. Thou shalt forget these "big four" methods for any nontrivial class.

2. Thou shalt declare and define thy destructor as virtual such that others may become heir to the fruits of your labors.

3. Thou shalt not violate the "is-a" rule by abusing the inheritance mechanism for thine own twisted perversions.

4. Thou shalt not rely on any implementation-dependent behavior of a compiler, operating system, or hardware environment, lest thy code be forever caged within that dungeon.

5. Thou shalt not augment the interface of a class at the lowest level without most prudent deliberation. Such ill-begotten practices imprison thy clients unjustly into thy classes and create unrest when code maintenance and extension are required.

6. Thou shalt restrict thy friendship to truly worthy contemporaries. Beware, for thou art exposing thyself rudely as from a trenchcoat.

7. Thou shalt not abuse thy implementation data by making it public or static except in the rarest of circumstances. Thy data are thine own; share it not with others.

8. Thou shalt not suffer dangling pointers or references to be harbored within thy objects. These are nefarious and precarious agents of random and wanton destruction.

9. Thou shalt make use of available class libraries as conscientiously as possible. Code reuse, not just thine own but that of thy clients as well, is the Holy Grail of OO.

10. Thou shalt forever forswear the use of the vile printf/scanf, rather favoring the flowing streams. Cast off thy vile C cloak and partake of the wondrous fruit of flexible and extensible I/O.

Final Note

Just when you think you've discovered all the things C++ can do to you—think again. There are still more surprises in store.

Question 30-1: *Why does Example 30-1 think everything is two? (This inspired the final note.)*

Example 30-1. not2/not2.cpp

```
#include <iostream>

int main( )
{
    int number;

    std::cout << "Enter a number: ";

    std::cin >> number;

    if (number =! 2)
        std::cout << "Number is not two\n";
    else
        std::cout << "Number is two\n";

    return (0);
}
```

Answers to Chapter Questions

Answer 30-1: The statement (number =! 2) is not a relational equation, but an assignment statement. It is equivalent to:

```
number = (!2);
```

(Because 2 is nonzero, !2 is zero.)

The programmer accidently reversed the not equal !=, so it became =!. The statement should read:

```
if (number != 2)
```

## PART VI

Appendixes

ASCII Table

Table A-1 lists the ASCII equivalents in decimal, octal, and hexidecimal.

Table A-1. ASCII character table

Dec	Oct	Hex	Char	Dec	Oct	Hex	Char	Dec	Oct	Hex	Char
0	000	00	NUL	23	027	17	ETB	46	056	2E	.
1	001	01	SOH	24	030	18	CAN	47	057	2F	/
2	002	02	STX	25	031	19	EM	48	060	30	0
3	003	03	ETX	26	032	1A	SUB	49	061	31	1
4	004	04	EOT	27	033	1B	ESC	50	062	32	2
5	005	05	ENQ	28	034	1C	FS	51	063	33	3
6	006	06	ACK	29	035	1D	GS	52	064	34	4
7	007	07	BEL	30	036	1E	RS	53	065	35	5
8	010	08	BS	31	037	1F	US	54	066	36	6
9	011	09	HT	32	040	20	SP	55	067	37	7
10	012	0A	NL	33	041	21	!	56	070	38	8
11	013	0B	VT	34	042	22	"	57	071	39	9
12	014	0C	NP	35	043	23	#	58	072	3A	:
13	015	0D	CR	36	044	24	$	59	073	3B	;
14	016	0E	SO	37	045	25	%	60	074	3C	<
15	017	0F	SI	38	046	26	&	61	075	3D	=
16	020	10	DLE	39	047	27	'	62	076	3E	>
17	021	11	DC1	40	050	28	(	63	077	3F	?
18	022	12	DC2	41	051	29	)	64	100	40	@
19	023	13	DC3	42	052	2A	*	65	101	41	A
20	024	14	DC4	43	053	2B	+	66	102	42	B
21	025	15	NAK	44	054	2C	,	67	103	43	C
22	026	16	SYN	45	055	2D	-	68	104	44	D

Table A-1. ASCII character table (continued)

Dec	Oct	Hex	Char	Dec	Oct	Hex	Char	Dec	Oct	Hex	Char
69	105	45	E	89	131	59	Y	109	155	6D	m
70	106	46	F	90	132	5A	Z	110	156	6E	n
71	107	47	G	91	133	5B	[	111	157	6F	o
72	110	48	H	92	134	5C	\	112	160	70	p
73	111	49	I	93	135	5D	]	113	161	71	q
74	112	4A	J	94	136	5E	^	114	162	72	r
75	113	4B	K	95	137	5F	_	115	163	73	s
76	114	4C	L	96	140	60	`	116	164	74	t
77	115	4D	M	97	141	61	a	117	165	75	u
78	116	4E	N	98	142	62	b	118	166	76	v
79	117	4F	O	99	143	63	c	119	167	77	w
80	120	50	P	100	144	64	d	120	170	78	x
81	121	51	Q	101	145	65	e	121	171	79	y
82	122	52	R	102	146	66	f	122	172	7A	z
83	123	53	S	103	147	67	g	123	173	7B	{
84	124	54	T	104	150	68	h	124	174	7C		
85	125	55	U	105	151	69	i	125	175	7D	}
86	126	56	V	106	152	6A	j	126	176	7E	~
87	127	57	W	107	153	6B	k	127	177	7F	DEL
88	130	58	X	108	154	6C	l				

Ranges

Tables B-1 and B-2 list the ranges of various variable types.

Table B-1. 32-bit Unix machine and Windows-32 systems

Name	Bits	Low value	High value	Accuracy
int	32	−2,147,483,648	2,147,483,647	
short int	16	−32,768	32,767	
long int	32	−2,147,483,648	2,147,483,647	
unsigned int	32	0	4,294,967,295	
unsigned short int	16	0	65,535	
unsigned long int	32	0	4,294,967,295	
char	8	System-dependent		
unsigned char	8	0	255	
float	32	−3.4E+38	3.4E+38	6 digits
double	64	−1.7E+308	1.7E+308	15 digits
long double	64	−1.7E+308	1.7E+308	15 digits

Table B-2. Older MS-DOS compilers and most other 16-bit systems

Name	Bits	Low value	High value	Accuracy
int	16	−32,768	32,767	
short int	16	−32,768	32,767	
long int	32	−2,147,483,648	2,147,483,647	
unsigned int	16	0	65,535	
unsigned short int	16	0	65,535	
unsigned long int	32	0	4,294,967,295	
char	8	−128	127	
unsigned char	8	0	255	
float	32	−3.4E+38	3.4E+38	6 digits

Table B-2. Older MS-DOS compilers and most other 16-bit systems (continued)

Name	Bits	Low value	High value	Accuracy
double	64	−1.7E+308	1.7E+308	15 digits
long double	80	−3.4E+4932	3.4E+4932	17 digits

Operator Precedence Rules

The tables in this appendix summarize the precedence rules for operations in C++.

Standard Rules

Table C-1. Standard C++ precedence rules

Precedence	Operators				
1	( )	[ ]	->	.	
	::	::*	->*	.*	
2	!	~	++	--	(type)
	– (unary)	* (dereference)			
	& (address of)	sizeof			
3	* (multiply)	/	%		
4	+	–			
5	<<	>>			
6	<	<=	>	>=	
7	==	!=			
8	& (bitwise AND)				
9	^				
10	|				
11	&&				
12	||				
13	?:				
14	=	+=	-=	etc.	
15	,				

Practical Subset of the Operator Precedence Rules

Table C-2. Practical operator precedence rules

Precedence	Operator		
1	* (multiply)	/	%
2	+	–	

Put parentheses around everything else.

Computing Sine Using a Power Series

This program is designed to compute the sine function using a power series. A very limited floating-point format is used to demonstrate some of the problems that can occur when using floating point.

The program computes each term in the power series and displays the result. It continues computing terms until the last term is so small that it doesn't contribute to the final result. For comparison purposes, the result of the library function sin is displayed as well as the computed sine.

The program is invoked by:

```
sine value
```

where *value* is an angle in radians. For example, to compute sin(0) we use the command:

```
% sine 0
x**1      0.000E+00
1!        1.000E+00
x**1/1! 0.000E+00
1 term computed
sin(0.000E+00)=
  0.000E+00
Actual sin(0)=0
```

And to compute sin(π) we use the command:

```
% sine 3.141
x**1      3.141E+00
1!        1.000E+00
x**1/1! 3.141E+00
  total   3.141E+00

x**3      3.099E+01
3!        6.000E+00
x**3/3! 5.165E+00
  total   -2.024E+00
```

```
x**5        3.057E+02
5!          1.200E+02
x**5/5!  2.548E+00
   total     5.239E-01

x**7        3.016E+03
7!          5.040E+03
x**7/7!  5.985E-01
   total    -7.457E-02

x**9        2.976E+04
9!          3.629E+05
x**9/9!  8.201E-02
   total     7.438E-03

x**11       2.936E+05
11!         3.992E+07
x**11/11!  7.355E-03
   total     8.300E-05

x**13       2.897E+06
13!         6.227E+09
x**13/13!  4.652E-04
   total     5.482E-04

x**15       2.858E+07
15!         1.308E+12
x**15/15!  2.185E-05
   total     5.263E-04

x**17       2.819E+08
17!         3.557E+14
x**17/17!  7.927E-07
   total     5.271E-04

x**19       2.782E+09
19!         1.217E+17
x**19/19!  2.287E-08
   total     5.271E-04

x**21       2.744E+10
21!         5.109E+19
x**21/21!  5.371E-10
11 term computed
sin(3.141E+00)=
   5.271E-04
Actual sin(3.141)=0.000592654
```

Example D-1 lists the *Makefile* for Unix.

Example D-1. sin/makefile.unx

```
#
# Makefile for many Unix compilers using the
```

Example D-1. sin/makefile.unx (continued)

```
# "standard" command name CC
#
CC=CC
CFLAGS=-g
sine: sine.cpp
        $(CC) $(CFLAGS) -o sine sine.cpp -lm

clean:
        rm sine
```

Example D-2 lists the *sine.cpp* file.

Example D-2. sin/sine.cpp

```
/*******************************************************
 * sine -- compute sine using very simple floating     *
 *        arithmetic.                                   *
 *                                                      *
 * Usage:                                               *
 *        sine <value>                                  *
 *                                                      *
 *        <value> is an angle in radians                *
 *                                                      *
 * Format used in f.fffe+X                              *
 *                                                      *
 * f.fff is a 4 digit fraction                          *
 *        + is a sign (+ or -)                          *
 *        X is a single digit exponent                  *
 *                                                      *
 * sin(x) = x  - x**3 + x**5 - x**7                     *
 *             -----   ----   ----  . . .               *
 *              3!      5!     7!                        *
 *                                                      *
 * Warning: This program is intended to show some of    *
 *        problems with floating point.  It not intended*
 *        to be used to produce exact values for the    *
 *        sin function.                                 *
 *                                                      *
 * Note: Even though we specify only one-digit for the  *
 *        exponent, two are used for some calculations. *
 *        This is due to the fact that printf has no    *
 *        format for a single digit exponent.           *
 *******************************************************/
#include <iostream>
#include <cstdlib>
#include <cmath>
#include <cstdio>

int main(int argc, char *argv[])
{
    float   total;  // total of series so far
    float   new_total;// newer version of total
```

Example D-2. sin/sine.cpp (continued)

```cpp
    float   term_top;// top part of term
    float   term_bottom;// bottom of current term
    float   term;   // current term
    float   exp;    // exponent of current term
    float   sign;   // +1 or -1 (changes on each term)
    float   value;  // value of the argument to sin
    int     index;  // index for counting terms

    char    *float_2_ascii(float number);  // turn floating-point to ascii
    float   fix_float(float number);       // round to correct digits
    float   factorial(float number);       // compute n!

    if (argc != 2) {
        std::cerr << "Usage is:\n";
        std::cerr << "  sine <value>\n";
        exit (8);
    }

    value = fix_float(atof(&argv[1][0]));

    total = 0.0;
    exp = 1.0;
    sign = 1.0;

    for (index = 0; /* take care of below */ ; ++index) {
        term_top = fix_float(pow(value, exp));
        term_bottom = fix_float(factorial(exp));
        term = fix_float(term_top / term_bottom);
        std::cout << "x**" << static_cast<int>(exp) << "     " <<
                float_2_ascii(term_top) << '\n';
        std::cout << exp << "!      " << float_2_ascii(term_bottom) << '\n';
        std::cout << "x**" << static_cast<int>(exp) << "/" <<
                static_cast<int>(exp) << "! " <<
                float_2_ascii(term) << "\n";

        new_total = fix_float(total + sign * term);
        if (new_total == total)
                break;

        total = new_total;
        sign = -sign;
        exp = exp + 2.0;
        std::cout <<"  total   " << float_2_ascii(total) << '\n';
        std::cout <<'\n';
    }
    std::cout << (index +1) << " term computed\n";
    std::cout << "sin(" << float_2_ascii(value) << ")=\n";
    std::cout << "  " << float_2_ascii(total) << '\n';
    std::cout << "Actual sin(" << atof(&argv[1][0]) << ")=" <<
            sin(atof(&argv[1][0])) << '\n';
    return (0);
}
```

Example D-2. sin/sine.cpp (continued)

```
/**********************************************************
 * float_2_ascii -- turn a floating-point string         *
 *       into ascii.                                      *
 *                                                        *
 * Parameters                                             *
 *       number -- number to turn into ascii              *
 *                                                        *
 * Returns                                                *
 *       Pointer to the string containing the number      *
 *                                                        *
 * Warning: Uses static storage, so later calls           *
 *              overwrite earlier entries                 *
 **********************************************************/
char *float_2_ascii(float number)
{
    static char result[10];     //place to put the number

    std::sprintf(result,"%8.3E", number);
    return (result);
}
/**********************************************************
 * fix_float -- turn high precision numbers into         *
 *              low precision numbers to simulate a       *
 *              very dumb floating-point structure.       *
 *                                                        *
 * Parameters                                             *
 *       number -- number to take care of                 *
 *                                                        *
 * Returns                                                *
 *       number accurate to 5 places only                 *
 *                                                        *
 * Note: This works by changing a number into ascii and   *
 *       back.  Very slow, but it works.                  *
 **********************************************************/
float fix_float(float number)
{
    float   result;     // result of the conversion
    char    ascii[10];  // ascii version of number

    std::sprintf(ascii,"%8.4e", number);
    std::sscanf(ascii, "%e", &result);
    return (result);
}
/**********************************************************
 * factorial -- compute the factorial of a number.      *
 *                                                        *
 * Parameters                                             *
 *       number -- number to use for factorial            *
 *                                                        *
 * Returns                                                *
 *       factorial(number) or number!                     *
 *                                                        *
```

Example D-2. sin/sine.cpp (continued)

```
 * Note: Even though this is a floating-point routine,  *
 *        using numbers that are not whole numbers      *
 *        does not make sense.                          *
 *******************************************************/
float factorial(float number)
{
    if (number <= 1.0)
        return (number);
    else
        return (number *factorial(number - 1.0));
}
```

Resources

This appendix provides URLs and brief descriptions for several C++ resources.

Compilers

GNU g++ Compiler (http://www.gnu.org)

The GNU g++ compiler is one of the highest quality compilers out there. It works on most Unix and Linux systems.

Cygwin (http://www.cygwin.com)

Cygwin is a Unix-like programming environment for Microsoft Windows systems; it includes a copy of the g++ compiler.

Borland C++ Builder (http://www.borland.com)

Borland supplies a free copy of the command-line version of their compiler. This is a stripped-down version of the integrated development environment they sell commercially. This is one of the best compilers for the Microsoft Windows environment.

Standard Template Library

SGI (http://www.sgi.com)

A reference on the Standard Template Library. Be careful, this reference includes extra containers that are not part of the standard library.

Standards

ANSI (American National Standards Institute) (http://webstore.ansi.org)

A place where you can purchase the ANSI C++ standard. This is a very difficult read if you don't know C++ well.

Programming Tools

Freshmeat (http://www.freshmeat.net)
> This web site contains a searchable directory of almost all of the open source tools, including programming tools.

Source Navigator (http://sources.redat.com/sourcenav)
> An IDE and source browser for both Unix and Microsoft Windows.

CScope (http://cscope.sourceforge.net/index.html)
> A source indexing and browsing tool.

Linux Cross Reference (http://lxr.sourceforge.net)
> A cross-reference and browser that is designed for the Linux kernel, but works with any large software project.

Indent (http://www.gnu.org)
> The indent command indents C++ programs.

Vim (Text editor with built-in indenting) (http://www.vim.org)
> A text editor similar to the standard Unix vi editor, but with lots of programming related commands including a very smart indenter. This editor works on both Unix type systems and Microsoft Windows.

Emacs (editor) (http://www.gnu.org)
> Another programmer's editor.

a2ps (Pretty Printer) (http://www.gnu.org)
> Prints nicely typeset programs.

Index

Symbols

/* */ comment markers, 24
{ } (curly braces), 53, 77
   and structures, 181
( ) (default class function) operator, 324
   overloading, 507
[ ] (index) operator, 323
( ) parentheses
   with macro parameters, 154
   and simple operators, 37
-= (decrease) operator, 71, 318
+ (addition) operator, 37, 316
& (address of) operator, 223, 316, 317
& (bitwise AND) operator, 161–163, 316
&& (logical AND) operator, 77, 320
&= (AND into) operator, 318
= (assignment) operator, 41
   for classes, 204
   versus == (equal to) operator, 85
\ (backslash)
   as escape character, 44
   in preprocessor directives, 146
~ (bitwise NOT) operator, 164, 317
| (bitwise OR) operator, 163, 316
   to merge flags, 259
>> (character-to-number) operator, 254
-> (class member) operator, 324
, (comma) operator, 324, 506
: construct, 506
? construct, 506
-- (decrement) operator, 71, 318
* (dereference) operator, 222, 317
diagnostic tag, 97
/= (divide into) operator, 71, 318

/ (division) operator, 37, 43, 316
. (dot) operator, 354
== (equal to) operator, 77, 317
   versus = (assignment) operator, 85
^= (exclusive OR into) operator, 318
^ (exclusive OR) operator, 164, 316
- (for command-line options), 236
& (for reference variables), 67
> (greater than) operator, 77, 317
>= (greater than or equal to) operator, 77,
   317
+= (increase) operator, 71, 318
++ (increment) operator, 71, 318
   x++ vs. ++x, 72
>> (input) operator, 51, 266, 315, 320
<< (left shift) operator, 165, 316
< (less than) operator, 77, 317
<= (less than or equal to) operator, 76, 317
! (logical NOT) operator, 77, 320
|| (logical OR) operator, 77, 320
%= (modulus into) operator, 71, 318
% (modulus) operator, 37, 316
* (multiplication) operator, 37, 316
*= (multiply by) operator, 71, 318
- (negative) operator, 317
!= (not equal to) operator, 77, 317
<< (number-to-character) operator, 250
|= (OR into) operator, 318
<< (output) operator, 38, 266, 315, 320
->* (pointer to member) operator, 324
+ (positive) operator, 317
# (preprocess) operator, 156
' (quotation mark), 45

We'd like to hear your suggestions for improving our indexes. Send email to *index@oreilly.com*.

Numbers

A

B

double-linked lists, 357
do/while loops (see while loops)
dynamic data structures, 348
dynamic_cast operator, 388–389

E

%e conversion, 268
ease of use as a design goal, 448
economy as a design goal, 448
editing programs, 477
elements, array, 48
else statements, 77
#endif directive, 151, 512
endl I/O manipulator, 252
end-of-line puzzle, 255
end-of-string character, 231
end-of-string marker, 58
ends I/O manipulator, 252
enum (enumerated) datatype, 185–186, 215
equal to (==) operator, 77, 317
   versus = (assignment) operator, 85
errors
   bounds errors, array, 54–57
   calculations, 346
   eliminating from code (see debugging)
   handling within programs, 393–400
   infinite recursion, 140
   messages, 446
   null effect warning, 38
   roundoff (floating-point), 340
   runtime (see runtime errors)
   stack overflow, 120
escape character (\), 44
evaluation order, 72–74
exceptions, 393–400
   in C, 501
   destructors, 399–400
   formatting, 395
   runtime library, 400
   for stacks, 394
   throwing, 396–399
exclusive OR (^) operator, 164, 316
exclusive OR into (^=) operator, 318
executable programs, 9, 10
execution, 395–396
   Makefile, 408–412
expandability as a design goal, 449
explicit class constructors, 205
exponential notation, 43

expressions
   simple, 37–38
   testing, 504
   typeid function, 509
extended precision, 67
extern modifier, 402–404
extern variable class, 69
external number formats, 311

F

%f conversion, 267
\f (form-feed character), 45
"//fall through" comment, 113
fast prototyping, 92
fclose (file close) function, 265
fgetc (get character) function, 265
fgets (get string) function, 266
file formats, comments on, 27
filenames, headers, 404–405
files
   ASCII, 254
   binary, 254, 264
   changing modification date of, 411
   core, 299
   designing formats for, 262–264
   directing debugging information into, 282
   disk, 246
   headers, 152, 404–405
   identification numbers for, 263
   include (see include files)
   input_file class, 473
   integer.h, 427
   I/O with (see I/O)
   main.cpp, 427
   multiple (see modules)
   object (see object files)
   output file functions, 248–250
   program, 478–496
   source (see source files)
   square.cpp, 427
   square.h, 427
   standard unbuffered, 259
   variables for, 264
file-specific namespaces, 123
fixed point class, 326–335
fixed point numbers, 310, 314
flags
   conversion, 251
   open, 249, 259
float datatype, 66, 70, 343
float keyword, 43
float.h include file, 343

floating-point numbers, 42, 66
  arithmetic, 337–346
    accuracy of, 341–346
    guard digit, 338
    overflow and underflow, 340
    roundoff error, 340, 342
    speed of, 343
  converting to integers, 43
  dividing, 43
  versus integers, 308
floating-point precision arithmetic, 343
flush command, 300
flush I/O manipulator, 252, 257
fopen (file open) function, 264
for statements, 5, 107–110, 121
foreach algorithm, 435–436
formatting
  dividing tasks into modules, 417
  exceptions, 395
  files, 262–264
  fixed-point numbers, 311
  floating-point numbers, 337
  Makefiles, 408–412
  programs, 31–33
  requirements, 469–470
form-feed character (\f), 45
FORTRAN, 9
fputc (put character) function, 266
fputs (put string) function, 266
fractional numbers, 42
fread routine, 270
free function (C language), 498–500
free library routine, 498
friend classes, 211–213
friend directive, 212
fscanf function, 269
fstream class, 246
fstream.h file, 246
functions, 5, 125–139
  body of modules, 406
  callback, 137
  calling, 252
  calloc, 499
  as class members, 197
  code, 429
  constant, 213–214
  declaring, 128
  generic, 420–422
  getline, 248
  inline, 137, 156, 306
  K&R style, 497
  length of, 33

longjmp, 501
  and namespaces, 129
  naming conventions, 135
  as operators, 315–324
  output files, 248–250
  overloading, 135
  parameters of, 126–139
    arrays as, 134–135
    const, 130
    reference, 130–134
  pop, 394–400
  prototypes, 128, 498
  push, 394–400
  qsort, 5
  recursive, 139–140
  return(0), 36
  setjmp, 501
  single-function programs, 36
  specialization, 423
  standard, 5
  static, 217
  templates of, 420
  trigonometry, 344
  typeid, 509
  virtual, 378–383
fwrite routine, 270

G

g++ compiler, 12, 408
-g (compiler option), 12
gdb debugger, 283–287
  example of using, 290–299
generality as a design goal, 449
generating templates, 420
generic functions, defining, 420–422
getline member function, 248
global namespaces, 123
global variables, 118–120, 452
goto statements, 504
  programming without, 31
graphics
  bitmapped, 169–174
  histograms, 412
greater than (>) operator, 77, 317
greater than or equal to (>=) operator, 77, 317
guard digits, 338
  (see also floating-point numbers)
guidelines
  coding, 453
  design, 451
  modules, 417

About the Author

Steve Oualline wrote his first program when he was eleven. It had a bug in it. Since that time he has studied practical ways of writing programs so that the risk of generating a bug is reduced. He currently works as a software engineer in Southern California. His spare time is spent on real engineering on a steam train at the Poway Midland Railroad.

Colophon

The animal on the cover of *Practical C++ Programming* is an Eastern chipmunk, a striped ground squirrel found mostly in eastern North America. Eastern chipmunks have five dark and two light stripes on their backs, extending from head to rump, and two stripes on their long, bushy tails. They are distinguished from other ground squirrels by the white stripes above and below their eyes. The coloration of chipmunks throughout North America varies, but is quite uniform within regions.

Chipmunks often make their homes in sparse forests or farms, where they can build the entrances to their lodges in stone walls, broken trees, or thick underbrush. The lodges consist of a maze of tunnels leading to a large leaf-lined nest. Chipmunks spend most of the daylight hours outdoors, but head for their lodges before nightfall. Although they are excellent climbers, chipmunks live primarily on the ground.

Chipmunks eat nuts, seeds, insects, and occasionally birds' eggs. Like all ground squirrels, they have large cheek pouches, sometimes extending as far back as their shoulders, in which they can store food. They collect and store nuts and seeds through the summer and fall. When the weather starts to get cool, all the chipmunks in a region will suddenly disappear into their lodges where they begin hibernation. On warm winter days one can often see chipmunk pawprints in the snow, as they will sometimes wake up and leave their lodges for brief periods when the temperature rises.

Mating season for Eastern chipmunks is mid-March to early April. The gestation period is 31 days, after which a litter of three to six is born. Baby chipmunks leave the lodge after one month, and are mature by July.

The chipmunk most likely got its name from the noise it makes, which sounds like a loud "cheep." You can occasionally see a chipmunk hanging upside down from a tree branch "cheeping" its call.

Edie Freedman designed the cover of this book, using a 19th-century engraving from the Dover Pictorial Archive. Emma Colby produced the cover layout with Quark XPress 4.1 using the ITC Garamond font.

David Futato designed the interior layout. Mike Sierra polished the final book files in FrameMaker 5.5.6. Leanne Soylemez copyedited the text. Octal Publishing, Inc., prepared the index. Jane Ellin provided quality control and production guidance.

The text font is Lintotype Birka; the heading font is Adobe Myriad Condensed; and the code font is LucasFont's TheSans Mono Condensed. The illustrations that appear in the book were created by Robert Romano and Jessamyn Read using Macromedia FreeHand 9 and Adobe Photoshop 6. The tip and warning icons were drawn by Christopher Bing. This colophon was written by Clairemarie Fisher O'Leary.

Related Titles Available from O'Reilly

C and C++ Programming

C Pocket Reference

C++ in a Nutshell

C++ Pocket Reference

C++: The Core Language

Mastering Algorithms with C

Objective-C Pocket Reference

Practical C Programming, *3rd Edition*

Programming Embedded Systems in C and C++

Secure Programming Cookbook for C and C++

STL Pocket Reference

O'REILLY®

Our books are available at most retail and online bookstores.
To order direct: 1-800-998-9938 • *order@oreilly.com* • *www.oreilly.com*
Online editions of most O'Reilly titles are available by subscription at *safari.oreilly.com*

Keep in touch with O'Reilly

1. Download examples from our books

To find example files for a book, go to:

www.oreilly.com/catalog

select the book, and follow the "Examples" link.

2. Register your O'Reilly books

Register your book at *register.oreilly.com*

Why register your books?
Once you've registered your O'Reilly books you can:

- Win O'Reilly books, T-shirts or discount coupons in our monthly drawing.
- Get special offers available only to registered O'Reilly customers.
- Get catalogs announcing new books (US and UK only).
- Get email notification of new editions of the O'Reilly books you own.

3. Join our email lists

Sign up to get topic-specific email announcements of new books and conferences, special offers, and O'Reilly Network technology newsletters at:

elists.oreilly.com

It's easy to customize your free elists subscription so you'll get exactly the O'Reilly news you want.

4. Get the latest news, tips, and tools

www.oreilly.com

- "Top 100 Sites on the Web"—PC Magazine
- CIO Magazine's Web Business 50 Awards

Our web site contains a library of comprehensive product information (including book excerpts and tables of contents), downloadable software, background articles, interviews with technology leaders, links to relevant sites, book cover art, and more.

5. Work for O'Reilly

Check out our web site for current employment opportunities:

jobs.oreilly.com

6. Contact us

O'Reilly & Associates
1005 Gravenstein Hwy North
Sebastopol, CA 95472 USA

TEL: 707-827-7000 or 800-998-9938
(6am to 5pm PST)

FAX: 707-829-0104

order@oreilly.com
For answers to problems regarding your order or our products. To place a book order online, visit:

www.oreilly.com/order_new

catalog@oreilly.com
To request a copy of our latest catalog.

booktech@oreilly.com
For book content technical questions or corrections.

corporate@oreilly.com
For educational, library, government, and corporate sales.

proposals@oreilly.com
To submit new book proposals to our editors and product managers.

international@oreilly.com
For information about our international distributors or translation queries. For a list of our distributors outside of North America check out:

international.oreilly.com/distributors.html

adoption@oreilly.com
For information about academic use of O'Reilly books, visit:

academic.oreilly.com